BELL
PLAC

Groundwork of
Biblical Studies

Groundwork of Biblical Studies

David Stacey

London   EPWORTH PRESS

© David Stacey 1979
First published 1979
by Epworth Press
All rights reserved

No part of this publication
may be reproduced, stored in a
retrieval system, or
transmitted, in any form or by
any means, electronic, mechanical,
photocopying, recording or
otherwise, without the prior
permission of Epworth Press

7162 0293 X

Enquiries should be addressed to
The Methodist Publishing House
Wellington Road
Wimbledon
London SW19 8EU
Printed in Great Britain by
The Garden City Press Limited,
Letchworth, Hertfordshire SG6 1JS

Contents

CONTENTS

Note for Methodist Local Preachers on trial studying for the Connexional Examinations in the Old and New Testaments.
Groundwork of Biblical Studies has as its companion volumes *Studying the Old Testament* and *Studying the New Testament* and the student, whether taking a correspondence course or not, should pay careful attention to the Study Schemes printed at the end of the companion volumes. These Schemes indicate the passages of the Bible required to be read.

It is to the student's advantage to read the whole of *Groundwork of Biblical Studies,* though the passages in smaller print are for reference only. The chapters referred to in the Study Scheme for the Old Testament (Studies 3–10) and in the Study Scheme for the New Testament should be read with special care as they provide essential background knowledge.

Preface

BIBLICAL study is endless. This is a large book and many who are beginning the study of the Bible will not want to read it all. But it is well to begin by recognizing how big the task is. After a while, most students will find this book inadequate, and they will turn to other books dealing with smaller areas. That process will go on throughout the whole of their studying lives. For this reason, a little book that gave the impression that in it was all a young student needed, would be the biggest deception possible. It is hoped that the beginner will not be lost here. If he finds some things difficult, it is best to leave them and come back to them. Or maybe some other book will make them more clear. The fact has to be faced, however, that some parts of biblical study are difficult. The study of religious texts created by very serious people two to three thousands years ago in a, distant land and expressed in a language that is far more foreign to us than French or German, can hardly be easy. None the less the keen student will not be easily put off, and he can be encouraged by the fact that the most learned divine who ever lived was once a beginner and maybe even heaved a sigh at books like this one.

Important

All cross-references in this book are expressed so: 14c, 28g. The number represents the chapter. The letter represents the paragraph or group of paragraphs indicated by that letter in the left-hand margin. The letters occur at regular intervals through the book. Where there are more than 26 sections in one chapter, capital letters are used for 27 onwards.

Acknowledgments

THIS book has been a long time in the writing and many people have contributed to it, some without being aware of the fact. If I tried to give the complete list, it would be absurdly long, which is a good enough reason for not attempting it. I must, however, put on record my gratitude to the various members of the Methodist Local Preachers' Studies Board who read the typescript and made dozens of suggestions, most of which I have adopted. A special debt of gratitude goes to my brother, the Reverend John Stacey, Local Preachers' secretary in the Division of Ministries, for his encouragement, his advice and his almost saintly patience. My wife, Professor Morna Hooker, has done her best to correct my errors and improve my argument. The blemishes that remain must be put down to my stubbornness rather than to her oversight. I am grateful to Mr Albert Jakeway of the Methodist Publishing House for his enthusiasm and the speed with which he has seen this book through the press. Another friend whose capacity for work amazes and humbles me is the Reverend Walter Selby, who produced the index for this book almost overnight and even claimed to have enjoyed doing it.

My first book, published more than twenty years ago, was dedicated to my parents. Since then I have made no use of dedication. But during the time I have been writing this book my life has undergone a complete change and it is now appropriate to look back in gratitude. So I dedicate this book to Baudine, with love and gratitude for the twenty-five years we shared together.

Wesley College, Bristol. 1979   DAVID STACEY

10

Section 1

The Student and his Approach

Chapter 1

Introduction

a Why study the Bible at all? That is the first question. Broadly
speaking there are two kinds of answer.

1. Because it is a deep and fascinating book covering the
whole range of human experience; because it has proved
itself able to move and inspire millions; because it is a
corner-stone of our culture; because it contains passages
of matchless beauty; because it has something to offer
everyone.

2. Because it is God's word; because it records the most
significant events in human history; because it is not only
inspiring but inspired; because its theme is God's self-
revelation; because, alone of all the books in the world, it
presents an authoritative account of the words and deeds
of the Son of God himself.

Many who give answers of the first kind would not give
answers of the second, whereas those who give answers of the
second kind are usually happy to give answers of the first kind
as well. To put it another way, there are good reasons why
every serious person should study the Bible, but there are
further reasons why people of Christian faith must do so.

We have, therefore, to think of different aims in studying
the Bible: in one case, to be enriched, informed and stimulated, in the other, to be confronted with the divine word.
Appropriate methods are available under both headings, but
they are different and it is well not to confuse them.

There are many people in the second category who would

13

not, in other connexions, regard themselves as students. They may have no academic experience. They may not be well equipped for study in the technical sense. Their motive, however, may be stronger than that of an ordinary student. Ordinary students simply find knowledge or personal enrichment in their study, whereas those who come in the second category believe that they will find eternal life. For this reason they are willing to persevere, even when the going is hard.

b   The going, at times, is hard for, from many points of view, the Bible is a difficult book. It arose from a culture distant from us in time and space. Its languages and idioms tend to be foreign to us. Its view of the physical universe is radically different from that which is current today. Hours of hard work are necessary to uncover the meaning of some words and phrases and some remain obscure to the end.

The fact that the Bible has been so important to our civilization means, of course, that thousands of scholars have devoted their lives to it, so we have the advantage of learning from those more competent than ourselves. But the very rigour with which Bible study has been pursued brings its own difficulties. On the one hand biblical study has become technical and many of the most authoritative books are beyond the common man. This is awkward, but it is something to be grateful for. Books that faithfully expound ancient Semitic texts are bound to be complex. There is no easy way of doing this task properly and we can be reassured that biblical scholarship generally has not shirked the difficulties or been content with over-simplifications. On the other hand, in so difficult a field where so many have worked for so long, disagreements inevitably appear. No doubt there would be disagreements if the matter were simple, but where information is sparse and difficult to assess, divergences multiply. The result is that the biblical library seems vast and daunting and the student may well wonder if he will ever learn very much from it.

Fortunately there are factors that tend in the opposite direction. Like all great books—and like all great works of art—the Bible can be studied at different levels. Shakespeare rewards Professors of English Literature, but not all who

14

crowd into Stratford upon Avon are professional students. Shakespeare is also able to stir the non-technical public as, indeed, he was able to stir the unschooled masses of Elizabethan England. So, too, the Bible rewards all who turn to it seriously. One does not need to have read all the books nor to have found answers to all the queries. One simply has to open the Bible and read.

Again, because the Bible is so widely read a large number of aids to Bible study exist. There are dictionaries, concordances, commentaries and many books that aim to distil for the common reader the findings of more technical scholars. There are dangers in simplifications but not all simplification is bad. It depends how it is done and for what it is used. No one would want to climb the Eiger with the map on the picture post-card as his only guide, but the post-card does serve a purpose. The important point is to know when to tear it up and to move on to something more detailed. A simplification is bad if it gives the impression that, simple as it is, it is adequate. It can be useful if it continually points out the problems and indicates where it is generalizing, where it is tidying up an untidy area. Words like 'briefly', 'broadly speaking', 'in general', tedious as they may seem in print, are in fact tokens of good faith in a simple and popular book. They are indications that there is more to be said, that, when the reader has digested the argument as it stands, he must go on to look for a more profound treatment elsewhere. Bad simplifications are those that delude the reader into thinking that the truth is simple and that, having understood the book, he has grasped all that matters.

c   This book is an attempt to put things simply. Wherever possible charts and maps and diagrams are used so that people beginning biblical studies can quickly grasp the facts, the methods, the hypotheses that every biblical student must understand. In very few cases is the information contained here final in the sense that there is nothing more to say. Almost every page is a simplification. The issues are nearly always more subtle, more elusive than at first sight appears. The wise student, having mastered the groundwork, will press on to read some of the longer and more scholarly works

15

referred to in the bibliographies. Groundwork is necessary but groundwork by itself profits little. It is what we build when the ground has been cleared that really matters.

There is one sense in which the metaphor of building is not helpful for it suggests a large but finite task. Clearing the ground is the beginning, completing the building is the end. There is no end in biblical studies. There are no areas in which we can say that there is nothing more to be known or nothing more to be thought. The enquiry goes on for ever. This is true of all study in the humanities. There is no 'last word' on Hamlet or the Choral Symphony, and there is no graver error than to launch out on a study of the Bible in the belief that it will soon provide finite and final answers to all our questions.

Difficulties and the Word of God

d   It may be that some devout people—who would certainly give the second of the two reasons for studying the Bible—will be disturbed by the suggestions that there are grave difficulties to be overcome in biblical studies and that there are no clear-cut and final answers. They may want to say that the Holy Spirit gave the word in the first place and the Holy Spirit guides the faithful student. The Holy Spirit is not a God of confusion but of truth. Therefore no difficulty is insuperable to the devout, and a clear and final word is available to them in Holy Scripture.

There are two arguments against making this bold, confessional affirmation. In the first place it assumes that there is unanimity among the devout, and there is not. Sincere people find different things in Scripture. Roman Catholics, Methodists, Salvationists, Orthodox, all believe that they understand Scripture correctly. Differences of opinion are one of the facts of life in all serious study including biblical studies. It is well to recognize this from the beginning and to think again about whether the work of the Holy Spirit really involves unanimity of this kind.

In the second place the person who makes this affirmation surrenders the opportunity of discussing questions of biblical meaning with those who have a different starting-point. In dialogue the parties must take each other seriously. Each must reckon on the possibility of learning from the other. In the situation described above one party is absolutely confident and asks the other to surrender his position altogether. There is little chance of progress that way.

Those who make this affirmation will say that faith is superior to reason. Faith is god-given. Reason is the work of man. It is right that the man of faith should call upon the man of reason to surrender his logic in order to know the truth. This implies a harsh opposition between faith and reason; but God gave us reason as well as faith, and reason is indispensable in religious discourse. It cannot be written off as corrupt and untrustworthy. Moreover there are many men of deep religious faith who do not make the affirmation we are discussing, and it would be wrong to suggest that such people do not really believe. It is surely wiser to recognize the difficulties that are there, to put both faith and reason to the test and to build up a doctrine of the Holy Spirit which takes full account of the facts of the case.

Criticism and the Bible

e In common usage the word 'criticism' has negative overtones. One criticizes that which has fallen short or that needs amendment. In personal relationships one must be careful about criticism. Yet it is common to talk of criticizing the Bible. The word is unfortunate. In the world of biblical studies criticism means investigation. One simply asks questions. Why are there two men in dazzling apparel in the Lukan resurrection story and only one young man in white in Mark? Why was man created after vegetation and the animals in Gn. *1* but before them in Gn. *2*? Why does Galatians differ from Acts in recounting Paul's visits to Jerusalem? There is nothing 'critical' in the sense of mean or bitter or aggressive about these questions. They are not sceptical either. They are questions one must ask if one is to have a reasonable and honest approach to Scripture.

The whole critical programme with all its ramifications simply follows from this. Very early in his course, therefore, the biblical student is confronted with this choice. Either he

17

asks the questions or he does not. If he does not, he loses touch with those who do. Public discussion becomes impossible. Moreover he must stifle the questioning impulse where Scripture is concerned, which is not an easy thing to do. On the other hand, if he does ask the questions, he must be willing to accept the answers to which the evidence points, and that may well mean revising his original notion of the nature of Holy Scripture.

People often begin biblical studies with the idea of Scripture as a timeless truth, universal in relevance, capable of answering the questions of men of every age and place. But there is one sense in which Scripture is not timeless. Every word of it was first spoken or written on a particular day. Every word was first written on a particular piece of material by a particular man with a particular tool. Thereafter every passage was copied, carried around, passed on through the generations, amalgamated with other passages and eventually translated. All this is normal with ancient books. And at every stage accidents can happen. The evidence suggests that accidents happened with the Bible too. How could it be otherwise? The scribe could grow tired, the parchment could fray, the pen could wear out and become blotchy. Time, the climate and the carelessness of ordinary people could damage the scrolls, so that the Bible we have today is not an exact account of what was first said or written, even supposing that no other complications are involved.

What then? At the very least this means that technical studies are necessary. We must study the languages to find out what is the best translation. There will never be a perfect one. We must study the literary history of the books to find out how they were put together, by whom, and when. We must study the text to see what mistakes might have crept in. We may still believe that the heart of the message is timeless, but a lot of work has to be done before we can be sure what the heart of the message is. Thus criticism—or investigation—is not sceptical. It is both necessary and constructive, necessary in that the questions are there and have to be answered, constructive in that the purpose of criticism is to find out what the Bible really does say.

18

Unfortunately most of the questions that we ask about the Bible cannot be answered with 100 per cent certainty. This leads to scholarly debates and differences of opinion. Was the author of John familiar with the Synoptic Gospels? What did the term 'the Son of Man' mean? How can we explain all those references to the king in the psalms? Opinion on matters like these has swung to and fro and there have been wide divergences among scholars. We shall never know for sure who is right. That means that in many cases we have to be content with probability and we have to assess that probability ourselves. It is no use saying that this is unsatisfactory. This is how it is. Not knowing for sure is an uncomfortable situation to be in, but wishing will not change it. The fact is that the answers to many critical questions cannot be known for certain and we have to proceed on the understanding that it will always be so.

f   Let us now return to the two reasons for studying the Bible. Those who come in the first category may well find themselves asking critical questions, but it is not essential that they should. The Bible can be deep and fascinating to a person who asks no questions at all. Just as it is not necessary to study Shakespeare to enjoy his plays, so it is not necessary to understand technical matters to profit from the Bible. Nevertheless great literature repays study and the Bible is no exception. Questions such as the following arise and, if they can be answered, the meaning of the text is greatly enhanced.

Concerning a book:
   What were the historical circumstances when the book
      came into being?
   Under what precise circumstances was it composed?
   Can the author be known? If so, who was he?
   Did the book make use of previously existing materials?
   Has the book undergone editing or other changes in trans-
      mission?
   In what language was the book first written?
   What is its literary style? Is it prophecy, psalmody, apoc-
      alyptic, or something else?
   To what audience was the book addressed?

19

What purpose was it supposed to fulfil?
On what occasions and under what conditions was it to be
  read?

Concerning a passage:
  To what literary category does the passage belong?
  Did it exist before the book as a whole? If so, in what form
    and for what purpose?
  How does it relate to the rest of the book?
  Has it any peculiar features?
  What is the argument of the passage? Does it cite or echo
    passages elsewhere?
  Must it be read in conjunction with related passages in
    other biblical books?
  Does it deal with any particularly interesting or difficult
    notions?

Concerning a verse:
  Does it make clear sense?
  Are there any problems regarding the text? Do all the
    ancient manuscripts give the same version of this verse?
  Are there any difficulties of translation?
  Do any terms need explanation?
  Are there any allusions to people, places or events that
    need to be looked up and clarified?

Some of these questions are critical questions, that is to say
they are concerned with investigation of the literary and
historical background. Others are expository, that is to say
they are concerned with sense and meaning. Critical and
expository are not opposed to each other. No sharp line can
be drawn between them. Both contribute to our understanding. Exposition is easier and fuller after critical questions have
been answered.

None of these questions presume the divine inspiration of
the Bible. Neither do they exclude it. In this regard they are
neutral. They treat the Bible as a book that came into being in
the course of human history, through the medium of ordinary
human beings, and as a book that has suffered its share of

historical accidents. Given all that, they try to search out what the words mean.

g   Here is an example:

Bel boweth down, Nebo stoopeth; their idols are upon the beasts, and upon the cattle: the things that ye carried about are made a load, a burden to the weary *beast*. They stoop, they bow down together; they could not deliver the burden, but themselves are gone into captivity (Is. *46*.1–2 RV).

A person who had never read these verses before and who knew little about the Bible would not find the sense entirely clear but he would be able to draw some positive conclusions. The prophet is speaking disrespectfully of idols. He is saying that they are helpless, that they have to be carried about, that, far from delivering their devotees, they are suffering a humiliating fate themselves.

Further investigation would reveal that chs. *40–55* of the book of Isaiah are almost certainly not to be attributed to Isaiah the son of Amoz who prophesied in Judah in the days of Ahaz (735–15 BC) and Hezekiah (715–687 BC) but to an unnamed prophet who prophesied in Babylon towards the end of Israel's exile there, that is to say, around 540 BC. At that time the armies of Cyrus the Mede were on the march. He had already subdued Medea, Persia and Lydia and was about to fall on Babylon. The exiled Jews were delighted as, under Cyrus, they expected to be allowed to return home. In the British Museum is a clay cylinder on which the story of Cyrus' conquests has been written by one his obedient scribes. It includes a reference to Cyrus' policy of allowing refugees to return home. Babylon was in a state of disunity and fear. The Jews, who had been distressed by the apparent triumph of Babylonian gods when Jerusalem fell in 586 BC, were amused at the discomfiture of the Babylonians as Cyrus approached. Bel and Nebo were Babylonian gods, carried high through cheering multitudes in the New Year processions, but now being manhandled hurriedly to a safe place. Bel was an ancient Sumerian deity taken over by the

Babylonians and assimilated to their god Marduk. (The word Baal, which occurs frequently in the Bible as the name of a Canaanite god, is really the same word as Bel.) Bel was known as king of the world and master of the fates of men. All earthly kings were supposed to be his deputies. But, when the usurper Cyrus appeared, Bel bowed himself out. Nebo, or Nabu, was Marduk's son who engraved divine decisions of life and death on sacred tablets. He could extend or shorten life at a stroke. He was not so prestigious as Bel-Marduk, but he shared in the victory procession—and in the rout. The verse is not easy to translate with precision. There are one or two grammatical difficulties and minor variations between the ancient manuscripts. The word 'beast' at the end of v. 1 does not occur in the Hebrew original. It was added by the translators of the AV and later the RV in order to make better sense. The Jerusalem Bible catches the spirit of the original very well. It makes two small adjustments to the text and produces this translation.

> Bell is crouching. Nebo cringing.
> Their idols are being loaded on animals, on beasts of burden,
> carried off like bundles on weary beasts.
> They are cringing and crouching together,
> powerless to save the ones who carry them,
> as they themselves go off into captivity.

Investigations of this kind add enormously to the meaning of a passage and this is the task that is carried out by the good commentaries. The task is called exegesis, which simply means explanation. From one point of view the commentator, or exegete, is trying to put his readers in the position of the earliest hearers or readers. He is trying to establish what the prophet actually said or wrote, what was in the mind of his audience at the time, and what the words meant to them. This again cannot be done with complete accuracy at this range, but enough can be achieved to justify the scholarly labour.

h   It will be obvious from the example that the exegete draws on the findings of scholars working in many different fields. Archaeologists, historians, linguists, philologists, anthropologists, sociologists, all provide grist for his mill. These various experts may or may not be religious believers. One does not have to be a Christian to be fascinated by the history of the Persian empire and to become an authority on it. The exegete himself need not be a man of faith either. He can explain what Is. 46.1–2 is saying without any religious beliefs other than that the Bible is a very interesting book. The fact that most exegetes are devout men is due to the tendency of devout men to study the Bible. But others can do so just as well. The quality of the exegesis depends on the depth and breadth of the exegete's scholarship, not on his religious faith. We need to sit at the feet of the best historians, not the most saintly ones.

Interpretation

i There is, however, another discipline over and beyond exegesis to which we must now turn our attention. Most of the people who study the Bible come in category 2. They believe that the Bible is the word of God. Consequently they are not satisfied to know what the words meant to the original audience. That is important, but they also believe that the Bible has a message for today. Supposing Is. 46 meant all that we say above, the vital question remains, what are we to make of it now? This is a question of a different kind. This is a believer's question. A person reading the Bible for pleasure, as in category 1, would not ask it.

Here we come up against the notions of revelation and authority. All great works can influence us. We can be stirred and changed by what we read as we can by the people we meet, but we do not allow these books and people to have complete authority over us. As far as the believer is concerned, however, God does have complete authority. God's word, if it can be known, is absolutely binding. Christians of all kinds hold that the Bible, *in some way or other*, represents God's word. (One has to italicize *in some way or other*, because the relationship between the Bible and God's word is infinitely debatable, but at this stage we are merely enunciating the principle.) So the new discipline emerges—how to translate what was said and written long ago into an authentic

23

word for us and our world. At this point exegesis stops and interpretation takes over.

The interpreter must be a man of faith. That is a primary qualification. The men who dig up the manuscripts, piece them together, date them, emend them, read them, translate them need only be experts in their various techniques. Their work is available to men of all faiths and none. But the man who interprets the Bible for the present day must be a believer and his work has significance only for those who share his faith.

j   How we get from 'what it meant then' to 'what it means now' is a complicated matter. We cannot unfortunately take the words just as they stand and transfer them into our day and age.

There are two reasons why simple transfer is impossible. In the first place, the greater part of the Bible deals with specific situations, not with generalizations. The author of our example was mocking Babylonian idols on one particular day. Very few people who read Is. *46* today have anything to do with Babylonian idols. If the words are to have any present sense, they must be interpreted. So too the law, the history, the myth, the legend of the OT, and much of the Pauline epistles in the NT, cannot be believed and acted upon in London and New York, just as they stand. The question must always be, 'if this was said then, what must we say and do now?' That is the interpreter's question. Much more than simple transfer is involved.

There is a further, far-reaching reason. There is a tendency to think of the language of the Bible as changeless, eternal truth. Times change, fashions change, but what is written in the Bible remains constant. The words that a student of NT Greek struggles with today are the very same words as those written on a page by St. Paul or his scribe in apostolic times. That statement is superficially true, but therein lies a danger. Words on a page may be static, but their meaning is not. What is set down in one sense may, with the passing of years, come to be understood in another.

Students of English know how subtly the meaning of words changes. In Renaissance times 'artificial' was a word of praise.

24

It meant 'well, cunningly or elaborately made'. Today it means 'not the real thing'. 'Glamour' originally belonged to the world of elves and fairies. It came to be applied to anyone who was fascinating and beautiful. Then the film-makers discovered it and now the word has a hollow ring. A good example from the Bible is 'charity'. There were excellent reasons why the translators of the AV used 'charity' and not 'love' in 1 Cor. *13*. They were not to know that the word would slide downhill.

k   It is not simply that the meanings of words change. The whole framework in which they are used changes too. The word 'heaven' meant a physical place in biblical times and 'the ends of the earth' were literally the places where the earth stopped. It is impossible, therefore, to read biblical statements about heaven and earth and set them immediately in a modern framework, because we comprehend the universe in a different way and so we understand these terms differently. In every direction that we look the same is true. One uses 'father' and 'son' according to the family structure in the society in which one lives. One understands 'summer' and 'winter' according to the climate of the place in which one lives. The use of 'bread' and 'wine' and 'water' depends upon one's everyday experience of these commodities. And so on. Transferring statements from apostolic times to the present day is thus more complicated than at first sight appears.

We are often led astray by the fact that words on a page do not change. This seems to be all-important, but it is not so. In any form of communication it is the participants that are primary, not the words they use. What is in my mind must be transferred to your mind, if we are to communicate, and, if that can be done, the medium is of secondary importance. Every individual has his own background and experience of life. He can only put forward ideas in terms of that background and experience. Equally he can only receive and digest ideas in those terms. So every communication is a case of a person from one world of understanding trying to send out signals that a person from another world of understanding will receive and grasp with the consequence that the sender intended. This process sounds complicated but it is relatively

25

easy when the two worlds of understanding are close together. It becomes more difficult as the worlds get farther apart. If you go into an English restaurant for a meal and make the sign of drinking, the waiter will bring you a glass of water. If you do the same in France, he will bring you a glass of wine. The signal is the same, but the worlds of understanding of the two waiters differ slightly.

Where the two worlds of understanding differ greatly, much care is necessary. Anthropologists find that only after living with a tribe for several years do they begin to understand what the tribe is saying in its various rites and ceremonies. The same diligence and care need to be applied to the Bible. Simple transfer is out of the question. There is a huge gulf between the biblical world and our own and much hard work is necessary to bridge it. Fortunately most of us do not have to do all this work ourselves. The exegetes and interpreters do it for us. To put it briefly—and over-simply—the exegetes map the biblical world of understanding, the interpreters relate that world to the present day.

1   The Wisdom literature probably raises fewest difficulties for the interpreter.

> Better is a dry morsel and quietness therewith,
> Than an house full of feasting with strife. (Prov. *17*.1 RV)

Whatever changes in environment, language and custom there have been since these words were first uttered, their truth has been unaffected. 'What it meant then' and 'what it means now' are almost identical. It is not the same with the Psalms. We still use them in worship, but we understand them differently.

> O give thanks unto the Lord; for he is good:
> For his mercy endureth for ever. (Ps. *106*.1 RV)

These words were originally addressed to Yahweh, the God of Israel, who had shown his mercy many times in saving his people from disaster. The modern Christian interpreter, however, would say that 'the Lord' is the God of all nations

26

and 'his mercy' is most clearly shown in the life of Jesus. In the case of the books of law, the difficulties are greater. What is the present meaning of this verse?

> Thou shalt not let thy cattle gender with a diverse kind: thou shalt not sow thy field with two kinds of seed: neither shall there come upon thee a garment of two kinds of stuff mingled together. (Lev. *19*.19 RV)

Simple transference would suggest that garments of mixed wool and artificial fibres are forbidden to Christians, which illustrates how unsound simple transference is.

To recognize facts like this is not to undermine Scripture or destroy its significance, but rather to be persuaded that there is an irresistible case for careful and diligent study of the Bible. In biblical studies there are no short-cuts.

Note on the terms 'exegesis' and 'interpretation'
We have used the words 'exegesis' and 'interpretation' as if they were clearly defined and easily distinguished. In fact it is not so. Different writers use the words in different senses and often the same writer will move in both areas at once. We have made a clear distinction so that the biblical student can recognize that there are different kinds of biblical study and that each kind requires appropriate qualifications.

A further complication is that there are other terms such as 'exposition' and 'hermeneutics'. These, too, lack clear definition. 'Exposition' is a general term that includes exegesis and interpretation. 'Hermeneutics' is a very technical word that has to do with interpreting the Bible in terms of contemporary ideas.

Chapter 2

The Basic Disciplines of Biblical Studies

a THERE are three basic disciplines which students of the Bible have to understand. They are the historical, the literary, and the theological. In various ways they will all be discussed later, but it will be convenient if a brief introduction is given here. All are technical, all are different, all have skills, methods, and approaches of their own.

1. Historical studies

Strictly speaking historical studies are not biblical studies at all. They use the Bible as a source and they throw a great deal of light on the Bible, but they are not directed to the Bible as such. They are directed to the people who gave us the Bible and to the culture and civilization within which those people lived and worked. This is an important point. Historical study of the Bible aims to establish *history*. By means of the Bible it hopes to go behind the Bible. It does not aim to establish the truth of the biblical history. At times it may in fact do so, but that is not the aim. The historian sets about his work ready to accept whatever conclusion the evidence shows to be most probable. He would not be a genuine historian if he reached his conclusions on non-historical grounds and then set about trying to prove them by historical means. So-called history has been written that way, but it is not worthy of much respect.

The area of historical enquiry could not be wider. Historians are interested in everything that belongs to the period they are studying. No greater calumny exists than that history is all to do with kings and battles. History includes a study of the climate of the period, the methods of husbandry, the economic system, legal and social structures, the appearance of the landscape, education, dress, even cosmetics and children's games. There is no such thing as a secular historian. How people think and talk about the beginning and the end of things and about the unseen forces that control everything is an important element in their culture. How they behave at the festivals is an important factor in their lives. And so on. It is, therefore, perfectly proper to have a historical enquiry into the beliefs of the Israelites, the way they sacrificed, the roles of prophet and priest and the common people in worship. The historian will not pass judgment on whether that worship was 'true' or not, but he will try to tell us in meticulous detail what actually took place. Similarly he will tell us what the primitive Christians believed about the Resurrection, how they celebrated the Resurrection and how they preached it. He will tell us what the historical probability of the story of the empty tomb is. Beyond that he cannot and would not wish to go. But enough has been said to show how great a contribution the historian makes to exegesis.

The raw material on which the historian works are records, archives, inscriptions, the more ancient the better, and artefacts, monuments, buildings, that have survived from the period. This is where the archaeologist becomes important. The archaeologist of today is able to uncover objects, date them, classify them and make deductions about the people who made them with remarkable accuracy. Gone are the days of the imaginative amateur. Today archaeology is a science.

Archaeological evidence is of two kinds. In the first place there are the objects that are uncovered, the houses, the temples, the altars and the broken pottery. In the second place there are the inscriptions, particularly, in the ancient near east, the clay tablets, of which thousands have come to light, and some scrolls that have amazingly survived. Immense skill is required to locate, uncover, clean, preserve and piece together fragments of a scroll, before ever the reading and translating begins. To all these must be added the skill of assessing the significance of a discovery. Inscriptions are not to be taken at face value just because they are ancient. Archaeologists today do not jump to conclusions as their predecessors did too readily. But at the end of the day some facts and many strong probabilities emerge and the historian is able to piece together his picture of the bygone age.

b **2. Literary studies**

Literary studies begin with the biblical text. Other ancient documents are useful for purposes of comparison but primarily the literary critic is concerned with the Bible. 'Literary studies' is a vague term covering many different concerns. Some begin with the parchments and work towards the final text. Others begin with the text and work backwards to the people who composed it.

The first task is to compare the many different versions of the biblical books which the chances of history and the labours of archaeologists have delivered up to us. This is an ever-increasing task because new fragments are for ever coming to light. The discovery of the Dead Sea Scrolls particularly gave the textual critics (see below 15e) an immense amount of work. The aim of this comparison is to work out the best, that is to say, what was most probably the original, version of every line in the Bible. Before any new translation can be launched, decisions must be made about the actual text to be translated. The variations are numbered in tens of thousands; many are trivial, but some are of great significance. A great textual scholar used to say, 'Anyone can tell you what the Bible means, but it takes a scholar to tell you what the Bible is.' An exaggeration, of course, but it makes the point that what the Bible is, word by word and line by line, has to be determined by laborious textual studies before we can have a translation to work on. Some new translations, notably the RV, were launched, not so much because a new version of the English was needed, but because so much more had been learnt about the text to be translated.

After the textual critic comes the translator or the translating panel. These people have to decide whether the new translation is meant to be read in church or on the train, whether it is to be a meticulously accurate version for students or a flowing, readable version for the common man. There is now no such thing as 'the Bible' but there is 'the Bible for this situation' and 'the Bible for that'. The existence of the AV on its own for 250 years gave the correct impression that the Bible does not change. The innumerable editions now on the market, read by different people in different circumstances for different ends, give the equally correct impression that the meaning of the Bible cannot be adequately expressed in a single English form.

Other literary scholars begin with the text and try to discover how the various books and passages came to take the form they finally achieved. If there are two accounts of one incident it is usually easy to see whether one borrowed from the other. From that one can deduce which is the older and what the particular interest of each author was. Where one man changes another man's story it is often possible to see why he made the change. The date of a piece of writing, its place of origin, its purpose, and the particular concerns of the author or authors is important for exegesis.

Another way of going about this literary task is to ask what situations in the everyday life of Israel and the infant Church would call for oral or literary composition. What situations in our life call for such compositions? Church services require hymns and prayers. Football matches need reports. Bereavements call for letters of sympathy, and so on. Our society is very literate and our literary needs are immense. The biblical communities were simpler, less literate, but probably more formal. Their needs would be few but probably stereotyped. They would be met by oral compositions for years before anything needed to be written down. Careful scrutiny of passages in the Bible enables scholars, known as 'form critics', to determine the situation for which a passage was composed and to guess at the earliest version of it. It is even possible to suggest how a passage changed as it was passed down through the decades, and also how the final editor who included the passage in his book put his own stamp on it.

This kind of enquiry brings home to the student the fact that the composition of the Bible was a long process in which many people, sometimes the whole community, were involved. Paul's epistles are not at all typical. Most of them were written on a day or over a few days by one man, though one suspects that, from time to time, even he made use of older material. There is no author in the simple sense for most of the other books of the Bible. We have to think, not so much of a man sitting down to write, but of a community using materials it has received from the past and passing it on, perhaps a little modified, to the next in line.

c **3. Theological studies**

The people who gave us the Bible had a robust faith and the Bible expresses it. The biblical theologian tries to find out what those people believed and how thay put it into practice. Even at this point it is still possible—and important—not to allow faith to determine what is discovered. There is a proper place for 'faithful' interpretation of that kind and we shall come to it in a moment.

In the first place the theologian studies the beliefs expressed in the stories of the Patriarchs, in Deuteronomy, in the prophets, in the books of Kings and Chronicles, in the Psalms, and in the NT. He must allow the biblical books to speak for themselves. He describes the beliefs and arranges them in a systematic way, but he tries not to impose on the books a system which is foreign to them. If they show an interest in atoning sacrifices, or rewards for the godly, or the signs of the end, so be it. That is the raw material of his study.

The theologian soon finds that there is not one system of belief and practice in the Bible, but many. The OT stands over against the NT, the prophet has different emphases from the priest, Kings differs from Chronicles, Psalms from Proverbs, the Synoptics from John, and so on. Moreover, not only is none of these books systematic in itself, but none offers a complete theology. Each is concerned with its own interests, and building perfect systems does not feature among those interests.

This brings the theologian to his final task, the task which

32

for many is the supreme end of biblical study, that is, to draw all this manifold material into a statement of faith that is, on one hand, true to the Bible and, on the other, relevant to the present. The biblical theologian draws on the work of those in the other disciplines. He must do his exegesis before he can interpret. He needs, therefore, to be a thorough-going biblical scholar. But, whereas all the other scholars could rely on interest in their subject and technical skill to fulfil their task, the theologian, that is to say, the interpreter as we can now call him, must have religious faith. He must believe, not merely that the Bible is an interesting old book, but that it is of profound concern to us now. He must believe that the Bible speaks to every age including his own. In short he must believe that, in the Bible, God addresses mankind. In all the other disciplines religious faith was not a relevant factor. Here it is not merely relevant, it is essential.

d **The authority of scholars**

There is a general tendency in biblical studies to clinch an argument by quoting the opinion of an eminent scholar. 'The greatest living authority on X said . . .' is usually the prelude to a bad argument. Scholarly judgments are of the utmost importance, but they need to be handled with more subtlety than this.

In the first place, scholarship is not like boxing. There are no world champions. In some fields there may be one who is pre-eminent, but it is more likely that there will be many whose opinions carry weight.

Secondly, scholars differ. Wherever there are difficult judgments to be made in biblical studies divergent views appear. If a famous scholar contends that Ezra preceded Nehemiah, another will soon appear to argue that Nehemiah preceded Ezra. On the face of it, it seems confusing. What is the good of scholarly opinion if it is contradictory? Indeed, what is the point of scholarship if nothing can be established with unanimity?

The answer is that one must know how to make use of scholarly opinion. It is also necessary to emphasize again that, in the great majority of cases, all that can be established is probability, not certainty. By careful use of scholars' researches a student can make his own judgment on the various issues he encounters in biblical studies. These judgments will be satisfactory in that they will contribute to his own mental map of the biblical area, that is, the particular layout of biblical issues that the student finds most positive and helpful. It will not be a perfect map. It will need to be redrawn from time to time. But it will enable him to read the Bible with greater and greater understanding.

Perhaps the greatest misconception of those new to biblical studies is the notion that there is a perfect answer to every problem, that the contradictory views are due to the machinations of sceptics, that it is only necessary to find a scholar of integrity for all one's problems to be solved. This is wishful thinking. One would like certainty. Therefore one imagines it can be found. It cannot. Honest and able men differ. The proper conclusion is that, in the kind of world in which we live, one must carry out one's exegesis—and, therefore, one's interpretation—on other grounds than cast-iron certainty. There is nothing alarming about this. In other areas of human studies—art and literature—cast-iron certainty does not exist. In other areas of faith—systematic theology and moral philosophy particularly—there is no unanimity. It would be anomalous indeed if biblical scholars were able to supply a complete series of unanimous and irrefutable answers.

How, then does one proceed? Before launching into a discussion authors commonly survey the field. They quote the opinions of their predecessors and strike some kind of balance. They then add their own reflections and any new evidence there may be and reach their own conclusion. For them that part of the map is then fixed for the time being. Every student has to do something similar. He has to find out what has been said. He has to weigh opinion being careful to give greatest weight to the best argued positions and not to those he finds immediately attractive. And he has to reach his own tentative conclusion.

At this point excessive modesty is as bad as excessive confidence. While it is obviously wrong to be sure of one's conclusion before one studies the evidence, it is equally unprofitable to be unwilling to make a judgment at the end of the day. The modest student who says, 'Who am I to pass judgment on the work of these eminent men?' is really contributing to the same misconception as the over-confident one, the misconception that there is *one, true, final answer*, though he himself—the modest student—has not yet discovered it. The more profitable way is to reach a tentative conclusion in whatever state of awareness one may have achieved, recognizing that it is tentative, and being ready to move on if further light comes. If there are no conclusions at all, there will be no mental map, no grasp of the whole field, and little positive biblical study.

e   To sum up this discussion here are a few principles to guide the student in his attempts to make the best use of scholarly work.

1. *It is dangerous to accept a scholar's conclusion without following his argument right through.* This is a counsel of perfection. The student cannot read everything. But it is important for him to recognize the difference between a conclusion he accepts because he understands how it was reached and a conclusion he accepts on trust. He can be confident about the former. But he must be hesitant and restrained about the latter.

The danger rests in the exaggerated, almost mystical, respect that is sometimes afforded to biblical scholars. Their conclusions are good only because they are founded on good arguments, not because they have any formal authority. From time to time one reads in essays and examination papers sentences that begin, 'Scholars say that . . .' This often means that the scholarly conclusions have been noted, but the arguments on which they are based have been ignored. From time to time a sentence like this occurs, 'The books of Chronicles and Kings were compiled by different editors or schools, so there are obviously going to be major differences in the style of the books.' Here there is a complete reversal of the proper method of study. The sentence begins with the conclusion—based on what the scholars say—and then goes searching for facts to support it and even assumes that they must be there. In fact 'the major differences' provide the facts and 'the different editors' are a scholarly hypothesis to explain the facts.

To follow the arguments of a scholar is to give him proper respect. To accept his conclusions uncritically is to misuse his work and to give him a status that is not proper to his function.

f 2. *It is necessary to recognize the varying degrees of probability that attach to scholarly conclusions.* If it is an error to treat scholars with exaggerated respect, it is equally wrong to reject their conclusions out of hand. There is no simple rule. In the case of some biblical problems the data (that is, the basic evidence) are complicated and many hypotheses have been put forward, each with a few supporters. In other cases a single hypothesis commands the support of almost everybody. In the former case it is right for the student to be unsure; in the latter he can follow with confidence. Knowing the data and the arguments enables the student to know which is which.

In the field of biblical studies, very few conclusions can be stated baldly as proven. There is always the possibility that they might be varied in the future when new facts come to light. It is good to remember this when we talk about Pentateuchal criticism or the Synoptic problem. In both cases the study of oral tradition has led to a softening of the hard lines of the original theories. It is difficult for a student not to take the priority of Mark as a fact when nearly every book he reads assumes it, but it is wise for him occasionally to remind himself that scholarly work moves on and that very little is so firmly established that it can never be modified.

On the other hand a few hypotheses are so well supported by the facts, and, therefore, so widely agreed among scholars, that it would be perverse not to use them as a basis for study. One has only to compare the account of the construction of the Ark of the Covenant in Dt. *10*.1–5 with those in Ex. *25* and *37* to realize that something needs explaining. The hypothesis of two sources, a simple narrative source and a complex priestly source, is unassailable. There are other such cases in biblical studies. The problems and the solutions are so well known that authors tend to assume that their readers are familiar with them.

g 3. *In the realm of interpretation presuppositions are all-important.* Interpreters of the Bible differ even more than the critics. Interpreters include liberals, conservatives, Roman Catholics, Christian Scientists, Jehovah's Witnesses, and many others. They all work on the same material, but they come up with different conclusions, because they do not begin in the same place.

Everyone has presuppositions. In the case of interpretation these presuppositions relate to the deepest beliefs about God and man. However brilliant an interpreter may be, those who do not accept his presuppositions will not be able to accept all his conclusions.

This puts the student in a quandary. He may find himself having to choose between a learned and widely-applauded work by one whose starting-point he rejects and a meagre volume by one with whom he is in sympathy. The experienced student will have less difficulty, because he will be able to read the better book making allowances for the unacceptable point of view. This is not easy for a beginner.

It is, therefore, necessary for every student to think carefully about his own position, to find out as much as possible about the position of the author whose work he is reading, to be willing to modify his own position if the impact of the book as a whole is persuasive, and, in any case, to be able to learn from those from whom he differs.

h 4. *Authority cannot be transferred from one area to another.* A person who is distinguished in one field merits the most careful attention in that field, but what he has to say in other fields may not be nearly as authentic. As a rule scholars are wary of making pronouncements about matters outside their field. NT scholars are reluctant to comment on OT issues, and vice versa. This is quite proper, but it can happen that in preaching or in popular lectures a man may go outside his area. He will know what he is doing and he will doubtless warn his audience, but audiences sometimes do not appreciate fine distinctions. A biblical scholar is a biblical scholar to them. The student must not be misled. There is no reason why an expert in Botany should be heeded if he makes provocative remarks about the Pauline epistles or the resurrection narratives.

i 5. *Beware of quoting secondhand.* It is good to be able to quote from great authorities, but their books are sometimes heavy going. So there arises another collection of books that tell us in simple terms what the authorities mean. Such books usually include quotations. It is unwise to make use of them without having seen them in their original context. Sometimes it is inevitable if the book is in a foreign language, but it is regrettable. There is no substitute for first-hand knowledge and the student is better advised to struggle with difficult original work than to read other peple's summaries. There are cautionary stories to be told about misapprehensions that were passed right down the line because nobody bothered to check the original. Moreover there are good educational reasons for attempting the difficult rather than the easy task.

Chapter 3

The English Versions of the Bible

a   Every Bible student will be interested in how the Bible came to be translated into English, and every student will also need to choose a working Bible of his own. The purpose of this chapter is to give an account of the major translations that have appeared, to discuss how translations are to be judged, and to enumerate the needs of a student who is choosing a Bible to work from.

English versions fall into two groups, the early ones of which the last and greatest was the AV of 1611, and the modern ones of which the first was the RV of 1881. Until 1881 the AV reigned supreme. The majesty of its prose and its secure position within the Church gave it a mystical quality that it has never lost. Small wonder that some Victorian clerics regarded the RV as an outrage. It is instructive to compare what was written about the RV by men such as J. W. Burgon, Dean of Chichester, with what was written about the Wycliffe Bible by such as Thomas More. Both men regarded translation as corruption, if not destruction, of the sacred text.

The student has to recognise, then, that the Bible appears under two guises. On one hand it has *meaning*, that deserves constant and careful scrutiny and ever new translation. On the other hand it is a *symbol* of the divine word to which all reverence must be given. Many people have found it hard to grasp that these two do not contradict each other. Only in the last few decades has it been easy to believe that the black, leather-bound volume, read with all solemnity from the lectern, can, in a different translation, be bound as a paperback and read briskly on the train.

Note on chapters and verses
Various systems for dividing the Bible into sections were in use in the Middle Ages. The present division into chapters originated in Paris in the early thirteenth century. It is ascribed to an Englishman, Stephen Langton. Verse divisions came with the Reformation. The present system goes back to Robert Stephanus' Greek NT of 1551. A similar division of the OT followed twenty years later.

---

b **The Wycliffe Bible**

John Wycliffe (1330–84) set the Bible against papal authority and urged that it be made available to every Christian believer. It is not clear how much of the actual work of translation he was able to carry out himself, but it is clear that what is known as the Wycliffe Bible was due to his inspiration. A first edition was produced in his lifetime. It was a translation of the Latin Vulgate and it preserved the contents and the order of the Vulgate (see below 14f). The first edition was very literal, that is to say, it followed the Latin word by word without any regard for flowing, English style. After Wycliffe's death, a disciple, John Purvey, produced a second edition that was more idiomatic, more like the written and spoken English of the day. Purvey's edition was completed in 1388, almost ninety years before Caxton set up his printing press in Westminster. The Wycliffe Bible was, therefore, handwritten and there was little chance of it being available to every Christian believer.

c **William Tyndale (*c*. 1494–1536)**

Tyndale lived in the age of printing. He also had the advantage of Erasmus' Greek text of the NT which was published in 1516 (see below 14g), but, due to the opposition of the English bishops, he had to work abroad. He translated

40

straight from Greek into vigorous, flowing English and his NT was completed in 1526. Notes were added to the translation proper, and these notes, Lutheran in tone, caused far more trouble than the translation itself. The Bishop of London had copies of the volume burnt at St. Paul's Cross. Other translators stole Tyndale's work and issued pirate editions, but in 1534 he produced his own second edition which became the basis of all English versions that were to follow. At the same time he set to work on the Hebrew OT and he managed to complete the Pentateuch and the historical books before he was arrested, perhaps kidnapped would be a better word, in Antwerp. He was imprisoned at Vilvorde, near Brussels, and executed in 1536. Tradition says that he died crying, 'Lord, open the King of England's eyes.' If so, he was probably in ignorance of the true state of affairs. Henry VIII had already permitted English translations. Tyndale's real enemy was Charles V, the Holy Roman Emperor.

d **Miles Coverdale (1488–1568)**

Coverdale learnt his trade from Tyndale when they worked together on the Pentateuch in Hamburg. The year before Tyndale died Coverdale had produced his own translation of the Vulgate, using Tyndale's and Luther's and other German versions as guides. Coverdale's was thus the first complete English Bible to be printed, though all the work was done on the continent. The Apocrypha was included but, following the Lutheran view, it was separated from the other books and given a section of its own. When the Bible appeared in England, it was dedicated to Henry VIII. The king, a student of some depth but alarming inconsistency, permitted the Bible to be distributed in England. A second edition in 1537 actually carried a royal licence.

e **Matthew's Bible**

The date of this Bible was 1537, but who was the author? Most historians are agreed that 'Thomas Matthew' was a pen-name for another associate of Tyndale, one John Rogers

41

who was martyred in 1555. Matthew's Bible follows Tyndale's closely as far as Tyndale's went. For the rest it relies on Coverdale. The Apocrypha appears as a separate section. Due to Cranmer's support and to Thomas Cromwell's political influence this Bible was given a royal licence, so, within a year of Tyndale's death, his work was being promulgated in England by the king himself. A greek scholar, called Richard Taverner, produced a second edition.

f The Great Bible

By 1538 the battle for an English version was over. Clergy of all persuasions began to make provision for English Bibles to be chained to their lecterns. The ideal version, however, had not yet appeared. Coverdale's was not a translation from the original languages and Matthew's Bible included notes that, like the notes of Tyndale, were more stridently Protestant than some bishops would allow. A royal injunction of September 5th 1538 required that a Bible should be available in every church by All Saints' Day, November 1st. What a stimulus for translators to provide a new and acceptable Bible! Coverdale was given the chief responsibility. He used Matthew's Bible as a basis. The Great Bible appeared in 1539 and a second, improved edition, with a preface by Cranmer, appeared in 1540. This was appointed by the king to be read in churches. All previous versions were thus superseded. In 1549 came the first English Prayer Book. The psalms in it were naturally taken from the Great Bible. Tyndale had died before he reached the Psalms, so the translation that appeared in the Great Bible was substantially Coverdale's. Coverdale's psalms survived through the various editions of the Prayer Book including the definitive one of 1662. This explains why the psalms in the Book of Common Prayer are different from those in the AV. The Great Bible was a milestone, but it had one flaw. It was still not in every part a translation from the original languages.

g **The Genevan Bible**

Geneva was the centre of Protestant scholarship after the year 1541 when Calvin began to establish himself as the supreme influence in that city. Theodore Beza, John Knox, Miles Coverdale, and many other reformers were attracted to Calvin's Geneva. There English refugees set about a new translation from the Hebrew and the Greek using the Great Bible as a model. It was completed in 1560. It included the Apocrypha as an appendix and, once again, notes were added strongly Calvinistic in tone. This ensured that, however scholarly the work might be and however popular it might become, it would never be adopted officially in an England seeking a middle way between Roman tyranny and Protestant excess. The Genevan Bible was set out in verses. It also introduced the valuable device of printing in italics those words which are necessary to make sense of the English but are not present in the original tongue. In this Bible Adam and Eve sewed fig leaves together and made 'breeches' in Gen. 3.7, hence the well-known 'breeches Bible'.

h **The Bishops' Bible**

In 1561, Matthew Parker, Archbishop of Canterbury, gathered a group of scholars, mostly bishops, to produce a Bible as scholarly as the Genevan but without the excessively Protestant associations. The Great Bible was again the basis. This time there were to be no notes. The work took seven years and there were numerous editions between 1568 and the publication of the AV. Scholarly opinion however has always been that the Bishops' Bible was technically inferior to the Genevan Bible. The Genevan Bible was certainly more popular. The Bible that was scholarly, popular, and universally acceptable had, therefore, still not appeared.

i **The Authorized Version**

King James VI of Scotland became James I of England when Elizabeth died in 1603. He summoned a conference to deal with Church affairs at Hampton Court in January 1604. Most of its business has long since been forgotten, but it passed one resolution that was to have inestimable influence over the religion and culture of the English-speaking world. It was that a translation of the whole Bible be made, without notes, from the original languages, for use in church. The AV was a literary miracle. Forty-seven men were involved, arranged into six panels. A smaller group reviewed the work as it was completed. To speak rudely of the literary productions of committees, as is customary today, is to forget the AV, for the panels produced one of the greatest works in the English tongue. Italics were again used for words added by the translators to make good sense of the English. Chapter headings were introduced, and paragraph signs (¶) which curiously disappear after Acts 20.36. There were also marginal references to parallel passages and to possible variant translations. The Apocrypha was included. In the course of time the chapter headings were abbreviated and the spellings modernized. Archbishop Ussher's dates were at one stage introduced into the margins, but happily they have disappeared now. Several features of the original have also been discarded. The Apocrypha was left out in the nineteenth century and many modern editions lack the marginal references, the preface, 'The Translators to the Reader', and the fulsome address to King James. The 1611 edition is commonly known as the Authorized Version, though it was never authorized by Act of Parliament. Its original authority rested on the king and the Hampton Court Conference. Tradition and the inherent excellence of the work provide all the authority it needs today.

Note on Ussher's Dates
In some old editions of the AV the supposed dates of the events recorded are printed in the margin. These dates first appeared in 1701 and they were taken from the works of James Ussher (1581–1656), Archbishop of Armagh, and a noted scholar of his day. By making use of the genealogies and taking the OT literally Ussher had

> *reached the conclusion that the Creation took place at 9.0 a.m. on October 26th 4004* BC. *Ussher's system is of only antiquarian interest today.*

j The Douai Bible

Roman Catholics of the sixteenth century had little regard for the English versions that were appearing. For them the Vulgate was the only authentic text and most of the translators were heretics. An English college for the propagation of the Roman Catholic faith was founded at Douai in northern France in 1568. Ten years later it moved to Rheims, returning to Douai in 1593. Gregory Martin, a professor of that college, translated the whole Latin Bible, preserving, of course, the Latin order, and adding notes that were as polemical on the Catholic side as the Geneva Bible's notes had been on the Protestant side. The NT was published in 1582, while the college was at Rheims, and the OT in 1609. The translation was very literal, in places unintelligibly so. Beginning in 1749 Bishop Richard Challoner made a number of revisions and a further revision was made in 1941. Until recent times the Douai version stood alone as the approved English Bible of Roman Catholics.

k The Revised Version

In some ways the AV was too successful. It gave to the English version a majesty and a permanence that are not proper to a translation. In many cases it improved on the original, turning wordy, halting Hebrew into matchless English prose. But scholars came more and more to realize that the AV was not perfect. On one hand, the actual Hebrew and Greek texts that were used by King James' translators were far from accurate. The two best manuscripts of the NT in existence were not available in 1611. One was lying hidden in a monastery on Mount Sinai and not discovered until 1844. The other was stored away in the Vatican library and not much appreciated. So, when the great Victorian textual scholars, B. F. Westcott and F. J. A. Hort, set to work to prepare their text, they were able to make use of documents of which the Jacobean translators had never heard. On the other hand, the normal processes of travel, discovery and research had greatly improved the understanding of biblical languages. It had become clear that, in some places, the AV was incorrect. Great courage was needed to launch a new translation and the fifty-four churchmen nominated for the task wisely proceeded with modesty and caution. They were concerned about accuracy. They did not want to give Scripture a new look. They decided to revise and not to re-translate. Their revisions were to be composed in AV style—no 'modern English' for them. Even when they corrected the AV, they put the old translation in the margin if it had any justification at all. The RV printed poetry as poetry and introduced paragraphs without cutting out chapters and verses. Only the chapter headings were discarded. The ecumenical nature of the undertaking comes as a surprise. Anglican scholars joined with Scottish Presbyterians and Free Churchmen. A Unitarian was included. Cardinal Newman was invited but was unable to accept. Help was given by thirty American scholars in hopes—unfulfilled—of a single version. The NT was published in 1881, the OT in 1885, the Apocrypha in 1896. In 1898 an edition with cross-references to parallel passages was published, after which the variant translations were put at the bottom of the page. No translation that has ever been made has been more concerned with scholarly accuracy, which is one reason why the RV is still regarded by many as the best English version for the biblical student.

1 R. F. Weymouth's New Testament

Dr. R. F. Weymouth was headmaster of Mill Hill School in north London. A Classical scholar, he produced his own version of the Greek NT. He aimed to produce a translation of the NT for private reading, not for reading in public. It appeared in 1903. It was much honoured and, in 1924, long after Weymouth's death, it was revised and re-issued.

m **James Moffatt**

Few men in the history of biblical scholarship have had the vigour and the learning to translate the whole Bible single-handed. James Moffatt was cᴝe. He produced *The New Testament: a New Translation* in 1913 and *The Old Testament: a new Translation* in 1924. A single-volume edition appeared in 1926. Moffatt's was no revision but a new translation and a fine example of a new theory in translating the Scriptures. Moffatt thought first of the effect the words had on the original readers and then tried to produce English that would have the same effect on his contemporaries. If meticulous accuracy did not produce clear, pungent English, he was prepared to compromise a little for the sake of the striking phrase. The Moffatt Bible is a Bible for Scots right down to the bagpipes in Dan. *3*.10 and 15. The work reveals certain idiosyncrasies and is generally liberal in tone. The Hebrew text is amended from time to time on the basis of conjecture only. There are rearrangements, most notably in the first verse of all which is transplanted from Gn. *2*.4a. There are double square brackets for passages which Moffatt rather over-confidently affirms to be editorial additions or later interpolations. The J source in the Pentateuch (see 21h) is printed in italics, though discussion about the precise limits of this source and even its existence as a source continues to this day. Yahweh, the name for God, is translated 'the Eternal', which is sometimes felicitous but sometimes cumbersome. 'Thee' and 'thou' become 'you' when biblical characters address each other but are retained when they address God. The Moffatt Bible was a landmark in biblical translation. It achieved a huge popularity and a whole series of commentaries, *The Moffatt New Testament Commentary*, was based upon it.

n **Ronald Knox**

Knox was a Roman Catholic priest, a chaplain at Oxford before the Second World War. A convert and a very orthodox Catholic, he insisted on translating the Vulgate despite his familiarity with Hebrew and Greek. As a man of letters and immensely gifted, he shunned the cliché and the ephemeral phrase. His NT, published in 1945, gained official approval beside Douai. His complete OT, including the Apocryphal books in their traditional Catholic positions, was issued a few years later. The use of the Vulgate makes it an unsuitable Bible for students. Perhaps due to its heavy style, it has never been very popular.

o **Revised Standard Version**

RSV has an American origin. It derives from the American Standard Version of 1901 which was the transatlantic parallel to the British RV. The project of revision was launched in 1937 with the admirable aims of being scholarly in text and translation, achieving a simple, direct, modern English style, and yet preserving some of the aura of the AV. Its translators were better equipped than any of their predecessors. If Knox had gone to one extreme in limiting himself to the Vulgate, the RSV scholars went to the other by looking at all the texts and versions and even, in a few places, translating what they thought must have been written originally when there was no concrete evidence to prove it. Unlike other translations RSV is published by a standing committee which is able to improve the work from edition to edition. The NT appeared in 1946, the whole Bible in 1952, the Apocrypha in 1957, and a cheap paperback edition of the whole in 1973. In 1966 there was a Catholic edition with the books arranged in Vulgate order, but more recently the standing committee has become not only international but fully ecumenical. An edition, called 'The Common Bible', is now accepted by all the major denominations. RSV introduced quotation marks for direct speech, set out the text in paragraphs, and attempted to make biblical poetry look and read like poetry. 'Thou' is used only when man addresses God. Such changes may seem simple and necessary but they raise many problems. The conventions of Hebrew poetry are very different from the conventions of our own. It is not always clear in the Bible what is direct speech and what is not. And should Jesus be addressed as 'thou' or 'you'? RSV has grappled with these problems and given us a revision which is scholarly, dignified and versatile. Every biblical student must have the RSV on his shelf.

p **J. B. Phillips**

Phillips' *New Testament in Modern English* was published as a complete volume in 1958, but most of the material had already appeared in parts, of which the first, *Letters to Young Churches* (1947), was undoubtedly the best. Phillips' intention was pastoral. He wanted to unravel Paul's intricate sentences so that ordinary people could read them with profit and pleasure. He was not writing for scholars and he was prepared to take liberties with the text in order to produce clear and lively English. He has been accused of paraphrasing rather than translating and that means calling on his own inventiveness and imagination to bring out the meaning. RV and Phillips between them illustrate the problem. Pure, accurate translation is flat and out of touch. Fresh, vigorous English may carry meaning that comes from the translator rather than the biblical text. The 1958 volume was revised in 1973. A better Greek text was used and some of the more imaginative renderings were removed.

q **The New Testament in Plain English**

This was the work of Charles Kingsley Williams, a NT scholar who taught in Madras and Ghana. He wanted to provide a version that could be read by those whose first language was not English. Williams' 'plain English' is not the same as basic English, but it does make use of a limited vocabulary. Sentences are short, syntax simple. There is a glossary to explain those words, less than 200, that are not to be found in the selected vocabulary the author was using. The work was published in 1952.

r **H. J. Schonfield**

Schonfield was a Jew and published *The Authentic New Testament* in 1955. It is rich in Jewish insights and nothing could be more necessary in a translation of the NT. It is in this sense that Schonfield's translation is claimed to be, and may in fact be, *authentic*.

s **New English Bible**

Up to this point all the Bibles we have considered were either offical revisions of previous, celebrated translations (AV, RV, RSV) or individual works by men of high literary skill with no official backing. An official translation which was not just a revision was still wanting. The idea of a new Bible came from Scotland in 1946 and it was put in hand by the British Church in the following year. The project was ambitious. Scholarly revision may well be done by a committee, but a new translation using modern vocabulary, modern English constructions, modern speech rhythms, is a different matter. Not since the AV had a committee attempted such a task and the outstanding success of that ancient venture was not necessarily encouraging. The aim was to bring the Bible to earth. In some instances the AV is more exalted, more resonant than the original. The NEB was not to make that mistake. It was to be the Bible in good, contemporary, common English. Like the RSV it is not tied to a single NT text. Choices were made of what Greek to read, and therefore translate, as the scholars proceeded. At the end of the undertaking a complete version of the Greek text they had constructed and then translated was published (*The Greek New Testament* ed. R. V. G. Tasker, 1964). The problem was not so great with the OT and a standard text was used, though from time to time the translators were ready to emend it, even by conjecture. Hence the occurrence of 'Prob. rdg.; Heb. . . .' at the bottom of the page which indicates that the translation is a scholarly construction because the Hebrew, a translation of which is then given, does not make sense. The NT was published in 1961 and the whole Bible, with a revised NT, in 1970. There are traditionalists who do not like the NEB. For them only the AV adequately represents the sublime mystery of the faith. Others argue that Christians must work out their faith in relation to the harsh, secular, late twentieth-century world. The NEB is for them.

t **Jerusalem Bible**

The Jerusalem Bible is more than a translation. It includes exegetical footnotes, introductions to sections, maps, historical charts, cross-references, headings. The aim is not simply to provide Catholics—and others—with a Bible in the language we use today but also to supply exegetical information so that the depth of biblical meaning can be more readily grasped. The Standard edition is large: it has over 2,000 pages, but there is a cheap editon without the notes. The name 'Jerusalem Bible' takes us back to the Dominican Biblical School in Jerusalem where a brilliant French Bible with cross-references and notes was made. It was published in Paris in 1956. It was so successful that an English version was contemplated at once. The translation was made from the original languages with the French version acting only as a guide, but the notes are a direct translation of the French save that they have been revised in the light of the Second Vatican Council. The English edition appeared in 1966. The JB is an excellent tool for Protestants as well as Catholics. It uses standard English nomenclature for biblical books and characters. The order of the books is the same as in the NEB save that the books of the Apocrypha are dispersed throughout the OT in appropriate places. Verse is regularly printed as verse. A real attempt has been made to allow the diversity of style in the original books to come through in the English in contrast, for example, to the AV where the best and the worst passages are all rendered into rich, Jacobean English. Unlike RSV and NEB, JB translates the sacred name for God as 'Yahweh', that is, by a simple transliteration. This is correct. The four letters do represent a name and not the word 'God' or the word 'Lord', but it may be some time before ordinary people grasp this fact. JB uses 'you' throughout.

u **Alan Dale**

Alan Dale was an educationist who was concerned that the Bible meant little or nothing to young people in secondary schools. He decided to produce 'The Heart of the New Testament in Plain English'. He called it *New World* and he published it in 1967. It was an immediate success and a similar volume dealing with the OT, *Winding Quest*, appeared in 1972. In the first place *New World* must not be confused with *The New World Translation* (1961), a product of the Jehovah's Witnesses. Both Dale's volumes are anthologies, that is to say, they consist of selections from the testaments, not the testaments complete. Both volumes are beautifully produced and brilliantly illustrated. A limited vocabulary is used. Allusions are brought up to date. So we have 'Captain Cornelius' and 'Doctor Luke'. Paraphrase is used readily. The style is vivid, poetic, lively throughout. All this makes the books admirable for hesitant adolescents but of only marginal use to serious students. Dale's books make an impact partly because of his great literary skill but also because the difficulties have been largely left out.

v The Cotton Patch Versions

Beginning in 1968, Clarence Jordan, a southern Baptist, issued several books of the NT in a version suggesting that they had been written simply for America's 'Deep South'. The language is scarcely credible for staid Britons. Local place names are substituted for biblical ones. The versions are interesting because they show just how far one would need to go to bring the Bible completely into the context of a modern, albeit deprived, community.

w William Barclay

With RSV, NEB and JB already on the market it might appear that the day of the individual translator was over, but William Barclay is one of the most widely read of modern NT scholars and it is not surprising that he should add his own translation to the ever-lengthening list of English versions. The two volumes of his NT came out in 1968 and 1969. It was to be a translation that needed no commentary, but can there ever be such a thing? Barclay originally arranged the books of the NT in what he thought to be their chronological order but later editions reverted to the traditional order. Barclay's translation tends towards paraphrase and he adds two appendices explaining particular words and passages. Commentaries exist to discuss these very matters of background, context and meaning. Is it better to telescope the two, as Barclay does, or to provide the translation first and the commentary separately? Most scholars would choose the second alternative. It is odd that the most prolific of modern commentators should choose the first.

x **The Living Bible**

The preface of this Bible states unequivocally, 'the theological lodestar in this book has been a rigid evangelical position'. This raises a serious question. Surely one ought to translate the Bible as accurately as possible and then form a theological opinion on the basis of what the Bible says. To form the opinion first is to pre-judge the issue in translation. This is exactly what happens in the *Living Bible*. The translator was an Illinois business man, Kenneth Nathaniel Taylor. He was not an expert linguist, and, though his style is vivid and clear, it is often inelegant, not to say vulgar. There is much paraphrase. Interpretations are constantly injected into the text by the translator. Despite the unquestioned sincerity of the author, the whole venture is dangerously superficial. It has, however, been a commercial success. The work was first published in a series of parts. The NT came out in 1967 and the whole Bible in 1971.

y **Good News Bible: Today's English Version**

Today's English Version of the NT appeared in 1966 with the title *Good News for Modern Man*. It was an immediate success. Fifty million copies were sold in ten years. A translation of the complete Bible in the same style was the natural consequence. The Apocrypha is due in 1979. It was carried out under the auspices of the United Bible Societies, but the American Bible Society had the chief responsibility, particularly Dr. Robert G. Bratcher, the director of the project.

GNB/TEV uses 'standard, everyday, natural English'. Technical terms, particularly religious and theological terms that are not in common use, are avoided. So too is slang. Measures are given in terms of the nearest modern equivalent. (The English edition differs from the American, so we read of 'pounds' not 'dollars'.) A centurion becomes a 'captain' or an 'officer'. GNB is really modern. The measurements of the Ark are given in metres. Apart from its brisk, contemporary style GNB has a number of splendid features. Chapter and verse numbers are retained for reference purposes, but the text is set in paragraphs—shorter and more effective than those of RV—and each section is given a heading. Beneath the heading, in brackets, are references to parallel versions of the same material. This is especially useful in the Gospels and for comparing Kings and Chronicles. Brief notes appear at the bottom of the page giving alternative readings and translations and also providing elementary explanations of a non-theological kind. Similarly there is a word list at the end, which is like a brief dictionary. It explains words like 'hyssop' and 'nard', but it does not provide an interpretive commentary. There is an index and a chronological chart. Each biblical book begins with a brief outline of its contents which beginners will find invaluable. Lastly, page upon page is enlivened by the most expressive line drawings. Text and illustrations are admirably matched. Here then is a Bible that is cheap, fresh, ideally suited to be in waiting-rooms. It was not meant to be a student's tool, but students, who will doubtless be working from another version, will find some use for it.

z **New International Version**

This is the latest of all Bibles at the time of going to press. It is another American venture, promoted by the New York International Bible Society. The OT appeared in 1978, the NT in 1973, and the whole, but without the Apocrypha was published in the UK in February 1979. It is an unofficial project but it has the support of scholars from many Protestant denominations. All the translators were committed to 'the authority and infallibility of the Bible as God's Word in written form'. Its aims were so ambitious as to be impossible. It was to be a completely new translation yet preserving continuity with the long tradition of English translations. It aimed at accuracy, clarity, and literary quality, as every translation should. It also aimed to be suitable for public and private reading, teaching, preaching, memorizing and liturgical use. What this means in practice is a translation that sticks close to the RV-RSV style and makes no attempt to be chatty. Dogma creeps in from time to time. 'Her iniquity is pardoned' in Is. *40*.1 becomes, 'her sin has been paid for', which is by no means a better rendering of the Hebrew. Compare, too, Ro. *3*.25 in this version, 'God presented him as a sacrifice of atonement through faith in his blood', with RSV and NEB, and it is clear that the translation serves a particular theological purpose. 'Thee' and 'thou' disappear throughout for the very good reason, given in the preface, that Hebrew and Greek had no special pronouns for addressing God. Poetry is printed as poetry and the whole volume is divided into sections with brief headings. This is particularly useful in the Gospels when one is leafing through looking for a parable without knowing the exact reference.

Choosing a Bible

A A century ago there would have been no problem. The Bible for English speakers was the AV. It was treated with deep reverence and used for private reading, public worship, study, prayer, for every situation to which the Bible could possibly be relevant. Today there are more English Bibles than can be counted and a new question emerges: which translation is most suitable for the purpose I have in mind?

We are concerned with study. It can be taken for granted that the student's motivation is strong. He does not need to be wooed with racy language or with illustrations, so he can put on one side the paperbacks that are meant for the uncommitted public. At the other extreme he can reject the AV, because its resonant prose does little to help the private student, and its blemishes, obscurities and inaccuracies do

55

much to hinder him. He will settle for something in between, a translation in straightforward, economical English that gives, as far as possible, the true sense of the original unadorned.

When it comes to the actual method of translation, again it is advisable to reject extremes. A literal, word for word translation can never be good English and it is bound to misrepresent the original authors. Fortunately, as far as the English language is concerned, such translations belong to the past. At the other extreme it is wise to reject paraphrase. Paraphrase means that the translator is pouring his own understanding into the text. That is entirely appropriate to the notes in a commentary, where the author's contentions can be recognized and disputed, but not at all appropriate to a translation, where they cannot be discerned at all save by the expert. We need a translation that is not slavishly literal and that uses the grammar, syntax and word order that is natural to English without introducing extraneous ideas.

Again we need to be convinced that our translation is based on the best possible texts. Here we are in the hands of the experts, though one or two obvious judgments can be made. The older the translation the more limited the textual background must be, for new discoveries relating to ancient texts and languages are taking place all the time. And the student needs to be suspicious of the non-academic translator who relies more on his literary flair than on knowledge of ancient languages. The only acceptable method of translation, as far as the student is concerned, is a scholastically rigorous rendering of the best possible text. Translations which are really a re-writing of the English in powerful language but without rigorous work on the ancient texts are not adequate.

A further relevant point is whether the translation is the work of one man or a panel of translators. It is said that committees do not produce great works of art and literature—though the AV is a glowing exception—but they can produce accurate work from which personal idiosyncrasies have been eliminated. The range and depth of scholarship represented by a panel of translators is also much greater than that of any single scholar. The presumption is, therefore, that, for the student's purpose, Bibles produced by groups are preferable to Bibles produced by individuals.

B   On the basis of these considerations the best Bible for the student is likely to be one of RV, RSV, NEB or JB. RV scores low in that it is old and merely a revision of AV, its language is old-fashioned, but its zealous accuracy is a point in its favour. NEB is more modern and tries to combine accuracy with a more flowing style. JB comes from a specific ecclesiastical background and one suspects that in a few places tradition has coloured the translation, as it certainly has the notes. RSV seems open to fewest objections, though, of course, each student must make a careful survey and then trust his own judgment.

Next remember that the student needs a version in which obvious quotations from the OT in the NT—there are many cases where quotation is possible but not certain—are printed in such a way that they are clearly recognizable and the origin of the quotation is put in the margin. JB does this best, setting all quotations from the OT in italics and giving the reference. RV and RSV indent large quotations so that they are clearly recognizable, but do not indent the shorter ones so that it is not always clear where the quotation ends. References are always given. The Standard edition of NEB puts OT quotations in single inverted commas but does not say where they come from. This is a decided disadvantage.

Every student must make up his own mind how much 'textual apparatus' he needs. That is to say, how much he wishes to know about the variations between the ancient copies of the books. Presumably he will want to know that Mk. *16*.9–19 does not occur in the oldest Greek manuscripts, but what of the smaller variations? There are thousands. All four Bibles we are considering deal with variations by notes at the foot of the page. RV provides many more than the others.

It is a matter of choice whether cross-references to subject matter are desirable. RV prints thousands in the vertical margins. Some students use them, others prefer to go their own way with concordance and commentary. JB adopts the same system as RV. RSV has many fewer and NEB does not provide subject references at all save that it does draw attention to parallels between Kings and Chronicles.

Translators debate whether it is advisable to print what is verse in Hebrew as verse in English. It is a difficult question because Hebrew verse does not observe the same rules of rhythm and rhyme as English poetry and the double task of both translating and constructing a literary form that reads like poetry in English is usually impossible. None the less it is valuable to know that the original is in verse when it is. English translations commonly print Psalms, Job and Proverbs as verse and more recent ones distinguish between prose and verse passages in the prophets. JB scores here in that its verse renderings are often very good and it has attempted, as the other three have not, to set out some of the speeches in John's Gospel in verse form, which witnesses to the important fact that, by the time John's Gospel was written, the words had been repeated over and over again and achieved a stylized form.

C   Finally there are the mundane matters of price, size and durability. A student's Bible is a tool and it must be functional. For that reason out go the leather bindings. Expensive bindings suggest that the Bible is precious, that it must be handled with care and expected to last for ever. I was given a Bible when I first went away to school, another when I left school, and another when I became a Church member. I have all three still. They are symbols and they are not mishandled. But no student will get far if he treats his working Bible with that kind of respect. He needs a Bible he can open and shut thousands of times. He must be able to leave it about the place, to pile other books on it, to push it into his briefcase and carry it around. A strong binding which is reasonably cheap is called for—strong enough to stand up to rough usage, cheap enough so that it can be battered without too much fear. One must be ready to replace one's Bible when it falls apart.

Another important factor is the quality of the paper. It is useful to be able to mark a working Bible with one's own marginal notes. Some students do this very extensively and Bibles have been produced with blank pages interleaved with pages of text so that there is ample space for personal notes.

Failing this, a Bible printed on paper strong enough to take writing from a soft pencil or ball-point pen is desirable. It is worth noting the quality of the paper carefully. The Bible is so large that printers tend to use a thin paper to keep down overall size. Smallness itself is no great advantage to the student. A pocket-sized edition is likely to have print too small and paper too thin for his purpose. Adequate editions of all the four versions mentioned above are available. It is well to remember that inserting one's own comments and headings in the margin is more difficult if the Bible is printed with two columns to a page. RV and RSV lose here. JB and NEB both have a single column to a page and provide just enough space for short personal notes.

Having chosen a Bible the student must be able to use it to the full. It is necessary to study the preface, the list of abbreviations, the 'Contents' page, the guides to the notes. Know your way round your own Bible. Search out its intricacies. That is one obvious way to make biblical studies easier.

It hardly needs to be said that, though a student will work from one particular version, he will find it useful to consult others. At the time of writing the GNB costs less than taking a good newspaper for a fortnight. It seems reasonable to suppose, therefore, that a biblical student will be able to possess three or four different translations. This goes some way towards making up the disability that most students feel in not being able to read Hebrew and Greek.

For further reading

F. F. Bruce, *The English Bible: A History of Translations*, 1961.

S. Kubo and W. Specht, *So Many Versions? Twentieth Century English Versions of the Bible*, 1975.

Chapter 4

Aids to Bible Study

Concordances

a NEXT to the Bible itself the most useful book for any biblical student is a Concordance. The name is not very informative. It means a book that lists the occurrences of all the words in the Bible, so that, if a student is interested in, say, the Pharisees, he can see at a glance all the places where Pharisees are mentioned. There are actually ninety-four instances in the NT, all but nine being in the Gospels, and none in the OT, which is at once very informative.

The Pharisees provide an easy example. As soon as we move on to other words, we shall see that difficulties arise. They can be overcome, but Concordances, like Bibles, have to be understood before they can be used properly.

The root of the problem is that the vocabulary of English is not exactly parallel to the vocabulary of Greek or Hebrew. For example, English has the single word 'temple' where Greek has two, *hieron* and *naos*. When we see 'temple' in an English version, we do not know whether it means the relatively small sanctuary building (*naos*) or the whole temple area including the surrounding courtyards (*hieron*). Conversely, every English speaker sees a clear distinction between 'sky' and 'heaven'. In Greek the same word, *ouranos*, has to serve for both, and the translator has to make up his mind which of the two English words is the more appropriate.

The biblical student can thus go astray in two different ways. If he wants to talk about the sanctuary building on Mount Zion he may unwittingly make use of texts that do not refer to the building at all. On the other hand, if he tries to understand what the biblical writer had in mind when he looked up into the blue, he might miss all those occurrences of *ouranos* that appear in his Concordance under 'heaven' and not under 'sky'.

Scholars who are competent in Greek get over this difficulty by ignoring the English and looking up the Greek words in a Greek Concordance. They are also able to use dictionaries which often do not simply define a word but also give every place where it occurs in Scripture.

Broadly speaking there are two possible solutions for the student who reads only English. One is to study only the English text and hope that commentaries and other books will indicate the points at which the difference in vocabulary is crucial. The other, for the more advanced student, is to come to grips with an *analytical* Concordance. Students in the former class must remember two things. One is that almost every Concordance is based upon one particular English version. The 'almost' is necessary because in 1976 there appeared a monumental work that can be used with all English versions. As it was published at £25, it is unlikely to find its way into many private homes, though it is worth noting that it might be found in libraries. But commonly a Concordance is based upon a particular version. It is necessary, therefore, to work from the two together. Many student hours have been lost in looking up half-remembered texts from one version in a Concordance that belongs to another. This is where the multiplicity of English versions actually works against the student. In the old days there was only one Bible to know and any text could be found in any Concordance. It is not so now. There is already a Concordance to the RSV on the market and doubtless NEB and JB will have their Concordances before long.

The other thing to remember is that one of the greatest merits of a Concordance is exhaustiveness. If one is studying a word one needs to know all that the Bible says about it. If one is searching for a text one wants to know that it must be there. For this reason selective and abbreviated Concordances invariably disappoint. They cannot be relied upon absolutely and the student does not, therefore, turn to them so readily. Of course complete Concordances are expensive. They run into hundreds of pages of small print. But in general it is better to find a library where there is a Concordance and use it until one can afford one's own rather than buy an incomplete book which sooner or later is bound to disappoint.

b   We turn now to the more complicated Concordance. *Young's Analytical Concordance* was first published in 1879. It was reprinted in 1974 when it sold at £7.90. It is based on the AV which means that anyone not familiar with that version is at some disadvantage in using *Young*, but the disadvantage is not crucial. *Young* lists the words in the AV in alphabetical order but sorts out the references according to what words are used in the original tongues. So, if we look up 'temple', we find that on nine occasions in the OT the AV uses 'temple' when the Hebrew is content to say 'house' (*bayith*). Then there are a large number of references where the Hebrew has *hekal*—which can be spelt in two ways—and the AV properly translates it 'temple'. Then there is a list of references in the NT where the Greek word is *hieron* and a further list where the Greek is *naos*. There is one case where the Greek simply says 'house' (*oikos*) and the AV translates 'temple'. The student who has noted all this is now in a position to follow up, not simply the cases where the English translators speak about the temple, but also the cases where the original authors speak *with greater precision than the English*.

That is not all. *Young* has a further use. At the back of the book there is a list of all the Hebrew and Greek words in the original text from which AV was translated. Beneath each one is a list of all the different ways in which that word is translated in AV. We can discover that *naos*, the temple building, is also, though only once, translated 'shrine'. That is in Ac. *19*.24 where it refers to silver models of an altar or sanctuary devoted to Diana. Similarly we can discover that about a fifth of the occurrences of *hekal* in the OT are translated 'palace' and not 'temple'. So we can build up a picture of how the original writers used their words.

The examples given so far are, of course, easy ones. More

complicated, but much more important are words like *ruach*, which means 'breath', 'the blowing of the wind', and 'the Spirit of God'. *Young* reveals this by telling us that *ruach* is translated as 'breath' twenty-eight times, as 'spirit' 232 times, and as 'wind' ninety times. There are other translations as well. The student will see at once that study of the word 'spirit', with a small initial letter or a capital, must begin here. God's Spirit is the unseen wind that blows into man giving him life and strength. Similarly the Hebrew *tsaddiq* and the Greek *dikaios* are adjectives describing a relationship with God that no English word properly expresses. They mean, 'correct, just right, proper, and as it should be'. *Young* sets us off on the right track by showing that *tsaddiq* is translated 'righteous' 164 times, 'just' forty-one times, and 'lawful' once, and *dikaios* is translated variously by 'just', 'right', 'righteous', and the old-fashioned 'meet'. Word study of this kind can go on for ever and all the time it takes us deeper and deeper into the minds of the biblical writers.

Two other facts about *Young* need to be noted. One is that all words are spelt both in their original Hebrew or Greek letters and in English letters so that not knowing the Hebrew and Greek alphabets is no barrier to using the book. The other is that inevitably technical grammatical terms occur in the second list. The student will have no difficulty with 'feminine' or 'plural', but mysterious words like 'piel', 'hiph.', 'niph.', 'kal' may worry him. These are simply parts of the Hebrew verb akin to our active and passive. They are important for the Hebrew scholar but it is quite possible for the ordinary student to make progress by recognizing that these words indicate usages of the same verb in different forms.

c **Dictionaries**

There are many kinds of Bible dictionary. The second part of *Young* is a dictionary of a kind. The primary use of a dictionary is to explain all the nuances of a word, especially for those translating from one language to another. Scholars use rather massive and expensive dictionaries like F. Brown, S. R. Driver, and C. A. Briggs' *Hebrew and English Lexicon of the*

Old Testament and W. F. Arndt and F. W. Gingrich's *A Greek-English Lexicon of the New Testament*. These can only be used by students who are familiar with the Hebrew and Greek alphabets and who know the word they are looking up in its original tongue. Many students have found it is not too difficult to learn sufficient Greek to use a Greek-English lexicon and the rewards are great. Hebrew is another matter. Hebrew is a difficult language for westerners and one needs to know something about Hebrew Grammar before one can even find the word one is looking for. Nevertheless some students could profitably find out where the nearest copy of these volumes is to be found so that they can refer to them, perhaps with help, from time to time.

Other dictionaries fall roughly into three groups, those dealing with words, those dealing with background and those dealing with theological themes. The lines are not clearly drawn between them, the first and third being particularly difficult to separate. None the less there is an important issue here. Simple definition of the way in which a particular word is used comes close to being a purely descriptive and objective exercise. That the Hebrew word for 'sin' is also used of a missile missing its mark is an undeniable fact. A dictionary that defines words according to usage, that is to say, one that comes very close to being a Concordance, is an invaluable tool for a student because it does not add anything external to the biblical evidence.

Dictionaries that deal with themes, however, tend to spread themselves. They consider the context of every occurrence and the presuppositions of the book in which it is found and they try to build up a complete account of the biblical idea of sin or salvation or whatever the theme may be. This is a very different exercise. The author of the dictionary is bound to introduce his own presuppositions into the account. A word translated 'salvation' occurs in each testament but the Greek word and the Hebrew word have rather different meanings. The author has to decide whether to consider OT and NT meanings on an equal footing or whether to give preference to NT meanings. The account of the theme will be different according to what he decides.

This does not diminish the value of dictionaries of biblical themes in general, but it does lay an extra task on the student. He must know the presuppositions of the compilers of the dictionary and also be able to assess them. For example, some recent dictionaries of theological themes come from the hand of conservative evangelical scholars and one or two come from Roman Catholics. Each may be excellent of its kind, but they will not appeal equally to all students.

Dictionaries dealing with background are invaluable and present no such problem. They are, to use the terms we have defined above (1e–l), concerned with exegesis rather than interpretation. They tell us how much a talent was, who the Samaritans were, all the things that Barnabas did, what kind of city Corinth was, and so on. The most famous dictionary of this kind was edited by James Hastings and first published in five volumes in 1898. A single volume abridgement was published in 1909 and that single volume was revised and re-issued in 1963, which proves its usefulness. There are many other similar volumes. Nearly all of them deal with words and themes as well as background material.

Commentaries

d The student of the Bible soon becomes familiar with com-
mentaries. At the very least they save him an immense amount of labour. Any verse of the Bible might raise questions of history, geography, text, language, literary form and style, religious rites and beliefs, social customs, contemporary affairs, and so on. To refer to books on all these subjects would be impossible for the average student. That is where the commentary justifies itself. All the relevant material is provided in one book and often on the same page as the text itself.

The aim of a commentary is to put the modern reader in the same position of understanding as those who first read the text in the place it was written all those centuries ago. It is an impossible aim. No modern Briton can ever feel like a Jew tending a few sheep in the harsh days of Manasseh nor like a Corinthian seaman under Caligula, but the very difficulty of

65

making the leap of understanding makes the commentary necessary.

Commentaries come in all shapes and sizes. Perhaps we ought to begin with the single-volume commentaries. The best known of all is *Peake's Commentary on the Bible*. This was first issued in 1919 and it became a classic. It was re-written and re-issued in 1962. It contains many articles as well as an introduction to every book in the Bible and notes on every chapter. It is exegetical rather than interpretive and it is written by scholars of great distinction. Other single volume commentaries are *The Interpreter's One Volume Commentary* (1972), an American work, the *New Bible Commentary Revised* (1970), which comes from a group of conservative evangelicals, and *The Jerome Biblical Commentary*, which was compiled by American Roman Catholics. The shortest of these books has 1,100 pages and the longest 1,500. They are expensive, *The Jerome Bible Commentary* especially so, but it is hard to see how a biblical student can make much progress without one of these books on his shelves, unless he has constant recourse to a good library.

After the one-volume commentaries come the series. They are manifold. At least ten more or less complete series are available. Supposing a student needs a commentary on Mark's Gospel what considerations should guide his choice? In the first place, unless he is extremely wealthy, it is not a good idea to try to build up a complete series. No series is even in quality. If one publisher's Mark is brilliant, another publisher's John is supreme. It may look nice to have a tidy row of volumes all the same size and colour, but a student is concerned with understanding the Bible and not decorating his study. Each individual book must be chosen for its quality alone and this is particularly true in the early days when the student can afford only one commentary on a biblical book.

Secondly, one must consider size and cost. One factor that may be forgotten at this point is that every student can expect to grow in understanding as the months go by. A book that is the right size and price now may soon be discarded. It may be worth going for something bigger in the hope that one will grow into it. Similar considerations apply to the degree of difficulty of the commentary. The most obvious distinction here is between those that are based on the Greek text—few OT commentaries are based exclusively on the Hebrew—and those that are based on an English translation. Moffat, Barclay, RSV, NEB, all have commentaries based upon them and some commentators produce new translations of their own. It is a superficial advantage to have the biblical text printed at the top of the page with the notes underneath, but, if one possesses the particular English text already, that space is wasted. It is better to buy a more serious commentary that works out a translation of its own and justifies the translation in the notes. In that way one gets most quickly to the heart of the text.

Thirdly, it is important for the student to understand the commentator's aim. All commentaries provide exegesis but some provide interpretation as well. Perhaps all do to a greater or less degree. One series, *The Interpreter's Bible*, divides its notes into two sections which it calls exegesis and exposition. The exegesis gives all the explanatory material, history, geography, religious background, etc. and the exposition provides theological and homiletical applications. The value of the former is unquestioned. The value of the latter depends upon whether the student finds the approach and preaching style of the author sympathetic or not. Once again the factors that govern interpretation must be stressed. To interpret the Bible one must have a point of view, an approach, an attitude, if you like, *faith* in the Bible of one kind or another. An interpretive commentary cannot be understood unless the reader becomes familiar with the point of view adopted by the author. A competent scholar, knowing nothing of an author, can judge his point of view in a few pages, but the student does not have that advantage. It is in his interest to find out something about the author first and to buy a commentary that will prove positive to him. It is not by any means suggested that one can only learn from authors one agrees with, but, particularly in the early days, a student learns most from authors with whom he has a certain sympathy. The ideal, of course, is to have four or five commentaries on Mark and to build up one's own interpretation on the basis of all of them and from other sources as well, but, for most readers of this book, that state lies far in the future.

e **Gospel parallels**

For Christians the most important books in the Bible are the Gospels. They present peculiar problems to the student because they are all telling the same story in their different ways, one of them, John, in a very different way. An obvious scholarly duty is, therefore, to compare the way in which an incident or a saying of Jesus is treated in the different Gospels. Turning over pages is wearisome and having four Bibles open at once is inefficient. Here the publishers have come to our aid by producing volumes in which the Gospels are printed in parallel columns. This kind of book is usually called a synopsis of the Gospels. Synopses are available on both the Greek and the English texts.

It is necessary to separate John from the first three Gospels and the usual practice is to print the Synoptics in three parallel columns with odd references to John on the right-hand side of the page. The term 'synoptic' refers to different viewpoints that are broadly in agreement. Matthew, Mark and Luke treat similar material in roughly the same way. John is quite different. So the first three Gospels are reasonably called Synoptics. And the books we are talking about treat the Gospels in the same way so that they can be seen together, so they are reasonably called synopses. To speak of a synopsis of the Synoptics sounds odd, but it makes good sense.

It is also possible to buy a synopsis in which John is printed in full on the left-hand page and references to the other three Gospels are printed in columns on the right. This is the method adopted in the second volume of the best known of the English synopses edited by H. F. D. Sparks under the general title of *A Synopsis of the Gospels*. Part I is called *The Synoptics with the Johannine Parallels* and is the first one to buy. It enables the student to make immediate comparisons between Matthew, Mark and Luke. Part II is called *The Gospel according to St. John with the Synoptic Parallels*.

The value of a synopsis cannot be over-rated. By it the

student is able to see what details Mark puts in, what details Matthew leaves out. Points where the Synoptics agree are clear. Points where they differ are equally evident. As one works through a synopsis, gradually the style and purpose of each individual Gospel begin to establish themselves in the mind. Soon the student can see for himself that Matthew is Matthew and Mark is Mark. By that time he will be making headway under full sail.

Section 2

Background Material

Chapter 5

Transculturization

a TRANSCULTURIZATION is an ugly word but there is no other that says quite the same thing. It refers to a difficult but absolutely necessary task with which every biblical student must be conversant.

In the first place let us be clear what we mean by culture. Culture refers to everything in the world that is man-made as distinct from what is part of the natural order. Culture includes towns and cities, language, tools, social organization and all the things which are the product of human labour and human inventiveness. Often the word 'culture' is used in a narrow sense to refer to symphony concerts, poetry readings and the like. They are certainly the product of human inventiveness, but we use the word more broadly to include *everything* that man invents. His imaginings are part of what he invents, so folk-lore, mythology, hopes for the future and reflections about the nature of the unseen world are all a part of culture.

It is abundantly clear that man imagines, invents, and manufactures different things in different places. Take the simple example of language. Language is a human invention. It is not a part of nature. The result is that hundreds of human groups in different places have manufactured different languages. Everyone who has ever travelled abroad realizes how trying this is. Why should it be? Everybody knows that the sun rises in the morning and sets in the evening. But different people render that same experience into different word forms. They say, 'Morning has broken' or 'Le jour se lève' or 'Es ist

Morgen geworden' or 'Het is nu morgen' or something far more complicated than any of those. Why all this variation?

b   There are, perhaps, two reasons. One is that the human imagination is intensely creative. No two five-year-olds would draw the sunrise in the same way if they were left on their own, and it is not really surprising that language works differently in different groups. The other is that different groups experience nature in different ways. The sunrise is not, in fact, the same thing to all men. It is one thing to the Afghan and another to the Eskimo; so the two imaginations do not have quite the same stimulus to begin with. Different stimuli on different creative imaginations may be expected to produce different results. And so it proves to be.

Every group manufactures its own culture. And everyone born into the group inherits the culture. His own imaginings are bound to follow the lines laid down by the culture. An Afghan child cannot begin to talk with a language of his own making. He has to learn Afghan from his parents and his creative power will be shown in the way that he subsequently uses that cultural tool. The same is true of every human act. A man learns from his culture about house building and then builds the house he wants. No matter how inventive he is, he inherits cultural attitudes and he expresses his originality within them.

c   What is true of language and houses is true of literary styles, worship, faith, prayer, indeed everything. The writers of the Bible had their culture. It was different from ours. But in the terms of that culture they constructed the great book that we study. It is true that they wrote about things that we also know, God, his mercy, his salvation, but, as with the sunrise, their experiences of those realities was different from ours. And, if the experience was different, the literary expression will be even more different.

This is the problem that we now have to sort out. We have to learn enough of Hebrew culture to try to understand what they meant when they wrote as they did. That means not simply a study of Hebrew life and language and thought forms but also a study of the things that shaped their culture, that is to say, the climate, the terrain, geography, topography, all the things that made the Fertile Crescent different from western Europe. In this way we can begin to discover what the biblical writers really meant.

In the following chapter, therefore, we shall consider the geography of the Bible lands, and then, in later parts of the book, see how those physical conditions—together with other influences too complicated for us to trace—produced a Hebrew culture complete with language, cosmology, mythology, social structure and, above all, a religious faith that was all its own. There is nothing tidy about this kind of study. One never reaches the point of saying, 'I now understand Hebrew culture'. Neither can one ever say that this feature in the climate gave rise to this or that religious idea. None the less the gains are great. The Bible is full of tantalizing sayings like, 'If they do these things in the green tree, what shall be done in the dry?' (Lk. 23.31) and 'The harvest is past, the summer is ended, and we are not saved' (Jer. 8.20). In cases like this a knowledge of the climate does help. And the more one knows of the culture, the more the difficult sayings are opened up.

Chapter 6

The Geography of the Bible

a THERE are two reasons why geography is important to the biblical student. First, because terrain influences *culture*. The water supply determines whether the occupants of an area become farmers or nomads. The way of life—agricultural or nomadic—influences the structure of society. Literary usage depends to some extent on the social structure. So the meaning of words like 'king' and 'father', which are important for theology, are influenced by a social structure which depends on an economic structure which depends on streams and rivers and oases. Secondly, more directly but perhaps less importantly, geographical features determine *historical events*, movements of people, settlements, battles, and so civilization. 'Jerusalem' and 'the promised land' are two potent images in the Bible. The study of geographical factors explains why they were first held in high esteem.

The biblical student needs to have an atlas near at hand. There are many to choose from. H. H. Rowley has edited the *Students' Bible Atlas*, which is brief and cheap—it was published by Lutterworth in 1975 at 60p—and at the other end of the market there are large and beautiful volumes which can be found in libraries. The *Oxford Bible Atlas* comes somewhere in between. Edited by H. G. May, it was selling at £3 in 1976. Most good atlases include coloured maps, photographs, notes on place names, and a commentary linking geography with historical events and with archaeological sites.

In addition to atlases there are books specifically on the geography of the Bible. The most famous is Adam Smith's

76

Historical Geography of the Holy Land, first published in 1895 and recently re-issued as a paperback. Despite its age, for which the student must make allowances, it is a most readable and enlightening book. More recently an American scholar, Denis Baly, has produced two books, *The Geography of the Bible* (1957 but recently revised) and *Geographical Companion to the Bible* (1963). Theological libraries usually have both of them. There is, too, a useful article in the 1962 edition of *Peake's Commentary on the Bible.*

Some Bibles have maps at the back and they vary enormously in their usefulness. Traditionally Bibles carried maps of the division of Palestine between the twelve tribes and of the journeys of St. Paul. Maps of that kind are of little use. They do not help one to understand and interpret the Bible. The fact that Asher was in the north-west and Reuben in the south-east adds little to exegesis, quite apart from the fact that the disposition of tribes is based rather woodenly on the account in Joshua which raises all kinds of historical queries. Similarly Paul's journeys are not important *as journeys.* The travelling is the least important thing about Paul's life. What matters is what Paul did and said in the cities where he lodged, and it is a thousand pities that generations of schoolchildren have been brought up to learn the journeys off by heart without much concern for the life and faith of the groups Paul left behind. Moreover there are good reasons for supposing that the journeys themselves are artificial creations of Luke to give literary form to the second half of Acts.

It is hard to resist the conclusion that maps of these things appear in Bibles simply because they are capable of being made into maps. If a map can be made, then there is some value in making it and some virtue in learning it. In much the same spirit children learned years ago to list the flowers of the Bible and the trees of the Bible as if any knowledge that related in any way to the Bible was *good* knowledge. Such notions are dangerous. Geographical study is more valuable than that.

First we turn our attention to the whole area in which the biblical story took place, an area which for many years has been known as 'the Fertile Crescent'.

b The Fertile Crescent

The OT world, the land between the Persian Gulf and the Nile delta, was cut off from the rest of the inhabited world by a ring of natural features that, if not impenetrable, was a fearsome obstacle either to the invader coming in or to the inhabitant going out.

In the east, beyond the Tigris and the Euphrates, were the Zagros mountains. Rising to a height of nearly 5,000 metres and running from the Gulf to the Caspian Sea, they were an effective barrier to both the merchants and the soldiers of the ancient world. In the north the same range turns and runs west to Asia Minor cutting off access to modern Russia via the land mass between the Caspian Sea and the Black Sea. In Asia Minor the range turns south and becomes the Taurus Mountains, still 3,000 metres high and intersected only by a famous pass, the Cilician Gates, in the south-east corner of Asia Minor. The Cilician Gates are famous simply because they represent one of the few entrances to the Crescent. Anyone passing to or from the west must use the pass. Cyrus used it, so did Alexander, so did Pompey, so did Paul.

The Mediterranean Sea provided a few exits, but only a few. The northern half of the Syria–Palestine coast is steep and rocky. It provides a few natural harbours—notably Tyre and Sidon—but only a few. The southern half is flat and almost useless for ships for they would run aground so far from the shore that they would be unable to deliver their cargo. In OT times Palestine proper boasted perhaps two sea ports, Joppa and Acco. In NT times Herod the Great built Caesarea with an artificial harbour some fifteen miles south of Carmel. But most dwellers in the Crescent in those days regarded the sea as an impassable barrier. It was certainly a psychological one.

In the south-west lay the Sinaitic peninsula and Egypt. Egypt was a terminus for a number of reasons. She was usually strong enough to discourage unwelcome visitors and the approach to Egypt was by a narrow corridor in north-west Sinai making free entrance impossible. And beyond Egypt lay the desert. There was no exit that way.

So much for the northern loop of the Crescent. The southern side consisted of the Arabian desert which spreads into Sinai in the west. This land was not entirely uninhabitable, but living in the desert required great experience and skill and it was impossible for large groups. Occasionally nomads from the desert came to raid the villages of the Crescent, occasionally they came to settle themselves, but the traffic was all one way. The farmers of the Crescent had neither the desire nor the ability to turn themselves into nomads.

All this means that the biblical area was a kind of closed arena. Within it tribes moved and settled, and moved and settled again. They often met and fought each other, but they were relatively undisturbed by forces from outside. The arrival of the Philistines from the Aegean in the thirteenth century was an exception, and in Jer. 4.6 we read of horsemen and bowmen from the far north who may well have been Scythians from the Black Sea area, but in biblical times the interruptions were few until Cyrus the Persian set out on his march of conquest in 550 BC.

Cyrus came from the mountainous kingdom to the east of the Crescent and he marched right through to subdue kingdoms beyond the Taurus Mountains in the west. From this time onwards the Crescent was never a closed arena again. The Persians kept trying to push further west into Greece and when, after 200 years, their empire fell, it was to a Greek, Alexander the Great, who was soon marching even more victoriously in the opposite direction. After the Greeks came the Romans, so the year 550 BC is really a critical one in Hebrew history. Before that year the Hebrews were a nation, a small one, sometimes victorious, more often defeated, but a nation among other nations within the Fertile Crescent albeit, at that precise moment, in exile. After that year they were merely a tribal group with a small stake of land under the dominion of a series of world empires.

It is worth taking time to become familiar with the map of the Fertile Crescent. The distance between the mouth of the Tigris and the Euphrates and the Nile delta is about 1,000 miles as the crow flies, though the journey through the watered valleys of the crescent itself was nearer 1,500. How long the journey took in Abraham's

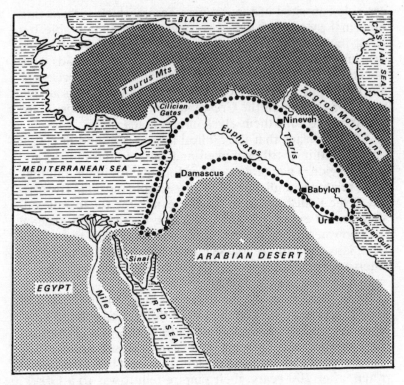

●●● FERTILE CRESCENT

The Fertile Crescent

day is hard to say. If he used camels, as some references suggest, he may have covered thirty miles or more in a day, but if he used asses—and asses were much more common— the journey would have been much slower.

The first place to notice is Ur, the city from which Abraham is said to have originated (Gn. *11*.31). Ur may have been a port in Abraham's day, because the Tigris and the Euphrates bring down so much silt that, over the years, they have pushed the land further and further into the Persian Gulf. Next notice Babylon, a city that was the centre of two kingdoms, one that flourished just after Abraham's day, and one, called the Neo-Babylonian Empire, that arose in 626BC, destroyed Assyria, and took the Hebrews into captivity. Next find

80

Nineveh, the Assyrian capital, on the southern slopes of the Zagros Mountains. Assyrian empires rose and fell, sometimes sending hordes of warriors west to plunder Syria and Israel. In 721 BC they took Samaria and destroyed the northern kingdom for ever. The areas occupied by Persia and Medea lay in the mountains to the east of the Tigris. As we have seen, Persia becomes important in Israel's history in 550BC when Cyrus began his march.

It is important now to locate the Cilician Gates in southeast Asia Minor. Immediately the course of one of the ancient trade routes becomes obvious. But, if the traveller from the east was bound for Egypt rather than the distant Aegean coast, he would need to turn left before he came to the mountains in the north. His route would take him through Damascus, the capital of Syria. Syria, properly called Aram, was Israel's north-eastern neighbour from the period of the Judges until Damascus was sacked by Assyria in 732 BC, eleven years before Samaria suffered the same fate. Syria and Israel were constantly at war, but in 735 BC Syria and the northern kingdom joined forces against Judah in the south.

The most important countries in the Crescent were at either end, in Mesopotamia and in Egypt. That was where the great rivers were and where agriculture was most secure. The rest of the Crescent was the link between the two. Palestine especially was a narrow corridor. Many a caravan passed through, regarding Israel's Holy Land as a mere staging post on the journey. Even more unfortunately kings bent on conquest had to use the same routes. Israel was often a battleground in other people's wars. No wonder that, in generation after generation, Israel sighed for the time when peace would cover the earth and she could rest in the land that God had given her.

c **Palestine**

We look now at Palestine or the land of Israel itself. The first thing to notice is its size. It was a small land tucked away in the south-east corner of the Mediterranean Sea. It was only a tiny fraction of the Fertile Crescent. Most of the Bible story relates to the area inside the rectangle marked on this map and the dimensions of that rectangle are 150 miles by 100 miles. Palestine. therefore, was rather smaller than Wales.

Names for the land of the Bible

Various names are used for the area in which most of the biblical events took place and none is completely satisfactory. The Holy Land is not much used today save in travel agents' brochures. It has a rather sentimental appeal and an image that is belied by the tragic history that has been enacted there. Canaan may be used for the land before the settlement of the Hebrews, but it is anachronistic afterwards. Israel is the name preferred by Jews, but this is a complicated term. See the note in 10c. Judah and Judaea refer only to the south. Palestine is probably the best, neutral term, though it is not entirely satisfactory.

Palestine derives from the Hebrew word for Philistine and in this sense it occurs four times in the OT. After the revolt of AD 135, Hadrian expunged the word 'Judaea' from the map and called the area Palestine, and this name has been preserved. The student needs to remember that, though the name is convenient for a book of this kind, it may give offence to Jews. Equally, of course, the name 'Israel' may give offence to Arabs, especially to those who regard themselves as 'Palestinians'.

One problem is what to include and what to leave out for the frontiers, if that is the right word, varied enormously through history. Solomon's empire at its greatest was 300 miles from north to south (see I K. *8*.65). At other times the Jews huddled together in a small space round Jerusalem and even that was not under their own control. But if we think of the Promised Land as an idea rather than a political territory, the traditional extremities were Dan, in the north, and Beersheba in the south (Ju. *20*.1; 1 Sam. *3*.20, etc.), two towns that were about 150 miles apart. The whole of the Promised Land would thus fall inside the rectangle.

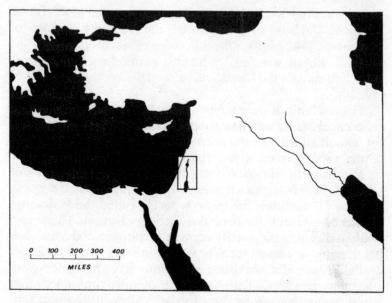

The map of Palestine is dominated by the two seas and the river that flows between them. Together they form part of the great rift valley, the deepest crack on the earth's surface. The river Jordan rises in the mountains of Lebanon and flows via Lake Huleh (also called Semechonitis) into the Sea of Galilee (also called Chinnereth, Gennesaret or Tiberias). The Sea of Galilee is about twelve miles by eight. It lies 212 metres below sea level. It supported a thriving fishing industry in NT times. Between the Sea of Galilee and the Dead Sea the Jordan meanders through a steep valley. We hear little about this valley in the Bible because unpredictable flooding made it almost useless for agriculture or habitation. In the south the Dead Sea is so dead that few people lived around its shores, except, of course, for the redoubtable monks of Qumran who gave us the Dead Sea Scrolls. The Dead Sea is about forty-three miles long and nine miles wide. It is 388 metres below sea level. It has no outlet. All the water that flows in evaporates, millions of gallons daily. Hence the great and growing mineral content which makes it impossible for a man to sink.

Many streams flow into the Jordan from the east. The two

largest are the Yarmuk, which is not mentioned in the Bible, and the Jabbok, which formed the northern border of Ammon. The brook Cherith, where, according to 1 K. *17*.1–7, Elijah was fed by ravens, is another. The Arnon, which flows into the Dead Sea, formed the northern border of Moab.

For the biblical story a much more important feature is the two valleys that, linking up, stretch from the Mediterranean at Mount Carmel to the Jordan. Names here are confusing. Strictly speaking the western part, drained by the river Kishon, is the Plain of Megiddo and the eastern part the valley of Jezreel. But sometimes the name Jezreel is given to the whole of it and sometimes the *western* part is called the Esdraelon which is a Greek form of the Hebrew Jezreel. These two valleys, running diagonally across the centre of Palestine, are of the utmost importance for Israel's history as we shall see.

Palestine has a backbone something like the Pennines in northern England. This backbone of hills runs north and south just to the west of the Jordan Valley. In the north, in Upper Galilee, the hills rise to 1,200 metres. Further south, in Lower Galilee, the slopes are gentle and the highest hill, Mount Tabor, is only 587 metres. Nazareth is built on one of these hills. The backbone is then cut through by the valley of Jezreel but the hills rise again immediately with Mount Gilboa where Saul made his last stand against the Philistines (1 Sam. *28*.4). Thereafter the ridge runs south, maintaining its height until it reaches the desert. The hills are 800 to 900 metres high. By comparison Snowdon is 1,085 metres, Ben Nevis 1,342, and Scafell, in the Lake District, 978. Many of the most important towns in the Bible story are located on this ridge.

Between the mountains and the Great Sea (the Mediterranean) there is a broad, fertile plain. Different parts of it have different names. In the south, opposite the Dead Sea, it is called the Plain of Philistia. Further north it is called the Plain of Sharon. Just as the hill country is slashed by the valley of Jezreel, so this plain is interrupted by the Carmel range of hills which runs along the southern side of the Plain of Megiddo. Travellers going from Egypt to Damascus or

84

further east naturally preferred the plain to the hill country because the Carmel range was the only obstacle. This meant, of course, that the pass through the Carmel range was of supreme importance. Whoever controlled that controlled all the traffic in the Crescent, whether going east to west or west to east. The ancient city of Megiddo stands on that pass. Many battles have been fought there or thereabouts. Deborah and Barak defeated Sisera near by (Ju. *4*). Pharaoh Thutmosis III defeated the princes of Syria there in 1468 BC. Josiah was killed there trying to prevent the Egyptians from gaining control of Syria (2 K. *23*.29 f.). It is not surprising that, according to Rev. *16*.16, the last great battle of history, Armageddon, will take place there.

d   There are other geographical features of Palestine that are important for the biblical student.

Mount Hermon: a snow-capped mountain in the far north, nearer to Damascus than to Galilee, 2,814 metres high. It sometimes appears in Joshua and Deuteronomy as the northern Limit of the Promised Land. It is a little further north than Dan.

Bashan: A fertile and wooded area south of Hermon and north-east of the Sea of Galilee. According to Nu. *21*.33 Moses defeated Og, king of Bashan as a prelude to the conquest. Bashan occurs in the prophetic books as a symbol of agricultural abundance.

Carmel Spur: the north western end of the Carmel range juts out into the sea forming a promontory and a bay. Elijah's contest with the prophets of Baal took place on the Carmel ridge (1 K. *18*).

Arabah: the Hebrew word for the great rift valley in which the Jordan and the Dead Sea lie. The Arabic name is el-Ghor.

Gilead: the area east of Jordan between the two seas. It was hilly but well-populated. Cattle thrived there though it was not proverbially fertile as was Bashan.

Wilderness of Judah: a barren area between the southern highlands and the Dead Sea. The road from Jerusalem to Jericho skirts the northern end. Only the most austere could survive in it. Amos lived on its edge at Tekoa (Amos *1*.1) and John the Baptist preached there according to Mt. *3*.1.

Shephelah: the area of low undulating country between the Judean Highlands and the Plain of Philistia. It was well wooded and fertile.

Negeb: the desert area south of Beersheba that links up with the wilderness of Sinai.

MEDITERRANEAN
SEA

Mountains of Lebanon

MT HERMON

Dan

BASHAN

L. Huleh

Sea of Galilee

Carmel Spur

MT TABOR

R. Yarmuk

Valley of Jezreel

Plain of Megiddo

Megiddo

R. Kishon

MT GILBOA

River Jordan

Brook Cherith

GILEAD

R. Jabbok

Plain of Sharon

HILL COUNTRY

Jericho

Jerusalem

The Wilderness of Judah

Dead Sea

Plain of Philistia

The Shephelah

R. Arnon

MILES

0   10   20   30

The Negeb

Brook Zered

Chapter 7

Climate, Seasons and Calendar

a WE began the last chapter by saying that geography, the lie of the land, influences both events and the way that people think about events. Now the same plea must be made for a study of the climate which is really a subdivision of geography. It may seem that phrases like 'living water' or 'the light of the world' or 'the bread of life' will mean the same everywhere, but it is not so. Only when one has struggled to understand the conditions of life of the people who used those phrases can one begin to grasp what they meant to them.

Climate

Palestine has the same latitude as California or Florida, but this can be misleading because latitude is only one element in climate. There are large variations in the same latitude.

Rainfall can be studied only with a map. The pattern is complicated. In Palestine rainfall decreases as you go south. The Hermon area has 60 inches a year (152 cm) against London's 23 inches (58·4 cm). Hebron has 20 inches (50·8 cm) and Edom only 11 inches (28 cm). Similarly, rainfall decreases as you go east. Twenty-five inches (63·5 cm) is common on the coast, but thirty miles east of Jordan the desert begins and 5 inches (12·7 cm) is the maximum. A further factor is that the rain-bearing winds come from the west and the eastern slopes of hills tend to be dry. Jericho, hidden in the Jordan valley behind the Judaean highlands, has only 4 inches (10·2 cm) and the Dead Sea even less.

The rain is not spread evenly around the year and much of it falls wastefully. The rain begins in October and reaches a peak in the period December to March. This is the 'former rain'. It then changes its character and April and May are two months of warm showers. This is the 'latter rain'. There are different words for the two kinds of rain in Hebrew. Summer is rainless and very hot.

Temperature is similarly variable. Upper Galilee is temperate ranging from 7°C in winter to 22°C in summer. On the coast further south the range is 10 to the upper 20s. Jerusalem, being higher, is slightly cooler. Frost is rare but not unknown there. The average is about the same as in Galilee. Down by the Dead Sea it is much hotter. Jericho, Qumran and Masada produce temperatures in the upper 30s and 40s. The suffering of the slaves who built the ramp at Masada cannot be imagined.

Apart from the heat there is a desert wind that scorches up all growing things. It blows in late spring and early autumn. The green grass withers when this wind blows (Is. *40*.6 f.). A plant, blasted by the wind and parched at the roots, provides a telling simile in Is. *53*.2. (See also Is. *27*.8; Ez. *17*.10; Hos. *13*.15; Jonah *4*.8.) On the other hand the west wind often produces sudden storms and does immense damage (1 K. *18*.44–45; Mt. *7*.24–7). There were also occasional earthquakes (1 K. *19*.11; Is. *29*.6; Am. *1*.1).

b **Seasons**

It follows from this that the pattern of the seasons is unlike that experienced by most readers of this book. It is as follows:

Autumn—the beginning of the year. It is a short season of transition. Rain falls and the world begins to look green again. There is a drop in temperature and general relief. Ploughing can start and people can look forward to the new spring.

Winter—the time of rain and a little privation, but it is cold only in January and February. This is a long season, the gestation time when the seed is sown and the world waits to bring forth.

89

Spring—the warm, soft rain has begun. Flowers bloom, the grain swells. A short, happy season when nature is at her best (Song 2.11 ff.).

Summer—the rain ceases. Then come the harvests, first barley, then wheat. Then the drought begins to bear heavily on the population (Ps. 32.4). Everything with shallow roots shrivels up. The land turns grey. It is the season of death. There is a great longing for coolness and rain. Only the trees whose roots are deep in the soil survive and produce their harvests of olives, grapes and figs. At the end of the long, hot summer, according to the understanding of the Hebrews, the creation is most at risk. If rain does not come then, all is lost.

c **Agriculture**

In the earliest times the Hebrews were semi-nomads, that is to say, they wandered around the edges of the desert driving their flocks and carrying what little goods they had on asses. Some more favoured clans may have had camels, but they would have been a minority. Semi-nomads differ from true nomads in that semi-nomads do not venture into the deep desert and they are always willing to settle if the chance arises.

After the Hebrews came into Palestine in the thirteenth century BC they ceased for ever to be semi-nomads. None the less the nomadic phase made a deep mark on the Hebrew consciousness. The nomadic life is austere. No one can possess anything that cannot be carried by a donkey. There is much hardship, few luxuries. Nomadic life has a strong communal quality. Nomads cannot split up and go their several ways. They must agree together and fight for each other. When all the flocks are driven together and all the drovers suffer the same hardships, it is impossible to have a privileged class. A single leader, albeit with advisers, but one whose decisions are obeyed without question, provides the only feasible style of government for a nomadic tribe.

When the Hebrews ceased to be semi-nomads and became settled farmers, their way of life changed. But there are many indications that loyalty to the desert virtues remained. The prophets tended to wear the desert herdsman's dress (2 K. *1*.8; Zech. *13*.4; Heb. *11*.37). John the Baptist did the same (Mt. *3*.4). They denounced the life of ease and luxury that farming made possible for the lucky few (Is. *5*.8: Am. *3*.15, *6*.8). Moreover there was a strong tradition that no Israelite should be either a slave or a king (Lev. *25*.39–41; 1 Sam. *8*.10–22; Ju. *9*.6–21). And the Rechabites continued to live by the standards of the desert right down to the Exile (Jer. *35*).

Most of the OT writings, however, reflect an agricultural manner of life. The festivals are linked with harvests, the law codes govern agricultural affairs, the images and metaphors used are derived from farming.

By no means all of Palestine was fit for farming. To the nomads of the desert, no doubt, it was 'a land flowing with milk and honey' (Ex. *13*.5), but, to the Hebrew hill farmer, it was anything but a paradise. Much of the land was steep and liable to erosion. It was exceptionally stony and much back-breaking work had to be done to clear a place to sow the seed (Is. *5*.2). Even today the visitor is struck by the tall piles of stones that are to be seen everywhere. There is a problem about collecting them and there is a problem about what to do with them when they are collected. There are five dry months in every year and, though drought is certain, the return of rain is not. Huge, underground cisterns had to be dug to supply the necessary water in summer (2 Chr. *26*.10). Then there were the plagues of locusts, the mildew, the scorching east wind.

But there were areas on the lowlands and on the gentler slopes which could be successfully farmed. Both barley and wheat could be grown, barley being harvested in late April and wheat a month or so later. The ploughing was done as soon as the rain fell in the autumn with a rudimentary plough that was little more than a metal spike to scratch the earth. The seed was then sown broadcast. Reaping was carried out with a hand sickle. In the early days of the settlement the sickle was made of a flint tied to a handle. The reaper grabbed the corn by handfuls and hacked it through at the base. More efficient sickles came with the use of iron about the time of

David. Am. *1*.3 contains a vigorous image derived from threshing. The corn was spread out and then thrashed by driving an iron sledge over it until husks were separated from the corn. The mixture was then thrown up in the air and the wind blew the chaff away (Job *21*.18; Ps. *1*.4).

Where there was any depth of soil vines, figs, olives and pomegranates could be grown. They could survive the summer drought and endure from year to year. The fruit was harvested in August and September. So much work had to be done then that the people made shelters out of the boughs of trees and ate and slept in them. These shelters were also used at the autumn feast of ingathering which was then called, rather clumsily, the Feast of Booths or the Feast of Tabernacles. In later times it was customary to build shelters for the festival even in cities (Neh. *8*.13–18). Lev. *23*.42 f. links the custom with life in the wilderness, and doubtless it did remind town-dwellers of their fathers' nomadic days, but a shelter is not the same thing as a tent. They are different words in Hebrew, and, while tents belong in the desert, shelters belong to Canaan.

It is also possible to grow flax for making cloth and rope and for other household uses (Jer. *13*.1; Ez. *44*.17 f.).

In those parts of the country that were too rough or barren for tilling, animals could still be raised. Sheep and goats occur frequently in the Bible story. They had many uses. They provided meat and milk, wool or rough hair for clothing, leather for wineskins and other domestic uses, a currency in that animals could be used in barter, and, of course, an offering for sacrifice. Sheep and goats roamed the hills and were rounded up together. Separating one from the other for different treatment was a common agricultural task. Why the sheep represent the righteous and the goats the ungodly, as in Mt. *25*.32 f., is not clear save that the sheep were softer, less aggressive and, probably, more pure in colour.

d   **Conditions of life**

It needs little imagination to see that life, even for the settled Hebrew, was hard, insecure and uncomfortable. This is an important fact that modern readers of the Bible have to recognize. The people who gave us the Bible were often hungry, bereaved, worn out and at risk. They worked harder than we do. They knew more pain. When they celebrated their festivals they had moments of pure joy, but the norm was bitter. They are the people who write about righteousness and truth. Not righteousness and truth when material needs have been looked after, but righteousness and truth when material needs may never be met at all.

It was not easy for the farmer, worse for the herdsman, and worst of all for those without possessions who lived by gleaning (Lev. *19*.9 f.; Dt. *24*.19–21).

The Hebrew was more involved in the natural world than we are. Or perhaps it would be truer to say that he could not escape his involvement as we can, or think we can. The rainy weather could be extreme and was always unpredictable. Yet every shower affected the Hebrew farmer's life. He had to work hard but he had no control over the crops and no defence if the crops failed. Failure meant selling himself and his family into servitude. A larger failure meant death by famine. It is small wonder that the times of harvest were times of wild rejoicing (Ju. *21*.16–25) and that expectations of a glorious future involved a natural world that brought forth abundantly without demanding too much work (Joel *3*.18; Am. *9*.13 f.).

It is interesting to note how these ancient farmers reacted to all their toil and trouble. There was one reaction among the Canaanites and another among the Hebrews. The Canaanites, impressed by the fact that they were totally involved with the circle of the seasons, concluded that the gods were similarly involved, and built up a picture of gods, men and the natural world all bound up together and all influencing each other. Their worship consisted of festivals at which they enacted what they wanted the natural world to do. At the end of the long, hot summer they wanted the creation to spring to life again. So they went through fertility rituals in the hope that that would stimulate the gods and so stimulate nature to bring forth again. The Hebrews, on the other hand, impressed by the fact that nothing that man could do could alter the

93

natural world, and also impressed by certain historical deliverances that had come their way when they least expected it, conceived of a God of absolute power before whom man could only tremble and express his dependence. Hebrew worship also moved with the year, but its themes were thanksgiving and submission. This contrast runs through the whole OT. (See below 18.)

e **Natural symbols**

In every language there are certain words that relate to basic, human experiences. Light, dark, bread, wine, blood, water, sun, summer, winter, day, night, these things belong to every kind of human existence. Shedding blood in China is much the same as shedding blood in Peru. These words, one might say, relate to the great universals of human life. But, basic as they are, their universality is only one part of their meaning. How they are understood will vary from place to place depending on the precise conditions of life at that place. We cannot take it for granted, therefore, that we understand what the Bible means even when it uses these universal terms. We understand their universal sense but not those peculiar nuances that belong to the biblical people alone. The more one studies Hebrew conditions of life the more the subtleties of the terms become clear to us.

Three examples must suffice. In our civilization we have all the light we need. Darkness can be banished at the touch of a switch. How different it would seem to the ancient herdsman or traveller who found himself benighted in the barren hills. A flickering light would then mean a tent and safety. It is instructive to re-read some of the biblical references to light with this in mind (Ps. 27.1, 43.3; Jn. 8.12). Similarly we all need water, but the life or death nature of water is hard to grasp when we are surrounded by taps. The Hebrew tongue is rich in words meaning springs of water. Water equalled life, no less. When God is described as a fountain of living water (Jer. 2.12, 17.13), it does not suggest the image of quenching the thirst on a hot day but of giving life to one under the threat of death. A common image for God in the OT is the Rock. He

94

is the rock of my salvation (Dt. *32*.15; 2 Sam. *22*.47; Ps. *89*.26, *95*.1). A rock is stable, immovable, a good foundation for building (Dt. *32*.4; Ps. *40*.2; Mt. *7*.24). A rock is a shelter from the storm (Is. *2*.10) and provides a shadow in the blazing sun (Is. *32*.2). But all these meanings are secondary in the Bible. The rock is pre-eminently a fortress, a high tower, a safe place to fight off the enemy. In the early days, the Hebrew settler was never really at peace. At any time raiders might come sweeping in and he would have to fight for his home, his family, his flocks. Villages were built on high ground even if it meant there were long walks to the fields. In the moment of crisis they were safer. Safest of all was Jerusalem, the rock that Yahweh had chosen for his temple. The rock was the safe presence from which the Hebrew could face the world unafraid.

Such nuances attach to all natural symbols. We err if we assume that we can understand these images perfectly because the whole human race is one.

f **Calendar**

This is a complex subject. The problem is that the time the earth takes to rotate once, which establishes the length of the day, and the time the moon takes to wax and wane, which, in many calendars, though not ours, establishes the length of the month, and the time the earth takes to circle the sun once, which establishes the length of the year do not fit very well together. For example, a year is actually $365\frac{1}{4}$ days, and twelve months, based on the moon, make up only $354\frac{1}{4}$ days. Our own solution is to have unequal months and occasional leap years. In ancient times there were many different systems and several of them show up in the Bible. There is no such thing, therefore, as 'the biblical calendar'.

The commonest solution was to have the year based on the earth's rotation round the sun and then to adjust the months to ensure that they fell roughly at the same time each year. That meant that, every few years, an extra month was put in to make up for the ten days by which the twelve lunar months fell short of the complete solar year. This is called

95

intercalation and it is almost certain that the Hebrew adopted some such system.

There are three different ways of describing the months and a large problem about whether the year began in the spring or the autumn. Before the Exile it appears that Canaanite names for months were used. Only four of the twelve actually occur in the Bible, Abib (Ex. *13*.4, *23*.15, *34*. 18; Dt. *16*.1), Ziv (1 K. *6*.1, 37), Ethanim (1 K. *8*.2), and Bul (1 K. *6*.38). The Canaanite year began in the autumn. Around the time of the Exile a new system of calling the months by numbers appears and the numbers were reckoned on the Babylonian system of a new year beginning *in the spring*. These numbers were then applied to the Canaanite names, which make Abib the first month and Ziv the second whereas, in fact, they came in the middle of the Canaanite year. Then later the twelve Babylonian names were used together with the numbers. All twelve names occur in Jewish tracts and seven of them occur in the OT or the Apocrypha. The system was as follows. The year, of course, begins in the spring:

1. Nisan (March–April) (Neh. *2*.1; Esth. *3*.7)
2. Iyyar (April–May)
3. Sivan (May–June) (Esth. *8*.9)
4. Tammuz (June–July)
5. Ab (July–August)
6. Elul (August–September) (Neh. *6*.15)
7. Tishri (September–October)
8. Marcheshvan (October–November)
9. Chislev (November–December) (Neh. *1*.1; Zech. *7*.1)
10. Tebeth (December–January) (Esth. *2*.16)
11. Shebat (January–February) (Zech. *1*.7)
12. Adar (February–March) Ezra *6*.15; Esth. *3*.7)

A slight complication is that, in 2 Macc. *11*.30, 33 and 38, Nisan appears with the Greek name of Xanthicus.

This acceptance of Babylonian numbers and names did not, however, upset the traditional notion that the year began in the *autumn*. The ingathering was at the end of the year (Ex. *23*.16, *34*.22). Thus, with the last crops in and the land completely dried up, the agricultural cycle had come to an end. What was needed was a new beginning. It was the natural time for new year because, when the rain came, the process started again. So one may suppose that the great celebrations of the new year took place in the autumn; the New Year's Day of modern Judaism is still in the autumn. No doubt there were other minor 'new years', when, for example, the first sheaves were cut. We have our financial year and our academic year beginning at other times than January 1st. So perhaps it is not so odd that, in post-exilic Judaism, the year begins in the seventh month.

Nothing is known about how the intercalations were made, though there must have been some system. The weeks are easier to understand, six working days and a sabbath rest on the seventh. They went on regardless of the problems over months. After the Exile at least, the days did not begin in the morning, as ours do. They began with sunset and the night came first. By Jewish reckoning, therefore, the Last Supper and the Crucifixion took place *on the same day*.

g **The sacred year**

The sacred calendar was dominated by three great feasts, Passover, Weeks and Booths (or Tabernacles; the Hebrew word is *sukkoth* and it means 'shelters'; see above under 'Agriculture'). All these feasts are ancient, they are mentioned in the Torah (13b), they all appear in the NT. They were the three 'pilgrimage feasts' that, according to Dt. *16*.16, all male Jews must attend. After the Dispersion, probably even before it, this requirement could not always be honoured. None the less Jews did their utmost to return to Jerusalem for the great feasts at least once in a life-time. Paul hurried back to be in Jerusalem for Pentecost (Weeks) in Ac. *20*.16.

These feasts were times of great rejoicings. The sacrifices involved communal meals and the worshippers were able to forget the hard times, to join in eating and drinking of rare

97

luxury, and to celebrate some aspect of Jewish faith and history. There is every reason to suppose that the temple rites were dramatic, colourful, exciting, and that they involved the fullest participation by the worshippers. Their significance, therefore, in the life and thought of the Jewish people cannot be over-rated.

The three pilgrimage festivals were not the only events in the calendar. In the course of time other feasts and fasts were added. By NT times the calendar was as follows:

h **Passover and the Feast of Unleavened Bread**

In the Bible these two feasts always occur together and both are securely linked to the Exodus from Egypt. There is widespread agreement, however, that two separate feasts, both older than the Exodus, have been joined together. The slaughter of the Passover lamb is an ancient nomadic rite and the annual banning of leaven, or yeast, is an agricultural custom.

Several accounts of the feasts are given in the OT of which Ex. *12.1–13*.16, Lev. *23*.4–8, Nu. *28*.16–25, and Dt. *16*.1–8 are the chief. The most notable difference between them is that the Deuteronomic account requires the lambs to be slaughtered on Mount Zion whereas Ex. *12*, located as it is in Egypt, assumes slaughter in the household. It is clear that, in NT times, the Passover was celebrated in Jerusalem (Mk. *14*.12–16), but in the periods when the Temple was destroyed, the full Passover rite could take place in the household.

The slaughter of the lamb took place on the evening of *14 Nisan*. According to Ex. *12* the blood was smeared on the lintels and the flesh was roasted and eaten by the company who were fully dressed for a journey. Anything not eaten was burnt before morning. In Exodus this reads like the description of what actually happened, but it is clear from Ex. *12*.25–7 that the chapter is also a prescription for how the Passover was always to be celebrated. From earliest times it had always been a celebration of the escape from Egypt.

98

Immediately following the Passover proper come the seven days of unleavened bread, *15–21 Nisan*. Every scrap of leaven has to be removed from the house. The custom was to use leaven from one day's baking to start the process the next day. The feast, therefore, meant a complete interruption of the process. After the feast it had to be begun again with fresh leaven from nature. The original occasion of the feast was the beginning of the barley harvest, but little mention of that is made in the biblical accounts and the link with the Exodus comes out strongly in Ex. *12* and Dt. *16*. Ex. *12*.14 speaks of the Passover day as a memorial and this is a powerful word in Hebrew. It has none of the sad and distant overtones of the English word. By making a memorial the Hebrew believed that he was bringing the past into the present. The later Passover was celebrated as if the celebrants themselves were in Egypt. It closes with the words, 'Next year in Jerusalem'. This has a bearing on the words of Jesus spoken at Passover time, 'Do this in remembrance of me' (Lk. *22*.19; 1 Cor. *11*.25).

i **Weeks**

Originally this festival took place seven weeks after the first sheaf of barley was cut (Dt. *16*.9 f.) which gave it a variable date. Later it was fixed at seven weeks after the beginning of Passover, which means *6 Sivan*. Reckoning inclusively, seven weeks make fifty days, hence the Greek name Pentecost which means fiftieth. It was the second great pilgrimage feast as is evident from the gathering recorded in Ac. *2*.

At this point the Hebrew Calendar and the Christian Calendar come close together. The Crucifixion coincided with the beginning of Passover. According to the Acts of the Apostles, Whitsun coincided with Pentecost, fifty days later.

Throughout the OT, Weeks was an agricultural festival celebrating the end of the wheat harvest. It lasted a single day and its main feature was the offering of two leavened loaves (Lev. *23*.15–21). It was also associated with the practice of offering 'firstfruits' (Ex. *34*.22; Nu. *28*.26) The notion of firstfruits rests upon the belief that the whole crop was holy.

Man had worked hard, but the mystery of growth was beyond his ken. It was an act of God. So the crop was sacred and not to be used for food. The firstfruits were, therefore, offered representing the whole. Once they were accepted the rest of the crop could be given over to common consumption. It appears that the feast of Weeks was the most popular occasion for firstfruits but that they might be presented at any time during the summer before the feast of Tabernacles.

In the inter-testamental period the feast became associated with the Covenant between God and Israel. The book of Jubilees (*6*.17) states that the feast is, in fact, an annual renewal of the covenant made between God and Noah. Jubilees *1*.1 also draws attention to the fact that, in Ex. *19*.1, the Law was given on Sinai in the third month (*Sivan*). Later Judaism certainly celebrated the Sinatic covenant at the feast of Weeks.

j **Trumpets**

This is a rather mysterious feast that took place on *1 Tishri* and was celebrated by the blowing of trumpets. Our authorities are Lev. *23*.24 f. and Nu. *29*.1–6. The difficulty is that Jewish writings of the post-biblical period make it clear that *1 Tishri* was also New Year's Day. It was called Rosh Ha-Shanah, ('head of the year') and it has been New Year's Day ever since. We have discussed above under the heading 'Calendar' the appropriateness of a new year at this season. But there is, in fact, no *biblical* evidence of a New Year's Festival on *1 Tishri*. It is a controversial area. Scholars have made many elaborate hypotheses about New Year festivals in the autumn but nothing is certain.

k **Day of Atonement**

Not a feast but a fast. There is no evidence of the fast before the Exile but afterwards it became a day of deep significance to Jews. It still is. The date is *10 Tishri* and the chief biblical passages are Lev. *16*, *23*.26–32, and Nu. *29*.7–11. This fast has given to the English language the word 'scapegoat' because, during the ritual of this day, a goat was chosen to bear the sins of the people. The reason a new word had to be invented by the AV translators was that the Hebrew phrase is not clear. The goat is described in Lev. *16*.10 as the goat 'for Azazel'. This goat was not sacrificed on the altar. The high priest confessed over it all the sins of Israel and then it was taken away into the wilderness there to die a natural death. According to later Jewish tradition the goat was pushed over a cliff. The meaning of Azazel is uncertain, though it probably means a demon. The name Azazel occurs frequently in 1 Enoch for the leader of a group of fallen angels. Even so it would not be a sacrifice to Azazel but rather a symbolic way of letting evil return to its source. There is no precise reference to the goat for Azazel in the NT, but references to the imagery of the Day of Atonement are unmistakable.

1 **Booths**

We have already discussed the name. The Hebrew is *sukkoth*. It means shelters made from branches of trees. Tabernacle is an old-fashioned word that means little to anyone, so we are left with Booths, which is little better. There is a tendency to refer to it nowadays as the Autumn Festival. Sometimes it is called the Enthronement Festival, but here the student has to beware. Scholars who use that name argue that the Autumn Festival was an enthronement festival, but that is not generally agreed, so Enthronement Festival begs an important question.

The date was *15–22 Tishri*. The chief authorities are Lev. *23*.33–44, Nu. *29*.12–40, and Dt. *16*.13–15. It was a pilgrimage feast. The fact that, at this time of the year, the grapes and the olives would just have been gathered in and that Ex. *23*.16 and *34*.22 refer to a festival of ingathering which must be the same festival means that the Feast of Booths was primarily a harvest festival, the chief and final one of the year. The worshippers lived in shelters as was customary in the fields at harvest time. As we have seen, this part of the ritual was given a historical meaning in Lev. *23*.42 f. The Israelites were thus reminded of their days in the wilderness.

101

All this is plain sailing. The great question is: did the festival mean more, much more, than this? There is a hint of something more in Zech. *14*.16 f. Non-attendance at the festival meant no rain. Does that imply that the feast had something to do with rain-making? Rites in which water is poured out in order to cause rain occur all round the world. According to later Jewish texts there was a water rite in the Feast of Booths. (Jn. 7.27 f. may be relevant too.) But this, of itself, means little. The water pouring could be a celebration of rain to come rather than an attempt to bring rain.

We now need to refer back to something we said in 7d. There we pointed out that the basic purpose of Canaanite religion was to exert influence over the gods and so over the natural order (a process which is sometimes described as sympathetic magic). The basic purpose of Hebrew religion was to glorify a God who was beyond human control. This distinction may be clear to us, but there is no doubt that in the minds of the common people of Israel the two views were mixed up. The Hebrews did borrow from their neighbours, constantly and perhaps deeply. And if they did, what kind of festival was this?

To take the most extreme thesis, the answer would be that, in the autumn the earth was in the power of the god of death. The king, who was a sacred and not simply a secular figure, took the part of the god of life, contended in ritual drama with the god of death and was slain. His consort then stepped forward, pursued the god of death, laid him low, and restored her beloved. The restoration was celebrated sexually by king and consort and by all the people in shelters constructed for the purpose. So death was overcome and fertility of the land for the next season ensured. There was a triumphal procession and the king, still representing the god of life, was installed upon his throne securely for another year.

It is impossible to discuss any of this here, but no one can read far in the OT area these days without coming across some reference to sacral kingship, or ritual magic, or an enthronement festival. We have stated the thesis in its extreme form in order to mention all the details, but very few scholars would accept it in this form. Nevertheless some elements of the thesis occur in most treatments of the Autumn Festival.

m Dedication of the Temple

There is no reference to this festival in the OT because the occasion for it did not arise until after the OT was complete. The Greek ruler, Antiochus IV (Epiphanes) sacked Jerusalem and desecrated the Temple in 167 BC (1 Macc. *1*). Three years later Judas Maccabaeus had driven him back and was able to reconsecrate the temple site (1 Macc. *4*.36–59). Each year a celebration of this event began on *25 Chislev* and lasted eight days. The feast is mentioned in Jn. *10*.22. It is also called Hanukkah or the Feast of Lights.

n Purim

The origin of this feast is to be found in the book of Esther especially *9*.17–32. The story tells of the villainous Haman, a Persian prime minister, who intrigued against the Jews. Fortunately the Persian king, Xerxes, had a Jewish queen and she and her cousin Mordecai intervened and saved their people. Haman was hanged on the gallows prepared for Mordecai on *13 Adar*, so *14 Adar* became a day of rest and celebration. The feast has a chauvinistic flavour and a carnival atmosphere. The name comes from the lots (Hebrew, *purim*) cast, as a means of determining policies at the Persian court.

In addition to these special days there were Sabbaths, about which so much is said in both testaments, and New Moons (Nu. *28*.11–15). There were special regulations for the seventh year (Ex. *21*.2–6, *23*.10f., Lev. *25*.1–7; Dt. *15*.1–6) and for the fiftieth year of jubilee (Lev. *25*.8–55, *27*.16–25). And there were the occasional sacrifices and fasts when heads of families performed vows or made acts of thanksgiving.

o **The sacred year at a glance**

Names	Season	First day	Length in days	Biblical references
Passover and Unleavened Bread	Spring	14 Nisan 15 Nisan	1 7	Ex. *12*.1–*13*.16 Lev. *23*.4–8 Nu. *28*.16–25 Dt. *16*.1–8
Weeks Pentecost	Early Summer	6 Sivan	1	Lev. *23*.15–21 Nu. *28*.26–31 Dt. *16*.9–12
Trumpets New Year's Day Rosh ha-Shanah	Autumn	1 Tishri	1	Lev. *23*.24 f. Nu. *29*.1–6
Day of Atonement Yom Kippur	Autumn	10 Tishri	1	Lev. *16* Lev. *23*.26–32 Nu. *29*.7–11
Booths Tabernacles Succoth Ingathering Autumn (Enthronement)	Autumn	15 Tishri	8	Lev. *23*.33–44 Nu. *29*.12–40 Dt. *16*.13–15
Dedication Hanukkah Lights	Winter	25 Chislev	8	1 Macc. *4*.36–59
Purim	Early Spring	14 Adar	1	Esth. *9*.17–32

For further reading

R. DeVaux, *Ancient Israel: Its Life and Institutions*, 1961.

Chapter 8

Biblical Cosmology

a THE word 'cosmology' means 'an account of the structure of the universe'. We do not talk much about cosmology today because we have learnt so much about the universe that questions about its size and shape no longer make sense. It was not so in biblical times. For all the majesty and mystery of the creation, the biblical writers still thought that the broad lines of its construction could be roughly grasped. The universe had foundations beneath the earth, a middle area where human life took place, and a roof, and it was natural that, when talking about God or the heavens or the dead in their tombs, the biblical writers should think and write with this construction in mind.

They were not, of course, geographers, physicists or astronomers, so they do not speak in those technical languages. And we, of course, do not submit biblical ideas on cosmology to modern scientific tests. We are not concerned to judge biblical cosmology. We do not judge Shakespeare negatively because ghosts appear in his plays, though we tend to talk about guilty consciences rather than spirits of the dead. Similarly we do not judge the cosmology of the Bible. We try to understand it and learn from it.

The biblical writers formed their cosmology not from scientific observations but from experience, imagination and faith. And the cosmology thus formed becomes an essential element in their language. There is no alternative, then, but to try to see how they worked it out. We must put out of our minds what we know, or think we know, and try to see the universe as they saw it.

b   The story of Creation in Gn. *1* provides the best clues to biblical cosmology and we can usefully follow it through the first few verses. In the first stage, before creation began, there was only a shapeless chaos of water. The spirit of God blew over it in the form of a wind. E. A. Speiser's translation in the *Anchor Bible* puts it very well, 'When God set about to create heaven and earth—the world being then a formless waste, with darkness over the seas and only an awesome wind sweeping over the water . . .'

Already we are in difficulties. How can one talk about something existing *before creation*? What does it mean to say that whatever existed was a shapeless chaos or a 'formless waste'? (The Hebrew *tohuwabohu* is very expressive.) And why water? Why do we begin with an image of a dark ocean?

Would that we could answer these questions with confidence. Water occurs in the cosmologies of many peoples, perhaps because in storm and flood it is uncontrollable, perhaps because until it is put in a container it is essentially shapeless and disorderly. It may be, too, that the Hebrews' memory of actual floods led them to think of the waters as a lawless enemy ever threatening to rise up and destroy their civilization. Clearly they preferred to think of creation as an act whereby God brought order into the chaos of things rather than an act of creation *from nothing*. If we are honest we have to admit that an act of creation from nothing is impossible for us to conceive. It is hardly surprising, therefore, that the biblical writers leave the problem unsolved.

c   We begin, then, with an unbounded waste of ocean, dark and sterile. Only God is outside it, over it and above it. Diagrammatically we may represent as in Fig. 1.

God's first act was to bring light, which calls for little comment. Those who criticize Genesis on the grounds that it speaks of day and night before there was a sun seem not to be aware of the kind of writing we are dealing with. Would such critics refuse to watch Hamlet or Macbeth?

d   The next act introduces us to the strange word 'firmament'. It is sometimes translated 'vault'. It actually means a large

Fig. 1

roof-like dome that is introduced into the middle of the ocean. The Hebrew word is used of beating out metal and the image suggests one of those large, round lids one sometimes sees on meat-dishes. It is not put on top of the ocean, but in the middle, so that there were some waters above and some below. See Fig. 2.

It is useful to compare the account of creation in Gn. *1* with a somewhat similar passage in Prov. *8*. Prov. *8*.27 refers to a 'circle' on the face of the deep. This is a different Hebrew word but it refers to the same idea.

e   The next act is to push the waters back to let dry land appear. There is so much water that the dry land is constantly threatened, so the Bible often speaks as if one of God's constant duties is to keep the seas back so that they do not flood in and reduce everything to the chaos from which it began (Job *26*.10, *38*.8–11; Ps. *104*.5–9; Prov. *8*.29; Jer.

107

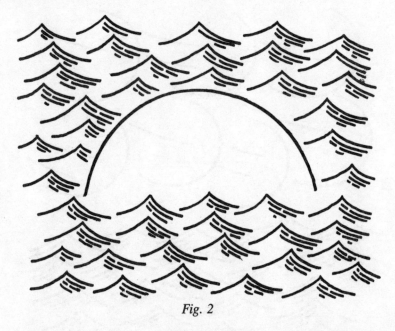

Fig. 2

5.22). Job *38* is particularly interesting because it draws an analogy between the creation of the earth and the birth of a baby from the waters in the womb. Perhaps this has something to do with the common occurrence of water in primitive cosmologies.

The diagram is now as in Fig. 3.

f   From this point onwards Gn. *1* goes on to speak about the creation of vegetation and then eventually fish, animals and man, but we must not miss the important detail on the fourth day when the heavenly bodies are created. They are described as 'lights in the firmament' and one gets the impression from v. 17 that God fixes them on the roof of the world in order to give light and to separate day and night.

Before we come to the final diagram we must look at other details of the cosmology that are found outside the Creation story in Genesis. In the first place, a universe of this kind has a natural crown to it. There is a place on the top of the dome which is the highest point in the whole creation and from it everything on earth and in heaven can be seen and controlled.

Fig. 3

This is where one would expect to find God enthroned and that is exactly how it is in the Bible. In the height of heaven, higher than the stars, God is enthroned (Job *22*.12; Ps. *103*.19; Is. *66*.1; Mt. *5*.34; Acts *7*.49; Rev. *4*.2). From that position of majesty and power he looks down upon men and they are helpless before him (Is. *40*.22). Height is used as a symbol of importance in every society. We still set important people on a platform. At the Olympic Games the winner has the highest stand. Holy places are set on hills and at the top of steps. It is not surprising that, in the Bible, God should be set in the highest point in heaven. From that position he is able to look down and see exactly what is going on (Ps. *33*.13; Lam. *3*.50). He can see his servants in need and come to their help (Ps. *80*.14, *102*.19; Is. *63*.15). He can note the virtuous, he can pass judgment, he can bless (Ps. *11*.4, *14*.2; Dt. *26*.15).

Secondly, the earth has foundations. It does not float like a raft on the waters. It is upheld by foundations that go down to the roots of the mountains. Just how the foundations relate to

109

the sea that surrounds everything is not made clear. The earth is founded on the floods (Ps. *24*.2). This may seem an extraordinary idea to us, but we can only repeat that our knowledge of marine engineering can be a positive barrier to getting inside the Hebrew mind. The Bible is not interested in engineering. It is anxious to give God his proper dignity. So he pushed back the sea and laid the foundations of the earth (Job *38*.4; Ps. *98*.11, *102*.25, *104*.5; Prov. *8*.29; Is. *48*.13, *51*.13, 16; Zech. *12*.1; Heb. *1*.10).

Thirdly, despite the firmness of the foundations, fountains spring up on earth from the waters that are below. Springs are to be found throughout the Fertile Crescent. They are both precious and mysterious. At times they dry up, at times they flood. Who is in control? The Bible suggests that God regulates the springs so that the earth is watered, usually for man's good but on occasion for his destruction (Gn. *7*.11, *8*.2; Prov. *8*.28; Am. *5*.8, *9*.6).

Similarly the waters above the earth occasionally break through as rain. English versions usually speak of windows in heaven, but the Hebrew word used for these heavenly openings is not the usual word for window. It rather suggests some kind of latticed opening through which smoke can escape. Hos. *13*.3 uses the word in this way. We have, therefore, to think of gratings in the sky which act like inverted drains or fountains acting in the same manner as the springs below. God controls them, sometimes for man's benefit (Ps. *78*.23, Mal. *3*.10), sometimes for his destruction (Gen. *7*.11, *8*.2; Is. *24*.18).

g   Finally and most important the cosmology includes a place for the dead. The Hebrew name is Sheol. The translators of the AV made the mistake of applying their own views on life after death to the OT and so the more painful references to Sheol they translated 'hell'. This is quite improper, as we shall see, and there is general agreement now that the word is best not translated at all. It is best used as a proper name.

The notion of Sheol is complicated and this is not the place for a long exposition, but something must be said to make the cosmology clear. With very few exceptions the Hebrews of OT times did not believe in a positive form of life after death

(Ps. *6*.5, *30*.9, *115*.17; Job *7*.10, *10*.21 f.). They shovelled their dead into a cold, dark ҕrave and left them. It was no secret that the grave was a place of corruption. The unconscious form was simply eaten by worms. The grave was, therefore, a place to be dreaded, and lucky the man who was blessed with a good long life.

It is not difficult to understand that, in the course of time, the thought of all these individual graves gave rise to a metaphorical notion of a land of the dead. The conditions of existence in the grave were simply transferred to this imaginary land. The land was given the name of Sheol and it was a place of darkness and corruption. The final step was to fit this imaginary land into the cosmology. It had to be beneath the earth because the bodies of the dead were down there away from the light of the sun. It had to be cold and cavernous because that is how graves appeared. So Sheol was envisaged as a great pit or cavern beneath the earth at the foot of the mountains.

There are more than sixty references to Sheol in the OT and they tell a consistent story. Sheol lies at the bottom of the universe in the deepest place imaginable (Dt. *32*.22; Job *11*.8; Prov. *9*.18). There the dead are unable to communicate with the living, or with each other, or with God (Ps. *6*.5, *30*.9, *31*.17, *115*.17; Eccles. *9*.10; Is, *38*.18). Their existence is joyless (2 Sam. *22*.6; Ps. *18*.5, *116*.3). It ends in corruption (Job *26*.6; Ps. *16*.10, *49*.14; Prov. *15*.11, *27*.20; Is. *14*.8–11). Ps *88*.1–12 gives a complete account of this baleful place.

h   In this chapter we are concerned with cosmology only. This is not the place to discuss the biblical view of life after death but perhaps a few brief notes regarding common misconceptions are in order.

1. The story of the witch of Endor in 1 Sam. *28* sometimes causes problems. Samuel had not long been dead and the witch managed to bring him back from Sheol just long enough to pronounce Saul's doom. What was happening was very irregular. It was an offence against the religious beliefs of the day. It annoyed Samuel. His life was over and it was improper for a witch to interfere with the ways of

111

God. The story does not, therefore, contradict what has been said here about Sheol.

2. Elijah's translation to heaven in a whirlwind in 2 K. *2* appears to be an exception but it is not so. Elijah's life was so meritorious that he did not die as other men did. He was carried off upwards to heaven, instead of downwards to Sheol. This is an exceptional incident but it does not contradict the cosmology.

3. Occasionally there are references to God redeeming the soul from the power of Sheol (Ps. *16*.10, *30*.3, *49*.15, *86*.13; Hos. *13*.14). On the face of it they seem to refer to a resurrection but careful study suggests that Sheol is being used in these references as a metaphor for serious illness or deep despair. They refer to recovery rather than resurrection.

4. There is a biblical view of life after death. It appears only at the end of the OT period. It rests upon a divine intervention to break open Sheol and restore and release its inhabitants.

We come then to the final diagram (Fig. 4).

i Against this background certain biblical ideas are easy to understand. The Ascension of Jesus was much like the ascent of Elijah. He just rose up to where God was beyond the clouds. The similarity between the Exodus and the creation narrative in Gn. *1* is underlined because God brought his people out of the waters of the Red Sea much as he brought the earth out of the watery chaos on the first day. This adds to the significance of NT baptism. The believer was plunged into the water as if he were going down into the great abyss, into death, as it were. He is brought up as a new creation out of the water. Something similar can be said of the Flood story. See 1 Pet. *3*.20 f. All this and much more follows from a careful study of biblical cosmology.

There remains, however, a serious problem. The diagram

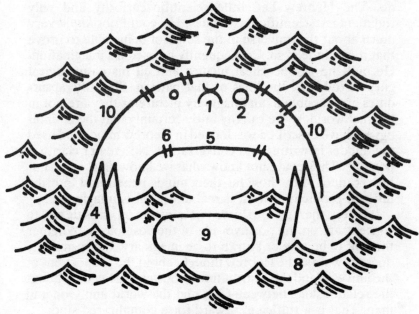

1   The throne of God
2   The sun and the heavenly bodies
3   The 'windows' of heaven
4   The foundations of the earth
5   The earth
6   The fountains
7   The waters above the firmament
8   The waters below the earth
9   Sheol
10 The firmament

Fig. 4

just does not make sense. Mountains do not float on the sea. Rain comes obviously from clouds not from windows in the heavens. The dead are not in a cavern beneath the earth. They are in the graves where they were buried. Could the Hebrews have actually believed that the structure of the universe was like this?

The question is unanswerable. It is not even clear what kind of answer could be given. Certainly neither yes or no would

113

do. The Hebrew had little scientific curiosity and only rudimentary scientific techniques. He could not *know* very much about the universe in the sense of being able to prove that it was indeed so. Consequently he used his imagination. He built up a theoretical picture and all his cosmological guesses followed the lines of that pattern. Scientific absurdities are possible in an imaginary picture as they are not in the real world, so we can say fairly certainly that the cosmology we have described was lodged in Hebrew minds and used as a model in writing and conversation. No greater clarity is possible. They could not know what we know, and we, in our turn, cannot know how far their minds penetrated into the difficult problem of what is real and what is imaginary.

It is best, therefore, to leave this question on one side and to concentrate on the positive side of the cosmology. Whether thought to be true or known to be imaginary, the cosmology does show what the Hebrew thought about the proportions of the universe and the distribution of power, particularly about the relationships between God and the world and God and man. That is a sufficient reward for a complicated study.

Chapter 9

Social Structure

a THE study of Hebrew social structure reveals a number of concepts which are significantly different from similar concepts rooted in our own society, for example the concepts of king, father, redeemer, and communal solidarity, to name but four. The best way to study the matter is to look at the social pyramid as it developed from nomadic beginnings to the absolute monarchy of Solomon's day. Thereafter the concept of the people of God over-rides all others, though remnants of the tribal system remain.

The smallest unit was the *family*, called in Hebrew 'the father's house'. This consisted of husband and wife, all children whether married or not, servants and their families, single relatives who had no father's house of their own, together with whatever wanderers had taken up a temporary dwelling in the house. There was a deadly fear of solitariness in ancient Israel and disconnected people, whether bereaved or far from home, were incorporated into families. The OT has strict laws on this matter. 'The stranger that is within thy gates' appears in the Ten Commandments. The head of the house was responsible for him as for all the others.

The patriarchal narratives refer to families on the move, but most of the references in the OT relate to a time after the settlement. The house means a physical dwelling as well as a family relationship. It is a place where the whole family can gather for the Passover (Ex. *12*.3 f., 46). When the father died, the property was divided and the sons founded houses of their own.

The position of the head of the house is thus pivotal. The son looked upon his father, in the first place, as his source and origin. Lacking any biological knowledge the Hebrew assumed that the man gave life and the woman incubated it. Consequently the child owed his being to his father. He expressed this by calling himself X son of Y. Thus the individual's identity was defined in terms of his father. The father had supreme authority. In early days this amounted to the right of life and death (Gen. *38*.24), but in later times it was limited to an authority under the law. At the same time the father was responsible for protecting every member of his household.

The concept of father is thus a rich and many-sided one. It embraces elements that, in other societies, are more widely distributed. This is important when one considers what the Bible means when it speaks of God as father.

b   A group of related families made up a *clan*. This was a unit large enough to defend itself in nomadic times. After the settlement it could be broadly equated with the village. The clan was ruled by the heads of the families who were called elders. In the deuteronomic code they had the right of life and death (Dt. *21*.18–21). Rule by elders is inefficient in war which explains why the 'judges' emerged. The judge was properly one of the elders, who therefore administered justice, but who also had charismatic gifts of leadership. No doubt others arose to lead who were not elder-judges, but they had pre-eminence only in battle. The patriarchal structure of society was not easily overturned. The clan was also the unit for worship in at least one case (1 Sam. *20*.6, 29).

The most important aspect of the clan, however, was its solidarity. On the level of the clan we meet the figure of the 'redeemer'. The Hebrew word *go-el* is untranslatable so we must consider his functions. Because of the solidarity of the clan, harm done to one member was harm done to all. In many cases the wounded party was not capable of revenging himself, but he had no need. The clan was outraged and so the *go-el* stepped forward to take responsibility for levelling the score (Nu. *35*.19). This was the soil in which the blood feud grew and blood vengeance worked havoc among these

116

ancient groups (see Dt. *19*.6; Jos. *20*). It was not all blood, however. The *go-el* was responsible for those in the clan who had fallen into debt. When they were on the point of selling themselves into servitude the *go-el* steeped in to buy them back (Lev. *25*.47–9). Similarly when property which was part of a member's patrimony was due to be sold, the *go-el* had to buy it so that it did not leave the clan (Lev. *25*.25). Jeremiah acted the part of the *go-el* when he bought the field of his cousin in Anathoth (Jer. *32*.6–15).

All this throws light on Job's famous utterance, 'I know that my redeemeth liveth' (Job *19*.25). God is also described as *go-el* in Ps. *19*.14 and Ps. *78*.35 and the verbal form occurs in Ps. *69*.18, *72*.14, *74*.2, *77*.15, *103*.4, *106*.10, and *107*.2. In all these cases God is protecting the worshipper from oppression, outrage, disease or death. Different verbs are used to translate the Hebrew in the English versions, redeem, deliver, rescue, claim back, vindicate, avenge, showing how complex the notion is and how much is being asserted when God is called *go-el*. The majority of usages, however, appear, not in Psalms, but in Second Isaiah. There are fifteen examples in Is. *40–55*. Perhaps the word was especially suitable because Israel was then in exile and needed redemption. Perhaps Second Isaiah's notion of God was more profound than that of his predecessors. In either case, careful study of this word throughout the OT is one way of discovering what the OT affirms about God.

So far we have spoken of family or father's house and clan. Unfortunately the terminology, especially in English, is not always clear. The reason is that 'family' in modern English usually means the small unit of father, mother and children. But it can mean a much larger body, 'the extended family', including aunts and uncles and distant relations, as in the phrase 'one of our oldest county families'. In this book we have called the former 'family' or 'father's house' and the latter 'clan'. NEB does the same. Jos. *7*.14–18 supplies the clearest definition of the three tier structure within the nation. NEB uses the terms tribe, clan and family. RSV, however, has tribe, family and household. In English versions, therefore, the word family might mean father's house or it might mean

117

clan. Problems of this kind are inevitable when we are not dealing with the original language.

c   So we come to the *tribe*. In theory a tribe is a group of clans who trace their descent from a common ancestor. This is an important symbol of tribal solidarity, but there is inevitably something fictional about it. In fact, in nomadic times, the tribe was a unit large enough to be an efficient fighting force, but small enough to travel easily and to subsist on what water-holes and oases provided. Oversized tribes subdivided and small groups coalesced to keep the over-all size right. Moreover there was a constant traffic of detached persons and groups who joined themselves to new tribes. Actual descent from a common ancestor was thus improbable in any biblical tribe, but the fiction was important. Blood relationship within the tribe was assumed whether it was fictional or not.

Ancestors were also used to explain relationships between tribes. The twelve tribes of Israel, who became a nation under David, explain their unity in terms of the twelve sons of Jacob. Edom, a related but hostile group, was explained as the descendants of Jacob's brother, Esau (Gen. *36*.43). The Ishmaelites were regarded as descendants of Abraham but through a son born to Sarah's maidservant, Hagar.

There is no rigid rule in the OT regarding leadership of the tribes. Again the terminology is not consistent in the English versions, but it is probably sound to think of a chief, much like an Arab sheikh, who had the final authority after consulting heads of clans (Nu. *1*.16, 44, *7*.2, etc.). Even after the settlement such leadership was necessary because, though each tribe had its territory, disputes were frequent and sometimes the whole tribe had to be rallied against persistent marauders.

Solidarity within the tribe was as real as solidarity within the clan. Abimelech appeals to his blood relations to support his bid for kingship in Ju. *9*. The words he uses suggest that he and they share a common existence. Responsibility did not end with the individual. It passed on to the family and, if it was serious enough, to the tribe and on to the next generation. When Achan broke a strict law and stole from the ruined city of Jericho, it was said that Israel had sinned (Jos. *7*.1, 11), and it may well be that his whole family was put to death, though the text is not clear on the point. There is no room for doubt in Ex. *20.5* f, however. The sins and the virtues of the fathers pass on down the generations and 'thousands' bear the loss or share the gain. 2 Sam. *21* provides the best example of this way of thinking. Israel is afflicted by famine and David eventually decides that the cause was Saul's gratuitous murder of Gibeonites some years before. The Gibeonites must be recompensed, even though the guilty person is long since dead. David asks their price and they demand seven of Saul's sons. David does not hesitate. The seven men are delivered and duly hanged and Israel has peace. Responsibility passes from Saul to Israel and to the seven and no one suggests that this is not perfectly just. Dt. *13*.12–15 makes it a matter of law. If certain men in a city turn to false gods and begin to entice their neighbours, the whole city must be put to the sword *including the cattle*.

On the same basis rests the assurance that the promises made to Abraham still apply. Through Abraham's faithfulness all his descendants are blessed. Similarly, according to 2 Sam. *7*, the choice of David means the choice of his people for ever. His name, his throne, his land will always be secure. This kind of thinking makes the notion of representation very easy to understand. Abraham and David are both individuals, but they both stand for all Israel. Adam was an individual according to Genesis but, through him, the whole human race entered into sin and death.

On this basis the Pauline doctrine of atonement is easier to comprehend. We are all where we are because Adam, our first representative, sinned. Through him we have been brought into sin ourselves. But Jesus is also one of us. He bears our flesh. He is a member of our tribe, the human race. He is our representative in his victory over sin and death. So, as we were brought down through Adam, we may be released through Christ (1 Cor. *15.22*).

Just how the tribal system operated in Israel is difficult to say. Some would argue that tribalism belongs to the desert and that there can be no real tribal system in an agricultural country. Others would say that the system of twelve tribes in

Israel was an artificial construction deriving from a shrine that imposed a division into twelve upon its devotees (see 10e). One cannot be sure. Relics of tribalism remain even in NT times (Lk. *2*.36; Ro. *11*.1), but there is little doubt that, after the settlement, the tribes increasingly gave way to the nation. Farmers have to be individualists. One man's errors do not spoil another man's crops. Gradually people began to think of themselves as bound together by the territory they occupied rather than by common ancestors. So, when Solomon divided the country for his levy (1 K. *4*), the boundaries did not coincide with what were supposed to be the tribal boundaries.

d   This brings us to the final unit, the *nation*, and its ruler, the king. In political terms Israel was a united nation for only two reigns, those of David and Solomon. After that there were two nations, Israel and Judah. After Samaria fell, there was one nation again, but it was only a remnant and it never regained political power.

Consequently Israel is represented in the OT much more as a religious community than as a nation. The patriotism of the OT has a religious slant. The Hebrews were saved at the Red Sea because they were to be a holy nation, a peculiar treasure, a kingdom of priests (Ex. *19*.5 f). The Canaanites were to be subdued for religious reasons according to Dt. 7. 1–11. Their altars were to be laid in ruins so that the chosen people might move in and establish the true Yahwistic faith. Whatever the facts of the case may have been, capturing Canaanite farms for basic economic purposes, was, according to the OT, very much a secondary consideration.

There was a strong tradition that, because Yahweh was sovereign in Israel, she should have no earthly king. Samuel rejects the first requests to appoint one (1 Sam. *8*). And when the king came, he was to be no oriental despot. In reality, many Hebrew kings behaved just like any other tyrant, but this did not affect the theory of kingship which persisted down to the Exile and is still to be seen in the Messianic hope.

In the first place the king is to be chosen by Yahweh. Saul and David were so chosen through the intermediacy of Samuel, but thereafter the king is described as Yahweh's chosen, even though he may have come to the throne by heredity (Ps. *89*.3, 19). The king's throne rests on a divine promise, he is supported by a divine covenant (2 Sam. *7*; Ps. *2, 89*). He leads the people in worship. David planned the Temple and Solomon built it and consecrated it (1 K. *8*). Many royal psalms show how the king represented the people in prayer (Ps. *20, 72, 110, 132, 144*). It is not surprising that, on one or two occasions, the king is given special status as God's son (2 Sam. *7*.14; Ps. *89*.27).

Chapter 10

The History of the Biblical Period

a   THE present chapter does not provide a history but a brief
outline. Nothing is said about Gn. *1–11*, for, whatever the
nature of those stories, they do not provide a basis for *historical* study. That is not to say that there is no history in them. No
doubt there was a flood, perhaps several, but one cannot write
a historical account of it from the material we have in Genesis.

The patriarchal narratives are rather different. However
difficult it may be to reconstruct that period, we can be
reasonably sure that actual events lie behind many of the
narratives. In the organization of the history, this is where we
begin, though some other history books begin with the
Exodus. The purpose of this chapter is to break the biblical
history down into ten sections, the general character of which
can easily be grasped. The tenth and longest section covers
the times of Jesus and the primitive Church.

b   **1. The patriarchs**

This is the period of Abraham, Isaac and Jacob, and Jacob's
family. The narratives are recorded in Gn. *12–50*. They end
with Joseph and his brethren in Egypt.

It can be readily agreed that there is a historical basis to the
narratives of the patriarchs. Ancient extra-biblical texts have
revealed that semi-nomadic chiefs having names and customs
similar to those of the patriarchs did roam the Fertile Crescent in the second millenium BC (see below 11 g, h). But that
does not mean that we are now in a position to establish how

122

much of Gn. *12–50* is historically accurate. For it is equally clear, from the genealogical framework of these chapters, that the narratives present an idealized account of the relationship of the tribes of Israel to their neighbours. Gn. *22*.20–4 tells us where Aram, or Syria, fits into the family pattern. Gn. *25*.1–4 places Midian, *25*.13–6 the Ishmaelites, and so on. Somewhere behind this artificial arrangement the real historical figures lie, but the true historian who studies events, their dates, their causes, their consequences, and the connexions between them is bound to reach the conclusion that no continuous account of the history of the period is possible.

Among scholars the narratives are known as sagas or legends. Sagas and legends deal with real persons and places, but their purpose is not so much to record fact as to affirm national identity, inspire national confidence and reiterate national aspirations. Legends are distinguished from sagas only in that they are especially concerned with the religious sphere.

Far from making these chapters useless, this realization concentrates attention on the fundamental importance of the Abraham stories. The religious ideas of Gn. *12–50* are, in any case, inescapable. And the message that comes clearly from them is that *Abraham knew God*, and knew him by trusting him. In Gn. *12–50* Israel defines herself as the nation that looks back to an ancestor whose supreme quality was personal religious faith.

One historical misapprehension that arises from following the patriarchal narratives too closely is that all the tribal groups related to Jacob (that is, Israel) went down into Egypt. Historically this is most improbable. Making sense of the stories of the Exodus and the entry into Canaan would be all but impossible if it were so.

c **2. The Exodus, the wilderness wanderings, and the entry into Canaan**

This is a period in which there are more questions than answers. We can speak with confidence of a dramatic Exodus, a profound religious experience for the group on the holy mountain, years of wandering in the desert, an entry into Canaan from the east across Jordan, and a linking up with other related groups who had entered Canaan in other ways. So the outline of the story is clear. The questions, however, concern large matters and not simply details. Unfortunately Egyptian sources make no reference to an Exodus at all.

To raise the questions and supply trite answers without giving the evidence would be an invitation to the student to pursue the path of prejudice. There is, however, no space to examine the questions properly. So what we shall do is simply point out the issues and leave the student to pursue them with the help of other books.

The first concerns the *date*. Much ink has been spilled on this in the past. There are various figures in the Bible (Gn. *15*.13–16, *50*.23–6; 1 K. *6*.1) and a few hints from outside. It is possible to come to a number of different conclusions but nowadays there is general agreement that the Exodus took place at some time in the thirteenth century BC.

Secondly, there is the question of *what actually happened* and where it happened. It is clear that the figure of 600,000 men plus children and flocks and herds, given in Ex. *12*.37 f., cannot be right. Sinai could never have supported a tenth of that number. We have to think of a small Exodus of a thousand or two, but it is clear that something profoundly impressive happened to them at the Red Sea because the history of the Jews has been coloured by it ever since.

Two explanations are combined in Ex. *14* which suggests that two different accounts have been woven together. Verse 21 speaks of a strong east wind making the sea go back so that the Israelites could walk on the sand whereas the Egyptian chariot wheels dug in and stuck. Verse 22 is more miraculous. The waters were pushed back forming a wall on either side. Verse 25 follows from v. 21 and vv. 28 f. follow from v. 22. It has also been suggested that both accounts are wrong and that an earthquake took place raising the bed of the sea for a short time. This question cannot now be settled on historical grounds. We have to be content with hypotheses.

It is clear that what we now call the Red Sea was not the site of the deliverance. The Bible actually refers to a 'sea of reeds' (Ex. *10*.19, *15*.4, etc.), which is wrongly translated 'Red Sea'. Where this sea of reeds was is not clear. The northern tip of the Gulf of Suez, which is on the west of Sinai, is too far south to fit the story. Some scholars suggest a crossing of Lake Menzaleh, which is that part of the Mediterranean nearest to Goshen. Some suggest the Bitter Lakes in the middle of the present Suez Canal. Some suggest Lake Sirbonis where there is a natural causeway a little way off-shore that is easily flooded. The last probably has the strongest support.

Thirdly, there is the question of the *route*. Ex. *13*.17 says that they did not go 'the way of the land of the Philistines' but by 'the way of the wilderness' (which is the strongest argument against Lake Sirbonis). Many place names are mentioned, but few can be identified now. The problem hinges on the site of Sinai, which is also called Horeb and 'the mountain of God'. The traditional Sinai is in *the far south of the peninsula* where the mountains rise to 2,500 metres. This is the site of the famous monastery of St. Catherine. The place has been hallowed as Sinai since the fourth century AD. But it has been contended that Sinai was volcanic. There was a pillar of cloud and a pillar of fire and the mountains quaked (Ex. *19*.18). In this case a site in *north-western Arabia* is to be preferred as traditional Sinai is not volcanic. The north-western Arabia site would put the mountain in Midianite territory which suits the Burning Bush story (Ex. *3*.1). Dt. *33*.2 and Ju. *5*.4, however, locate the mountain in *Edomite* territory and this fits in well with Elijah's journey 1 K. *19*.1–8. It is hard to say which of the three sites has the best claim.

One possible solution to the uncertainty is that the Israelites in the wilderness were not a single band but several, and that, when they came together in the Holy Land, they pooled their traditions leaving us with a composite route and a composite mountain.

Fourthly, there is the question whether the entry into Canaan was properly a *conquest or a settlement*. According to Joshua, Canaan was conquered by swift concerted action and then shared out between the twelve tribes, whereas Ju. *1* suggests a slow, piecemeal entry by several groups, spread over a long period. Some historians see the entry as a slow and partly peaceful infiltration of many different clans that discovered a unity, called themselves Israel, and adopted a twelve-tribe structure only after they had been settled in Canaan for some time. There is plenty of archaeological evidence of the destruction of Canaanite cities at this time but linking the archaeological evidence to the biblical text is difficult and many controversial issues arise. The understanding of this period is one of the points at issue between John Bright and Martin Noth, two leading OT historians.

The name 'Israel'

This name often causes confusion because it is used in so many different ways.

1. *It is a new name given to Jacob in Gn. 32.28.*
2. *It is the name of the covenant people throughout the OT and, indeed, throughout history. Terms like 'my people Israel' and 'the children of Israel' illustrate this.*
3. *It is the name of the land in which that people lived.*
4. *It is the name of the northern kingdom after the schism of 922 BC. As such Israel is set over against Judah, the southern kingdom.*
5. *Following on from 2 above it is the name given to the southern group after the northern group went out of existence in 722. It is thus possible to speak of 'Israel in exile in Babylon', even though the ancestors of those people, two centuries before, would have been called Judah and not Israel according to 4 above.*
6. *It is the name of the modern Jewish state.*

The real confusion arises from 4. A kingdom that existed for only two centuries bore the name that belonged to the whole people. The Assyrians destroyed Israel in one sense, but Israel in another continues to this day.

---

d   **3. The judges**

This is a period of 200 years concluding with Saul being made king around the year 1020 BC, during which the Israelite tribes had to discover their identity and assert themselves in Canaan.

The book of Judges records the events of these years in a schematic way, that is to say, it makes the history fulfil a certain pattern, clearly set out in 2.11–3.6, as follows:

1. Israel forsook its God and worshipped the gods of Canaan.
2. Yahweh then sent a foreign nation to oppress Israel.
3. Israel then appealed to its God and Yahweh raised up a judge to deliver Israel. (See below 22a.)

The application of this pattern implies that one judge followed another in continuous succession and that Israel acted throughout as one. Not surprisingly the judges were twelve in number and, with a little difficulty, they can be made into two groups, major and minor. The exploits of the major judges are recorded, the minor are simply mentioned.

Major

Othniel (*3.7–11*) overcame king Cushan-rishathaim from Mesopotamia.

Ehud (*3.12–30*) murdered king Eglon of Moab who, with Ammonite and Amalekite help, had captured Jericho.

Deborah (*4, 5*) with the help of Barak and six of the tribes destroyed Sisera, the commander of a Canaanite alliance.

Gideon (*6, 8*) led a group of northern tribes against the Midianites.

Jephthah (*10.6–12.7*) defeated the Ammonites, but is chiefly remembered for the rash vow which involved sacrificing his daughter.

Samson (*13–16*), a wild man, made several heroic, if ineffective, sallies against the Philistines.

Minor

Shamgar (*3.31*) killed 600 Philistines.

Tola (*10.1 f.*)

Jair (*10*.3–5)
Ibzan (*12*.8–10)
Elon (*12*.11 f.)
Abdon (*12*.13–15)

Jephthah's name occurs in *12*.7 with the same formula as the last five minor judges and it is notable that Shamgar is not described with this formula. So perhaps Shamgar should be made into a major judge and Jephthah into a minor one. If that is done, all the minor judges are said to have judged Israel for a period of years, which runs counter to the picture of the major judges as temporary, heroic, charismatic leaders. This has led some to say that the so-called minor judges were really the first officials of Israel.

One person from this period who was not a judge was *Abimelech*. His father, Gideon, refused to be made king (Ju. *8*.22 f.), but Abimelech rashly tried to seize his chance in Shechem and murder all possible rivals. According to Judges, Yahweh was king over Israel and Abimelech was presumptuous. Judges records with satisfaction the pretender's death at the hands of a woman (*9*.53 f.).

e *The 'amphictyony'*
This word crops up regularly in the study of this period. It means a group of tribes or cities who accept a common unity because they share in the worship at one, central shrine. What gave the tribes who had infiltrated into the Holy Land a sense of unity and identity as Israel? Martin Noth says it was the Ark and the shrine at which it rested. This accounts for the notion of twelve tribes, because, in an amphictyony, the worshippers were divided into groups, each group taking responsibility for the shrine for one month a year. The critical passage is Jos. *24*. There Joshua gathered the tribes at Shechem, gave them the choice of serving Yahweh or the gods of the land, and, because they chose Yahweh, sealed a covenant between Yahweh and the group. In this way those tribal elements that were not Yahwist before their settlement became Yahwist, and Israel as a covenant people was born. Amphictyonic unity lasted a century or two, but it proved

128

insufficient, so a monarchy was created, though the old covenant unity was still preserved. All historians take Noth's theory seriously, though many criticize it.

Chronology

Unfortunately precision in pre-exilic chronology is not attainable. The dates of Saul, David, and Solomon can be known only roughly. After Solomon it is possible to be a little more precise. There are about half a dozen different chronological schemes. The dates they give for important events do not differ at any point by more than ten years. Peake's Commentary *carries articles on the chronology of both OT and NT. The Chronological Charts at the end of John Bright's* ₁A History of Israel *are much prized by students because of their clarity. John Bright consistently follows W. F. Albright's scheme. Martin Noth follows Begrich, and Herrmann follows Andersen, which unfortunately means that the three history books recommended at the end of the chapter differ in their dating. For the death of Solomon, Bright gives 922, Noth 926, and Herrmann 932/31.*

---

f **4. The early monarchy**

This was a period of transition roughly from 1020–920 BC. At the beginning Israel had no political structure. At the end it was a great empire under a despotic king. Four names dominate the period, Samuel, Saul, David and Solomon. The chief threat to Israel was the Philistines, a warlike race who settled in the south-western corner of Palestine at roughly the same period as the Hebrew infiltrations.

Sources
The Deuteronomic History (see below 22a, 25) deals with the period in some detail. The whole of 1 and 2 Sam. and 1 K. *1–11* are given up to it. The Chronicler's History (see 25) also devotes 1 Chr. *10–29* to David and 2 Chr. *1–9* to Solomon. The sources behind these books are exceptionally complicated. Traditions of different kinds have been combined, especially in

1 Samuel, so that the book reveals different views of Samuel, Saul, David and the monarchy. On the positive side, it is probable that the first written sources date from this period. The court was wealthy enough to employ scribes who recorded events not long after they happened.

Samuel
Prophet, priest, seer, intercessor, king-maker. See 1 Sam. *1*.1–*25*.1. Some of the material relating to him is legendary.

Saul
There are two accounts of his becoming king and two accounts of his deposition. It is clear that he was never a proper king. He had no royal seat and he was always at war. He commanded only the northern tribes. David was able to win the loyalty of the south while Saul was still struggling with the Philistines. Saul was a tragic and unhappy character. His story is told in 1 Sam. *9–31*.

David
The greatest military and political figure in Israel's biblical story. When Saul died, Israel was a defeated and divided group of tribes with no king, no capital, no court and a Philistine overlord. When David died, Israel was an empire stretching from the approaches to Egypt to beyond Damascus. David gave Israel unity (at last north and south were brought under a single government), a strong capital and holy city (not until David's attack in 2 Sam. *5*, 6–10 did Jerusalem fall into Hebrew hands), and an empire. As he grew old there was trouble with the succession. Absalom, David's beloved son, rebelled and there was a danger of civil war before Solomon was eventually established on the throne. David first appears in 1 Sam. *16*.13. The whole of 2 Samuel is given to his reign and his death is recorded in 1 K. *2*.

Solomon
(See 1 K. *1–11*.) His reputation for magnificence was more merited than his reputation for wisdom. He was no warrior but a diplomat and an administrator. He had a large civil

service that helped him to thrive on taxes and trade. He built the Temple and a palace for himself. The Deuteronomic History is inconsistent about him. On one hand there are laudatory stories (1 K. *3*.5–15). On the other, the fact that he allowed his foreign wives to worship their gods on Mount Zion counts against him (1 K. *11*.1–8).

Religion
Prophecy comes to the surface in this period. Apart from the ecstatic groups (1 Sam. *10*.10, *19*.20), Gad and Nathan, advisers of David, appear. Moving the Ark up to Mount Zion and the subsequent building of the Temple were events of great importance. They prepared the way for the Deuteronomic belief that Zion was the place Yahweh had chosen for sacrifice and that there was to be no other.

g **5. The divided monarchy**

This was a period of 200 years between the death of Solomon and the end of the northern kingdom. It is recorded in 1 K. *12*–2 K. *17*, twenty-eight chapters to cover twelve Judaean kings and nineteen northern ones. 2 Chr. *10–28* covers the same period but deals with Judaean affairs almost exclusively. Both histories deal at length with the kings that interest them but say little about the others, which means that some important kings are almost ignored.

The kings of the two centuries were as follows:

South		*North*	
Rehoboam	922–915	Jeroboam	922–901
Abijah	915–913		
Asa	913–873		
		Nadab	901–900
		Baasha	900–877
		Elah	877–876
		Zimri	876
		Omri	876–869
Jehoshaphat	873–849		
		Ahab	869–850
		Ahaziah	850–849

131

Jehoram	849–842		
		Jehoram	849–842
Ahaziah	842		
		Jehu	842–815
Athaliah	842–837		
Jehoash			
(Joash)	837–800	Jehoahaz	815–801
		Jehoash (Joash)	801–786
Amaziah	800–783		
		Jeroboam II	786–746
Uzziah			
(Azariah)	783–742	Zechariah	746–745
		Shallum	745
		Menahem	745–738
Jotham	750–735		
		Pekahiah	738–737
		Pekah	737–732
Ahaz	735–715		
		Hoshea	732–724

Albright's dates have been given purely as a guide. Albright's is the simplest system but not necessarily the most accurate. See the note on Chronology.

Both Syria and Assyria were enemies of the Hebrew kingdoms in this period. Syria, especially under kings Benhadad and Hazael, was a constant nuisance to the northern kingdom and Assyria finally caused its downfall.

At least four northern kings are worthy of note. Omri gave order and stability to the kingdom and built Samaria as its capital. Ahab, the husband of Jezebel and the antagonist of Elijah, defeated Benhadad and then made an alliance with him against the Assyrians. Jehu was appointed by Elisha, perhaps because he was thought to be loyal to Yahweh. His idea of reform was to murder everyone in his way (see 2 K. *10*.18–31). He suffered at the hands of Hazael. Jeroboam II recovered territory lost to Syria and built up a prosperous kingdom just a few decades before the final blow fell.

Judah's history is less eventful. Asa and Uzziah were the most notable kings. Athaliah, Jezebel's daughter, attempted a murderous purge. She was eventually dealt with by Jehoiada, the priest.

One sad incident of the period is recorded in 2 K. *15*.37 and provides the background for the well-known prophecy of Is. 7.14. Pekah of Israel joined forces with Rezin of Syria to resist Assyria and together they tried to coerce Ahaz of Judah to join them. Ahaz refused, so Pekah and Rezin laid siege to Jerusalem. Ahaz did not listen to Isaiah but appealed to the arch-enemy Assyria for help.

Religion
It was a time of fierce struggle between those who subscribed to a strict Yahwist faith with Mount Zion as its only shrine and those who wanted to accommodate Yahwism to Canaanite practices and worship with fertility rites at shrines all over the country (the 'high places'). There was a series of great prophets, staunch defenders of Yahwism: Ahijah, Elijah, Elisha, Micaiah, Amos, Hosea, Isaiah, Micah.

h   **6. The kingdom of Judah alone (721–587 BC)**

See 2 K. *18–25* and 2 Chr. *29–36*. Assyria was triumphant during the first half of this period. Judah expected a siege and Hezekiah dug a tunnel 518 metres long to bring water into Jerusalem (2 K. *20*.20). The tunnel is still there to be seen. 2 K. *18* and *19* record that Sennacherib did come to Judah and besiege Jerusalem. It is not quite clear what happened, but he retreated and the city survived. (See also Is. *37*.)

There were eight more kings after Ahaz. (The dates here are Albright's. Unhappily there are problems with those given in 2 K. *18*.9. Only a careful study of the commentaries can sort out the chronology at this point.)

Hezekiah	715–687
Manasseh	687–642
Amon	642–640
Josiah	640–609
Jehoahaz	609
Jehoiakim	609–598
Jehoiachin	598
Zedekiah	598–587

After 650 there were uprisings and Assyria began to weaken. Nineveh fell to a joint attack of Medes and Babylonians in 612 and the rest of the Assyrian empire, although supported by Egypt, was defeated at Carchemish in 605. This meant that Nebuchadnezzar, the Babylonian king, had to secure his western frontier. Jehoiakim foolishly backed Egypt which meant that Jerusalem was attacked and taken. All the notables were deported including the new, young king, Jehoiachin. An uncle, Zedekiah, was set on the throne as a Babylonian puppet, but he too tried to rebel and Jerusalem was finally sacked in 587 BC.

Religion
Isaiah dominates the beginning of the period and Jeremiah its end. There was much kow-towing to Assyria, especially by Manasseh. This usually meant adopting Assyrian styles of worship. Hezekiah is credited with a religious reform in 2 K. *18*.3–6 and 2 Chr. *29–31*. The book of Deuteronomy was given its final editing in the first half of the seventh century and then hidden, to be discovered during Josiah's reform (2 K. *22–3*).

i **The Exile**

Ps. *137* gives a moving picture of the Jews in exile, but it appears that, after the first shock, they were able to survive quite well. (See Jeremiah's letter to them in Jer. *29*.) The poorest Jews were not deported (2 K. *24*.14, *25*.12; Jer. *40*.7). They intermarried with other stray groups and became 'the people of the land' that the returning Jews so heartily despised. (See the next section.) The Jews in Babylon were able to keep their national identity (Ezek. *8*.1, *14*.1, *20*.1) and even develop it further.

Babylon shared the Fertile Crescent with the Medean Empire. There was also the Lydian Empire in Asia Minor. In 550 Cyrus, ruler of a small Persian kingdom subject to the Medes, attacked and dethroned his overlord, Astyages, the Medean emperor. Next he went west and dealt with Lydia, by which time Babylon was ready to give up without a fight.

Cyrus took the city in 539. The Jews were free to go home, for Cyrus was a good colonizer who prized loyal vassals. His policies excluded deportations and religious bans. (See note on the Cyrus Cylinder in the next chapter on archaeology.)

Religion
There were two great prophets, Ezekiel and the unknown prophet responsible for Is. *40–55*. The Exile was a time of immense literary activity. New law codes were worked out. Old documents were revised and edited, chiefly by editors with a priestly interest. It seems likely that the synagogue, as a substitute for the distant and ruined Temple, emerged during the Exile.

j 8. The Persian period

The *Persian Empire* was different from its predecessors in the Crescent in two regards. It was a 'world empire' covering the whole of the world as it was known to the biblical writers. And it was well organized, attempting constructive government of subject peoples.

For the history of the Jews records are scanty. The chief biblical passage is Ezra *1–6*. We postulate a small and poor community, struggling to preserve its traditions but suffering considerable disillusionment.

Cyrus issued an edict allowing the Jews to go home (Ezra *1.2–4, 6.3–5*). No Jew was compelled to go and many did not, so that Babylon remained a centre of Jewish learning for centuries.

The first task was *the re-building of the Temple*. Cyrus gave his permission and those who did not return helped financially. The prophets Haggai and Zechariah gave moral support and encouragement. 'The people of the land' offered help but were spurned, so they did their best to impede the building. The dedication took place in 516.

Nehemiah and Ezra are the two great figures of the Persian period. There has been much argument about the date of Ezra and whether he preceded Nehemiah or followed him. The traditional view is that Ezra came first, that is in 458.

Others say 398. Nehemiah arrived in 444. Both men came from Babylon to Jerusalem to support the re-settled community.

Ezra brought a new version of the Law that had been worked out in Babylon. His story is told in Ezra *7–10* and Neh. *8–9*. Ezra was hard on Jews who had married 'people of the land'. To keep Israel pure he required both the parents and their children to be expelled from the community.

Nehemiah was appointed Governor of Judah and came to build a wall to make both the defence and the separation of the chosen people easier (Neh. *1–7*). 'The people of the land' tried threats, mockery and physical force to stop him, but he succeeded in building the wall—a part of which is still visible. On a second visit Nehemiah carried out religious reforms including the banning of mixed marriages.

'The people of the land' consisted of descendants of Jews left behind in 721 and 586 and of refugees from other areas deported *to* Palestine at various times, plus the 'polluted' half-Jews expelled by Ezra and Nehemiah. They were Yahwists and honoured their own version of the Law. After their repulse they built their own temple on Mount Gerizim. They became the *Samaritans*.

This period thus sees the beginning of an avowed policy of *separatism*. The logic of separatism was simple:

a. Yahweh has chosen Israel and given her his holy Law.
b. Israel had failed to grasp the import of this privilege and had followed practices, forbidden in the Law, that were learned from other nations not so chosen.
c. Israel was thus punished with exile, a time for thought and penitence.
d. Israel, released from exile, determined not to make the same mistake again. The definition of the chosen people must be made clear and absolute fidelity of the Law ensured.

This is the logic that has kept Israel distinct from other peoples to this day.

k   ## 9. The Greek period

While Jews were struggling to re-establish themselves in their own land, the Greeks were experiencing a golden age of culture. In the two centuries after 525 a brilliant succession of philosophers, dramatists, sculptors, scientists, statesmen and orators flourished. Socrates, Plato, Aristotle, Aeschylus, Sophocles, Euripides, Pheidias, Myron, Praxiteles, Pericles, Hippocrates, Demosthenes, all belong to these two centuries.

Alexander, one of the most brilliant generals the world has seen, was tutored by Aristotle. He conquered, not simply to gain wealth and glory, but to spread this brilliant Greek culture throughout the world. Therein lies the tragedy of the Greek period for the Jews. Greek culture and Hebrew faith did not easily mix.

Alexander, setting out in 336, conquered all the way from Macedonia to the Indus. Israel came under his sway in 333. He died of a fever in 323.

Alexander had no heir. His subordinates squabbled over the division of the empire. A clear pattern does not emerge until 301. One Greek general, called *Seleucus*, ruled over Syria and Babylon from a capital city he called Antioch (the Syrian one). Another Greek general, called Ptolemy, ruled Egypt from Alexandria, which Alexander himself had founded. There were constant disputes between these two kingdoms. For centuries Alexandria and Antioch were rival cultural centres as well as rival capitals.

Israel, at first under Ptolemy, was a small farming and trading community with a high priest and much concerned with her Law and her religious observances. She became deeply divided between those who wanted to profit from Greek culture, trade with the Greek world, and enjoy Greek pastimes, and those who wanted to preserve a strict separatism and have nothing to do with their conquerors. Under the relaxed rule of the Ptolemies this crisis was simply an internal matter.

Unhappily in 199, after the battle of Paneas, Israel passed from the Alexandrian empire to the Antiochan. The king, Antiochus III, was in trouble with the Romans whom he had

137

foolishly attacked. He had to pay a huge tribute so his subjects had to be squeezed. His son was Antiochus IV who called himself Epiphanes, meaning 'manifestation', the manifestation of God, that is. This immodest title was assumed in an attempt to unite the sagging empire under the king. It had exactly the opposite effect on the Jews.

Antiochus IV began meddling in the affairs of the Jews, outraging the faithful by appointing a Benjamite high priest. A rumour reached Jerusalem that Antiochus was dead so an attempt was made to replace the high priest with a man of proper levitical descent. Antiochus was not dead. He attacked Jerusalem in 167 and desecrated the Temple. Antiochus was losing his reason and the faithful among the Jews were in no mood to compromise. A Jewish uprising was inevitable.

The sources for this period are 1 Maccabees and Josephus, *Antiquities of the Jews* Book 12.

Josephus

The writings of Josephus figure largely in biblical studies. Josephus was a Jew who fought against the Romans in the war of AD *66–70, but afterwards managed to ingratiate himself with the emperors Vespasian and Titus, and so was able to live securely in Rome, following a literary career. His works were,* The Jewish War, *a full account of the causes and course of the war in which he had fought,* The Antiquities of the Jews, *a huge work, which tells the story of Israel from the Creation to the outbreak of the war with Rome, his* Life, *which is a defence of himself and his work against detractors, and* Against Apion, *which is a reasoned defence of Judaism against first-century anti-Semitism.*

References to Josephus are confusing because they appear in two different forms. There is a famous English translation by William Whiston that first appeared in 1737. In it the large works are divided into books, chapters, and paragraphs, so any reference has three figures, e.g. Ant. 13.8.4. Roman numerals are often used which makes it more difficult. Moreover the titles are often given in abbreviated Latin. In this guise the four works appear as, Bell. Jud., Ant., Vita., *and* Contra Ap., *or just* Ap. *Some books, however, quote from the Greek text, not from the*

Whiston translation. The Greek text is divided into books and sections only, so Ant. 13.8.4 in English is Ant. 13.249 in Greek. If one is using the English text, meeting references to the Greek is tiresome.

In 1959 a Penguin version of The Jewish War *appeared. It has its own system of chapters, but there are clear indications to enable the student to relate the translation both to the Greek text and to the Whiston version. Either kind of reference can therefore, be looked up in the Penguin edition.*

The rest of the Greek period is taken up with the account of the Maccabaean revolt and the Hasmonaean dynasty.

Occasion of the war: Antiochus did not understand Jewish monotheism. He himself recognized many gods but gave none absolute devotion. Gods were allies rather than masters. Consequently he interpreted Jewish unwillingness to sacrifice to his gods as treason. He sent soldiers to enforce pagan sacrifices. At the village of Modein, Mattathias, an elderly priest, killed the officer in charge and fled, calling the faithful to follow him. The Maccabaean war had begun.

Judas Maccabaeus, son of Mattathias and an ideal guerrilla leader, won victories at Emmaus and Beth-Zur, won back Jerusalem, re-consecrated the Temple, and set up a Jewish kingdom. But the war was by no means over and Judas died fighting in 160.

Jonathan, the next brother, profited from diplomacy rather than fighting. Antiochus was dead and the appearance of rival claimants for the Antiochan throne gave Jonathan the opportunity to advance the Jewish cause. It is likely that the community that gave us the Dead Sea Scrolls was formed at this time. (See 11s.)

Simon, another brother, won from Antioch an acknowledgment of Jewish independence. He was murdered by his son-in-law in the squalid manner of those days, but fortunately his son, John, managed to outwit the murderer and succeed his father.

John Hyrcanus I (134–04) was the first to call himself king and was the founder of the Hasmonaean line. Pharisees and Sadducees emerged as separate parties.

Aristobulus I (104–03) sympathized with the Greek party in Israel. He tried to secure his deeply divided kingdom by a policy of murder.

Alexander Jannaeus (103–76) was successful in enlarging the

139

kingdom, but the Hasmonaean kings were also high priests and, in this area, Jannaeus was a bungling amateur. There was an uprising against him which he put down with barbarous cruelty. *Alexandra* (76–67) was the wife of the two previous kings. Her eldest son, Hyrcanus, became high priest. There was trouble between the Sadducean and the Pharisaic parties. *Aristobulus II* (67–63), a younger son, ousted Hyrcanus, but allowed him to go free. He went off to Idumaea to intrigue against Aristobulus. Hyrcanus was just about to lay siege to his brother in Jerusalem when the Romans arrived.

l **10. The Romans**
Rome was supposedly founded by Romulus in 753 BC, about the time of Amos. At first it was a monarchy and it became a republic in 510. Expansion was slow. The chief enemy was Carthage in North Africa. At last, in 150, Carthage was erased from the map.

In 67 BC, Pompey came east to deal with pirates, but he took Antioch and Damascus. From there it was a short step to Jerusalem. After a great slaughter, he entered the Holy of Holies. He sent Aristobulus off to Rome and made Hyrcanus ethnarch. The whole land was reorganized. Hyrcanus governed those areas that were predominantly Jewish, Judaea, Idumaea, Galilee, and Peraea. Samaria was ruled from Syria and the Decapolis, an area east of Jordan consisting of self-governing cities, was created.

Pompey lost power to Julius Caesar who was murdered in 44 BC. The empire was then divided between Octavian in the west and Antony in the east. Antony fell fatally in love with Cleopatra, the surviving Ptolemaic monarch, who still coveted Judaea, which had been lost to Antioch in 199 BC.

Before Antony could give her Judaea one of Aristobulus' sons arrived from Rome and deposed Hyrcanus. He was Antigonus, the last of the Hasmonaeans, popular because he was the legitimate heir and because he was able to get rid of Hyrcanus' political 'advisers', who were Idumaean and roundly hated by the Jews.

m *Herod the Great*
One of these 'advisers' was Herod. He went to Rome and

140

whipped up support. In 37 BC he was back with a Roman force. He took Jerusalem, executed Antigonus, and was installed as king, under the Romans, of Judaea and Samaria. Antony, urged on by Cleopatra, tried to limit Herod's powers, but Herod managed to out-manoeuvre him.

Cleopatra quarrelled with Octavian, which was her undoing. In 31 BC Octavian defeated Antony at Actium and the lovers committed suicide. Herod made a bold bid for the emperor's support and Octavian increased his kingdom. In 28 BC Octavian was proclaimed Emperor Augustus.

The intrigues at Herod's court were too complicated and too horrible to be worthy of our attention. Herod built fortresses, including the one at Masada. He also rebuilt Samaria, gave it a temple of Augustus, and a new name, Sebaste (Greek for Augustus). He built Caesarea and gave it a theatre, hippodrome, and a large, artifical harbour. In Jerusalem he shored up the east side of the Temple area to make a huge platform where gates, porticoes, and markets were set up. The sanctuary was also rebuilt. For all this he gained little popularity with Jews other than the few known as Herodians.

Why did the Jews hate Herod?

Because he replaced a true, Jewish, levitical, Hasmonaean king.

Because he was Idumaean, that is, Edomite, by race.

Because he was a friend of the great oppressor, Rome.

Because he was murderous and ruthless.

Because he became crazy with fear and jealousy, killing his nearest and dearest on the flimsiest of pretexts. The slaughter of the innocents (Mt. 2.16) is entirely in keeping with his known character.

Almost everyone in Israel hated Herod. The Pharisees hated him for his foreignness but they also regarded him as a punishment sent from God. The Sadducees hated him because he had stolen their power, though they still had some power in the Temple. Some Jews decided that Yahweh would be more honoured if they removed the outrage. So the zealots came into being.

141

Herod the Great's successors
Jesus was born just before the death of Herod (Mt. *2*). Herod died in 4 BC and the kingdom was divided between three surviving sons, Archelaus, Antipas and Philip. Archelaus was to have most, that is, the whole of Judaea, Samaria, and Idumaea, and he was to bear the title ethnarch. Antipas and Philip were to have smaller areas and to be known as tetrarchs. Antipas was to have two separated areas, Galilee and Peraea. Philip was to have an area in the north-east made up of small territories called Gaulonitis, Trachonitis, Batanaea, Auraniitis, and Ituraea. A small area in the south-west, which, in days gone by, had been Philistine country was allotted to Herod's sister Salome. The large area called the Decapolis, which had never been under Herod's jurisdiction, was to remain under the control of the Roman officer in charge of Syria. We now look at the three areas and their rulers in turn, beginning with Galilee.

n   *Galilee and Peraea*
Galilee was the centre of the ministry of Jesus. Galilee was rather more prosperous than Judaea but it had a large Gentile population. Hence the sneer of Jn. *1*.46. Antipas is confusingly called Herod in the Gospels and one has to be careful to distinguish between Herod the king in Mt. *2*.1 and Herod the tetrarch in Mt. *14*.1. It is best always to refer to one as Herod the Great and to the other as Antipas or Herod Antipas. Antipas was a faithful servant of Rome. He built the town of Tiberias on the shore of the Sea of Galilee, naming it after the emperor. Antipas showed some interest in the reports of Jesus and, according to Luke, took some part in his trial (*23*.7–12). From the Jewish point of view Antipas sinned grievously by divorcing his first wife and marrying the wife of his half brother. John the Baptist denounced him for this. Hence John's execution (Mt. *14*.1–6; Mk. *6*.14–29). Two slighting remarks by Jesus about Antipas are recorded in Mk. *8*.5 and Lk. *13*.31 f. Intrigues and misjudgments eventually caught up with Antipas and he was banished in AD 39. Peraea, on the east of Jordan, is not mentioned in the NT.

o *North-east territory*
Philip was the best of the Herods. He ruled with moderation and tolerance until his death in AD 34. For this reason his territory was probably safer for Jesus and his followers than Galilee. A glance at the map shows that it was easy to cross from Galilee to Philip's territory by boat. Perhaps Mk. *6*.45 refers to such an escape. Philip built the town of Bethsaida Julias, from which the disciples, Philip, Andrew and Peter came (Jn. *1*.44), on the shore of the lake. He also built, further north, the town of Caesarea Philippi, where Jesus withdrew with his disciples at a critical point in his ministry (Mk. *8*.27). Jn. *12*.21 says that Bethsaida was in Galilee, but this is probably an error.

p *Judaea, Samaria and Idumaea*
The three areas that make up this territory are an unlikely combination. Jews and Samaritans had been enemies since the Jews returned from exile and refused all co-operation with the Samaritans. Idumaea was the Roman name for Edom. The inhabitants of this area, enemies of even longer standing, had advanced north during the days of Jewish weakness after the fall of Jerusalem in 586 BC. The fact that John Hyrcanus, one of the Hasmonean kings, had compelled Idumaeans to be circumcised in the second century BC made things worse rather than better, for the Jews had a special contempt for those who posed as co-religionists without being thorough-going servants of the Law. Archelaus was a disastrous ruler. According to Mt. *2*.22, it was through fear of him that Joseph and Mary went to live in Galilee rather than Judaea. He dismissed two high priests for disloyalty. Both Jews and Samaritans sent separate deputations to Augustus asking that he be deposed. He was banished in AD 6 and replaced by a Roman procurator, Coponius. *This explains why, during the ministry of Jesus, Galilee and Jerusalem were ruled in different ways.* Galilee was still under Herod Antipas, who, though a turncoat, came from the locality and had some Jewish blood. Judaea was ruled by a procurator, a Roman soldier, who might come from anywhere.
The procurators lived in Caesarea which was badly situated

143

for the territory they ruled, but it was a modern city and the nearest place to Antioch in Syria where the Roman legate who had oversight of the whole province lived. The procurators were responsible for security and all military affairs. They had ultimate responsibility for the raising of taxes and the administration of justice. They could, and did, depute some of their civil power to the Jewish Sanhedrin. There were seven procurators covering the period AD 6–41. Pontius Pilate (AD 26–36) is the best known. He was not a good ruler quite apart from his great mistake.

q *From AD 37 to the end of the NT era*
The crucifixion of Jesus falls clearly within the procuratorship of Pontius Pilate and the reign, in Galilee, of Herod Antipas. Not many years afterwards the government of Palestine underwent further changes. None of them brought any satisfaction to the Jews and the infant Church began its course in a political situation that was both insecure and charged with hatred. A Jewish rebellion was inevitable and it came in AD 66. In studying the NT it is always necessary to remember the general instability of the situation and the inescapable sense of overhanging doom that proved all too accurate. Two further rulers have to be noted.

Herod Agrippa I: grandson of Herod the Great and intimate of Caligula before and after he became emperor. In AD 37 Agrippa was given Philip's tetrarchy, and in 39 Antipas was deposed and Agrippa got his territory too. When Claudius became emperor Judaea, Samaria and Idumaea were added. Agrippa was happy to persecute Christians to please the Jews (Ac. *12*.1–3). Ac. *12*.20–3 records his death in AD 44. The whole territory was then put under procurators and ruled from Caesarea.

Herod Agrippa II: son of Agrippa I. He was not allowed to succeed to all his father's lands, but in AD 50 he was given Galilee and territory in the north-east. Procurators continued to govern the south. That is why Paul appeared at Caesarea

145

Emperors and procurators

One cannot always be sure of dates, but the following lists are as reliable as one can reasonably expect.

Roman Emperors

Augustus	BC 28–14 AD	(Lk. *2*.1)
Tiberius	AD 14–37	(Lk. *3*.1)
Caligula	37–41	
Claudius	41–54	(Ac. *11*.28, *18*.2)
Nero	54–68	

Galba, Otho and Vitellius all failed in attempts to seize power.

Vespasian	69–79	
Titus	79–81	

First group of procurators

Coponius	AD 6–9	
Marcus Ambibulus	9–12	
Annius Rufus	12–15	
Valerius Gratus	15–26	
Pontius Pilatus	26–36	(before whom Jesus was tried)
Marcellus	36–37	
Marullus	37–41	

Second group of procurators

Cuspus Fadus	AD 44–46	
Tiberius Alexander	46–48	
Ventidius Cumanus	48–52	
Felix	52–60	(Ac. *23*.24–*25*.14)
Porcius Festus	60–62	(Ac. *24*.27–*26*.32)
Albinus	62–64	
Gessius Florus	64–66	

---

before both a procurator and Herod Agrippa II (Ac. *25*.13–*26*.32).

r   *The war of AD 66–70*: It was a forlorn hope from the beginning. The Jews were hopelessly divided and, even united, they would not have been strong enough. They won a few victories, as guerrillas tend to do, but, as soon as the Romans

146

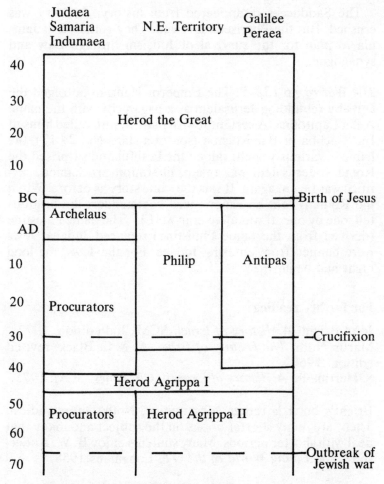

Chart showing the rulers of Palestine in the NT period

took them seriously, they had no hope. Nero sent Vespasian who carefully took city after city in Galilee. Then he came south and isolated Jerusalem. At this point he returned to Rome to become emperor, but his son, Titus, besieged Jerusalem and took it with much bloodshed in AD 70. A shrine to Jupiter was set up on the Temple site. The last act took place at Masada, ending with the famous mass suicide.

The Sadducees disappeared from history. Zealotry was crushed. But the Pharisees survived. They gathered at Jamnia to plan for the survival of Judaism through Law and synagogue.

s *The War of* AD *132–5*: The Emperor Hadrian outraged the Jews by rebuilding Jerusalem as a pagan city with the name Aelia Capitolina. A certain Jewish patriot, who called himself Bar-Cochba or Bar-Kochba (son of a star—Nu. *24*.17), the name is variously spelt, rallied the faithful and surprised the Romans. Jerusalem was taken, liberation proclaimed, sacrifice was begun again. It was the same story as before. When the Romans sent an experienced commander, the bastions fell, one by one. It was all over in AD 13*5*. The name Palestine (derived from the name Philistine) replaced Judaea. Jews were banned from entering Judaea. For the Jews, the long night had begun.

For further reading

John Bright, *A History of Israel,* SCM, 2nd edition, 1972.
Martin Noth, *The History of Israel,* A. & C. Black, revised edition, 1960.
S. Herrmann, *A History of Israel in OT Times,* SCM, 1975.

Bright's book is rather conservative, Noth's more radical. There are many shorter books on the subject and many that deal with shorter periods. Many students enjoy B. W. Anderson's *The Living World of the OT,* Longmans 1958.

Floyd V. Filson, *A NT History,* SCM, 1975.
Bo Reicke, *The NT Era,* A. & C. Black, 1969.
F. F. Bruce, *NT History,* Oliphants, revised edition, 1971.

A shorter book is E. M. Blaiklock, *The Century of the NT,* IVF, 1962.

Chapter 11

Archaeology and the Bible

a ARCHAEOLOGY is a modern science calling for much patience and skill. It is a valuable source of information to the historian. Each decade provides more 'finds', so the information provided by archaeology is always increasing. Occasionally there are 'sensational discoveries', beloved by journalists, but their importance is usually exaggerated. Archaeology is a far less melodramatic discipline than the man in the street realizes.

Broadly speaking, finds are of three kinds. There are the ruins of buildings, homes, temples, fortifications. Sometimes villages and whole cities can be uncovered. These reveal much regarding the culture, worship, social structure and manner of life of the original occupants. Sometimes it is possible to see how the buildings were destroyed and so to surmise about some catastrophic event in the people's history. Secondly, there are artefacts, pots, lamps, weapons, ornaments, that reveal something about wealth and culture as well as more homely facts about everyday life. Thirdly, there are inscriptions, what is known as epigraphic material. Here there is a double benefit. It is not simply possible to see how they wrote but also what they wrote about. Translating the texts provides the most valuable information both about historical events and about how the ancient people thought.

The two most important scripts were *hieroglyphs* and *cuneiform*. Most people have seen hieroglyphs in museums. Each word or syllable was represented by an object drawn in a simple way. In the course of time, the objects were so simplified that they are hardly recognized as objects at all and look more like letters. Cuneiform works by a different system. It is written on wet clay tablets with a tool, the head of which is shaped like a long, thin triangle. This triangle is stamped into the clay two or three times to make one letter or syllable. Thousands of tablets covered with cuneiform have been discovered. They provide information about the biblical world before 1000 BC. After that time alphabets with letters not made up of combinations of triangles begin to emerge and we are on our way to the Hebrew script known to biblical scholars.

b   Valuable as all this information is, two words of caution are necessary before one launches on a study of archaeology and the Bible. In the first place, much of what is discovered in Palestine has no bearing on the Bible at all. It is so easy to suppose that, because the Palestine is the land of the Bible, any important find must relate to the Bible. It is not so, and serious mistakes have been made by people who thought it was. The excavations at Jericho are an example. There, before the war, Professor John Garstang found a system of walls that had been violently destroyed. The news went round the world that the walls Joshua had flattened had been uncovered. It seemed impossible to believe that Jericho had any other walls. But, beginning in 1952, Dame Kathleen Kenyon excavated the whole site and discovered many Jerichos, all pre-dating the settlement of the Hebrews. Using modern scientific methods she was able to prove that when Joshua arrived, Jericho was a ruin. The flattened walls belong to some other, unknown disaster.

Secondly, we need to be cautious about what archaeology can *prove*. We can read an ancient text, but we cannot tell whether it is true or not. All we can tell is what the writer wanted the world to believe. Kings did falsify records for their own glory. Similarly, archaeology can provide evidence that an event happened, but it cannot show why it happened nor who was involved. It is, therefore, most useful for corroboration. The existence of a water tunnel from a spring in the Kidron valley to the Pool of Siloam, together with the inscription on the wall of the tunnel (now unfortunately removed), provides ample corroboration for 2 K. *20.*20. Even here, however, one has to be careful. A number of stables were found at Megiddo. Solomon fortified Megiddo (1 K. 9.15). He also built stalls for his many horses (1 K. 4.26). But the Megiddo stables were not Solomon's. They belong to a later period.

We now look briefly at some of the major epigraphic discoveries. This is not to underestimate the other finds of archaeologists. The remains of cities like Megiddo, Samaria, Hazor, Jericho, Shechem, and Lachish, and of settlements like Masada and Qumran are deeply impressive, but probably the epigraphic material is most informative.

c **Ebla Tablets**

Thousands of clay tablets were discovered at Ebla in northern Syria in 1975. They date from the third millennium BC, some centuries before the patriarchs. They include myths, legends, hymns and prayers as well as diplomatic documents. Many of the personal names include the syllable 'yah', which is a name for God in the OT (Ps. 68.4, 89.8). Does this mean that the origins of the name Yahweh go back a thousand years before the Exodus to Ebla? The full importance of these texts has not yet been worked out.

d **Execration Texts**

Cursing was an ancient art. The name of an adversary was scratched on a pot or figure and then it was smashed with an imprecation. Many fragments have been found from the Egypt of Abraham's time. Towns, like Jerusalem and Ashkelon, are mentioned on them. The name of chieftains reveal something about the gods being worshipped in the Canaan of that day.

e **Cappadocian Tablets**

Thousands of clay tablets were found at Kultepe in eastern Asia Minor. They show the Assyrians, untypically according to their militaristic reputation, engaged in trade and setting up trading posts far from home. They belong to the time of the patriarchs and they show that lengthy journeys were common in those days.

f Code of Hammurabi

Hammurabi was a king of the old Babylonian empire who lived some five centuries before Moses. On a stele (a tall pillar), found in 1902, is written his law code. It is long and detailed, ruling on behaviour and assessing punishments. It affords interesting comparisons with the law codes of Israel which have a greater interest in God's will (as distinct from social need) and are more humane.

g Mari Tablets

In 1935 André Parrot uncovered a palace at Mari on the upper Euphrates. It came from the same period as Hammurabi. Again, thousands of clay tablets with cuneiform writing were found. Their importance is that they refer to social customs that are similar to those found in the stories of the patriarchs. If the patriarchal stories were artificial compositions, the composer in a later century would be likely to make the patriarchs conform to the social customs of his own time. But that is not the case. The social customs of the patriarchal narratives are nearer to those of the Mari texts than to those of later Israel.

h Nuzi Tablets

Something similar can be said of the Nuzi or Nuzu tablets, found by two Americans away to the east of the Tigris, According to these it was legitimate for a husband who found his wife to be barren to take one of the maids, as Abraham did with Hagar. Birthrights could be sold for livestock. Deathbed blessings could not be revoked. The theft of the teraphim in Gn. *31* is explained by the fact that possession of the household gods was regarded as an indication that one was the rightful heir.

i Ras Shamra Tablets

Before 1929 the main source of our knowledge of the Baal

cult was the OT itself, which is strongly prejudiced against it. In that year, clay tablets in cuneiform were found at Ras Shamra (the ancient Ugarit) on the northern Syrian coast, which give us an extensive guide to the myths of the Phoenician Baal and his cult. There are also legends of two kings that tell us much about how kingship was understood. There are poems similar to our psalms. See especially what the commentaries say about Ps. *29*. There is plenty of scope, too, for comparative study of the meanings of particular words.

j **Tell el-Amarna Tablets**

These tablets were found in 1887 at a town on the Nile where the pharaoh, Amenophis IV (=Akhnaten 1377–60 BC), had his capital. They are letters written by vassal rulers to the Egyptian court. One comes from Jerusalem. They all tell the same story. The writers are under attack and they want help. The attackers are given various names including *Habiru*. At one time it was thought that these must be the Hebrews and that, therefore, the date of the conquest could be fixed. It is now clear, however, that *Habiru* were desert bandits who, from time to time, raided settlements and caused trouble.

k **Merneptah's Stele**

A black, granite column, found in 1906, gives us the first extra-biblical reference to Israel. It belonged to Pharaoh Merneptah (1223–1211). It celebrates Merneptah's victories over the 'sea peoples' who were part of that large shift of population that brought the Philistines to the Holy Land. There are references to distant insurrections that Merneptah had put down, one of them by 'Israel'. It has been argued that Israel was already settled in Canaan by 1220 and was thus rebelling against an Egyptian overlord. But the name 'Israel' might well refer to a few settlers only who subsequently gave their name to other tribes who had yet to arrive. There is no mention in the OT of Egyptian involvement in Canaan at this time to help us.

153

l **Black Obelisk**

The obelisk, a tall tapering stone, shows Jehu, the king of Israel, making submission to the Assyrian king, Shalmaneser III. Jehu is described as 'son of Omri'. In fact he was a usurper three generations later. The phrase 'son of' does not have to be taken literally, but it does show how important Omri, slighted by the author of Kings (1 K. *16*.21–8), appeared to Assyrian eyes. The OT makes no reference to this act of submission. The obelisk, found in 1846, is now in the British Museum.

m **Moabite Stone**

An interesting example of the selective memory of ancient historians. This stone was set up by Mesha, king of Moab, about 830 BC. It was found in 1868 and is now in the Louvre. It describes how Mesha freed himself from Israelite oppression begun by Omri and eventually won a great victory. 2 K. *3* describes what must be the same war. The coalition of Israel, Judah and Edom trounced the Moabites and Mesha was reduced to offering his heir as a sacrifice. Mesha evidently did not wish to record defeats and the OT omits reference to Mesha's successes. The power of Omri is again confirmed.

n **Lachish Ostraca**

An ostracon is a piece of broken pottery on which there is writing. Before paper became common, messages were frequently written with pen and ink on scraps of pottery. Some important ostraca were found at Lachish in 1935. They date from 590 BC when the kingdom of Judah was breaking up. An officer from an outlying station is sending reports to the governor of Lachish. Cities are falling to the Babylonians. The officer trusts in Yahweh and looks hopefully for the fire signals of Lachish.

o **Babylonian Chronicle**

Some clay tablets found in Babylon in the nineteenth century give us an interesting source for biblical events of the Babylonian period. The Chronicle records the fall of Nineveh in 612 BC, the final defeat of Assyria at Carchemish in 605, the capture of Jerusalem, and the rise of Cyrus. The tablets are now in the British Museum.

p **Cyrus Cylinder**

Ezra *1* records a decree made by Cyrus in 539 allowing the Jews to return. A clay cylinder has been discovered giving Cyrus' own account of this incident. Cyrus is told by his god, Marduk, that he is to rule the world. The fall of Babylon without a blow is described. Cyrus is so full of his own magnanimity that he does not actually mention the Jews, but he does speak in general terms about returning exiles to their former habitations and allowing sanctuaries to be restored.

q **Elephantiné Papyri**

Elephantiné is an island in the Nile near Aswan. Papyri were discovered there at the beginning of the century, a fortunate find as papyrus does not normally survive as clay tablets do. They come from the fifth century BC and they relate to a local Jewish colony. It is not clear when the Jews settled there, but it is clear that things were going on at Elephantiné that would have horrified Ezra and Nehemiah. In flat contradiction of Dt. *16* the colony had built a temple to Yahu (=Yahweh). Not only so, but Yahu had a consort, Anath-Bethel. None the less, one letter is an appeal to the Persian governor of Judah for help in rebuilding the temple which had been damaged. The Jews of Elephantiné seem unaware of their lawlessness, which raises the possibility that what they were doing was common practice in Israel at the time they left. Unhappily no one knows when that was.

r **Rosetta Stone**

One of Napoleon's officers found this stone by chance in the Nile delta. It records a sycophantic decree by the priests of

Memphis in honour of Ptolemy V. The subject matter is not the important point, however. The priests wrote their decree in three scripts, hieroglyphic and demotic Egyptian and Greek. The comparison enabled scholars to crack the hieroglyphic code and translate inscriptions that had previously remained obscure. The Rosetta Stone is in the British Museum.

s **Dead Sea Scrolls**

Everybody knows the story of Mohammed Adh-Dhib's search for a goat and of his finding a cave in the cliffs near the Dead Sea in 1947. Inside the cave were large pots containing scrolls. Since then, ten more caves have been discovered containing pieces of about 600 manuscripts. Moreover, ruins near by have been excavated revealing a monastery with a scriptorium where the scrolls were copied. From the scrolls and from finds at the monastery the history of the strange sect that lived there can be traced.

In 152 Jonathan, a brother of Judas Maccabaeus, ruled the little Jewish kingdom (see 10k). One of the contenders for the Greek crown in Antioch bought Jonathan's support by offering him the Jewish high priesthood, which had been vacant for seven years. Pious Jews were horrified at such insensitive bargaining. The Dead Sea community was founded by a Teacher of Righteousness who was incensed by the behaviour of a wicked priest. Coins found at Qumran, the site of the Dead Sea community, date from 135 BC. It is reasonable to suppose, then, that Jonathan's base act was the stimulus that led to the forming of the community and later to its withdrawal into the Judaean wilderness.

The first phase of the community lasted 100 years and was ended by an earthquake, signs of which can still be seen in flights of stairs cracked down the middle. The site was deserted for about twenty-five years and then the monks returned and stayed there until the awful days of the Jewish War (AD 66–70).

The monks believed themselves to be the true remnants of an Israel that generally had betrayed its trust. They alone

156

were faithful to the Law and their Teacher alone interpreted it correctly. They spent most of their time copying out the Law and commentaries on it. Benches, tables, even inkwells have been found. There is a pottery where the storage pots were made. Scrolls were made by sewing up parchments. There are few papyri. In a time of crisis, the scrolls, the community's greatest treasure, were hidden in caves and never recovered until 1947.

The scrolls include a Manual of Discipline for the running of the sect and a War Scroll which gives a detailed commentary on the final conflict which was imminent between the sons of darkness and the sons of light (the community). The conflict came, but it did not turn out as they expected. The monks were slaughtered and their monastery burned. Arrowheads and charred timber tell the story. At least the scrolls were safely hidden.

The value of the scrolls is inestimable. They cover the whole Hebrew Bible, save Esther, and they are about 1,000 years older than the most ancient copies previously available. Some of them provide a perfect example of the eschatological expectations of NT times. Comparative studies between the scrolls and the NT are pursued diligently by scholars now and the full import has yet to be known.

Perhaps the most extraordinary discovery is the copper scroll from Cave 3. This gives an account of a fabulous treasure hidden in various caches around Jerusalem. Of course it cannot be true, but why did they put all this strange information *on copper*? Nobody knows. 'In the sepulchral monument of Ben Rabbah, the Shalishian, there are a hundred bars of gold.' It is the Dead Sea enigma.

For further reading

John Gray, *Archaeology and the Old Testament World*, 1962.
H. T. Frank, *An Archaeological Companion to the Bible*, 1972.
G. Vermes, *The Dead Sea Scrolls in English*, 1962.

Chapter 12

The Languages of the Bible

a **The Old Testament**

THE common name for the language in which almost all the OT was written is Hebrew, but this name applied to a people rather than to a language until rabbis began using it for the language in the second century BC. In the OT the language is called 'the Jews' language' in 2 K. *18*.26, 28 and Neh. *13*.24, and, curiously, 'the language of Canaan' in Is. *19*.18.

Despite the fact that their sacred writings were in Hebrew, after the Exile the Jews began to change over to Aramaic. Aramaic was also a Semitic language, but it had a wider currency than Hebrew. Aramaic is sometimes erroneously called Chaldee. Hebrew continued to be used for religious purposes long after Aramaic became the predominant language of the area.

A few OT passages, written very late, are in Aramaic: Dan. *2*.4–*7*.28, Ezra *4*.8–*6*.18, *7*.12–26, Jer. *10*.11, and a few odd words.

The Hebrew text, including these few Aramaic passages, was and is the sacred Scripture of the Jews. They did not allow any change whatever but they did accept a change of script. The original Hebrew script was abandoned in favour of the square script of Aramaic, so *the Hebrew Bible is a Hebrew text, with a few Aramaic insertions, written throughout in Aramaic script.*

The Hebrew text of Gn. *1*.1 looks like this:

בְּרֵאשִׁית בָּרָא אֱלֹהִים אֵת הַשָּׁמַיִם וְאֵת הָאָרֶץ:

It reads like this: bereshith bara elohim eth hash-shamayim we-eth ha-arets. Hebrew reads from right to left so it is impossible to fit the English letters to the Hebrew letters without writing one of the lines backwards.

Hebrew was originally written without vowels, but this raised little difficultly as long as the language was in common use. Few people needed to write. But, as soon as it ceased to be a spoken language, that is, when Aramaic took over, there was a problem about preserving the proper pronunciation. At first (second century BC) an attempt was made to indicate the more important vowels by giving some little used consonants a second fuction as vowels. In the verse quoted above there are eighteen vowel sounds but only two of them are written in the script. This made things very difficult for Jews of later times whose first language was not Hebrew or Aramaic but Greek. So, in the sixth century AD, some Jewish scholars, called Massoretes, invented a complete vocalic system and added it to the text. (See below 14c.) They did not want to disturb the sacred text, however, so they wrote the vowels round the words rather than within them. This is called 'pointing the text'. So Gn. *1*.1, fully pointed, looks like this:

בְּרֵאשִׁית בָּרָא אֱלֹהִים אֵת הַשָּׁמַיִם וְאֵת הָאָרֶץ:

The most striking thing about Hebrew is the simplicity of its syntax. Subordinate clauses are not impossible, but Hebrew tends to shun them and put a lot of simple clauses together in a long chain: this happened and this and this and this. Look, for example, at the first chapter of the book of Ruth in the AV and count the number of sentences and clauses that begin with 'and'. Here is Gn. *22*.9–12: And they came to the place which God had told him of; and Abraham built an altar there, and laid the wood in order, and bound Isaac his son, and laid him on the altar upon the wood. And Abraham stretched forth his hand, and took the knife to slay his son. And the angel of the Lord called unto him out of heaven, and said,

159

Abraham, Abraham: and he said, Here am I. And he said, Lay not thine hand upon the lad . . .

Hebrew is an ideal language for telling stories, but not so good for abstract arguments. *This is a fact of the utmost importance for biblical studies.* The Hebrews tended to reduce everything to narrative form. Note, in this connection, the parables of Jesus.

b **The New Testament**

The NT is written in Greek. Although it has a different alphabet, Greek is much closer to English in grammar, syntax and vocabulary than Hebrew. The first verse of St. John looks like this:

ἐν ἀρχῃ ἦν ὁ λογος, και ὁ λογος ἦν προς τον θεον, και θεος ἦν ὁ λογος

en archē ēn ho logos, kai ho logos ēn pros ton theon, kai theos ēn ho logos

Because Greek is read from left to right, as English, it is possible to put the transliteration under each word. Greek is usually printed with accents, acute, grave and circumflex rather like French, but only experts need be concerned with them.

This Greek is not the same as the classical language of the golden age. It is sometimes called Hellenistic Greek, which is a strange name as the word 'Hellenistic' really means 'derived from Greece'. The explanation is that, when Alexander conquered the then known world, he spread Greek culture among people who were certainly not Greeks. This gave rise to the notion of a Hellenistic world and Hellenistic Age, that is to say, a world and an age that were not properly Greek but were deeply coloured by Greek culture. It is natural, then, that the form of Greek language used in the Hellenistic world should be called Hellenistic Greek.

Sometimes NT Greek is called Koinē Greek, which means common Greek, the Greek of everyday affairs. Koinē Greek could be written well with literary style. It could also be written crudely as it was spoken in the market-place. The

160

literary standard of the NT is not the same throughout. Mark
and, even more, Revelation are written in a very basic, sometimes ungrammatical style, whereas other books, 1 Peter,
Hebrews, Luke-Acts, have a good literary standard.

From time to time in the NT one encounters constructions
which are not Greek at all but Aramaic. Somebody, at some
stage, has been thinking in Aramaic and then putting the
thoughts, word for word, into Greek. This is difficult to inves-
tigate as we are now dealing with two foreign languages, but a
simple example is the AV's 'and he answered and said', which
is not Greek (or English), but which represents a common
construction in Aramaic.

Chapter 13

The Canon

a IF a collection of writings is held to be sacred by a religious community, it is important to define that collection with as much clarity as possible. That process, however, is not always easy. In this chapter we are concerned with the list of books that make up the Bible.

The word 'canon' originally meant a measuring rod, but it comes to mean any kind of standard. For our purpose it means the standard list of books in the sacred writings. We have, in the first place, to consider three canons, the Hebrew Bible, the Greek OT, and the Christian NT.

b The Hebrew Bible

The story of Josiah's reform shows how a book, probably Deuteronomy, was honoured in Israel before the Exile (2 K. 22.3–23.30), and it is clear that Ezra brought with him a book of law that was duly obeyed when he returned from Babylon (Neh. 8). These are indications that the process of canonization was proceeding slowly for many years before a definitive list appeared.

The Hebrew Bible has three sections and the three sections were given canonical authority at different times and to different degrees. The first section is the Law, or *Torah,* as Jews prefer to call it. The Torah consists of the first five books, Genesis, Exodus, Leviticus, Numbers and Deuteronomy. These books are also called the Pentateuch but Pentateuch is a name used in literary studies. It is not a religious or theological term. (See below 21a.)

162

The Torah reached its final form about 400 BC and thereafter became the cornerstone of Judaism. It has never been changed in any way since.

The second section is the *Prophets*. It is common to divide the Prophets into Former and Latter Prophets, though this distinction does not go back to the beginning. The Former Prophets may not seem to us to be prophets at all. They are Joshua, Judges, 1 and 2 Samuel, 1 and 2 Kings. They record the doings of early prophets like Gad, Nathan, Elijah, Elisha, but, more importantly, they narrate history in a prophetic way. The prophets look ahead and proclaim the justice and mercy of Yahweh; these histories look backwards, but the message is much the same. The Latter Prophets are Isaiah, Jeremiah, Ezekiel and the Twelve, the Twelve being Hosea, Joel, Amos, Obadiah, Jonah, Micah, Nahum, Habakkuk, Zephaniah, Haggai, Zechariah, and Malachi. The prophetic books had gained wide recognition by about 200 BC, though they never acquired the authority of the Torah.

The third section is the *Writings* and comprises Psalms, Job, Proverbs, the Five Rolls—Ruth, Song of Songs, Ecclesiastes, Lamentations and Esther—Daniel, Ezra-Nehemiah and Chronicles. This was the last section to be recognized. Recognition was not so much a formal act as a gradual process of acceptance, and, save for the Torah, which was universally honoured, there was no unanimity in Judaism in NT times. Sadducees and Pharisees differed about the importance of the second two sections. Jews of the Diaspora also honoured some of their own books. The Qumran community had Scriptures of its own. Arguments continued for some time about Ecclesiastes and Song of Songs and perhaps other books as well.

It seems likely that a group of Rabbis met at Jamnia (Jabneh) after the fall of Jerusalem in AD 70 and gave formal assent to the list set out in the last three paragraphs, though there is no direct evidence. Josephus, writing around the year AD 100, refers to the three sections, though he does not name all the books. He points out that, unlike the Greeks, the Hebrews have a fixed canon.

163

c **The Greek Old Testament**

With the conquests of Alexander, Greek came to the Holy Land. Greek could not be ignored. It was the language of commerce and government. It was a universal language. However repugnant Greek religion and culture were to faithful Hebrews, most of them had to know some Greek.

Moreover, from 722 BC onwards, Jewish families were 'dispersed' around the eastern Mediterranean by a number of historical accidents. Other nations suffered similar fates, but the next generation inter-married with their new neighbours and the nations lost their identity. The strictness of the Jews, their sense of being a 'peculiar people', saved them from this fate. Consequently Jewish colonies survived and eventually grew strong in places as far apart as Babylon, Egypt and Rome.

Jews of the Dispersion (the Greek word is Diaspora) struggled to keep up their Hebrew so that they could read the sacred Scriptures, but their everyday language had to be the language of the local population. In most cases this was Greek, because, after Alexander, Greek became the common language of the empire. The coming of the Romans did not shake the cultural status quo and Greek remained the universal language.

There was, therefore, a need for a Greek version of the Jewish Scriptures. Doubtless it all began with informal, oral translation in the synagogue, but it is clear that written versions of parts of the OT in Greek began to appear from the third century BC onwards.

The myth of the Greek version
Late in the second century BC there appeared a work called the *Letter of Aristeas* which purported to give an account of how the Greek version of the OT was written. It was as follows. Demetrius, the librarian of Alexandria, approached Ptolemy II (285–46), his monarch, and asked that the famous library should promote a Greek translation of the Jewish Law. The king agreed and the High Priest in Jerusalem was asked to send six translators from each tribe. The seventy-two

translators were installed on the island of Pharos and, appropriately produced their translation in seventy-two days. It was read to the king, who deeply impressed, loaded the translators with gifts.

There is no need to take this story seriously, but it has provided us with a name for the first Greek version of the OT. It is called the Septuagint from the Latin word for seventy. There were seventy elders present with Moses on the sacred mountain in Ex. *24*. It seems probable that the reference to six translators from each tribe is an attempt to get as near as possible to the traditional number of seventy. Compare the seventy in Lk. *10*. Septuagint is commonly abbreviated to LXX.

The facts about the LXX

The Pentateuch was translated into Greek in Alexandria in the third century BC. To this extent the myth is correct. The translators appear to have known Hebrew better than they knew Greek and the translation is fairly literal. The other books were translated sporadically over the next 100 years. They vary considerably in style. Some stick closely to the original Hebrew, others are in flowing Greek. Some make no concessions to the ideas of Greek civilization, others try to reconcile the two worlds.

The communities of Greek-speaking Jews in Alexandria and elsewhere were not content simply to translate the old books. They added new books of their own, some of them written in Greek by Jews of the Greek-speaking world. So the Greek Bible comes to be longer than the Hebrew.

d ### The LXX in the Christian Church

Christian preachers like Paul had considerable success among Jews of the Dispersion. Many of their arguments were based upon references to the Scriptures, quoted from the Greek version. Christian communities not only used the LXX for their own purposes, they also made it their own and added to it. Inevitably Judaism repudiated the LXX. None the less, at the Reformation the Reformers decided to go back to the Hebrew Bible, because some of the Roman doctrines, with

165

which they disagreed, were based on passages that were in the LXX but not in the Hebrew.

The clearest example of Christian influence in the LXX is to be seen in the *Nine Odes of the Greek Church,* a book that was inserted between Psalms and Proverbs. The odes include the Magnificat and the Benedictus, and an appendix includes the Nunc Dimittis and the Gloria in Excelsis.

Other Greek versions
Having rejected the LXX, the rabbis took steps to provide other Greek versions uninfluenced by Christianity. The best known are those attributed to Aquila, Theodotion, and Symmachus. (See below 14f.)

e   **The contents of the LXX**

(This material is complicated and difficult to remember. It is included here for reference purposes.)

Put simply, the LXX consists of the books of the Hebrew Bible plus some others that were composed originally in Greek. The details, however, are very complicated indeed. Below we list the books that appear in the LXX as it is studied today (*Septuaginta,* edited by A. Rahlfs, 1935). Five preliminary points must be made. The less important matters are added as notes.

1. The divisions of the LXX are different from those of the Hebrew. Here we have Laws, Histories, Poetical Books, and Prophetic Books—a more accurate classification than that of the Hebrew.

2. The order is different. The LXX puts all the Histories together and brings the Poetical Books before the Prophetic Books.

3. The names are different. The Hebrew Bible has Hebrew names for the books. The LXX makes use of both Latin and Greek names. To save trouble the list below uses names that are familiar to readers of the English Bible, which are not without complications themselves.

4. The list of contents of the Greek OT was never fixed

definitively as the contents of the Hebrew Bible were, so the word canon is not strictly correct in relation to the LXX or the other Greek versions.

5. Normally the contents of each *book* are the same in Hebrew and Greek forms, but in some books there are variations.

Laws
Genesis
Exodus
Leviticus
Numbers
Deuteronomy

Histories
Joshua
Judges
Ruth[1]
1 Samuel
2 Samuel
1 Kings
2 Kings
1 Chronicles
2 Chronicles
a *Esdras[2]
2 Esdras (=Ezra-Nehemiah)
Esther[3]
a *Judith
a *Tobit
a *1 Maccabees
a *2 Maccabees
*3 Maccabees[4]
*4 Maccabees[5]

Poetical Books
Psalms
*Odes[6]
Proverbs
Ecclesiastes (Eccles.)
Song of Songs
Job

[a] *Wisdom of Solomon
[a] *Ecclesiasticus (Ecclus) or Ben Sira or Wisdom of Jesus, son of
Sirach
*Psalms of Solomon[7]

Prophetic books
Hosea
Amos
Micah
Joel
Obadiah
Jonah
Nahum
Habakkuk
Zephanaiah
Haggai
Zechariah
Malachi
Isaiah
Jeremiah
[a] *Baruch
Lamentations
[a] *Letter of Jeremiah
Ezekiel
[a] *Susanna
Daniel[8]
[a] *Bel and the Dragon

Notes
Books not in the Hebrew Bible are marked with an asterisk (*).

Books which appear in the Apocrypha of our Bibles are marked
with an 'a'. Usually books which have an asterisk also have an 'a'.

1 The Hebrew puts Ruth in the Writings, not with the historical
books. The LXX moves it to follow Judges because the book is
set in the period of the Judges. The Hebrew is correct. Ruth is
a tale. It is not part of the Deuteronomic History.

2 The books of Ezra and Esdras, the Greek form of Ezra,
present the most daunting muddle in the whole area. A much
simplified explanation is as follows:

168

The 1 Esdras of the LXX is not in the Hebrew at all. 2 Esdras is Ezra-Nehemiah run together as one book. Protestant Bibles put Ezra and Nehemiah in the OT as separate books, 1 Esdras from the LXX in the Apocrypha, and another book altogether in the Apocrypha as 2 Esdras. So the 2 Esdras of the Apocrypha is not the same as the 2 Esdras of the LXX.

3 The Greek version of Esther is longer than the form in Hebrew.

4 3 Maccabees is a misnomer. It tells the story of a persecution of Jews in Egypt and their miraculous deliverance some thirty years before the Maccabaean revolt.

5 4 Maccabees is a lecture on fidelity to the Law in all circumstances. It makes frequent reference to the Maccabaean struggle by way of illustration.

6 A series of hymns of much later date than the rest of the LXX showing that the Christian Church had taken it over.

7 A collection of psalms probably originating from the Pharisaic party in Jerusalem.

8 The Greek version of Daniel is longer than the Hebrew in that it includes in chapter 3 the section from our Apocrypha known as 'The Prayer of Azariah and the Song of the Three Young Men'.

f **The Protestant version of the Old Testament**

As we have seen, the Reformers went back to the Hebrew Bible and relegated most of the extra books of the LXX to the Apocrypha, which was then described as a kind of second class Scripture. Article VI of the Book of Common Prayer says that these books 'the Church doth read for example of life and instruction of manners; but yet doth it not apply them to establish any doctrine'. The Apocrypha went into eclipse for a long time in Protestantism, but in more modern versions, such as RSV and NEB, the Apocrypha is usually included.

Nearly all the Apocrypha comes from the LXX, the only exceptions being 2 Esdras and the Prayer of Manesseh. The contents of the Apocrypha are as follows:

169

1 Esdras[1]
2 Esdras[2]
Tobit
Judith
Additions to Esther[3]
Wisdom of Solomon
Ecclesiasticus (Ecclus) or Ben Sira, or Wisdom of Jesus, son of
    Sira[4]
Baruch
Letter of Jeremiah[5]
Prayer of Azaraiah and the Song of the Three Young Men[6]
Susanna or Daniel and Susanna
Bel and the Dragon or Daniel, Bel and the Snake
Prayer of Manasseh[7]
1 Maccabees
2 Maccabees

Notes

1 1 Esdras in the Apocrypha is the same as 1 Esdras in the LXX. It is composed largely from excerpts from the Chronicler's writings. Sometimes called Greek Ezra.

2 2 Esdras does not come from the LXX. It is sometimes called the Ezra Apocalypse and consists of a series of visions. It is also, alas, sometimes called IV Ezra.

3 A number of insertions were made into the book when it was translated into Greek in order to give it a more profound religious character. The Apocrypha has tended to print the insertions separately, but the NEB and JB give the full LXX version of Esther.

4 It is important to distinguish between Ecclesiastes of the OT (abbreviated Eccles.) and Ecclesiasticus of the Apocrypha (abbreviated Ecclus.). Both words mean 'the preacher'.

5 This letter, addressed to captives on their way to Babylon, sometimes appears as ch. 6 of Baruch. LXX and Apocrypha make the letter into a book on its own, but JB includes it in Baruch.

6 Four additions to Daniel exist: the Prayer of Azariah, the Song of the Three Young Men (or Holy Children), Susanna, and Bel and the Dragon. JB Daniel includes all four additions. LXX Daniel includes the first two but makes the second two

separate books. The Apocrypha does not, of course, include the main part of Daniel, which is in the OT, but it includes all four additions, the first two as one book.

7 2 Chr. *33*.10–13 recounts that Manasseh had a change of heart before he died and *33*.18 refers to a prayer that he made. This book is an attempt to supply the text of it.

g **The Roman Catholic version of the Old Testament**

The early Church had trouble making up its mind about the books we now describe as the Apocrypha. Jerome, who was responsible for the Vulgate (See 14f), refused to regard them as canonical, whereas Augustine made no distinction between them and the books of the OT. When the reformers rejected the Apocrypha, the Council of Trent responded by including it firmly in the canon. In RC Bibles, such as JB, the books of the Apocrypha are scattered throughout. They do not appear as a section on their own. Consequently the list of contents of JB comes close to that of the LXX. 1 Esdras, 3 and 4 Maccabees, Odes, and Psalms of Solomon are in LXX but not in JB, and there are a few differences of order.

h **The Pseudepigrapha**

Many books were written within Judaism in the period 200 BC to AD 200 which were not included in either the Hebrew or the Greek canons. They are nevertheless important for the modern student. They are usually loosely described as Pseudepigrapha. A pseudepigraphical work is one in which the true author disguises his identity under a famous pseudonym. To the modern reader this seems like forgery, but it was probably more of an act of humility. The author believed that he was writing in the spirit of a great figure of the past and wished to ascribe the credit where it was due. Many of the non-canonical Jewish books of this period were pseudepigraphical, but some were not. To classify the whole literature under the heading of Pseudepigrapha is, therefore, imprecise. There are also pseudepigraphical works, like Daniel, which are canonical and not included in this literature.

In 1913 R. H. Charles published two large volumes called *The*

171

Apocrypha and Pseudepigrapha of the Old Testament, which gave an English translation of the texts together with a commentary. Both volumes have recently been re-issued. The former is not so important as much has been written on the Apocrypha, but the second volume is still the best collection of Pseudepigrapha available.

The contents of Charles' second volume are as follows:

Jubilees
Letter of Aristeas
Books of Adam and Eve
Martyrdom of Isaiah
1 Enoch
Testaments of the XII Patriarchs
Sibylline Oracles
Assumption of Moses
2 Enoch or Secrets of Enoch
2 Baruch or Syriac Apocalypse of Baruch
3 Baruch or Greek Apocalypse of Baruch
4 Ezra
Psalms of Solomon
4 Maccabees
Pirke Aboth
Story of Ahikar
Fragments of a Zadokite Work

3 and 4 Maccabees and Psalms of Solomon are not in the Hebrew Bible. They occur in the LXX but were never taken over by the Christian Church or included in the Apocrypha. They have a right to appear in the 'other literature' that Charles has collected but surprisingly, Charles deals with 3 Maccabees in his first volume. 4 Maccabees and Psalms of Solomon occur properly in his second.

Charles' volumes do not cover all the Jewish literature of this period. There are other books of importance and there is the massive library of the Dead Sea Scrolls, of which Charles knew nothing. Nevertheless, his collection and its commentary is a most valuable tool for the biblical student.

i **The Mishnah**

The same period, 200 BC to AD 200 saw the appearance of the Mishnah, a collection of Jewish tractates second only to the Scriptures in authority. The Pharisees believed that not only the written Law, the Torah, was delivered by God to Moses on Sinai, but also the oral Law, that is to say, the means whereby the Torah could be applied to the manifold situations of everyday life. The oral Law was passed down from generation to generation by the elders of Israel, and it became known as the 'Tradition of the Elders'. As such it was a point of controversy between Pharisees and Sadducees, for the Sadducees honoured Torah alone. After AD 70, however, the Pharisees were left to build up Judaism and the Tradition flourished. It was gathered together in the Mishnah. Much of the Mishnah has to do with a way of life that was no longer possible for Jews, but this did not affect the care with which the rabbis taught the ordinances and interpretations contained in it.

For the modern student the Mishnah provides a valuable insight into the mind and spirit of the Judaism of the NT period, though not all the rulings can be held to be contemporary with the NT. The Mishnah was further expanded in the Talmud, a vast work which comes in two forms, the Jerusalem Talmud and the longer, and more influential, Babylonian Talmud, but this carries us beyond the period with which we are concerned. A very good translation of the Mishnah was published by Herbert Danby in 1933.

j **The New Testament**

The existence of a canon of Scripture in Judaism and its regular use in worship had considerable influence on primitive Christianity. The earliest Jewish Christians held fast to the OT and used it as Christian Scripture, that is, as divinely attested writings witnessing to Jesus as Lord and Christ. Soon Christianity provided its own writings of various kinds, but there was no suggestion that they were to be regarded as Scripture. One has only to read a chapter or two from a Pauline epistle to realize that there was no thought in Paul's mind that his writings would in time become Scripture on a par with, and, in the judgment of many devout Christians, superior to, the OT.

173

At the end of the first century the first moves towards a Christian canon were being made. It is reasonable to suppose that two influences were at work. In the first place, Christianity was centred in Jesus. What he said and did had a binding authority and, when his earthly life began to drift into the past, the need for a stable and permanent record was obvious. Secondly, there is every reason to suppose that authentic writings were needed for Christian worship. In the middle of the second century, Justin Martyr says so explicitly. Paul expected his letters to be read to the particular churches, presumably when they were gathered for worship, and he even suggests exchanging letters (Col. 4.16). The letters were soon gathered together for this purpose, though we cannot be certain what letters were in the collections known to people like Ignatius (about AD 110) and the author of 2 Peter. (See 2 Pe. 3.15 f.)

Paul himself and the early Church as a whole, however, recognized the supreme authority of Jesus. Neither OT nor epistles was sufficient. Most necessary and most important were writings that represented what the Lord himself, in his life, death and resurrection, had said and done. (See 1 Thess. 4.15; 1 Cor. 7.10, 9.14, 11.23, and especially 1 Cor. 7.25.)

Not only Paul could write letters and not only those who had been close to Jesus could write about him. Consequently, from early times, a Christian literature emerged that included fanciful works that enjoyed great popularity, at least in their places of origin. During the second century, Gnosticism, a strange religious philosophy which blended all religions into one and indulged in the wildest speculations, was making rapid progress and producing a considerable literature of a quasi-Christian kind. The need for an authentic list of Christian writings became obvious.

The first evidence of a list of approved writings comes from Rome around the year AD 144. It was not an official canon but a list put forward by a heretic called Marcion, who is often suspected of having Gnostic leanings. It included only an edited version of Luke and ten Pauline letters and it expressed Marcion's anti-Jewish notion of Christianity. Irenaeus, the chief defender of the faith against Gnosticism in the late second century, stressed the authority of the four Gospels, and added thirteen epistles of Paul, 1 Peter, 1 and 2 John, Revelation, the Shepherd of Hermas, and Acts. Tertullian and Clement of Alexandria are equally firm on the four Gospels, though their lists of other books differ from that of Irenaeus. Thirteen Pauline epistles, Acts, 1 Peter, 1 John and Revelation were common. After that there was considerable uncertainty.

The first official list is one now known as the Muratorian Canon from its eighteenth-century discoverer, one Muratori. The document is damaged and badly written, but it does go back to the late second century. It lists the books accepted as apostolic and worthy to be read in church. They are the four Gospels (almost certainly, although the document is damaged at this point), Acts, thirteen epistles of Paul, 1 and 2 John, Jude, Revelation, and the Apocalypse of Peter. By a strange error the Wisdom of Solomon from the LXX is also included.

In the third and fourth centuries the discussion was in full swing. In the writings of Origen and Eusebius, three classes emerge, undisputed books, disputed books, and rejected books. Hebrews, James, 2 Peter, 2 and 3 John, Jude and Revelation were all disputed at one time, while the Shepherd of Hermas, the Epistle of Barnabas, 1 Clement and the Didache had their defenders.

Eventually the factor that settled the issue was the provenance of the book. Those which were thought to come from the apostles themselves or from sources close to the apostles were accepted. Those which originated outside the immediate circle of the apostles were rejected, regardless of how profound or highly prized they were. The list of the twenty-seven books that now make up the NT first appeared in the Festal Letter of Athanasius in AD 376. The collection was called a canon and nothing was to be added or taken away. Confirmation came from a council held in Rome in 382 and the Synod of Carthage in 397. Some discussion continued. Manuscripts were produced that left out Hebrews and that incorporated an epistle to the Laodiceans; but the contents page of the NT has never been seriously challenged since the end of the fourth century.

175

k **New Testament Apocrypha**

Apart from the books that were widely approved and ultimately included in the canon, there are a number of documents, such as the Diadache, the Letters of Ignatius, and the
Epistle to Diognetus that arose out of the on-going life of the
Church and made no claim to dominical or apostolic authority. Though not canonical themselves, they often quote
canonical books and they provide valuable information about
life in the early Church. These sub-apostolic writings are *not*
to be regarded as NT Apocrypha. That term is reserved for a
substantial collection of documents that originated
within and just outside the main stream of Christianity. These
documents follow the same literary format as the canonical
books, that is to say, they appear in the form of Gospels or
Acts or Epistles or Apocalypses. They present teaching that is
at best peripheral to the Christian faith and at worst heretical.
All were ultimately excluded from the canon.

The subject can be studied in M. R. James, *The Apocryphal
New Testament* (revised edition 1953) or the large, two-
volume *New Testament Apocrypha,* originally edited by
Edgar Hennecke and afterwards by Wilhelm Schneemelcher,
and translated into English by R. McL. Wilson and others
(1963 and 1965).

For further reading

E. J. Roberts, 'Canon and Text of the Old Testament', article
in *Peake's Commentary* (1963), p. 73.
J. N. Sanders, 'The Literature and Canon of the New Testament', article in *Peake's Commentary* (1963), p. 676.

Chapter 14

The Ancient Manuscripts

a FOR nearly 300 years English-speaking Christianity was served by the AV, a fixed and unalterable standard to which the faith was securely tied. The AV itself was hallowed as the word of God and few who read it ever thought much about the Hebrew and Greek originals that lay behind it. In modern times we have had many new translations which suggests that no English version is absolutely authoritarian and there are different ways of understanding the Hebrew and the Greek. We must now go one step beyond this and ask what we mean by 'the Hebrew' and 'the Greek', and we shall find that 'fixed' and 'unalterable' are not very helpful words.

Since the invention of printing in the fifteenth century it is reasonable to speak of texts being fixed and unalterable. Misprints are possible (there is the appalling story of the 1631 edition that left the word 'not' out of the seventh commandment), but proofs can be checked so that one can fairly say that an AV published in 1950 would be identical with one in use in 1650. But this unfortunately cannot be said about the Bibles copied by hand in the fifteen centuries before printing became common. Hundreds of manuscripts (the usual abbreviation is MS, plural MSS) of both testaments have been discovered and the variations between them run into tens of thousands. Many are relatively trivial. Words or letters are added or subtracted without affecting the sense at all. But many others are important. The first verse of Mark's Gospel in AV and RV speaks of 'Jesus Christ, the Son of God', but many ancient MSS, including the famous Codex Sinaiticus, leave out 'the son of God' leaving us with the question whether later scribes added the phrase for reasons of their own.

A great scholarly industry exists, therefore, called 'textual criticism'. Most biblical students know little about it. They simply take the Bible as it comes to them in their own tongue. But we need to remind ourselves that the book that appears in print so clear and tidy, albeit with marginal readings here and there, is actually produced by scholars of great patience and learning comparing dozens of ancient MSS, many unclear, many damaged, many incomplete, and making their own scholarly judgments about what the original probably was. The text of the Bible, it must be firmly stated, is a matter of probability not certainty.

b   The original document written by a biblical author is called the *autograph*. All autographs of both testaments have long since been destroyed. In the case of Paul's letters it is easy to think of a single autograph, dictated by the apostle on a single occasion. It is not so easy with the writings of the prophets. They give the impression of being revised and collated several times. It is equally difficult in the case of the Gospels, for they went through many stages in composition, and, in each case, the edition that has survived to our day was not the first and may well not have been the last.

Most ancient MSS were written on papyrus. Papyrus was first made in Egypt by weaving and sticking together strips of the stem of the papyrus plant. No matter how carefully it was done nor how much the sheets were polished, writing on papyrus must have been a laborious business. Around the second century BC parchment or vellum came into use. Parchment is made of the skins of animals. The skins were scraped and rubbed smooth and were easier to write on and longer lasting than papyrus. These were the only writing surfaces that could be used for books. Clay tablets had served their turn. They were stacked in ancient libraries, being too heavy to be carried around. Scraps of pottery, called *ostraca*, were used for short messages but not for books. Copper was much too expensive for more than exceptional use.

Sheets of papyrus or parchment were stuck together or sewn together to make a long scroll. The scribe wrote in columns across the scroll and then rolled it up. The reader proceeded by rolling up what he had read and unrolling the rest as he went along. The Torah is still read in the same way in the synagogue sabbath by sabbath. The most famous of all scrolls were those found near the Dead Sea in 1947 and the following years. Because of that find, most people now know what an ancient scroll looks like.

Scrolls were not easy to use and by the second century AD Christian scribes were making use of the *codex*. The codex (plural, codices) is simply a book made by folding the sheets of papyrus or vellum down the middle and stitching them, much as we make a modern book. All forms of writing material were expensive which explains why they were sometimes used more than once. Parchment can be cleaned and used again. The resulting writing is called a *palimpsest*, which simply means 'rubbed smooth again'. In one or two cases the writing underneath is more interesting than that on top and we have good cause to be grateful to the scribes who failed to clean the pages properly. Modern methods of photography can be used to bring what was almost expunged to light.

THE OLD TESTAMENT

c **The Massoretic Text**

The preservation of the Hebrew Bible, which Christians call the OT, was largely due to the labours of some Jewish scribes who assembled at Tiberias in Galilee in the sixth century of the Christian era. Those scribes were called 'Massoretes', from a word, *massorah*, meaning 'tradition'. Their aim was to produce an exhaustive codification of traditional Jewish learning. Uppermost in their minds was the intent to give the world a perfect text of the Hebrew Bible embellished with extensive notes and commentary. Not only did they succeed in this but they also devised means of supplying vowels to the consonants in the sacred text so that it could be read with ease (see above 12a). Their text is called the Massoretic Text (abbreviated as MT). The Massoretes laid down a list of stringent rules to govern the work of copying and checking.

179

On account of these rules the MT survived with a minimum of variations until the invention of printing and so to the present day. A modern scholar trying to discover the original text of the Hebrew Bible must begin with the MT.

d **The Dead Sea Scrolls**

Until 1947 the oldest MSS of the OT in our possession dated from the ninth and tenth centuries AD. That means that, if the last book of the OT to be written, that is Daniel, comes from the second century BC, more than 1,000 years separate the autographs from the copies we possess. On the face of it this looks serious. A thousand years suggests numerous copies of copies of copies. How many mistakes crept in? Even if the Hebrew scribes treated the text with extreme reverence, would that preserve them from error? The finding of the Dead Sea Scrolls in 1947 and the following years to some extent answered the questions. The scrolls provide an admirable test for the MT. Some portion of every book in the OT save Esther has been discovered at Qumran. In some cases complete scrolls of a book have been found, in some cases many copies of the same book. Some of these scrolls date from before the Christian era. They carry our knowledge of the Hebrew text back almost 1,000 years. Substantially they vindicate the Hebrew scribes. Careful comparison reveals many minor variations, but it is remarkable how few modifications or scribal errors found their way into the text in the six or more centuries that stretch between the Qumran covenanters and the Massoretic scribes.

e **The Samaritan Pentateuch**

When the Jews returned from the Exile at the end of the sixth century BC they found their homeland populated by people of mixed race who preserved Jewish traditions and wished to join in worship with the returning exiles. Under Ezra and Nehemiah the 'people of the land' were driven out and they became the Samaritans. (See above 10j.)

The Pentateuch was complete before the separation

became final so the Samaritans took it with them, which means that, from about 400 BC, the Pentateuch was being used and copied in two different contexts. Mediaeval MSS of the Samaritan Pentateuch still survive. Some deliberate alterations appear to have been made to favour the Samaritans, but there are many other variants that can be used to check the MT.

f **The Versions**

Long before the MT was thought of, the OT, or parts of it, was translated into other languages for the benefit of faithful Jews who lived abroad and no longer understood Hebrew. These translations are called *Versions* and many of them have survived in whole or in part. A modern scholar trying to work backwards beyond the MT to the original text will sometimes need to consult these Versions. If the MT does not make sense, the reason may be that the text was corrupted at a very early stage. But there is a chance that the translator of one of the versions used a text that had not suffered that particular corruption, in which case his Version will point to a better reading than the MT. Of course the translator might have had a corrupt text and corrected it out of his own imagination, in which case his Version would actually lead us astray. This illustrates the complexity of the task. Reaching a scholarly conclusion in a matter like this is difficult, technical and never assuredly free from error.

The most important Versions are:

1. *The Greek Versions*: The most important is the LXX (see above 13c–e). Also to be noted are *Aquila*, a Jewish answer to the LXX and a very literal translation of the Hebrew dating from the second century AD; *Theodotion*, a version of mysterious origins more used by Christians than by Jews; and *Symmachus*, from a literary point of view the best of the Greek translations; only fragments of it survive; Jerome made considerable use of it in translating the Vulgate.

2. *The Targums*: The fact that, after the third century BC, fewer and fewer people could understand the Scriptures when they

181

were read in Hebrew led to the practice of giving a translation into Aramaic as the Hebrew was read. It may be that we see the beginning of this practice in Neh. *8*.8. The translations were informal at first so that no official Aramaic version could challenge the sacredness of the Hebrew text. The translation of the Torah was given after each verse, so there was no chance of getting it wrong. The books of the prophets were not quite so sacred, so the translation was made after every three verses. The translations were called Targums (or Targumim). In time they became fixed, though they never challenged the Hebrew as the sacred text. There is a Babylonian and a Palestinian or Jerusalem Targum. (The Targums are not to be confused with the Talmud (see above 13i), which also has Babylonian and Palestinian or Jerusalem versions.)

3. *The Peshitta*: A Version in Syriac, an eastern dialect of Aramaic, dating from the fifth century AD. The Peshitta includes the NT and is the authorized Bible of the Syrian Church.

4. *Coptic Versions*: They come from Egypt and there are several of them (e.g. Sahidic, Bohairic) because, at the beginning of the Christian era, there were several dialects in Egypt. Coptic is the ancient Egyptian tongue written in Greek letters. The Coptic Versions were based on the LXX. They also include the NT.

5. *The Latin Versions*: They also cover both testaments. There is the *Old Latin*, a very early translation of the LXX. (Versions which are based on the LXX are of less use to the textual scholar because they are translations of translations.) Most important is the *Vulgate*, the work of Jerome (AD 346–420), whose name also appears as Hieronymus. Jerome began by producing three different versions of the Psalter, known as the *Roman*, the *Gallican*, and the *Hebrew*. The first is a slight revision of the Old Latin, the second a more thorough revision, and the third a completely new work based on the Hebrew. It is clear that, as Jerome progressed, he came to put more and more faith in the Hebrew text for the OT and less and less in the already existing translations. This may seem obvious to us, but we must remember that Christians had used the Greek and its Old Latin counterpart in worship for centuries.

182

The Hebrew Bible, if known to them at all, was the book of another religion. In the course of time Jerome translated the whole Bible from the original tongues into Latin and his work has been the standard RC Bible down to modern times.

The modern scholar has the task of comparing all these different texts and versions, studying their history and their relationship, and then producing what, in his judgment, is the best representation of the original texts. Most theological libraries contain several Hebrew Bibles compiled in this way in recent times. Three need to be mentioned. The first was produced by C. D. Ginsberg in 1894. Bound in mouldering brown leather, it can occasionally be seen in secondhand bookshops or in the studies of elderly ministers today. Ginsberg's edition was re-issued by the British and Foreign Bible Society (BFBS) in 1926. A more important work is *Biblia Hebraica*, published by Rudolf Kittel in 1926. It has been through many editions (the seventh came out in 1951) and is the Bible used by serious students because of its extensive 'critical apparatus'. (A critical apparatus is a list, at the bottom of the page, of all the more important variants found in the various MSS, so that the translator can decide for himself which reading he wishes to translate. The apparatus also contains suggested readings for places where none of the MSS make very good sense.) Finally there is the more recent BFBS text produced after almost a lifetime's labour by Dr. Norman H. Snaith, a former President of the Methodist Conference. This Hebrew Bible is within the reach of every student. Despite the massive labour that lies behind it, it is currently on sale for a few pounds.

g **THE NEW TESTAMENT**

In 1633 two brothers in Leiden, called Elzevir, published the second edition of a Greek text of the NT which they described as the text 'received by all in which there is nothing altered or corrupt'. The impression they were trying to convey was that the Greek NT had been passed down the centuries unchanged and that they were in the happy position of being able to print it and give it to the world. No doubt this was good for trade. Their claim was widely accepted and it gave rise to the term 'received text' (Latin, *textus receptus*) which was taken on every hand to mean the text that had come down from antiquity. A similar notion had gained currency in Britain and the same term is now used of the text produced by Erasmus in 1535 and published in Paris by Robert Stephanus in 1550.

The truth is rather more complicated. The MSS used in the sixteenth century were not very old. Their text had certainly not come down from antiquity unaltered. Neither were they all in agreement, but scholars at the time of the Reformation were not aware of the extent of the problem. They believed too readily in the soundness of the relatively few MSS that they had to hand. And they could, of course, know nothing of the MSS that lay buried in ancient lumber rooms. Erasmus used no more than seven or eight MSS when he produced the first printed Greek NT in 1516. It was rather a bad publication and he revised it several times using further MSS as they became available to him.

In 1627 the Patriarch of Constantinople made a present of an ancient MS, called Codex Alexandrinus, to the British royal house. This MS was centuries older than the sources Erasmus had used. Other MSS followed. The most famous is probably Codex Sinaiticus, found in 1859 by Count von Tischendorf at a monastery on Mount Sinai where the monks were about to use it for lighting fires. Codex Sinaiticus is a complete NT dating from the fourth century. Today the textual scholar has the advantage of being able to consult hundreds of different MSS, thought it must be remembered that they are not all different witnesses. If MS x was copied from MS y and both survive, we do not have two separate witnesses but only one.

It is clear that texts of the NT were preserved and copied in the great cities of the ancient world. Consequently we can speak today of the Alexandrian type of text, the Byzantine, the Caesarean (probably), and the Western, but it must be remembered that these terms represent groups or families, not an actual text. The Byzantine type, which predominated until the Reformation was what is called an 'ecclesiastical' text, that is, one that had been adapted and 'improved' for use in church. Difficult passages tended to be smoothed out and contradictions removed. Modern scholars are more fortunate in that some MSS have come to light (‭א‬ and B, for example; see below 14i) that appear not to have been accommodated to the needs of the Church. Westcott and Hort believed that the Alexandrian type reproduced the originals most faithfully. Consequently they gave the name 'neutral text' to those of this type.

Before we come to list the more interesting MSS, there are one or two other points to note. All ancient MSS were written without punctuation. The oldest, called *uncials*, are in capital letters throughout. A smaller script, in which the letters are joined together so that the scribe could proceed quickly without taking his pen off the page, came into use in the ninth century. MSS with this script are called *cursives* or *minuscules*. Most MSS are written on parchment, but some of the earliest are on papyrus. These papyri are numbered and given the prefix P.

Occasionally one sees a reference to the Chester Beatty papyri and the Bodmer papyri. In 1930–1 Sir Chester Beatty acquired three papyri in Egypt. They are sometimes called Chester Beatty I, II, and III, and their other designations are P45, P46, and P47. Similarly P66, P72, P74, and P75 were acquired by Martin Bodmer of Geneva some twenty years later.

A list of the more interesting MSS follows. They are in three groups, papyri, uncials, and minuscules or cursives. Broadly speaking this is the chronological order in which the texts were written. It is not, however, the order in which they were discovered.

h **Papyri**

P45 Chester Beatty I. Originally it contained all four Gospels and Acts, but it is much mutilated and only about thirty pages out of 220 have survived.

P46 Chester Beatty II. A third-century papyrus codex of eighty-six pages edited by F. G. Kenyon in 1936. The number of pages in a codex can be worked out from its construction. This one was originally 104 pages long. It contained Romans, Hebrews, 1 and 2 Corinthians, Ephesians, Galatians, Philippians, Colossians and 1 and 2 Thessalonians, in that order. Parts of Romans and the Thessalonian letters are now missing. Points of interest are the eminence given to Hebrews, the absence of the Pastorals (1 and 2 Timothy and Titus), and the appearance of Ro. *16.25–7*, the final doxology, at the end of Ch *15*, thus implying that Romans originally ended at *15.33*.

P52 The oldest MS of any part of the NT that we possess. Found in Egypt in 1920 but not recognized until 1934, it consists of only Jn. *18.31–3*, 37 f., but its date is probably the early part of the second century. This is immensely significant. John's Gospel was probably written in Ephesus, but this fragment shows that it was revered and copied in Egypt by about AD 130. This means that the fourth Gospel can hardly be dated later than the turn of the first century. P52 is now in the John Rylands library in Manchester.

P66 Bodmer II. Its present home is Geneva. It dates from about AD 200. 104 pages have survived. They contain John's Gospel with large gaps.

P75 A text of Luke and John from around AD 200. 102 pages out of 144 have survived. It is the earliest copy of Luke and one of the earliest of John.

i **Uncials**

אַ Codex Sinaiticus. Dating from the fourth century. א is the only complete surviving copy of the NT in uncial script. It also includes much of the OT. א belongs to the Alexandrian type of text. The secondary nature of the doxology to the Lord's Prayer (Mt. *6.13*) and the last twelve verses of Mk. *16* is demonstrated by the fact that they are missing from א. The symbol for Sinaiticus is *aleph*, the first letter of the Hebrew alphabet. Codices other than papyri were given letters of the alphabet to identify them. It appears that Tischendorf was convinced of the primary importance of his find, but the letter A was already taken by Codex Alexandrinus. Rather than accept a lower letter he turned to another alphabet. Just how Tischendorf persuaded the monks to present ℵ to the Czar is a matter of some doubt, but he did so, and, after the revolution, the U.S.S.R. sold the codex to the British Museum for £100,000.

A Codex Alexandrinus. An early fifth-century codex containing both testaments, almost complete. It originated in Egypt, arrived in England in 1627, and is now in the British Museum. Most of the NT represents the Alexandrian type but the Gospels are closer to the Byzantine. It is interesting, among other things, for the corrections made by a second scribe soon after the work was completed, a reminder to us that no one ever expected scribes to work without error. Corrections of this kind are common in ancient MSS. Until ℵ and B became available in the nineteenth century, A held the field as the most important NT MS.

B Codex Vaticanus. A fourth-century Greek Bible with some severe mutilations, preserved in the Vatican. 759 pages out of 820 remain. Though in the Vatican library, it was not made available for study until the latter part of the nineteenth century. It was the chief authority for the revisers of 1881, was greatly prized by Westcott and Hort, and is still the best example of the Alexandrian text. B brings Mark to an end after *16*. 8 and places Hebrews after 1 and 2 Thessalonians. Whatever may have come after Heb. *9*. 14 is now lost.

C Codex Ephraemi. A palimpsest (see above 14b) of the fifth century, now in Paris. Originally it contained both testaments, but, in the twelfth century, some theological vandal (or so he seems from the NT scholar's point of view) tried to erase the writing and copy out the homilies of one St. Ephraem of Syria on top. Many of the original pages were thrown away.

D Codex Bezae. A fifth or sixth century text now in Cambridge University Library to which it was presented by the great French scholar, Theodore Bezae, in 1581. It contains most of the Gospels and Acts plus a few verses from 3 John in Greek and Latin in parallel columns. D differs markedly from all MSS of the Alexandrian and Byzantine types, especially in Luke and Acts. For example, in Lk. 6, after v. 4, D inserts, 'On the same day, seeing a man working on the sabbath, he said to him, Man, if you know what you are doing, you are blessed; but, if you do not know, you are accursed and a transgressor of the law.' Again, in Lk. 22.19, D omits everything after 'This is my body' together with the whole of v. 20, thus removing altogether the cup which comes after supper. (In Luke alone there is mention of two cups, one before the bread and one after.) In Acts the D additions are very extensive. D is the principal representative of the Western Text.

j **Minuscules or cursives**

There are approaching 3,000 minuscule texts and the number continues to grow. They are identified by simple Arabic numbers. The great majority represent the Byzantine text, hence the notion that a single text had come down from antiquity. Some minuscules obviously related to each other are grouped in families and the families are identified by the number of the first minuscule in them. So 1, 118, 131, 209, and a few others make up family 1, and 13, 69, 124, 346, with others make up family 13. These are the two best known families. They also have names and signs. Family 1 is the Lake group, sign λ, family 13 is the Ferrar group, sign φ.

k **Modern editions**

The AV of 1611 was based on the so-called 'received text' which consisted of late and much adapted MSS. The revisers of 1881 broke new ground and also called forth much criticism by deserting the traditional text and making use of older and better MSS. Much of the credit for this is due to two members of the panel, B. F. Westcott and F. J. A. Hort. They had worked together on the Greek text of the NT for twenty-eight years and supplied the other translators with proof copies of their work which they were able at last to publish in 1881. The Westcott and Hort edition (WH) is one of the most important products of British NT scholarship.

Westcott and Hort made the far-reaching judgment that the Byzantine text (or, as they called it, the Syrian) was much inferior to the newly available ℵ and B. This outraged the. traditionalists who could not accept the notion that the much revered AV had been based on poor MSS. The Dean of Chichester, John W. Burgon, launched a ferocious attack on Westcott and Hort and the RV. This might seem an obscure, technical debate but in fact a fundamental issue is involved. Burgon affirmed, on the ground of his own theological convictions, that God would not have allowed the text of the Bible to be corrupted. Westcott and Hort argued that careful comparison of the traditional text with ℵ and B showed that it had in fact been so corrupted. It was a case of theological affirmation versus critical argument. Few would go with Burgon today, though the same issue has a way of cropping up in many other guises.

All more recent editions owe a lot to WH. Alexander Souter produced a student's volume in 1910 (second edition 1947) which consisted of the Greek text that lay behind the RV together with a critical apparatus giving the more important variants suggested by the ancient MSS and the Versions. Souter's edition is rather conservative because the RV did not depart from the AV unless it was compelled to do so. It is much nearer to the traditional, received text than WH itself.

A common sight in ministers' studies is the Nestle text, for the third edition of that text was adopted by the BFBS in 1904 and given free to ministerial students. Based on three contemporary editions, including WH, it had originally been published by Eberhard Nestle in 1898. Since then it has been continually revised, first by Erwin Nestle, Eberhard's son, and then by Erwin and Kurt Aland. It has now reached its twenty-fifth edition.

In 1954, to celebrate the BFBS's 150th anniversary, a

second BFBS edition of Nestle was begun by G. D. Kilpatrick with help from Erwin Nestle. It appeared in 1958 with an excellent critical apparatus.

When the NEB was translated no existing text was regarded as satisfactory. At each particular point the variations between existing texts were considered on their merits. The text actually translated was published afterwards by R. V. G. Tasker in 1964. This kind of text is called 'eclectic' because it consists of a large number of selections from different texts rather than a revision of one.

Most recently, in 1966, appeared the United Bible Societies text, edited by Kurt Aland, Matthew Black and others. It was especially prepared for translators and the critical apparatus is designed to give the relative degree of certainty for each variant adopted.

All this information makes it clear how daunting is the task of preparing a text of the Hebrew OT or the Greek NT even for the professional scholar. Every year that goes by makes it more difficult as fresh MSS are discovered and published. For every line in the Bible the scholar must ask himself questions like these:

Does the line make good sense?
Do all the Hebrew/Greek MSS agree about it?
If not, can the variations be explained?
In the light of the explanation, which reading is to be preferred?
What do the Versions say?
If they also provide variants, what Hebrew/Greek reading are they translating? (To answer this question the scholar must be able to translate from the Version, Latin, Coptic, or whatever, back into Hebrew/Greek.)
Does this change the preferred reading?

And so on. It is clear that the Church owes an enormous debt to textual scholars. It must be remembered that their work must be done before any translation into a modern tongue can take place. And if the translator is also the textual critic, then he has a double claim on our gratitude.

.**For further reading**

D. R. Ap-Thomas, *A Primer of Old Testament Text Criticism*, 1965.

F. Kenyon, *Our Bible and the Ancient Manuscripts*, 1958.

B. M. Metzger, *The Text of the New Testament*, 1964.

Chapter 15

Critical Methods

a THE difficulty with studying an ancient text—and this applies with works of art, too—is that we cannot study it *as it is being put together.* If we could do that, we could understand the finished product much better. But unfortunately only the finished product is available for study. If we are to understand it we must try to work our way back to the previous stages using logic and knowledge and as little guesswork as possible. That is what the critic does.

Criticism is usually a positive process in that it adds to understanding, but it may sometimes produce negative results. Critics may, for example, reach the conclusion that the apostle Peter did not write 2 Peter or that some parts of the Book of Isaiah were not written by Isaiah, the son of Amoz, who is named in *1*.1. In these circumstances it is possible to take one of four attitudes.

(a) One can say that the Bible is God's Word and that it is wrong to scrutinize it or ask any questions about it. Criticism of every kind and all critical conclusions are thus rejected.

(b) One can allow criticism but pre-judge the issue, that is to say, ask the questions, but know beforehand what one intends to find as the answer.

(c) One can allow criticism but be unwilling to accept conclusions that overturn traditional positions unless the evidence is overwhelming.

192

(d) One can follow the logic of criticism and accept the conclusions to which criticism points as firmly or as tentatively as the evidence suggests.

There is little one can say about the first attitude. People who hold it rarely listen to arguments, and they are unlikely to be reading this book. The second attitude is like the first only it is less honest. Those who take it pretend to ask questions, but, in fact, do not. They would be wiser either to affirm attitude (a) and make no pretences about criticism or to take attitude (c) and accept the risks. The third attitude might be called conservative. Conservatives are slow to respond to criticism, but, if logic absolutely requires it, they will modify their traditional views. They may maintain that logic rarely requires it, but they do not rule out critical conclusions from the beginning. All the views, (a), (b) and (c) rest in varying degrees upon the belief that the Bible cannot be treated like any other book. The fourth attitude pays less respect to traditional views. Those who hold it simply say that, with the Bible as with everything else, what is most reasonable is most worthy to be accepted.

There are many different kinds of criticism. In this chapter we shall deal briefly with historical criticism, textual criticism, source criticism, form criticism, traditio-historical criticism, and redaction criticism. First, however, we must clear out of the way two or three terms that are commonly but rather loosely used in biblical studies. They are 'literary criticism' and 'higher' and 'lower' criticism.

b *Literary criticism* is used in a number of different senses. It can be used for the rigorous study of a famous work to find out what was in the author's mind when he wrote it. It can also be used of the judicious assessment of new books by literary experts. In biblical studies it can mean the former, never the latter, and often some or all of the particular techniques discussed below. Because of this vagueness it is not a useful term for our purposes.

c *Higher and lower criticism* are now old-fashioned terms. Higher criticism meant going back to the source, finding out

193

who wrote a book and why and in what circumstances. Lower criticism was concerned with the text and whether we should read this word or that when there is doubt. In place of these two terms we now use six, which enables us to be more precise and more technical.

d Historical criticism

Historical criticism of a text is concerned with the historical circumstances in which the text came into being. With some literary forms those circumstances do not matter very much. For example, nobody knows who first said, 'A rolling stone gathers no moss'. Nobody cares either, for the statement is a universal and timeless truth. That is not so, however, with the statement, 'the Lord Jesus in the night in which he was betrayed took bread'. This statement belongs to a time and place. Its significance depends upon our knowing who said it, on what authority he said it, for what purpose he said it, who the Lord Jesus was, what his taking bread meant, what the relevance of the betrayal was, and so on. Historical criticism tries to provide the answers.

Scholars of all points of view engage in historical criticism. Some are more enthusiastic than others. Some say that there are few 'timeless truths' in the Bible and that everything must be studied against its historical background. Others reckon much of the Bible to be universally true but allow that historical criticism can often help to clarify statements. The difference is seen in a text like 1 Cor. *15*.52, 'the trumpet shall sound, and the dead shall be raised incorruptible'. Some scholars immerse themselves in first-century Judaism and try to understand why Paul thought of survival of death in this particular way. Often they go on to ask how Paul's convictions would sound if he were able to utter them in twentieth-century Europe. Other scholars take the view that there is no need to carry historical criticism so far. It is interesting to know why Paul thought there would be a trumpet on the last day, but the real point of the statement stands as securely now as it did when Paul first wrote it.

Historical criticism also fulfils a second, narrower function.

194

When a document refers to particular events as having happened, historical criticism tries to ascertain whether the events did indeed happen as they are said to have done. This means enquiring into the intention of the author, how he would have been understood by his first readers, and also how he got his information. Was he an eye-witness? If he wrote at a great distance from the event, what were the links in the chain that connected him with the original happening? Was he really writing to record the past accurately, or was he not rather addressing his contemporaries by means of a recitation of bygone events?

Historical criticism is a wide-ranging and complex discipline. It is much broader in its terms of reference than the other types of criticism which follow in this chapter. Moreover it makes use of those other types to elucidate texts, determine their background, and assess their historical reliability. For that reason it ought to come last, but it is the oldest form of biblical criticism, indeed, almost as old as Christianity. Origen, who died about AD 254, studied the style of Hebrews and compared it with that of the other epistles and concluded that Paul did not write it. Dionysius of Alexandria, Origen's contemporary, established, by similar methods, that Revelation was not written by the author of the Fourth Gospel and was not, therefore, apostolic in origin. And so it has gone on ever since. One cannot help asking questions and seeing difficulties. Historical criticism is an attempt to pursue that kind of study as rigorously and as honestly as can be.

About its usefulness five things can be said. In the first place, useful or not, it is inevitable. An honest man cannot avoid asking questions. Someone said that the reason for climbing Everest was because it was there. It is the same with historical criticism. The questions are there to be asked. One must ask them.

Secondly, it rarely provides proof. It deals rather in probabilities. It is almost certain that Isaiah contains large sections not written by Isaiah; it is probable that 2 Corinthians is made up of two or three different letters; it can hardly be doubted that Mark was completed before Matthew. None of these statements is absolutely certain, but it may be profitable to

195

make such assumptions. Scholarship would be easier if there were such a thing as absolute certainty, but we do not live in that kind of world.

Thirdly, historical criticism achieves both positive and negative results. It makes Mosaic authorship of the Pentateuch unlikely, which might be called negative, though not necessarily so, but it adds greatly to our understanding of the prophets, which is surely positive. It is wrong to regard it as essentially negative. It weakens some traditional positions, but it confirms and consolidates others.

Fourthly, its methods and arguments are not limited to Christians. Anyone can pursue them and anyone can see the force of their conclusions. This means that, in this area, discussion between believers and unbelievers can take place with profit. This is not true of all discourse about the Bible. In some areas believers and unbelievers simply have to differ because they have different presuppositions.

Fifthly, it serves the cause of Christian faith without ever producing an irresistible argument for it. Historical criticism does not prove the Bible to be factually accurate at every point. Nothing can. It does, however, establish certain events, such as the life and death of Jesus, on a basis of firm probability. That is a reasonable and important contribution.

e **Textual criticism**

Much has been said on this subject in the preceding chapter. The textual critic begins with the MSS that have survived and tries to work his way back to the original. P46 is a very old MS of Paul's letters, but there is still a gap of at least two centuries between Paul and the scribe who wrote P46. Quite a lot could go wrong in those two centuries.

MSS suffer in three main ways. They are liable to scribal error, that is to say, a weary scribe might make mistakes unintentionally. They can be altered deliberately by someone anxious to make them more relevant or, as he thought, more accurate, and they can be damaged accidentally by age or misuse or accident.

There is nothing the textual critic can do about accidental

196

damage. The gaps simply have to be supplied from other MSS. But it is possible sometimes to detect deliberate altera- tions. Deliberate alterations were made with the best inten- tions, to make the text more clear and helpful. For example, there are four accounts of the institution of the Lord's Supper in the NT. Matthew and Mark are very similar, Luke and 1 Cor. *11* are different. There will be a natural tendency on the part of the teacher to harmonize them, to make them all say the same thing. According to D, Luke mentions a single cup before the bread. Other MSS introduce a second cup after supper. Is this to bring Luke more into line with the others?

Similarly scribal errors can be understood because we all make mistakes when copying texts ourselves. A common one is *dittography*. That simply means writing the same thing twice, an error that the author has made several times in typing this book. *Haplography* is the opposite, omitting some- thing in the mistaken belief that you have already written it. Once one is familiar with the effect of errors like this one can begin to see explanations for some of the problems that occur in ancient MSS.

Textual critics work in two main ways. One is to study the history and relationship of texts in general. This means put- ting texts into families and associating them with particular places. This helps to prevent the gross error of settling textual matters by counting the MSS as if each MS had one vote. A hundred Byzantine MSS can be wrong and a single Alexan- drian right if some fifth-century Greek patriarch has intro- duced a modification into the text from which the hundred were copied. By this means the strength of particular texts is assessed.

The other method is the painstaking comparison of read- ings. Why does A say this if B says that? After considering the ways in which MSS get altered it is possible to make the rule that the more difficult reading is likely to be the more original. Teachers and scribes both tend to make the text easier. So, if one MS has a difficult phrase and another an easy phrase, the former is likely to be original. People called Roberton often get bills addressed to Robertson, for even the modern scribe tends to change the unfamiliar into the familiar.

197

Textual criticism is a technical, onerous, but very necessary, task.

f Source criticism

Source criticism is the study of books in the Bible to discover what sources, if any, the author used. Authors can be brilliantly original and have no traceable sources at all, or they can be simply editors combining pre-existing sources into a coherent whole. If the latter is true, source criticism can be useful as it enables the scholar to trace the material back to an earlier, and, therefore, perhaps more authoritative stage.

The best known example of source criticism is the work that has been done on the synoptic Gospels. We know from Lk. *1*.1 that Luke had many predecessors in Gospel writing and it is reasonable to suppose that he and other evangelists made use of the work these predecessors had done. There is nothing improbable, therefore, about the idea that our Gospel writers had sources. Then, as soon as one looks closely at Matthew, Mark and Luke, it becomes clear that they are very closely related. They tell the same stories, often in the same order, and often using the very same words. Various explanations are possible. All three might have used a common source. Or two of them might have used the third as a source. In fact the position is rather more complicated than this in that Matthew and Luke have passages in common that are not in Mark. They also have passages that are peculiar to themselves alone.

The source critic's task is to sort all this out by careful comparison and reach a conclusion about the sources used by each evangelist. More will be said about this when we deal with the Synoptic problem.

It is equally likely that other books of the Bible had sources, though it is not so easy to be sure as it is with the Synoptic Gospels. Here the source critic looks for sudden changes of style and vocabulary, differences in background between one chapter and the next, the appearance of what look like beginnings and endings in the middle of a book. The pursuit of this kind of argument has led to the conclusion that the Pentateuch had four sources, that Is. *1–66* is really a collection of books, that even Is. *1–39* is made up of various sources, that Luke had several sources in writing Acts, and so on.

Source criticism is valuable, but it can be overdone. Perhaps the worst mistake is to assume that everything must come from a source, that all sources must be documents, and that the final editor simply cut up his sources and stuck them together to make a new book. On the contrary, some sources may well have been oral and there is every reason to suppose that the editors used them with great subtlety for theological purposes of their own. (See below 15r.)

g **Form criticism**

Unlike textual criticism and source criticism, form criticism is not primarily concerned with documents. It is concerned with the community that produced them. Form critics begin with the assumption that every primitive society had need of certain types of verbal expression, myths, songs, sagas, war cries, and so on. Each of these types belongs to a particular occasion in the life of the people, the myth to the shrine, the song to the festival, the saga to the fireside. Moreover, with the passage of the years, each type achieves its own particular fixed form. There evolves *a right way* of reciting a saga or presenting a song.

There is nothing unreasonable about any of these assumptions. Even a very literate society like our own provides illustrations. There is a right way of telling a fairy story which includes even the tone of voice. 'What big eyes you have, grandmama!' The particular occasion for that little recital is the nursery at bed-time, or what passes for the nursery in these days. Adults also have their occasions. Games players will be familiar with the sing-song in the coach on the way home. The *form* of the song is all-important. It must be simple, repetitive, climactic and funny.

Two questions can, therefore, be asked about the people who gave us the Bible. The first is: what kind of forms did they need? And the second: how does the material that has survived to our day match that need?

We need to be clear straightaway that the answer to the second question is: only partially. It would be absurd to suggest that all or most of the OT consists of songs or fireside tales, or that the Gospels can be immediately divided up into forms for specific occasions. The question is not whether form criticism gives an exhaustive account of the biblical material, but whether it can add illumination. Here a much more confident yes can be given. It is extremely positive to see the Psalms, the Pentateuch and the Gospels as a repository of living traditions of a believing community.

The term 'form criticism' comes from a German word *Formgeschichte*, which means 'a history of form' and it draws attention to the form critic's belief that the evolution of the form is significant. The form helps to create the occasion, but the occasion also helps to determine the form, so that, in time, form and occasion become a perfect match. This explains why form critics are often regarded as radical critics in the NT. They tend to argue not simply that the Gospel forms (to which we shall return) created the Church, but also that situations in the primitive Church helped to create the Gospel forms. It is also implicit in the name that forms evolve and flourish and then fade and are replaced by documents. This notion has more relevance to the OT where the development went on for centuries than to the Gospels where the oral period lasted only a few decades.

h The pioneer of form critical studies in relation to the Bible was Hermann Gunkel and he applied the method to Psalms and to Genesis. In Genesis he showed how the simple folk-tale developed into the legend and finally into a complex series of episodes. In Psalms he discovered five types, the communal hymn of praise, the communal lament, the individual thanksgiving, the individual lament, and the royal psalm. The last is defined more by subject matter than by form. It is easy to see the occasions for these five types, victories or good harvests, national disasters, personal good fortune, sickness or accident, coronations, royal weddings, etc. Gunkel had hopes that his method would furnish the material for a complete social and religious history of Israel. These hopes have not been fulfilled, but every writer on the religion of Israel is willing to recognize that he stands in Gunkel's debt.

i The form critical study of the Gospels began in Germany after the First World War with Martin Dibelius and Rudolf Bultmann and it was introduced to England by Vincent Taylor and R. H. Lightfoot. The argument rests on the fact that the Synoptic Gospels are made up of many brief, independent units called *pericopae* (or pericopes; the word is pronounced as four syllables with the accent on the second). Save in the passion narrative, these pericopae are not related to each other by means of any continuing thread. They can easily be separated, and then one can ask the question: do they fall into obvious categories, and, if so, can one determine the occasion on which each category was used?

What were the occasions in the life of the early Church that corresponded to the festival or the fireside or the nursery bed-time, the occasions when particular verbal forms were needed? This question is no sooner asked than answered. *Preaching* in the market square on the basis of some text relating to Jesus, *controversy*, especially with Jewish antagonists, when it was necessary to make positive affirmations about Jesus, and *teaching* within the community, when a fuller account of Christian belief and practice could be given. Each of these provides an occasion. (It is usual to use a German phrase, *Sitz im Leben*, 'setting in life'.) The question then is: do the Gospels provide the verbal forms for such occasions? Is this what the pericopae are for?

There have been several attempts to sort the Gospel pericopae into categories and the categories have been given long and forgettable German names. Moreover, they do not exactly coincide as one passes from scholar to scholar. What follows is a simplified pattern using English terms.

j *1. Pronouncement stories*
These are brief anecdotes, devoid of local or personal detail, which lead straight up to a saying of Jesus on a matter of some import to the first Christians. If the form critics are right, the saying is of more importance to the primitive Church than to the original hearers. Mk. *12*.13–17 is an example. The

Pharisees and the Herodians try to ensnare Jesus. He asks for a coin, points out the image and says, 'Render to Caesar the things that are Caesar's and to God the things that are God's.' Not a very conclusive answer in the debate with the Pharisees but a good general principle to guide the primitive Church. Similarly, in Lk. *12*.13–15, a probate dispute is brought to Jesus. There is no precise reply but a pronouncement of far-reaching relevance, 'A man's life does not consist in the abundance of things he possesses.'

k   *2. Miracle stories*
These are slightly fuller anecdotes with some circumstantial detail beginning with the description of the sufferer, moving on to the cure by Jesus and finishing with the effects on the sufferer or the bystanders. In Mk. *1*.40–5 a leper appears kneeling to Jesus and begging him to help. Jesus heals with a touch and a word. The rest of the story is the result. Despite being asked to say nothing, the healed man spreads the good news so that Jesus is embarrassed by the crowds that come to him. Similarly in Mk. *4*.35–41, the scene is set with some care, the lake, the boat, the disciples, the storm. The miracle is accomplished with a word. The result is not simply a great calm but a question in the minds of the disciples; who is this that even the wind and the sea obey him? The function of these stories seems to be to make bold affirmations about Jesus, to show him doing what only God can do, and doing it with God-like confidence.

l   *3. Legends*
Legends are stories about Jesus that show him in the light of a holy man, and, therefore, as an example to follow. The aim is not pure history but the reinforcement of his character. That does not mean that the stories are purely fictitious, but representation of what actually happened is secondary to presenting him as a figure worthy of honour. Other characters are also included in the stories so that their virtues can also shine forth. The story of the boy Jesus in the Temple is a good example (Lk. *2*.41–51). The wisdom and precocity of the

child mark him out as someone of exceptional virtue. Dibelius includes the Birth and Resurrection stories in this category.

m *4. Myths*

Myths are stories that deal with the actions of the gods, either on earth, or in some other world that appears like an idealized earth. Very little of the Gospel is mythology. The Pronouncement stories certainly are not in that they represent Jesus as a teacher. Similarly miracle stories and legends represent him as an outstanding and powerful human figure rather than a god. In three places, however, according to Didelius, the Gospel passes into mythology. They are the Baptism, with its accompanying miracle, the Temptation, in which the Devil figures so largely, and the Transfiguration. It seems odd that Dibelius does not include the Birth and Resurrection stories here, but he is quite clear on the point. (See *From Tradition to Gospel*, pp. 269–71.)

n *5. Sayings*

This is the large category of sayings of Jesus that provided the basic teaching material of the primitive church. There is great diversity within this category. Dibelius notes maxims or proverbs, metaphors, parables, prophetic oracles, short commandments and extended commandments. Bultmann subdivides the sayings into wisdom sayings, prophetic and apocalyptic sayings, legal sayings and church rules, 'I' sayings, and similitudes of various kinds including parables. In all these cases the words of Jesus provide the ground rules for the life of the Christian and the church. The occasion for their use would thus be the instruction of converts.

Biblical students often have difficulty with form criticism because it never seems to 'click' in the way that source criticism does. So let it be firmly understood that form criticism is not nearly as precise a method as some of the others we are considering in this chapter. The whole idea of 'form' is rather vague. Strictly, there are only two clear forms in the above list, the pronouncement story with its climactic saying and the miracle story with its three phases, description, cure and results. Moreover, much of the Gospel material does not fit

GROUNDWORK OF BIBLICAL STUDIES

easily into any of the categories. And some categories are confused. Mk. 2.1–12 is both a pronouncement story and a miracle story. Dibelius includes it in the former group. There is also the question of the historical scepticism of some form critics. This rests on two suppositions, *first* that the primitive Church modified the Gospel material to make it more useful for its ongoing purposes, and *secondly* that it modified it by secularizing it, that is, by making the narratives conform more readily to the types of narrative already current in the Hellenistic world. The second supposition is controversial. The production of the Gospels might well have been a unique, Christian phenomenon. The Jesus stories need not have been conformed to any contemporary type at all. And the first supposition can be put positively as follows. So seriously did the first Christians take the resurrection and the work of the Spirit among them that the words of Jesus were to them not historic pronouncements made long ago, but living realities that continued to speak to them in the developing situations. Scholars who take this view argue that the recovery of what Jesus actually said in the first place is much more difficult than at first seems, but that does not mean that they are to be written off as unbelieving sceptics. Perhaps, in the end, it is a question of balance. Attention has to be given to both the situation in which Jesus spoke and the situations in which his words were used in the primitive Church.

Finally, form criticism does provide valuable insights into primitive Christianity. It lodges an objection to the idea that Gospel writing was a solitary pursuit of certain literary men who wrote pieces that were later cut up and rearranged by other solitary editors. Form criticism sets the process of Gospel composition in the context of the teaching and preaching of the Church. The Gospel grows out of the working life of the Christian community and expresses its faith. This realization is a great gain.

o **Traditio-historical criticism**

Form criticism naturally leads to traditio-historical criticism, for, once the separate units have been isolated, attention naturally turns to the way the units develop as they pass through time. Traditio-historical criticism deals with the history of blocks of material, whether large or small, oral or written, and it tries to explain how the material changes. The underlying supposition is that whatever changes take place will reveal the circumstances, not of the original composition, but of the period in which the change is made. So it is often said, regarding OT material, that it tells us more about the time in which it was edited than the time which it purports to be about, and, with regard to the NT, more about the time of the early Church than the life of Jesus.

The pursuit of the traditio-historical method is easiest in the case of a block of material that occurs twice in different forms. Then, either one can be seen to be a developed form of the other, or, more probably, both are developed forms of a common original, the developments having taken place in different places and circumstances. A good example from the OT is the Decalogue, that is, the Ten Commandments. The Decalogue occurs in Ex. *20*.2–17 and in Dt. *5*.6–21. Both of them present the same list of basic commands but make rather different comments upon them. That suggests an original simple form, perhaps to be declaimed in worship, and a more complicated form for teaching purposes. Those who know the style of the book of Deuteronomy will recognize deuteronomic touches in Dt. *5* which are not present in Ex. *20*, such as the reason given for observing the sabbath in Dt. *5*.14 f. Similarly in Dt. *5*.21 the wife comes first followed by house, field, servant, cattle. Exodus puts the house first. This suggests that Dt. *5* has suffered a deuteronomic adaptation that Ex. *20* has escaped. On the other hand Ex. *20*.11 supplies a reason for sabbath observances that comes straight from Gn. *2*.1–3. At some stage this priestly teaching was added to the basic commands. It is in this fashion that traditio-historical criticism proceeds. Very important for the study is the social and religious context (e.g. prophetic or levitical group) in which the development took place.

In the NT, the period of time in which the traditions could develop was much shorter than the long centuries of Israel's history. Within forty years of the ministry of Jesus much of the

Gospel material was already written down. None the less, these years provide several different contexts in which changes could happen. There was the early Church in Jerusalem, various Jewish-Christian communities in Palestine and the Diaspora, various mixed communities, and some predominantly Gentile-Christian churches. These are the factories in which the Gospel units were modified, if not made. The traditio-historical critic tries to discover what happened to a unit as it passed from one stage to another and then on to appear in one of the Gospels.

p   Before looking at particular examples, another nettle has to be grasped. We have spoken, in the previous section, of the communities modifying but not making the units. Many scholars want to go further and say that some units, though attributed to Jesus, were actually created in the Christian communities. The argument is put like this. So conscious were the early Christians of the reality of the Resurrection that they expected the Risen Lord to be present at their worship. So when Christian prophets spoke 'in the Spirit' at the communal Eucharist, it seemed proper to assume that this was the voice of Jesus speaking through them. So, it is argued, the Gospels include words of the Risen Jesus put on the lips of the pre-Easter Jesus. If this argument is accepted, the traditio-historical critic has the further task of working out, not simply how units changed, but at what point they were created.

The traditio-historical critic looks first for different accounts of the same incident or different versions of the same idea. For example all three Gospels recount the incident at Caesarea Philippi, but they all put different replies on Peter's lips (Mk. 8.29; Mt. 16.16; Lk. 9.20). It is inconceivable that all three represent separate incidents in which Peter gave three different replies. So one has to ask which, if any, of the replies is original and how the others arose. Again, the Resurrection narratives provide different accounts of what is meant to be the same event. The account of the visit of Mary to the tomb in Mk. 16.1–8 tells of Mary's female companions, a young man in white at the tomb, the announcement that Jesus is risen, and the flight in fear. It does not mention a meeting with the risen Jesus. In Jn. 20.1–18 Mary comes alone, she goes back to fetch Peter and another disciple, two angels appear, there is no announcement but a meeting with Jesus himself. Whatever the original happening, the divergences between these two accounts need to be explained, and this is what the traditio-historical critic tries to do.

The traditio-historical critic also notes passages in the Gospels that appear not to fit properly into the ministry of Jesus. For example the parable of the wedding feast in Mt. 22 accords well with the teaching of Jesus. The guests who refuse are the Pharisees and the publicans and sinners are those invited to take their place. But the ending in vv. 11–14, where the guest without the wedding garment is thrown out, does not fit in either with the rest of the teaching of Jesus or with the rest of this parable. But if one imagines a later day when the guests who refuse represent unbelieving Israel and those invited to take their place as the Gentiles, then you have a more formal, ecclesiastical setting in which the idea of an unacceptable interloper is a little more comprehensible.

q   There can be no doubt that the questions raised here need to be answered, but the answers need not be destructive. It is unfortunate that many critics in this field have not been content to explain the data. Having decided that the primitive Church was capable of modifying Gospel material and even creating new units, they have tended, unnecessarily, to assume that most of the Gospel material was produced in the primitive Church. From that point onwards it becomes a question of finding ways of attributing anything to Jesus at all.

Certain criteria are suggested for judging whether a unit can be reasonably taken back to Jesus. If it occurs in more than one Gospel source and if, in content and style, it has the true Aramaic flavour, then it might come from Jesus. If a saying has no parallel, as far as we know, in contemporary Judaism and if it could not have originated in a primitive Christian community, then it may reasonably be attributed to Jesus. (Considerations of this kind have led to the enunciation of the so-called 'criterion of dissimilarity'.) But how little can go through this net! None the less, that little is regarded as the basic core. To this can be added whatever else can be held to be entirely coherent with the core. (That is the *'criterion of coherence'*.)

Various criticisms spring to the mind. The process seems unnecessarily loaded in favour of the primitive Church. It is very subjective, especially in judging what is coherent and what is not. It requires that the hard core of Jesus' teaching cannot have had anything in common with contemporary Judaism, which is absurd.

This kind of argument seems an aberration on the part of traditio-historical critics. It is one thing to try, modestly, to track the development of tradition. It is quite another to be so confident in the results that one is ready to diminish the creative influence of Jesus. Traditio-historical criticism is a necessary but uncertain discipline. It can make useful suggestions, but it loses its way when it begins to dogmatize.

r **Redaction critism**

Form critism and traditio-historical criticism lead logically to redaction criticism. The first attempted to analyse the Gospels into units (or pericopae), the second to trace the history of the units. Redaction criticism concentrates on the final editing of the units into the complete Gospel. 'Redaction' is the process whereby the final editor selects, adjusts and links together his sources. Redaction criticism studies the process and tries to explain what the editor's motives were.

In the past the differences between the Gospels has been a source of some embarrassment to Christians. The variations were put down to the inadequacy of human memory or the inevitability of minor errors in transmission. The source critics had little positive to say. Why, if one evangelist was copying from another, did he not copy accurately? The source critics were never quite sure of the answer. But, for the redaction critics, the differences are crucial. They are not due to forgetfulness or error. They represent a subtle but deliberate moulding of the material by the evangelist for his own particular end.

The evangelists are, therefore, not mere 'scissors and paste' men, but creative thinkers according to the redaction critics.

They concentrate their attention on three features of the Gospels: first, the material selected by each evangelist, secondly, the arrangement of the material selected, and thirdly, the changes in the material made by the evangelist when these can be determined. These are all editorial matters and they must have been carried out by a particular editor. By careful study of them the redaction critic hopes to ascertain what the purpose of each editor-evangelist was. It might be argued that what looks like the work of one man might be the work of three or four men, for who can say that all the editing of Matthew was done at one time and for the one version that we possess? Redaction critics would answer that the final editor was the most responsible, because, even supposing he had predecessors, he still chose to reproduce those predecessors' work.

Once all the changes made by the editor-evangelist are noted and his 'editorial policy' made clear, it is a short step to fit him into a particular context in the early Church and to see him as a positive theologican relating the Gospel to that context. This the redaction critics attempt to do. And so Willi Marxsen sees Mark's Gospel as an eschatological tract linked to Galilee just before the Jewish War; Bornkamm interprets Matthew's Gospel as an attempt by a Jewish Christian to persuade Pharisaic Judaism that the law had been transcended in Christ and Hellenistic Christians that the law was still in force; and Hans Conzelmann sees Luke's Gospel as an attempt to spell out the historical pattern of salvation for the Gentile world. It will be seen that the whole method is speculative and, therefore, very controversial.

The reader will have noticed that once again the word 'context' has crept into the discussion. This is not surprising. Any study of any scrap of verbiage must concern itself with the context to which the words belong. But by now we have accumulated three different contexts in this present chapter. There is the context in the life of Jesus, the precise occasion—often difficult to establish—on which the words were first used. There is the context in the life of the early church, which is not so much a precise situation as a series of situations in and for which the words were preserved. And there is the context of the evangelist himself, the precise place where he worked and the audience to which he addressed himself.

The chief difficulty with redaction criticism is being able to ascertain with confidence that a particular editor did in fact make the change that appears in the text. That is not easy with Matthew and Luke, despite the fact that we have one of their sources, that is, Mark, available for comparison. But it is even more difficult with Mark, because it is impossible to say what his sources were and, therefore, what editorial changes he made. Again, where two accounts of an incident occur, it is possible to assess the slant of the two redactors, but often there is only one account and then establishing a redactional pattern becomes a matter of guesswork. Moreover the theological position of the evangelist is not expressed simply in the changes that he makes. The use of a tradition *as it stands* may, in fact, be a better witness to the evangelist's position, but how is one to know? Considerations of this kind lead us to be hesitant in accepting the more confident conclusions of redaction critics. None the less, both the value and the necessity of the method must be recognized.

The technical meaning of the word 'Introduction'

The introduction to a book is usually a general chapter that brings the ordinary reader to the point where he can get to grips with the specific issues with which the book is concerned. An introduction to Hamlet would tell us something about the plot, something about Shakespeare, something about Elizabethan England and the Elizabethan stage, and so on. In biblical studies the word is used in a much narrower sense. It is chiefly concerned with critical matters, and is often very technical. Consequently a book called 'Introduction to the New Testament' is unlikely to be a book for beginners. It is more likely to be a difficult book discussing technical questions for advanced students if not for experts.

S **Conclusion**

All these various kinds of criticism have a useful function, but they must not be regarded as infallible. From time to time one comes across the cliché, 'the assured results of criticism'. In fact, no results of criticism are absolutely assured. Criticism provides hypotheses, and hypotheses are more or less probable, and that is as far as we can go. That does not mean that one can ignore criticism, for the uncritical position, that Matthew wrote Matthew entire, that Mark wrote Mark, etc. is equally an hypothesis, and a very improbable one. So, whether we like it or not, we are plunged into the world of hypotheses. The arguments have to be pursued and the conclusions assessed. Some will appear more probable than others. This is a laborious task and there are no shining certainties, but that is the true state of affairs in biblical studies.

For further reading

I. H. Marshall (ed), *New Testament Interpretation*, 1977.

Section 3

The Old Testament

Chapter 16

The Political Map in OT Times

a   OLD atlases used to contain maps showing how Palestine was parcelled out between the twelve tribes. These maps were misleading. They were based on the details given in the second half of the book of Joshua, and, even if those details are substantially correct, they are not sufficient to provide accurate maps. Who, for example, could define the border between Lancashire and Yorkshire in a few verses? And that leaves aside the difficulty of identifying all Joshua's place names. Moreover, clear lines on a map suggest frontiers, and frontiers, as we know them, did not exist. Boundaries there certainly were, but expansion and encroachment were so common that a map suggesting a static situation has to be rejected.

    Another weakness of the old maps is that they imply tribal sovereignty within their boundaries, but there is little in the OT to suggest that every tribe had a political structure which embraced all the people in a defined area. On the contrary we know the Israelites lived cheek by jowl with the Canaanites so that, in the early days of the settlement, social and political loyalty would vary from village to village.

    There is one further difficulty. It is not clear when the twelve tribes came into being, when they became aware of themselves as twelve separate groups. Nor is it absolutely clear who the twelve were, as twelve groups are given a share of land in Joshua and Levi is in addition (Josh. *13*.14), being the priestly tribe without land. Fortunately the identity of the tribes does not matter very much and tribal boundaries even less, but two political factors do matter and they must be given careful attention. They are the division between the northern and the southern tribes and the location of Israel's neighbours, particularly in their periods of ascendancy.

b **1. The kingdoms of Israel and Judah**

History-books commonly speak of the years 922–721 BC as the period of 'the divided kingdom' which implies that a unified kingdom was the norm. The truth is, however, that, whatever religious unity Israel had, political unity of the whole people lasted only two reigns, those of David and Solomon. The division between north and south that came about on Solomon's death (1 K. *12*) was but the latest manifestation of a long-standing division that David's genius had temporarily overcome.

There are strong reasons for supposing that the group of clans later known as Judah came into the Holy Land from the south and not across Jordan as did Joshua's army. Then, once settled, geographical features, such as the Jordan and the valley of Jezreel, separated the people into what John Bright calls 'little cantons' (*A History of Israel*, p. 155). When threatened they united to repel invaders, but very rarely in the period of the judges did the land rise up as one. Saul, the first king, was of the tribe of Benjamin and operated chiefly in the hill country north of Jerusalem (still held by the Jebusites). David came from Bethlehem in Judah and south of Jerusalem. How much this had to do with Saul's antipathy to David is hard to say, but, when David became an outlaw, his kinsmen rallied to his side (1 Sam. *22*.1), and, at the final, fatal battle of Saul against the Philistines, David and the Judahites were in the enemy camp. David as king united the country by his military and administrative genius, but that the old enmities persisted is seen in 2 Sam. *20* where Sheba, another Benjamite, played on the old tribal feeling to raise a revolt against David. Solomon divided the country into areas for taxation purposes and Judah appears to have been given special treatment (1 K. *4*.1–20).

After 922 BC we have to think of two separate kingdoms,

but it is not easy to define them either in terms of tribes or territory. 1 K. *11*.29–40 makes no pretensions to precision. There the twelve tribes are divided into two groups of ten and one! 1 K. *12*.20 describes Rehoboam's kingdom as the tribe of Judah only, but the very next verse speaks of a rally of Judah and Benjamin. There is also the matter of Simeon, a tribe in the very far south, that must, by this time, have been incorporated in Judah. Territorially the border varied through the two centuries. Jerusalem was clearly in the southern kingdom and Bethel· in the northern. They are a dozen miles apart. From 1 K. *15*.17 we learn that Baasha, a northern king, fortified Ramah so that he could control his southern frontier. Ramah is five or six miles from Jerusalem.

For the rest it is best not to think of frontiers but rather of land that could be tilled and villages that could be defended when raids took place. There was frequent hostility between the two groups through the two centuries of their co-existence.

c **2. Israel's neighbours**

The political map of the OT was never static. Power was constantly changing hands. Different countries became involved with Israel at different times. And we must distinguish between local neighbours, small groups like Israel herself, and the great world empires whose soldiers came from afar. The local neighbours were Syria, Phoenicia, Philistia, Edom, Moab and Ammon.

d *Syria*: properly called Aram. A kingdom to the north and north-east of Israel from the period of the judges to the advent of Assyria. Its capital was Damascus, an important junction of trade routes. David incorporated most of Syria in his empire (2 Sam. *8*.5 f.), but it became free at the division of the kingdom. Syria constantly harried the northern kingdom, but, on one occasion in 735 BC, Rezin of Syria and Pekah of Israel (that is, the northern kingdom) allied themselves and attempted to force Ahaz of Judah to join them in resistance to Assyria (2 K. *15*.37; Is. *7*). Assyria sacked Damascus in 732

217

and that was the end of Syria, though the name re-appears during the Greek empire.

e *Phoenicia*: a coastal land stretching some 100 miles from just north of Carmel towards the river Orontes and Syria. Phoenicia lay between the Lebanon Mountains and the sea. It had two famous ports, Tyre and Sidon, and it is by the name of these ports that the country is known in the OT. Hiram of Tyre was an ally of both David (2 Sam. *5.*11 f.) and Solomon (1 K. *5*). Cedars growing on the slopes of Lebanon were cut down by Hiram and sent southwards for both David's house and Solomon's temple.

f *Philistia*: the Philistines were a war-like people who came to the Holy Land, probably by sea, in the thirteenth century BC. They set up five independent cities on the coastal plain in the south-west. From here they spread out and, in Saul's day, Philistine garrisons were all over the land. The Philistines had an advantage in that they had mastered the use of iron. They defeated Saul, but David subdued them (2 Sam. *8.*1). The name Palestine is derived from the name Philistine.

g *Edom*: a barren country to the south of the Dead Sea. According to Nu. *20.*14–21, Edom refused to allow the Israelites coming from the Wilderness of Sinai to pass through her territory. Enmity between the two nations lasted through history. David savaged Edom (1 K. *11.*15). The name Idumaea is derived from Edom. Herod the Great was an Idumaean which was one reason why he was disliked.

h *Moab*: the country on the east of the Dead Sea between the Brook Zered and the River Arnon. In times of prosperity Moab advanced both north and south of these borders. The god of the Moabites was Chemosh. The Moabites were implacable enemies of Israel. During the period of the judges Eglon, a Moabite king, seized some Israelite territory, but Ehud, the judge, murdered him and defeated his troops (Ju. *3.*12–30). David included Moab in his empire (2 Sam. *8.*2).

i   *Ammon*: the country north of Moab between rivers Arnon and Jabbok. In Ju. *10* the Ammonites attacked Israel across the Jordan, but Jephthah defeated them. Their god was Milcom, though Ju. *11*.24 suggests that they also worshipped Chemosh. Saul struggled against Ammon (1 Sam. *14*.47), but David's captain, Joab, defeated them (2 Sam. *10*). The ensuing ritual (2 Sam. *12*.26–31) seems barbarous, but it was simply typical of the tribal warfare of those days. The capital city of Ammon was called Rabbah or Rabbath-Ammon. It was while Joab was beseiging Rabbah that David seduced Bathsheba and sent his infamous command that Uriah, her husband, was to be deserted in the thick of the battle.

In addition to these more or less settled neighbours there were nomadic tribes who traversed large, mostly unproductive territories and occasionally made raids against settled populations, particularly when the harvest had just been gathered in. The two most important groups were the Amalekites and the Midianites.

j   *Amalekites*: they covered the area of northern Sinai and southern Negeb. A fierce battle took place between the Israelites and the Amalekites in Ex. *17*.8–16. Saul was sent to deal with the Amalekites in 1 Sam. *15*, but they continued their harassment of Israel until David's apparently final attack (2 Sam. *1*.1). After David's time they do not appear again in the Bible story.

k   *Midianites*: the records are a little confusing. It is clear that Midian is a territory in the north-west corner of Arabia, just across the Gulf of Aqabah from Sinai. Yet Midianites often appear as nomads. Similarly, Moses fled to Midian and found a wife there in Ex. *2*.11–22. But in Nu. *25* the Midianites are said to lead the Israelites astray and a man who took a Midianite woman was speared to death. Nu. *31* recounts an awful slaughter of Midian. In Ju. *6* they appear as camel nomads who swept into the fertile areas and stole or destroyed both crops and cattle. Gideon's great feat was that he dealt with the Midianites and they did not return.

There are, of course, many other clans, tribes and peoples in the OT, such as Kenites, Ishmaelites, Hittites, Amorites. Some represent small, almost unknown groups, others great civilizations. There is no simple way of classifying these names and it is best to look them up in dictionaries or in commentaries.

That brings us to the greater powers, located further away, but powerful enough in their turn to make a devastating effect on Israel's history.

1 *Egypt*: Egypt was a great and powerful nation before Israel ever emerged. Great civilizations arose and disappeared there long before the Hebrew slaves escaped. Egyptian history is reckoned in dynasties and Kingdoms which are groups of dynasties. The Old, Middle and New Kingdoms, comprising the first twenty out of a total of thirty dynasties (the last ten dynasties were relatively feeble and do not count as a Kingdom) had finished their course before David became king. The Egypt that interferes in biblical history is, thus, an Egypt in decline, separated from the Egypt of the pyramids by 1,500 years or more.

Egypt's strength rested on the fact that she was not dependent on fitful rains for her agriculture but on the flooding of the Nile which was regular and on irrigation from the Nile which was easy. Thus she became the granary of the ancient world. Her frontiers were easily defended, particularly that on the north-east where the Suez canal is today. Invaders from the east had no choice but to attack Egypt through this narrow strip of land which was easily defended.

Israel's relations with Egypt were ambivalent. On the one hand she was a large and dangerous neighbour always liable to interfere. On the other she appeared a useful ally against predatory forces from the east (Assyria or Babylon). In fact her value as an ally proved again and again to be illusory.

Around the year 1100 BC the New Egyptian Kingdom collapsed. The land of Israel was freed from the imperial yoke and this, in time, made David's empire possible. Solomon allied himself with Egypt (1 K. *3*.1) but this did not prevent

Egypt from plundering the Temple in Rehoboam's time (1 K. *14.25 f.*). Hezekiah was tempted to seek Egypt's help against Assyria, despite Isaiah's strictures (Is. *20* and *30*), but, in the event, he appears to have been saved from his folly. Josiah, as we have seen, met his death fighting against Egypt at Megiddo in 609. Four years later Nebuchadnezzar inflicted a decisive defeat on the Egyptians at Carchemish.

In the OT period, therefore, Egypt can best be described as meddlesome and unreliable. When the Greeks came in 332 BC, they subjugated Egypt, founded a new capital at Alexandria, and administered a large part of their conquered lands from it. Unfortunately another administrative capital was set up at Antioch in Syria, so the Jews once again found themselves occupying the critical frontier space between two larger forces.

m   *Assyria*: a great civilization flourished in the north-eastern sector of the Fertile Crescent in the second millenium BC. Assyrian empires, centred on the old capital of Asshur, rose and fell many times, but it is difficult to link any of this history with what we know of the Israelite tribes at the time. In the ninth century, however, Assyria emerged as a ruthless, military power, centred on Nineveh and savaging all the lands around including Israel. In 853 BC Syria and Israel (the northern kingdom), normally enemies, joined forces to try to prevent the Assyrian king, Shalmaneser III, advancing west. This battle at Qarqar is not mentioned in the Bible, but we can learn of Ahab's participation from an Assyrian inscription. The inscription is interesting because it assures us that the Assyrians won, though it is fairly certain that they did not, because they withdrew. National records do not always tell the truth. A century later, Tiglath-pileser III, called Pul in the Bible, came west again. He inaugurated the cruel policy of deporting whole populations from conquered territories. This was the occasion when Rezin of Syria and Pekah of Israel tried to force Judah to join them. Judah refused, Pekah defected and Syria had to face Assyria alone. Damascus fell in 732 BC. Samaria, Israel's capital, survived a little longer but fell to the Assyrian king, Sargon II in 722. So ended the northern kingdom (2 K. *17*.1–6). Judah survived and, even more surprisingly, survived an Assyrian siege in 701 (2 K. *18*.13–*19*.37). The seventh century BC belongs to Assyria. She was enormously successful, conquered Egypt, and built up a huge empire, but Assyrian kings were conquerors rather than colonizers. They created havoc rather than stable government. Nineveh fell to an army of Babylonians and Medes in 612 and finally at Carchemish in 605 Assyria was defeated to be heard of no more. The book of Nahum celebrates Assyria's downfall.

n *Babylon*: there was an ancient Babylonian empire in the second millemium BC, but the biblical story is mainly concerned with the Neo-Babylonian empire which emerged as the Assyrians weakened. Nabopolassar, who crushed the Assyrians, was its first king. Nebuchadnezzar is the best known. 2 K. *24* and *25* tell the story of how he came against Jerusalem twice. The first time he carried away all the treasure and the king himself (Jehoiachin). The second time (586 BC) he sacked the city. Able-bodied Jews were carried away into exile in Babylon. There, according to Ps. *137*, they sat down and wept as they remembered Zion. But they did more than weep in exile and the years from 586 until the return began in 538 are of the utmost importance for Jewish history. The Neo-Babylonian empire soon weakened and it fell to Cyrus the Persian without a struggle in 539.

o *Persia*: hardly a neighbour of Israel since it was located outside the Fertile Crescent to the south-east, east of the Persian Gulf. Persia is often linked with Medea which lay further north and south of the Caspian Sea. Persia was the first of the three great empires that swallowed up the Crescent as part of greater conquests. However important these empires were to Israel, Israel was only a detail on these empires' strategic map. Cyrus, the founder of the Persian empire, was a small Persian monarch at the time when the Persians were vassals of the Medes. In 550 BC he rebelled, captured the Medean capital and dethroned the king. He left Babylon trembling and marched west to conquer Asia Minor before returning to receive the submission of Babylon. Cyrus is hailed in Is. *44*.28

and *45*.1 as 'messiah', an interesting and instructive use of that word. He allowed the Jews to return and build their temple. The Persian period in Jewish history lasted 200 years. It must be studied in the history books with the help of Ezra and Nehemiah.

p   *Greece*: hardly a neighbour of Isreal but another great power that took control of the land of Israel by means of Alexander's lightning conquests from 334 BC to his death in 323.

q   *Rome*: still further afield but the greatest of all the ancient empires. It began with Pompey's arrival in Damascus in 63 BC and lasted until long after the biblical period was complete.

Chapter 17

Cities, Settlements and Shrines of OT Times

a HUNDREDS of place names are mentioned in the Bible and the student need not trouble to learn where they all are. In many cases the present location is unknown. There are, however, some important places whose location is secure, and it is well to know them. They are all marked on the accompanying map, but that does not mean that they all prospered at the same time. Like every other land, Palestine was always changing. One static map cannot do justice to the changes brought about by 2,000 years of history.

b *Beer-sheba*: the southernmost extremity of Israel's territory. In Genesis it is linked with Abraham (Gn. *21*.22–34), Isaac (Gn. *26*.23–5), and Jacob (Gn. *46*.1). All these references suggest that there was a shrine there in the early days (see also Amos *8*.14).

c *Bethel*: this city has associations with Abraham (Gn. *12*.8) and it was here that Jacob had his famous dream. 'Surely the Lord is in this place; and I knew it not' (Gn. *28*.10–21). Jeroboam cunningly chose a site that was already holy in Israelite tradition as one of the religious centres of the northern kingdom (1 K. *12*.29). Amos denounced the shrine (Am. *3*.14) and Josiah destroyed it (2 K. *23*.15), but all the indications are that, until the conviction grew that Mount Zion was to be Israel's only shrine, Bethel was a shrine of the utmost importance.

d *Damascus*: an important junction of trade routes in the Fertile Crescent. Capital city of the kingdom of Syria which was Israel's neighbour from the time of Solomon to the fall of Damascus to the Assyrians in 732.

e *Dan*: the northernmost extremity of Israel's territory. When the kingdom divided after Solomon's death, Jeroboam established a shrine there to prevent his people going south to worship at Jerusalem (1 K. *12*.25–9). Amos denounced this shrine (Am. *8*.14).

f *Gilgal*: the first stop of Joshua's army on the west of Jordan according to Josh. *4*.19. Memorial stones were set up there (Josh. *4*.20–24). There was a shrine at Gilgal that Samuel often visited (1 Sam. *7*.16, *10*.8, *11*.15). Saul was made king in Gilgal (1 Sam. *11*.15). There was a guild of prophets in Gilgal of which Elisha was head (2 K. *4*.38). Hosea deplored the worship there (Hos. *4*.15, *9*.15, *12*.11) as did Amos (*4*.4, *5*.5).

g *Hebron*: Abraham lived there and built an altar there (Gn. *13*.18). He bought the cave of Machpelah in Hebron to bury his wife, Sarah (Gn. *23*). Later he was buried there himself (Gn. *25*.8 f.). Splendid tombs associated with Abraham and Sarah can still be seen there. Hebron was a fortress in the hill country and David made it his first capital (2 Sam. *2*.1–11). Absalom tried to raise a revolt against David in Hebron (2 Sam. *1*.7–12).

h *Jericho*: The city where, by tradition, the walls came tumbling down (Josh. *6*). Archaeologists, however, are convinced that Jericho was uninhabited and without walls when the Israelites entered the Promised Land. For solutions of this awkward problem, see recent history books. In the ninth century there was a prophetic guild at Jericho which Elijah and Elisha visited (2 K. *2*).

i *Jerusalem*: originally a fortress city surrounded on three sides by the Hinnom valley and the valley of the Kidron. At the time of the Settlement and throughout the period of the judges it was occupied by Jebusites. David captured it (2 Sam.

5.4–10) and made it his capital. Solomon built the temple there (1 K. *6–8*) and thereafter the city became the focus of Jewish national and religious feeling. It has remained so ever since. The hill on which it is built is sometimes called Ophel, but, whenever religious considerations are uppermost, the same hill is called Mount Zion.

j *Mizpah*: another ancient shrine and place of assembly for Israel (Ju. *20*.1; 1 Sam. *7*.5–12). Samuel frequented it (1 Sam. *7*.16). After the fall of Jerusalem in 586 BC Gedaliah was set up as a Babylonian puppet in Mizpah (2 K. *25*.23; Jer. *40*.7–10).

k *Philistine cities*: there were five cities in the plain where the Philistines settled. *Ashdod*, where the Philistines carried the 'ark of the Lord' after they had captured it in battle (1 Sam *5*.1–5); *Ashkelon*, the scene of one of Samson's exploits (Ju. *14*.19); *Ekron*, the city that refused to lodge the ark because of the havoc it had caused elsewhere (1 Sam. *5*.10–12); *Gath*, Goliath's home town (1 Sam. *17*.4) and a place where David found refuge during his dispute with Saul (1 Sam. *21*.10–15), *27*.1–4); *Gaza*, where Samson was blinded and imprisoned (Ju. *16*.21).

l *Samaria*: This city did not exist when the northern tribes broke with the southern group after Solomon's death. It was founded by Omri fifty years later (1 K.*16*.24). Thereafter it was the capital of the northern kingdom until it was taken by the Assyrians in 721BC (2 K. *17*.6). The Assyrians scattered the Jewish inhabitants and settled foreigners around Samaria (2 K. *17*.24). These people inter-married with such Jews as remained and they became the Samaritans of later history. Nehemiah and Ezra refused them access to Mount Zion, so they withdrew and built their own temple on Mount Gerizim near Shechem. Samaria has been well excavated. The brilliant work of Omri's masons can still be seen.

m *Shechem*: another ancient shrine. Abraham erected an altar there (Gn. *12*.6 f.). So did Jacob (Gn. *33*.18–20). Jos. *24*

226

records a very important event taking place at Shechem. The elders of Israel made a covenant to be faithful to Yahweh and to reject the gods of Canaan. During the period of the judges Abimelech made a bid to become king at Shechem (Ju. *9*). Rehoboam went to Shechem to proclaim his kingship after Solomon's death, but his foolish speech made Jeroboam's revolt possible. Shechem became Jeroboam's first capital instead (1 K. *12*).

n   *Shiloh*: another important shrine like Shechem and Bethel. All Israel assembled there according to Jos. *18*.1 and *22*.12. The ark was housed there (Jos. *18*.1; 1 Sam. *4*.3) and it was the chief centre for sacrifice in the period of the judges (1 Sam. *1*.3. *2*.14). The boy Samuel heard the call of God in Shiloh (1 Sam. *3*). Ahijah the prophet lived in Shiloh, perhaps at the shrine (1 K. *14*.1–4). Shiloh was apparently destroyed (Jer. *7*.12–14, *26*.4–9).

The multiplicity of shrines in ancient Israel raises a problem because it is well known that Deuteronomy, especially ch. *12*, insists that sacrifice should be offered in only one place, that is, Jerusalem. Why should places of noble tradition, like Gilgal, be roundly condemned by Deuteronomy and the prophets? The answer is that Israel's men of vision, prophetic and priestly, reached the conclusion that an absolute separation must be made between Israel's worship and that of the local people, the Canaanites, who occupied Palestine before them. However noble the origins of the shrines were thought to be, the shrines themselves were sullied by centuries of Canaanite practice. When all this became clear, the shrines were condemned, sometimes destroyed, and worship was concentrated at Jerusalem. But in the days of the judges and of Samuel and David and the early kings, all this lay in the future. Jerusalem was not even captured in Samuel's day. So we have a period when the shrines were mentioned quite respectfully in the surviving records and a later period when they were condemned. Josiah was responsible for a great purging of the shrines, but he did not begin to reign until 640 BC, some four centuries after Samuel.

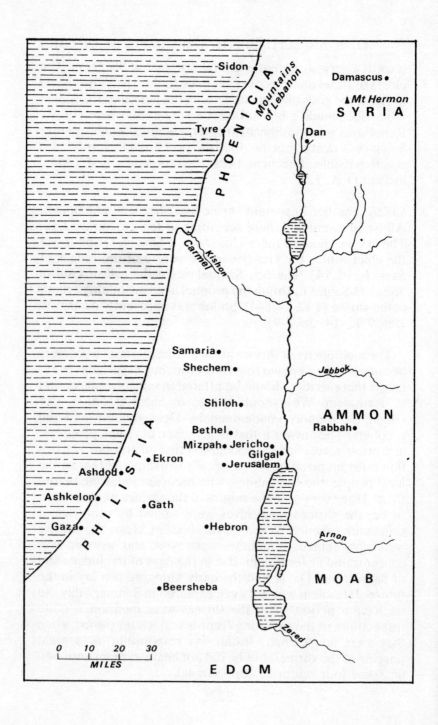

Chapter 18

Yahweh and the Gods of Canaan

a THROUGHOUT the OT, the opposition between Yahweh, the God of Israel, and Baal, the god of Canaan, is a constantly recurring theme. Condemnation is continuous both of the Canaanite cult itself and of the Hebrew renegades who trifled with it. So fierce is the language (see, for example, Dt. 7.1–6), that one can only think of the opposition in terms of a holy war. Israel's mission under Yahweh was to wipe the Canaanites and their religion from the face of the earth. Plainly it is necessary to understand something about this opposition if one is to study the OT seriously.

The Sacred Name Yahweh

The name, Yahweh, is interesting. It occurs in the OT in the form of four consonants, יהוה *. The first consonant, reading from the right, can be transliterated by either y or j, the third by either w or v. So the four consonants (they are called 'the sacred tetragrammaton') can be transliterated either YHWH or JHVH. There were, of course, originally no vowels (see above 12a).*

The sacred name was never pronounced. When the reader came to it in the text, he pronounced another Hebrew word, the word for 'lord' instead.

When the Massoretes added vowels to the Hebrew text, they did so in accordance with what was standard pronunciation in their day. But YHWH had no standard pronunciation, so no one knows to this day what vowels it ought to have.

The name, Jehovah, which occurs four times in the AV, is based on a misunderstanding. It is made up of the four consonants plus the vowels from the word 'lord', which were sometimes written down to remind the reader what he ought to pronounce at that point. Consequently, though we cannot say that Yahweh is the correct form, we can say that Jehovah is wrong.

The meaning of the name is obscure, though it is probably connected with the verb 'to be'. In Ex. 3.14 an attempt is made to explain it, but the attempt is not very successful. The word explained is, in fact, אהיה *which anyone can see is not the same as* יהוה.

The English versions vary in the way that they deal with the name. Usually they render it 'the Lord'. Moffatt has 'the Eternal'. JB simply says 'Yahweh'.

In the first place, the two communities represented different ways of life. The Israelites were semi-nomads, driving their flocks from place to place and never settling anywhere for long. The Canaanites were settled farmers. They tilled the land and lived off their crops. This difference is fundamental. It affects everything from diet to religion. Nomads are travellers, used to fighting and the hard life; they build no houses, have no luxuries, think and act always as a group, and have a very austere religion, for rich sanctuaries were no easier to build than houses. Farmers live better. They can build houses and temples and enjoy luxuries in good years. They are less inclined to band together, as each farmer has to make decisions for himself.

The initial settlement, therefore, represented a clash between two different cultures. Something similar happened in the United States in the last century when the cowboy, who rode the range, and the farmer, who put up fences, often came into violent opposition. In Israel's case it was made worse by the fact that the nomads were trying to take over from the farmers. Throughout the period of the judges, Israelite tribes were pushing into the country and trying to find room for themselves at the expense of the previous inhabitants and, in time, at the expense of other marauders who also coveted the comparatively fertile hill-sides.

If the settlement had been swift and complete, as the book of Joshua suggests, the problem might have been less. The Canaanite cult would have been destroyed and Yahwism would have been triumphant. But, in fact, Israelites and Canaanites shared the land for a long time. Doubtless they sometimes made common cause, when, for example, an invader, like the Midianites, threatened them all. The new settlers also needed to establish good relations with the local population, because they had to learn how to farm from those who were there before them. This, indeed, was the root of the trouble.

b   Farming techniques were all tied up with religion. The fertility of the land was due, so the Canaanites maintained, to the actions of certain divine figures, and the only way to farm successfully was to learn how to approach them. Canaanite religion was a fertility cult and we must take a little space to show what a fertility cult was.

First we must put out of our minds all notions of one supreme deity who is all-powerful and answerable to nobody. Canaanites did not believe in any such deity. Instead they believed that men, animals, the fields, and the gods were all joined together in the mystery of life, each one influencing the others and sharing the power between them. Each had his part to play. None had absolute responsibility.

Man played his part in the worship of the cult, which was far more important to the men of those days than good husbandry. The method used can be loosely called sympathetic magic. The idea of sympathetic magic is that all things that are like each other share in a common identity. An original and its effigies are really one thing. So, if you stick pins in one of the effigies, you harm the original, and vice versa. On this basis the fertility of flocks and fields can be brought about by fertile acts on the part of the gods and these in turn can be stimulated by fertile acts on the part of the worshippers.

This brings us to the heart of the fertility cult. It was thought that the miracle of fertility in the flocks and fields was caused by an act of sexual union between Baal, the lord of the land, and his consort, Anath (also called Ashtoreth, plural

231

Ashtaroth). This supremely fertile act conveyed fertility upon all the other coitions and germinations on which agriculture depended. The farmer, for his part, had to share in the action. So, in the worship of the shrines, acts of ritual intercourse took place to affect sympathetically both Baal and Anath and the flocks and the herds. Every shrine had a staff of ritual prostitutes for this purpose.

The sexual act did not take place in isolation. It had its place in a liturgy which included a recital of the myths of Baal, myths which, for the Canaanites, explained the cycle of the seasons. A great deal of information about Canaanite mythology was provided by the discovery, in 1928, of the Ras Shamra tablets. The texts tell us that the father of the gods was called El and that he had a consort called Asherah, but that the most important figure was their dashing young son Baal, whose adventures provide the basis of the Canaanite liturgy. In one of the myths Baal fights with Mot, the god of drought, desert and death. Mot wins and Baal is carried off into the underworld. The gods put on a great show of mourning and all nature wilts. (This represents the summer, for *summer* is the season of death in a hot land of low rainfall—see above 7b) Anath then sets out to find her lover. She meets Mot and batters him to death with a shovel. Baal is then resurrected. The lovers return to earth and celebrate their joy with an ecstatic marriage. Nature springs to life again.

This is a fairly common pattern in the ancient near east. The various texts tell many stories of dying and rising gods and the rites of mourning and jubilation that go with them. Notice how these myths bring together the activity of the gods, the pattern of the worship and the cycle of the seasons.

c From an Israelite point of view the objection to this was primarily theological and only secondarily moral. Yahweh, the God of Israel, was not one god among many. He shared his power with no one. He could not be constrained by man in any way whatever. He was not liable to death and resurrection. Baal was thus a false god and his worship was immoral. It is well to remember that prostitution was wrong because it was baalish rather than that baalism was wrong because of the prostitution.

It is important to realize, however, that the understanding of Yahweh that we have just outlined was not yet fully formed. Unfortunately it is impossible to be precise at this point. The question of how much of the single-minded Yahwism of Deuteronomy actually goes back to the historical Moses and how much of it was the discovery of later days is controversial and difficult to resolve. And beyond that, the degree to which the average Israelite understood and subscribed to pure Yahwist theology is quite beyond our knowledge. It does seem certain, however, because of all the denunciation of renegades in the OT, that a large number of Hebrews were more interested in agriculture than theology and were prepared to let the Canaanites teach them both.

d   The word used to describe the blending of two or more different cults is *syncretism*. Syncretism in this case was quite inevitable. Baalist Canaanites and Yahwist Israelites were living side by side for at least seven centuries. They could not help but learn from each other. Moreover, the Yahwist cult, in its early days, had no tradition of temple building and probably little idea of linking the religious festivals with the agricultural year. The Canaanites knew all about these things. Then there was syncretism carried out for political purposes. Solomon's Temple was built by a Phoenician architect (1 K. 7.13 ff.) and with Phoenician materials (1 K. 5). Within it he set up altars to foreign deities for the convenience of his wives (1 K. *11*.5–8). Theologically this was improper, but, no doubt, Solomon thought that it was good diplomacy.

Just how far syncretism went is hard to ascertain. Again, the matter is most controversial. Some scholars have argued that Yahweh was worshipped as a dying and rising god, that annually the king personated him in the ritual, pretended to die, was raised up by a consort, then married and re-enthroned. This is an extreme point of view and the evidence for it is scanty. But there is hard evidence for syncretism of a more obvious kind, like that of Solomon to which we have just referred. The historical books of the OT bitterly criticise kings, like Ahab and Manasseh, who followed a syncretistic policy. The prophets right down to Jeremiah and Ezekiel inveigh against Canaanite practice and interpret the troubles

233

of Israel as God's judgment on syncretism. Deuteronomy is completly devoted to stamping out baalism. Such a body of evidence would not exist if there were nothing to combat.

e   Opposition to syncretism showed itself in various ways. In the earliest days judges like Gideon (Ju. 6.25–32) fought against baalism for reasons of tribal identity. Yahwism became a rallying call to unite the Hebrews when the immediate danger was from Canaanites. This still seems to be the case in Deuteronomy, though there religious and theological reasons predominate. It is not clear when the Nazirites first appeared, but they were men and women whose repudiation of the grape expressed an anti-Canaanite attitude (Nu. 6). Similarly the Rechabites still followed the nomadic style and lived in tents and drank no wine. Jeremiah was much impressed by their firmness (Jer. 35).

From time to time brute force seems to have been used in the cause of religious reform. In the J Decalogue (Ex. 34) (see below 21h) the Israelites are exhorted to break down the Canaanite altars, smash their pillars and cut down their asherim. The asherah (plural, asherim) was made of wood. It was probably a pole. It stood by the altar and represented the female deity. The pillar was made of stone and represented the male. Dt. 7.5 and 12.3 give similar instructions. They were not always carried out for, as late as 622 BC, Josiah still found the land full of these syncretistic objects. The most appalling story comes from 2 K. 10.18–28. Jehu summoned all the worshippers of Baal in Israel to a great sacrifice and then surrounded the shrine and slaughtered them.

The word Baal often occurs in the plural, baalim, for Baal had many manifestations in many different areas. Hence there were many different baalish shrines or 'high places'. Dt. 12 demands that there be a single sanctuary in Israel. It does not mention Zion, but Zion is obviously 'the place which the Lord shall choose'. All other altars, whether dedicated to Baal or Yahweh, were to be destroyed. This did not ensure the end of syncretism, but it was an obvious step in the attempt to overcome it.

f   The real defenders of Israel against syncretism were the prophets. Some, at least, appear to have worn the hairy mantle and leather girdle, the common clothing of the desert, as a protest against the soft clothing of Canaan (see 2 K. *1*.8, Zech. *13*.4). Elijah challenged the prophets of Baal on Mount Carmel and demonstrated that Yahweh was God in Israel (1 K. *18*). Hosea protested against ritual prostitution (Hos. *4*.14), and argued that it was Yahweh and not Baal who gave the corn and the wine and the oil (Hos. *2*.8). And so we could go on.

The prophets were not content simply to attack baalism by affirming the majesty of Yahweh. They also worked out a peculiarly Hebrew view of God and his activity on man's behalf. All the religions of the Fertile Crescent were nature religions. They were concerned with the agricultural cycle and with little else. Yahwism was different. The crucial fact of Yahwism was the deliverance at the Red Sea. This was not part of the agricultural cycle. It was an event in history. Yahweh was thus understood as the God of history. He had acted in the past and he would so act again. He also showed his hand in the harvest, but it was as the God of history that he was best known. So the prophets talk at great length about Yahweh working out his will, both for Israel's chastisement and for her salvation, in history. So, too, the festivals of Israel are linked, not simply with the seasons, but with historical events. The Passover is a good example. A spring festival existed in Canaan before the Hebrews arrived. It was linked with the barley harvest. In Israel's hands the barley harvest receded into the background and the feast was linked primarily with the escape from Egypt.

By the time that the final editing of the OT took place, in the centuries after the Exile, the Yahwist faith had been fully worked out and the inadequacy of all other faiths demonstrated at least to the satisfaction of the editors themselves. They made sure that all references to the great enemy were condemnatory. They could not deny the fact of syncretism. They could ensure that it was regarded as apostasy. And so they did. Just how deeply the Canaanites influenced Israelite religion we shall never know. We can, however, be sure that the doctrine of the holy, merciful, covenant God of history is an Israelite discovery. There is nothing in the myths of the ancient near east to put beside it.

235

Chapter 19

Prophets, Priests and Kings

a   THE religious life of Israel was dominated by three figures, the prophet, the priest and the king. In later times there were scribes and lawyers, but they figure more in the NT than in the OT. We ought not to overlook the sages or wise men who coined proverbs and other wise sayings. Solomon is said to have been the doyen of sages, and this means, at least, that there were sages from Solomon's time onwards. It is difficult to say much about them, however, because their literary productions are late. Maybe the sages did help in the struggle with baalism. We simply do not know. The few references that exist from early days do not help very much (2 Sam. *14*.2, *20*.16).

There is, however, ample evidence of the parts played by prophets, priests and kings and we must give them some attention.

b   **Prophets**

The earliest records are confused. 1 Sam. *9*.9 suggests that prophecy did not exist in Israel until Samuel's time. Before that there were people called seers. The seer was originally a kind of clairvoyant. Saul regarded Samuel as a seer and came to him to ask about his lost asses (1 Sam. *9*). Prophecy was a different phenomenon, though Samuel was both seer and prophet. Later books tend to use the words interchangeably, which is misleading.

We need, therefore, to put out of our minds notions of

236

clairvoyance or 'second sight'. The prophet, in the early days, was a member of a group. From time to time he joined with others in a kind of ritual dance that led to great excitement and a state of ecstasy. In this ecstasy the prophets shouted out words and sayings that were not the product of their own rational thought. It was supposed that a spirit from beyond had taken them over and was speaking through them. These words constituted the earliest prophetic oracles. A group of this kind is mentioned in 1 Sam. *10*. They met at a 'high place', that is, a shrine, and they had musical instruments to help them. Saul joined in and he was 'turned into another man' (v. 6). The spirit of God came mightily upon him and he prophesied (v. 10). An even more informative story is found in 1 Sam. *19*.18–24. Notice that Samuel was in charge of the group, that the prophetic behaviour proved contagious, and that Saul reached such a state of abandon that he stripped off his clothes and took nearly a day to recover.

c   The question naturally arises: what has all this to do with the great men of prophecy? Did they live in groups? Did they meet at shrines? Were they ecstatic? These questions must be taken one at a time, but first note this. From the beginning prophecy was thought to be the word of the spirit from God. The very ecstasy witnesses to the fact that the prophet was not thought to be using his own sober judgment.

Groups of prophets existed in Israel, perhaps right down to the Exile. Obadiah saved 100 prophets from Ahab in 1 K. *18*.4. Elisha appeared to live with a group called 'the sons of the prophets' (2 K. *2*.15, *4*.1, 38, *5*.22, *6*.1, *9*.1). Ahab called on 400 prophets to advise him (1 K. *22*.6). On the other hand, Ahijah, Elijah and Micaiah appear to function alone.

The solution to this problem may be found in Am. *7*.12. Amos is accused by Amaziah of being a professional prophet and he hotly denies it. Yet he seems *to us* to be a prophet. Similarly Jeremiah launches into a seering attack on prophets in Jer. *23*, yet he seems to be a prophet himself. And Micaiah appears separately in 1 K. *22* when the crowd of prophets led by Zedekiah have finished speaking. From this we may guess that group prophecy was the norm in Israel, but that the groups were liable to corruption. They seemed to

237

manufacture prophecies to suit their patrons. Over against these there were a few outsiders who were unpopular because they sought the word of the Lord honestly. It is these outsiders that we know as the prophets. In their time they were usually (Isaiah is an exception) odd and outside the establishment, but it is they who have left the great books behind. The groups, for all their strength in manpower, have left no written records at all.

d   Fifty years ago it would have been taken for granted that, after the earliest period, prophets had nothing to do with shrines, nor with the Temple when it was built. On the basis of such passages as Am. 5.21, Is. 1.11 and Jer. 6.20 it was assumed that the prophets were opposed to sacrificial worship and stood for some kind of personal and inward religion. As long ago as 1892, Robertson Smith tried to halt this trend by saying that the prophets objected only to hypocritical sacrifice. His view has steadily been gaining ground. It is now argued that groups of prophets acted in Temple worship and that even some of the great solitary figures had a place in public worship.

There is no doubt that Canaanite prophecy (1 K. 18) and early Hebrew prophecy were linked to shrines. When David planned the Temple, he did not consult the priests but Nathan the prophet (2 Sam. 7) and, when it came to choosing the site, David was guided by Gad, not by a priest (2 Sam. 24). Of Elijah's prophetic stature there can be no doubt, but he is seen conducting a sacrifice on Mount Carmel (1 K. 18.20–35). When the woman of Shunem spoke of consulting Elisha, her husband questioned whether he should be consulted when it was neither new moon nor sabbath (2 K. 4.23), which suggests that prophetic activity was governed by ritual considerations. Priests and prophets are often linked as if they were colleagues (Is. 28.7; Jer. 2.26, etc.). Isaiah had his vision in the Temple (Is. 6) and Jeremiah often preached there. Ezekiel was a priest and in his last nine chapters he redesigned the Temple. After the Exile Haggai and Zechariah show great concern for the re-building of the Temple. The most tantalizing reference is Lam. 2.20. 'Shall the priest and the prophet be slain in the sanctuary of the Lord?' Evidently prophets belonged in the sanctuary, but in what capacity? The argument is inconclusive. There is little doubt that some prophets had a function in the Temple service, but there is hardly any evidence to suggest that the great prophets were of their number.

e   About ecstasy it is also difficult to be conclusive. The prophets functioned by something other than cool-headed shrewdness, and there is plenty of evidence of paranormal behaviour on their part, but few would argue that the great prophets always received their messages through ecstasy. How they received their message is really a theological question not a historical one. Here we are only concerned with appearances.

It is plain that they were all under a great sense of compulsion. Walking naked as a sign, as Isaiah did in Is. *20*, is hardly the action of a perfectly normal person. Ezekiel had trances. He was dumb for seven days after his call and on other occasions (*3.26, 24.27, 33.22*). He acted strangely and at times appeared paralysed. He had visions in which he felt himself transported from Babylon to Jerusalem (*3.14, 8.3*). This does not add up to a normal prophetic pattern. It simply means that the men who gave us the great prophetic books were unusual people, which does not establish a necessary link between prophecy and ecstasy.

f   The essence of prophecy is to be found in the belief that the prophets were speaking God's words. 'Thus saith the Lord' was their constant theme. They believed themselves called by God to the task. The OT contains many stories of calls, Samuel's (1 Sam. *3*), Amos' call that took him away from his flocks (Am. *7.14* f.), Hosea's call that came through his tragic marriage. Isaiah, Jeremiah and Ezekiel had visions (Is. *6*; Jer. *1*.4–10; Ez. *2*.1–*3*.9). Many passages in Jeremiah (see especially *28*.5–9) suggest that, if left to himself, he would have prophesied something different, but he could not. He felt himself under divine compulsion.

Because the oracles were regarded as God's words, they were regarded as being, not simply true, but powerful and able to achieve their object. So too were the signs that the prophets sometimes performed together with their words.

When Jeremiah broke the pot in Jer. *19* and prophesied the doom of Jerusalem, the city was as good as finished. If God says something through the prophet, it must be fulfilled. This raises a tremendous problem about false prophecy, for there were false prophets in both senses, prophets who were not honest, and prophets who proved to be inaccurate.

This was an agonizing question for the Hebrews. If the prophet was true, then, however awful his prophecy, the only thing to do was to accept it and act accordingly. But he might not be true. In Jer. *28*, Jeremiah and Hananiah meet as contrary prophets. Hananiah said the city would be spared, Jeremiah said it would fall. Both began with 'Thus saith the Lord'. Both spoke with passion. Both supported their words with dramatic signs. Yet both could not be right. At the time most people believed Hananiah and were wrong. There was no way of knowing the true from the false except by waiting to see what happened. In this sense we are more fortunate, for the oracles of the prophets who proved to be right have been preserved. The others, for the most part, were not worth preserving, but few people knew that at the time.

In view of the uncertainty it is surprising what authority the prophets had in Israel. They were able to speak to kings with remarkable candour and survive. Nathan, Elijah and Micaiah are but three examples out of many. See 2 Sam. *12*.1–15, 1 K. *21–22*. Ahijah and Elisha are both credited with inspiring revolts that led to new royal houses (1 K. *11*.29–31; 2 K. *9*.1–13). Prophets were often appointed as advisers to the king. Gad and Nathan had a place at David's court and Zedekiah was the leader of a band of prophets at Ahab's court. Isaiah was often in the king's company, but did not apparently reside at court. In later times there was a tradition that many prophets suffered martydom, but in fact the OT records only one such case and the prophet concerned was not among the great ones (Jer. *26*.20–23).

g   Most prophetic oracles had to do with the immediate future. They were concerned with the present state of the nation, with God's will for the people who heard the oracles, with the threats and promises implicit in the contemporary situation. In most cases it is a mistake to see in them references

240

to events that happened centuries later. Isaiah, for example, was looking a few months ahead, not seven centuries, when he spoke of the child called Immanuel in 7.11. But two comments have to be made on that. One is that an occasional prophecy about the distant future might be relevant to the present and, therefore, might be expected, whether the source was the Spirit or the prophet's own imagination. The other is that profound and serious language often has meanings at various levels. The oracle that was concrete for the day might also have meanings that were relevant to another day. While recognizing the immediacy of most prophecy it is wise not to limit its significance too severely.

h **Who's who among the prophets**

Ahijah—a tenth century prophet who helped Jeroboam in his revolt against Solomon and Rehoboam. He later prophesied against Jeroboam (1 K. *11*.29–40, *14*.1–18).

Amos—mentioned only in the book that bears his name. A herdsman from Tekoa in the south. He went to Bethel to prophesy against the northern kingdom in the middle of the eighth century when it was enjoying a period of great prosperity. He attacked neighbouring nations and Israel and Judah with the same destructive vigour. Amos claimed not to be a prophet (7.14), but he probably meant that he was not a corrupt professional. Most of his prophecies were fulfilled in the Assyrian invasion. The book closes with a promise of salvation (9.11–15) which some think comes from a later hand.

Deutero-Isaiah—this is the name given to the author of Is. *40–55*. He was a prophet of hope and is thought to have lived at the end of the Exile. The so-called Servant Songs are found in this prophecy.

Elijah—the first great prophet and one of the greatest of all. He is most famous for his opposition to Ahab and Jezebel in the ninth century. (See 1 K. *17*–2 K. *2*.)

Elisha—disciple of Elijah and his apparent successor. Many of the stories told about him are of a strange, magical kind that do not fit in well with the prophetic tradition. (See 2 K. 2–13.)

Ezekiel—son of a priest, he was among the first to be deported to Babylon in 597 BC. A profound and original thinker, but his book is difficult to understand because of the obscurity of language and imagery. He is not mentioned elsewhere. (See below 23e.)

Gad—an adviser of David from his time as a fugitive. (See 1 Sam. *22*. 3–5, 2 Sam. *24*.)

Habakkuk—known only from his book which was clearly written at a time of deep depression. The probable date is late seventh century. The first oppressors are the Assyrians. The Babylonians (called Chaldaeans) raise Israel's hopes as they attack Assyria but dash them again when they, in turn, become oppressors. Chapter *3*, a kind of psalm, has a different style from the rest of the book.

Haggai—a prophet concerned with the rebuilding of the Temple in the late sixth century. (Apart from his book, see Ezra *5*.1 and *6*.14.)

Hananiah—Jeremiah's opponent in Jer. *28*. He prophesied the destruction of Babylon and was wrong.

Hosea—a prophet of the northern kingdom just before the fall of Samaria in 721 BC. He is best known for the deep love he showed to a worthless wife and the use he made of this in his prophecy. Israel was the treacherous wife, Yahweh the ever-faithful husband. Hosea is mentioned only in his book.

Huldah—a prophetess whom Josiah consulted about the book that was found in the Temple (2 K. *22*).

Isaiah—son of Amoz, he began his prophetic work in 742 BC, 'the year that King Uzziah died'. He lived through the confederacy of Israel and Syria against Judah, the fall of Samaria, the Assyrian threat, the reforms of Hezekiah and the crisis of 701 BC. He rejected foreign alliances and taught that Judah should put her trust in Yahweh alone. There is a tradition that he was martyred by Manasseh in 687 BC. (Apart from chs. *1–39* of his book, see 2 K. *19–20*; 2 Chr. *26.*22, *32.*20,32. Also see below 23c.)

Jehu—a prophet who denounced Baasha, king of Israel (900–877 BC). (See 1 K. *15.*33–*16.*12.)

Jeremiah—he prophesied from 627 BC to some time after the fall of Jerusalem. An unspeakably sad yet noble man. When Jerusalem fell, he was taken to Egypt where he continued to prophesy. He is mentioned several times in the OT outside his book. (See also below 23d.)

Joel—known only from his book which cannot be dated, though the occasion appears to be a plague of locusts (See *1.*4 and *2.*1–11.) The first two chapters are a national lament, but at *2.*28 the theme changes, the prophecy becomes more like apocalyptic (20l). This perhaps gives a clue to date, some time in the fourth century when prophecy was ceasing and apocalyptic was taking over.

Malachi—the name means 'my messenger' and it may not be a proper name at all. The prophet is known only from his book which consists of six imaginary disputations between God and Israel, *1.*1–5, *1.*6–*2.*9, *2.*10–6, *2.*17–*3.*5, *3.*6–12, *3.*13–*4.*3. The book is usually dated in the first half of the fifth century. The people are disappointed and are neglecting their religious duties. The argument of the book is that this is short-sighted for judgment is sure even if it is delayed.

Micah—Micah's date is known from *1.*1. He was a contemporary of Isaiah. He is mentioned in Jer. *26.*18 f. He is especially hard on unworthy leaders (ch. *3*). Chapters. *4* and *5* interrupt the general condemnation and promise the overthrow of Israel's enemies.

Micaiah—the faithful prophet of Yahweh at Ahab's court (1 K. *22*).

Nahum—prophesied with glee over the fall of Nineveh in 612 BC but had no complaints to make about Israel. Known only from his book.

Nathan—David's court prophet. He prophesied a great dynasty for David, rebuked him over the Bathsheba incident, and helped to ensure Solomon's succession (2 Sam. *7*, *12*, 2 K. *1*).

Obadiah—known only from his book, a single chapter in which he attacks the hated enemy Edom.

Second Isaiah—see Deutero-Isaiah.

Shemaiah—warned Rehoboam against attempting to regain the ten tribes. (See 1 K. *12*.21–4, 2 Chr. *12*.)

Trito-Isaiah—a name given to the author or authors of chs. *56–66* of Isaiah.

Uriah—a prophet who took Jeremiah's side and was killed (Jer. *26*.20–23).

Zechariah—a prophet who helped to rebuild the Temple in the late sixth century. His oracles are found in Zech. *1–8*. The format is a series of eight visions. They all relate to the day of salvation which is very near. The second section of the book, Zech. *9–14*, does not mention Zechariah's name, and is sometimes called Deutero-Zechariah. It is difficult to date and, in places, hardly less difficult to understand.

Zedekiah—a false prophet at Ahab's court (1 K. *22*).

Zephaniah—the book comes from Josiah's reign (*1*.1), so Zephaniah was a contemporary of Jeremiah. He saw the Scythian invasion of the Fertile Crescent as a sign of doom.

Chapter *1* is a judgment on Judah, chapter *2* on other nations. The book concludes with a forecast of a purified nation living the good life on Mount Zion. Zephaniah is known only from his book.

Not included in this list are:

Daniel, who was not a prophet. The book of Daniel is not a prophetic book despite its position in our Bibles.

Deborah, who is called a prophetess in Ju. *4.*4 but was really a judge.

Jonah, who was a prophet of fiction rather than fact. The purpose of the story of Jonah is to rebuke those who wish God's mercy to be confined to Israel. It is, therefore, probably post-exilic.

One or two others, like Azariah, Eldad, Hanani, Iddo, Jahaziel, Medad and Oded, are omitted, but they are of no importance.

i **Priests**

In many societies the gods are thought to be so powerful and dangerous that the ordinary man cannot have dealings with them without courting certain death. This leads to the creation of a group of people who, by function and status, are immune to the awful danger. They police the frontier between this world and the world of the gods.

Israel, with her notions of one all-holy, all-powerful God, needed a priesthood more rather than less than all her neighbours. There are plenty of cautionary stories in the OT to show what happens to amateurs and trespassers. Poor Uzzah was only trying to do his best. He steadied the Ark when the oxen slipped, but he was struck dead for his pains (2 Sam. *6.*6–8).

The immunity of the priest made him the ideal intermediary. He was able to speak to God for the people and to the people for God. His main function was to offer sacrifice and play a leading part in cultic festivals. More will be said of this in chapter 22. He also had the function of teaching the people the law. In later times the scribes took over this function, but several references show that the priests had the responsibility until the Exile (Dt. *33*. 10; Mic. *3*.11; Jer. *18*.18; Ez. *7*.26). There were two kinds of law in Israel, the down-to-earth, practical laws that regulated the life of the community, and the categorical imperatives which were based, not on common sense, but on the supposed absolute will of Yahweh. (See below 20h.) The magistrates and judges had charge of the former, the priests of the latter. Perhaps summaries of this categorical law were declaimed in the Temple service.

A third function of the priest was to handle the sacred lot, *Urim and Thummim*. These were two objects carried by the priest in a front pocket of the priestly mantle. They were used to give a simple yes or no answer to a question, much as one might now spin a coin. (See Ex. *28*.30; Dt. *33*.8; 1 Sam. *28*.6 and probably 1 Sam. *14*.41 f.)

j The organized priesthood in Israel is probably no older than the settlement. In the patriarchal narratives heads of families sacrificed and this appears still to have been the case in the period of the judges. Gideon offered sacrifice at God's command (Ju. *6*.25 f.), Manoah, Samson's father, did similarly (Ju. *13*.19 f.). Anyone could be set aside for priestly duties but a Levite was preferred (Ju. *17*). The official priesthood traced its lineage back to Aaron (Ex. *29*), who was, of course, a Levite. According to Dt. *18*.1 f. any Levite could discharge the functions of a priest, but, one effect of the holy war against baalism (see above 18e) was the closing down of all the syncretistic local shrines and the centralising of worship at Jerusalem (Dt. *12*). This meant widespread unemployment for Levites, which explains why Deuteronomy often appeals for charity to be shown to them (Dt. *12*.12 f., 18 f., *14*.27, 29, etc.).

In the P source of the Pentateuch (see below 21k) the priesthood is limited to Levites of the family of Aaron (Ex. *28*.1). They had to be physically whole (Lev. *21*.16–24). Levites not of the family of Aaron had only subsidiary functions. Ezekiel would have limited it still further to the descendants of David's priest Zadok (Ez. *40*.46, *43*.19), though this was never put into practice.

Because priesthood depended on birth, it was not charismatic as was prophecy. The priests' separation from the profane world was radical and permanent. Their consecration and their vestments are discussed in Ex. *29* and Lev. *8–9*. They had to be especially careful about ritual purity and about the choice of a wife (Lev. *21*) and they had to abstain from strong drink, at least when on duty (Lev. *10.9*).

There was probably no high priest before the Exile. The title does occur four times but, in every case, it was probably read back by a later editor. The head of the hierarchy was the king. Only after the Exile, when there was no king, did a high priest become necessary.

The post-exilic cult had a service of consecration for all Levites (Nu. *8*). Their function was to help the priests and be in charge of the mundane side of Temple life. They looked after the furniture (Nu. *3*.8) and kept things clean (1 Chr. *23*.28). They may also have been choristers (Ezra *3*.10; Neh. *12*.27; 1 Chr. *6*.31). There was also a group of servants called *Nethinim*. They had a no priestly function but performed the meanest tasks. They are mentioned only in 1 Chr. *9*.2 and in Ezra and Nehemiah.

k   The king

It may seem strange to some readers that the king should be included in a category of sacral figures with prophets and priests, but perhaps that is because we tend to forget the sacred origins of kingship. In Israel there was no division between the sacred and the secular, and the king, as head of the nation, was head in both senses. In this discussion it must be remembered that there was a king in Israel only from the time of David to the Exile. The Hasmonaean dynasty falls outside the OT period. That means that there was a king for a little over 400 years, though the period covered by the OT is more than 1,000 years.

That the king was an important religious figure cannot be disputed, but that, alas, is as far as unanimity goes. The function of the king is, at present, the subject of the most acute controversy. We shall look very briefly at some of the arguments in a moment, but first let us see the evidence for saying that the king was an important religious figure.

1. It was believed that the king was appointed by God. The stories of Saul and David in 1 Samuel make this clear, but it is no less true of Solomon and his successors. Indeed, Solomon had an elder brother, Adonijah, who was rejected, so he believed, by God (1 K. *2.15*).

2. Kings were anointed at the beginning of their reign. Samuel anointed Saul and David (1 Sam. *10.*1, *16.*13; see also 2 Sam. *2.*4, *5.*3; 1 K. *1.*32–48; 2 K. *11.*12). Anointing is a cultic ceremony in which a man is consecrated for a special sacral function. Elijah was told to anoint two kings and a prophet in 1 K. *19.*15 f. Priests were anointed according to the P source (Ex. *40.*12–5). In the case of Saul and David the anointing produced charismatic results.

3. As 'the Lord's Anointed' the king had a sacrosanct personality. David spared Saul's life for this reason (1 Sam. *24.*6–10, *26.*9–11) and he also slew the Amalekite soldier who had killed Saul, even though the man had acted at Saul's own request (2 Sam. *1.*14–6).

4. Because the safety and security of the people rested to a large extent on the vigour of the king, his health was a vital factor in the covenant between Yahweh and Israel. The king had a special place in the covenant (2 K. *11.*17). In the psalm in 2 Sam. *23* the anointing, the gift of the spirit, the king's safety, and the covenant are all tied together. When he grew old, David was not allowed to go to battle in order that 'the lamp of Israel' should not be quenched (2 Sam. *21.*17; see also Lam. *4.*20).

5. In the early monarchy, at least, the king supervised worship. The Temple was really a royal chapel. David, wearing the ephod (a priestly garment of some kind), escorted

248

the Ark up to Jerusalem (2 Sam. *6*) and, when the site of the Temple was chosen, David offered the first sacrifice (2 Sam *24*.25). Solomon presided at the consecration of the Temple (1 K. *8*).

6. The Psalter shows how important the king was. How many of the psalms relate to the king is a matter of controversy. The most important, *2* and *110*, are unfortunately not clear, but there can be little doubt about *21* or *45* or *72*. Most scholars recognize a category of royal psalms.

The controversy arises from the fact that the kings of neighbouring states had further functions in their cults. Scholars have been able to piece together the myths and rituals of these cults and have reached the conclusion that there are pronounced similarities between them, so much so that they claim to see the same pattern repeating itself all over the ancient near east. The great question is whether this pattern is to be seen in Israel as well.

At one extreme it might be said that the religion of Israel was a unique gift from God and that it owed nothing to Israel's neighbours at all. At the other it might be said that Israel's cult was simply part of the pattern. In between these two there is room for every kind of theory. There is no need to repeat what is said under the heading of the feast of Booths in 71 except to say that, if there was an 'enthronement festival' in Israel, it would be the king who played the central part. Even if there was not, the importance of the king in the Hebrew cult cannot be gainsaid.

Chapter 20

Literary Types in the OT

a IT is normal to think of the OT as a collection of *books*. Some books, like the prophets, form a group, but really each book has an identity of its own. Genesis is Genesis and Numbers is Numbers. If one is to study them, they must be studied as individual books.

In fact, this is not necessarily the best way to approach the literature of the OT, for two reasons. First, the books as we have them represent the end product of a long process, in some cases lasting centuries. Genesis did not begin as a book. It began as a mass of oral units that were slowly collected and linked together. Now, while the final edition of Genesis is naturally interesting, the best place to begin is with the original units. Secondly, the original units can be classified into different literary types, legends, laws, oracles, etc., and these types occur in many different books. Genesis has no monopoly of legends. To study the literary components of Genesis properly it is necessary to study those components as they occur all through the OT literature. So, in this chapter, we are not dealing with the books themselves but with the literary types that make them up. Study of the books will be more profitable after these types have been sorted out.

There is no finite and agreed list of literary types. It is possible simply to make broad distinctions, say between prose and poetry, or it is possible to make complex and technical distinctions that will produce scores of different categories. What follows is a list of a dozen or so types that are obviously distinct and easily recognized.

b **Myths**

The word 'myth' is a widely used technical term in the study of religion. It causes a lot of trouble because people do not realize that it is a technical term. In common parlance myth means a rumour or a tall story that some people continue to repeat but which, in fact, is not true. Politicians tend to accuse each other of repeating myths and they mean stories that are impressive but false and, therefore, dangerous. Obviously, to say that the Bible is full of myths in this sense is to be both offensive and inaccurate. We, however, are concerned with the technical meaning of myth.

Even so it is not simple. In the study of religion generally myths have four characteristics:

i.   though they have the form of stories, they represent an event that keeps recurring in the experience of men, for example, the cycle of the year, the appearance of spring flowers, and so on;

ii. the stories are staged outside time and space altogether, often in the world of the gods;

iii. the characters in them are divine and not human, despite the fact that they tend to behave in a very human way;

iv. the stories are dramatised or recited in worship at a shrine in the belief that acting out the myth will ensure that the recurring event will happen again.

This matter is discussed at greater length in the chapter on 'Yahweh and the Gods of Canaan'.

Myths of this kind are to be found all over the ancient near east and there can be no doubt that the ancient Hebrews were familiar with the myths of their neighbours, but no Hebrew myths of this kind appear in the OT. The reason is that Israel adopted a theology which made the kind of thinking outlined above impossible. It was a theology of the one Almighty God, Yahweh, who continually showed his hand in the course of history.

Though Israel developed an advanced theology of this kind, that theology still had to be set out in the style of ancient

251

Hebrew (see above 12a), so narrative, that is to say stories, remained the medium for expressing the nation's faith. Some of these stories originated in Israel, others were borrowed and adapted. When we speak of myths in the OT, therefore, we mean myths in yet another sense. We mean stories that may have had a mythological beginning but that have been transformed by the OT writers so that they now express Hebrew theology. Gn. *1–11* is full of such stories.

Myths in the OT are, thus, best described as the Hebrew faith in narrative form. The myths are true as the faith is true. Myths do not stand or fall according to whether they are true historically any more than the parables of Jesus do. Parables are not the same as myths, but they have a similar function in that they speak about God by telling stories.

We can summarize by pointing out three characteristics of myths in the OT:

i. they have the form of stories and they deal with the sovereign activity of Israel's God, Yahweh;

ii. they are concerned, not with fantastic happenings in an unseen world of the gods, but with Yahweh's dealings with his people;

iii. the stories were, without doubt, dramatized or recited in Hebrew worship but more to *celebrate* what God had done and would do than to ensure that this or that would happen.

Often one comes across the term *'aetiological myth'*. An aetiology, sometimes spelt 'etiology', is simply an explanation. The aetiological myth is one that is told to explain a phenomenon that cannot be explained in practical terms. Why does the sun rise? Why is the sea salt? Why does summer give way to winter? On a more serious level, the first of the two creation myths in Genesis (*1*.1–*2*.4a) provides an aetiology for the sabbath in *2*.2 f.

c **Legends**

The word 'legend' is also used in common parlance for an

unreliable story, and the statement that a large part of the OT is properly called 'legend' is liable to mislead. In technical discussion of the OT the word 'legend' is used for a narrative with the following features:

i. unlike the myth, the legend is grounded in this world, it concerns real people in a real, but distant, time and often in a known and named geographical location;

ii. the legend often has a historical core, though this is not the most important fact about it;

iii. the legend explains some feature of contemporary life, usually by recounting a story about its supposed origin; by extolling the virtues of heroic and godly men of the past, the legend affirms contemporary beliefs and values.

There is no universally accepted distinction between legend and saga in OT studies. Sometimes the words are used interchangeably. It is common, however, to use 'legend' for narratives that deal with sacred places or persons and 'saga' for stories that concern geographical areas or names or tribal matters.

Like myths, legends often have an aetiological function. Sanctuary legends explain why particular sites were considered sacred. For example, Bethel depended on the legend of Jacob's Ladder (Gn. *28*.10–22), and Gilgal on the story of Joshua's action in setting up memorial stones (Josh. *4*.20–4). Other cult legends explain the origin of particular rituals. There are no less than three legends relating to circumcision, Gn. *17* linking it with Abraham, Ex. *4*.24–6 linking it with Moses, and Jos. *5* linking it with Joshua.

Many of the narratives about the great religious figures such as Samuel, Elijah, and Elisha, might be considered here. Often historical elements, artistic exaggeration, positive interpretation, and moral and theological teaching are mixed together; see, for example, the legend of Elijah overcoming the prophets of Baal on Mount Carmel in 1 K. *18*.

d **Sagas**

If legends are properly understood, little more need be said

253

about sagas. The Sodom narrative in Gn. *19* is an aetiological saga explaining the saline rocks that surround the Dead Sea and the general barrenness of the area. The Dead Sea is part of the Great Rift Valley and a massive subsidence within folk memory is by no means impossible. This may provide a historical kernel for the Sodom narrative. The story of Cain and Abel in Gn. *4* has to do with tribal origins. The two figures are symbols of two different ways of life. Abel stands for the semi-nomadic herdsman and Cain for the settled farmer. Abel's offering was accepted, but not Cain's, which illustrates the Hebrews' ancient distrust of agricultural religion and the preservation of the nomadic ideal long after Israel herself was settled in Palestine. Similarly, Israel's relationship with the Ishmaelites is explained by the story of Abraham and his two wives in Gn *16* and the enmity with Edom is traced back to the quarrel between Jacob and Esau (see Gn. *36*.19). Other sagas tell stories of tribal heroes, Moses, the judges, David. Others provide explanations for place names.

e   **Other stories**

There are many other stories in the OT that do not fit into any of the categories named so far. Various attempts have been made to classify them using terms such as anecdotes, fables, fairy-tales, folk-tales and *Novellen*. This last is a German term meaning a fictional story. There are certainly some stories larger than life, but lacking the dignity of the legend. For example, the accounts of Samson's exploits in Ju. *15*.1–*16*.3 are exciting rather than edifying. Perhaps they are best called simply anecdotes. Of the true fable, that is a moral tale in which animals and plants are the chief actors, there is scarcely a sign in the OT. Jotham's fable in Ju. *9*.8–15 and Jehoash's message to Amaziah in 2 K. *14*.9 are the only possible exceptions. Most cultures preserve fairy-tales in which men and animals are mixed up, minor deities sometimes appear, and crises are resolved by magic, and it is remarkable that none find their way into the OT. There are magical elements in otherwise sober stories, such as Moses' miraculous rod (Ex. *4*) Elijah's mantle (2 K. *2*.8), and Elisha's remarkable powers, but these are no more than are to be expected in a pre-scientific culture. The fact is that Israel recorded no fairy-tales of its own and greatly modified any that it borrowed. However difficult the Elisha stories are, they are stories about a real man and their purpose is not amusement but serious proclamation.

f **Genealogies and lists**

The OT preserves various list of nations, cities and persons. The genealogies are most important. They are a witness to the deep sense of national unity in Israel. There is a census list in Nu. *1* and another in Nu. *26*. 1 Chr. *1–9* attempts to provide a complete genealogy of Israel from Adam to Saul. Ezra *2* has a list of those who returned from exile and Neh. *3* a list of those who helped to repair the wall. There are many other smaller lists.

g **Histories**

Much of the OT reads like history. Some of the material has already been discussed under the headings of legend and saga. About the time of the monarchy a new kind of writing emerged. It was the work of court scribes and it provided an official record of important events. There are allusions to such writing in 1 K. *11*.41 (the acts of Solomon) and 1 K. *14*.19 and 29 (the chronicles of the kings of Israel, or Judah). It is possible that the account of the building and consecration of the Temple in 1 K. *6–8* comes from one such record.

The difference between history, even of this elementary kind, and legend and saga is significant. History depends on sources that have some claim to reliability and on the ability to criticize and make use of them. That does not mean that history is free from didactic purpose, but that historical composition is a more technical and sophisticated form of writing than saga.

The earliest extended piece of history writing in the OT is the pssage known as 'the succession narrative' in 2 Sam. *9–20* and *1–2*. The author was probably an eye-witness, his interests were political rather than cultic, and his purpose was to validate Solomon's succession to the throne. That this is history and not legend is shown by the masterly true-to-life descriptions, the careful exposition of events in terms of cause and consequence, and the linking of separate incidents into an organic whole. The story of David's rise in 1 Sam. *16*.14–2 Sam. *5*.25 exhibits similar characteristics.

The casual reader of the Bible, however, will point out that there is much more history in the OT than this. Leaving aside the Pentateuch, the books of Joshua, Judges, Samuel and Kings appear to be historical throughout. There may have been sources but the final product is a continuous record beginning with Moses' death and ending only with the departure of the Hebrews into captivity in 586 BC. Moreover, there is a similar record in 1 and 2 Chronicles, beginning with David and ending, if Ezra and Nehemiah are added, with the community reinstated on Mount Zion and reformed in the fifth century BC. These two records are called the *Deuteronomic History* and the *Chronicler's History* respectively. They merit a chapter of their own (see below ch. 25). Here we simply note that the historical record is a very important literary category in the OT, though, like the myth and the legend, it needs to be understood in OT terms and not in terms of common, modern usage.

h **Laws**

Every society needs laws, partly to regulate its day to day affairs, partly to restrain wickedness and vice, partly to protect the weak, and partly to proclaim to the world at large the ideals and values, and, therefore, the true identity of the society. Israel had laws which fulfilled all these purposes.

In the first place there are many laws dealing with personal injuries, theft, damage to property, marriage rights, and so on. Many of these were borrowed from neighbours, especially the Canaanites. They are set out in the form of, 'if anyone does this, then he must do that, or he must be punished in such and such a way'. Examples are to be found throughout the Pentateuch (e.g. Ex. *21*; Dt. *15*.12–18, *22*.13–29). Law of this kind is built up on the basis of previous cases and it was administered in Israel by elders of the tribe sitting as magistrates in the open space just inside the gates of the cities, hence Amos' complaint about the absence of justice 'in the gate' (Amos 5.10–15). These laws are often described as *casuistic* since the work, published in 1934, of a German scholar called Albrecht Alt. Casuistic laws were gathered together in the major towns and so collections appear, of which the *Book of the Covenant* (Ex. 20.22–23.19) is the best known.

Alt, however, also recognized a different kind of law in the OT. These are laws of an absolute character referring to offences so awful that no fitting punishment could be conceived. They are set out in the form, 'Thou shalt not . . .' or, 'Cursed be he that . . .' Alt called these laws *apodeictic* and examples are to be found in Ex. 21.12, 15–17, Lev. 18.7–17, Dt. 27.15–26, and many other places. The distinction between casuistic law and apodeictic is a valuable one and is widely recognized, but Alt went further and suggested that apodeictic law was uniquely Israelite, that it was commonly expressed in short series of ten or twelve commands, that these series were recited by priests at the sanctuaries as a summary of Israel's duty under the covenant, and that the people gathered at the festivals to hear them and to renew their covenant pledge. All this is rather controversial, but there are good grounds for distinguishing between magistrates' (casuistic) law and priests' (apodeictic) law. Since death under a curse seems to be the only sentence for the apodeictic law-breaker, the sanctuary with its holy and supernatural associations is a more probable context for the proclamation of these categorical commands than the sober, calculating, almost secular, atmosphere of 'the gate'. The Decalogue (Ex. 20; Dt. 5) is in apodeictic form. There is much to be said for the suggestion that the Decalogue represented the badge or symbol of Israel and the heart and kernel of its law. In that case the sanctuary was the appropriate place for it.

There is a third kind of law in the OT, a rather technical kind dealing with priestly duties, sacrifice, clean and unclean, and so on. No doubt in early days these laws were very simple, but, by the time the OT was completed, they had evolved into several complex systems. There is priestly law in Deuteronomy (e.g. chs. *14–18*) and Ezekiel tried his hand at devising a new system for the time when the Exile was over (Ez. *40–8*), but Leviticus is pre-eminently the book of priestly law, especially chs. *17–26* which comprise the *Holiness Code.*

i **Secular songs**

There is little doubt that the Israelites loved to sing at harvests, at weddings, at work, and so on. Yet, though there are snatches of songs in several places in the OT, there are few perfect examples. The reason is to be found in the thoroughly religious intention of the compilers of the OT. Israel had a secular life, though it was a much smaller fraction of the whole than is the case today, but the compilers show little interest in it. And much of what was originally secular has been given a religious meaning or been preserved in a religious context. The 'Song of the Well' in Nu. *21*.17 f. was probably a working song, though it now appears as a religious song commemorating the fact that Yahweh gave the people a particular well when they were in need. The best example of this process is the Song of Songs which was originally a collection of love songs but which owes its place in the OT to the fact that it was interpreted as a symbolic account of Yahweh's relationship to his people.

One would expect to find battle songs and there are indeed one or two victory refrains, Miriam's song in Ex. *15*.21 and the Israelite women's song in 1 Sam. *18*.6 f. Perhaps Jos. *10*.12 f. refers to another. The Song of Moses in Ex. *15* and the Song of Deborah in Ju. *5* are more formal compositions and suggest official, probably cultic, celebrations. There are two laments or dirges, the brief one for Abner in 2 Sam. *3*.33 f, and the longer and most moving one for Jonathan in 2 Sam. *1*.19–27. But the best examples of songs are to be found in the Psalter where they have been adapted to a religious function. Ps. *45* is a possible exception. This song for a royal wedding seems to have escaped the process of adaptation.

j Cult songs

Elements of songs taken from a cultic setting are to be found here and there in the prophetic books (Jer. *14.7–9, 14.*19–22), but the Psalter provides an abundance of incomparable material. There are hymns of praise to be sung at festivals (Pss. *145–50*). There are individual thanksgivings to be sung on occasions of personal deliverance (Pss. *30, 92, 116, 118, 138*), which often begin with an account of the worshipper's previous state and conclude with thanks to Yahweh who has restored him. There are communal laments for occasions of famine or defeat (Pss. *44, 74, 79, 80, 83*). Here the usual pattern includes a recital of past mercies and calls for a further demonstration of Yahweh's power. The most common type in the Psalter is the individual lament (Pss. *3, 5, 6, 7*, etc.) which begins with a description of the affliction, sometimes includes the claim that it was not deserved, and continues with a plea for deliverance often including the destruction of personal enemies. In some (Pss. *6, 31, 54, 71*) the mood changes in the middle from despair to fulfilment. This has led some people to wonder whether some cultic action took place between the first half and the second to give the worshipper the conviction that all was now well.

These are the four major groups in the Psalter, but there are other ways of grouping psalms, some of which cut right across the one given above. There is a large number of royal psalms linked with various occasions in the king's life, coronation, marriage, battle, etc. (Pss. *2, 18, 20, 21, 45, 101, 110, 132*). There are the Songs of Zion (Pss. *46, 48, 76, 87*) and the Songs of Pilgrimage (Pss. *84, 122*). And there is that most controversial of all categories, the Enthronement Psalms (Pss. *47, 93, 96–9*), which are said by some scholars to relate to Yahweh's enthronement, not the king's, and to belong to an annual festival at which some rite of death and resurrection was worked through. See the chapter on 'Yahweh and the Gods of Canaan'.

k Prophetic oracles

Unlike most of the material we have considered so far,

prophetic oracles begin on the lips of a single person, perhaps even a known person. None the less, the prophetic books cannot be seen as long recitals by the prophets whose names the books bear. Most oracles are relatively short and few were written down at the time of their first utterance. They were remembered and passed on and collected by disciples. Then the collections were edited into books. The book of Amos provides some of the best examples of the short, direct oracles of which the prophetic books are made.

l **Apocalyptic visions**

Apocalyptic is sometimes regarded as the successor to prophecy. The word means 'revelation'. Strictly speaking Dan. *7–12* and Zech. *9–14* are the only apocalypses in the Ot, but Joel *2*, Is. *24–7* and Ezek. *38–9* come very close to the genre. Apocalyptic was written rather than uttered. It claimed to recount the details of a vision invariably concerned with approaching catastrophe and the end of the world. Its purpose was to encourage the faithful in times of acute suffering and it does so by speaking in lurid terms of the destruction of the wicked and the salvation of the righteous. Unlike the prophets, the apocalyptists see no hope for this world and they expect God to work his salvation by destroying this world and creating a new age and a new earth. Their writing is full of weird symbols and obscure imagery, perhaps to confuse contemporary persecutors. Apocalyptic proper belongs to the years 200 BC to AD 100, though it had its roots in certain kinds of prophecy. Few apocalyptists reveal their identity. They prefer to write pseudonymously.

m **Proverbs**

All cultures manufacture wise sayings, epigrams, riddles and the like. Israel was no exception. There is a well-known riddle in Ju. *14*.14 that Samson devised and then revealed to his wife. But more important are the sayings that express profound human wisdom in a terse, colourful and rhythmic way. 'Let not him that girdeth on his armour boast himself as he that putteth it off' (1 K. *20*.11) has lost none of its meaning over the years. In ancient cultures there appear to have been specialists who devised and collected such wise sayings, and it may well be that Solomon's reputation for wisdom rests on the encouragement that he gave to such people. The book of Proverbs is the result of this industry together with Ecclesiasticus, the Wisdom of Solomon, Job, and certain psalms.

This list by no means exhausts the categories. One could go on to speak of blessings and curses, oaths, and so on, but we have said enough to show the kind of bricks out of which the OT books were made. Sometimes the bricks fit tidily together. The Psalter, for example, consists almost exclusively of cultic songs. Other books, however, are made of many different kinds of bricks and their construction was elaborate and slow. The essential point to remember is that *every completed book represents a process*. No one ever sat down and wrote an OT book. On the contrary, the books grew. In this chapter we have tried to begin at the beginning and see what the elements were like in their earliest stage.

Chapter 21

The Pentateuch

a THE word 'Pentateuch' comes from two Greek words and simply means 'five volumes'. After the Exile all five books were attributed to Moses. This tradition passed into Christianity and remains in the headings of AV and RV. In Judaism these books constitute the Torah, a word that is hard to translate but which includes the ideas of legal ordinance, practical instruction, and fatherly counsel. For Judaism, the Torah represents the complete guide to belief and conduct, whether civil or religious, individual or social. A great gulf separates the books of the Torah from the other books of the Bible, holy as those books may be.

A modern reader may find this exaltation of the Torah, or the Pentateuch as non-Jews prefer to call it, difficult. It is not simply law or instruction. It is full of myths, legends, battle songs, and so on, and it is hard to see how it is essentially different from the rest of the OT. Literary study of the next book, Joshua, does not suggest that Joshua is on a lower level altogether. This has led some scholars to give up the Pentateuch as a unit of study and talk about the *Hexateuch*, or the first six books. Others point out that Deuteronomy is quite different from the other four, so they leave out Deuteronomy and talk about the *Tetrateuch*.

Moreover the Mosaic authorship is impossible to accept. This was a great issue in biblical studies a century ago. For doubting it William Robertson Smith was removed from his chair in the Free Church College, Aberdeen, in 1881. Even more famous was John William Colenso, bishop of Natal, who was deposed in 1863 for the same reason. Today this seems very wrong. Mosaic authorship was doubted by Carlstadt as long ago as the sixteenth century. And, if there is any such thing as unanimity among modern biblical scholars, it is to be found here. Moses could not have written five books that are so diverse in style and content and background and that refer to facts that took place long after his death.

Let us look briefly at the contents of the five books.

b **Genesis**

The name means 'beginning' or 'birth'.

1–11 deal with the primaeval world—the Creation, the Fall, Cain and Abel, Noah, the Tower of Babel—and some genealogies.

12–50 deal with the patriarchs, the legendary fathers of Israel, Abraham in *12–25*, Isaac in *26–8* and Jacob and his twelve sons in *29–50*. The book ends with Joseph's death in Egypt.

c **Exodus**

The name means 'departure'.

1–19 deal with Israel in Egypt, the plagues, the Passover, crossing the Red Sea, the wilderness wanderings and the arrival at Sinai.

20–3 provide social laws, including the Decalogue (*20*.1–17) and the Book of the Covenant (*20*.22–*23*.19).

24–31 deal with matters of priestly ceremonial—Ark, priesthood, sacrifice, Tabernacle. These things look very odd amidst the simplicities of desert life. See, for example, the description of the Ark in Ex. *25*.10–22 (see also Ex. *37*.1–9).

32–40 give the story of the golden calf, another Decalogue different from Ex. *20*, and an account of the work of Bezalel, the craftsman.

d **Leviticus**

The name is derived from Levi who was regarded as the father

263

of the Hebrew priesthood. The whole book is concerned with priestly legislation.

1–7 give instructions relating to the various kinds of sacrifice.

8–10 describe the consecration and induction of priests.

11–15 give laws of ritual cleanliness.

16 describes the Day of Atonement.

17–26 is the Holiness Code (called H) dealing with sacrifice, social legislation and calendars.

27 deals with priestly dues.

e **Numbers**

The name derives from the repeated lists and genealogies contained in it.

*1.1–10.*10 is priestly legislation.

*10.*11–*20.*13 is the continuation of the story of the wilderness wanderings and includes some passages of legislation.

*20.*14–*36.*13 deals with the struggles of the Hebrews on the east of Jordan.

f **Deuteronomy**

The name seems to suggest a second law (*deuteros* means 'second' in Greek), but actually it means 'a copy of the law' (see Dt. *17.*18).

1–4 survey events from Horeb to Jordan.

5–11 contain exhortations to worship Yahweh alone. There is another version of the Decalogue in Dt. *5.*6–21 and the *Shema*, a famous Jewish prayer, is found in *6.* 4–9.

12–28 contains a complete system of laws for Israel in her new home. The Deuteronomic Law is characterized by the following features:

    a. firm belief in the election of Israel,

    b. firm belief that there must be one sanctuary only in Israel at 'the place which the Lord your God shall choose' (Dt. *12*),

    c. firm belief in a law of justice and rewards and punishments working in history,

d. strong advocacy of humanitarian attitudes in social relationships.

29–30 contain an exhortation to observe the covenant.

31 deals with the appointment of Joshua.

32 is the *Song of Moses* and is an explanation of Yahweh's actions.

33 is the *Blessing of Moses* in which he blesses the children of Israel before his death.

The literary form of Deuteronomy is seven addresses given by Moses to Israel during the last forty days of his life. Dt. *34* is a conclusion recounting the death and burial of Moses.

g   Modern study of the Pentateuch begins by noting the evidence of diversity within it.

1. In Genesis God is sometimes called Yahweh and sometimes Elohim. Certain passages seem to belong to each. This suggests two different sources coming from two different localities, one of which used Yahweh and the other Elohim. Ex. *3*.14 and *6*.3 seem to explain how the name Yahweh first appeared, but Gn. *4*.26 traces the name back to the second generation from Adam. (Note, too, what is said about the Ebla tablets in 11c.)

2. Not only God has two names. Leviticus and Numbers talk about Sinai, Deuteronomy about Horeb. Moses' father-in-law usually occurs as Jethro, but sometimes as Reuel. The inhabitants of Canaan are sometimes Canaanites, sometimes Amorites. Two Joseph stories seem to be amalgated, for he is sold to both Ishmaelites and Midianites in Gn. *36*.27 f, 36.

3. There are different accounts of important matters. In Gn. *1*.1–*2*.3 man is created by Elohim, both sexes at the same time, on the sixth day as the climax of creation. In Gn. *2*.4–25 a single man is formed by Yahweh out of the dust, livestock follow and woman after livestock. In Dt. *10*.1–5 the Ark is a simple box to keep the tablets of the law in. Ex. *25*.10–22 and *37*.1–9 speak of an elaborate construction with gold plate, rings, and cherubim. In the story of Noah, one pair of each

kind appear in Gn. 6.19, but seven pairs of clean and one pair of unclean appear in 7.2.

There is an immense amount of material of this kind and the only explanation seems to be that the Pentateuch is an amalgamation of different sources. For the moment it does not matter whether the sources were oral or written documents; we have to think of separate sources slowly brought together as the years went by and not united into the present five books until the Exile at the earliest.

Modern study of this problem goes back to Julius Wellhausen, who flourished just over 100 years ago. What he suggested seemed radical at the time. It was a reversal of the supposed order of things in the OT. The previous belief was that Moses was responsible for the law and that the prophets based their message on it. Wellhausen suggested that, in the days of the prophets, the law was still being worked out in different ways in different places. The prophets were original thinkers and the final edition of the law rested on their teaching. Wellhausen has been proved wrong on many things, but his basic theory about sources in the Pentateuch has survived, and it is impossible to study the Pentateuch today without taking it seriously.

The starting-point of the argument is Ex. 6.2–8. Whoever wrote that believed that the name Yahweh was first revealed to Moses just before the Exodus. Before that God was known as Elohim. On the other hand there was another source that knew nothing of Ex. 6 and innocently used the name Yahweh all through Genesis (Gn. 4.26). So we begin with two sources.

Then it appears that the source that used Elohim was not homogeneous. Parts of it were engagingly simple, other parts were ornate, stylized and full of priestly intricacies. So the Elohim source can be divided into a simple Elohim and a priestly Elohim.

Once the three sources are separated their distinctive features can be noted, and once their distinctive features are noted they can be traced through the rest of Pentateuch after Ex. 6.

There is one further complication. Deuteronomy does not

fit into this picture at all. It operates by rules of its own, so it is best to regard Deuteronomy as a special source.

The argument of these last four paragraphs leads to the supposition that there were four main sources for the Pentateuch and they have been given the symbols J, E, D, and P.

h **J**

This is the source that uses the name Yahweh from the beginning. It is called J from Yahweh, J and Y being the same letter in Hebrew. J also speaks of Sinai and Canaanites. Its style is simple and vigorous. It is full of anthropomorphisms, that is to say, it speaks of God in human terms (see Gn. *3*.8, *7*.16, *8*.21, *11*.5). It covers the Creation, Eden, the Fall, Cain and Abel, Noah, Babel, the patriarchs, the Exodus and Moses. It appears to be interested in the southern towns of Israel, Ai, Sodom and Gomorrah, Beersheba, Hebron, etc.

J in its earliest form suggests folk-lore, but to treat it as folk-lore is to miss the point completely. The raw material of folk-lore has been skilfully edited into a homogeneous document that proclaims a positive faith. The story deals with Creation, man's sin, God's judgment and, over all, God's faithfulness. God's faithfulness is shown in his loyalty to the promises made to the patriarchs, despite the fractiousness of Israel and the attempts of Israel's enemies to destroy her.

J was probably compiled in the southern kingdom. It is difficult to determine the date, but some time in the century after David's reign is most likely.

i **E**

This is the more straightforward Elohist source. It speaks of Horeb and Amorites. It is also simple and vigorous, though perhaps not so lively as J. It is mainly interested in northern towns, e.g. Dothan and Shechem. It appears that E is not as well preserved as J, because, as far as we can see, it begins only in Gn. *15*. One suggestion is that E is a northern source parallel to J with its own account of the creation, but that, after the fall of the northern kingdom, a southern editor combined the two and left out the E version whenever it suited him to do so.

E also has a theological viewpoint. Its doctrine of God is a little more sophisticated than that of J. There are less anthropomorphisms. God reveals himself through dreams and visions and angels.

Again it is not easy to be precise about date. Some time before the fall of Samaria in 721 BC and yet after the composition of J seems to be indicated. The best guess is around the year 800.

j **D**

D is not folk-lore. It is an independent literary work with its own distinctive style and ideology. It stresses Israel's position as the chosen nation and the demand for faithfulness, obedience and true worship that goes with that privilege. It shows implacable hostility to Canaanites and their cult. It argues that Yahweh shows his graciousness in history by rewarding the faithful and punishing the disobedient. It has a strong humanitarian streak in its social legislation.

D is later than E because it revises some of E's provisions. In Ex. *21*.1 f. a Hebrew slave can go free after seven years, but in Dt. *15*.12–14 he must go free and be liberally provided for. But the question of dating may be answered by the story of the discovery of a law book in the Temple in 2 K. *22*. Immediately after discovering it, Josiah began a reform which followed strictly deuteronomic lines. This leads to the conclusion that the book was, in fact, Deuteronomy, and that it had been written in the dark days of Manasseh's reign and hidden in the Temple for safe keeping. In this case D is a seventh-century book that emerged in 621 BC.

k **P**

This is the more ornate source that used the name Elohim in Genesis. It makes use of incidents that also appear in J and E, but it uses them for its own special purpose, that is, to give a sound, traditional basis for institutions such as the sabbath, the food laws, circumcision, sacrifice, and the priestly affairs, in which the editor was so deeply interested. P was the last of the four sources to be written, probably about the time of Ezra and Nehemiah. According to Neh. 8, Ezra brought a book with him when he came to Jerusalem. If we compare Nehemiah's story with the teaching of the P source, it appears that Ezra may well have brought P, or even the whole of the Pentateuch, with him. It is quite impossible to be certain, but this is as good a guess as it is possible to make.

The process of compilation of these four probably went something like this. J and E were originally separate sources. After 721 BC J and E were combined by an editor who gave preference to J. D was written in the seventh century by someone who was familiar with J and E, either as separate documents or combined. J, E and D were brought together during the Exile. P was written after the Exile and, when all four were brought together, P was the foundation document. This theory is all based on Wellhausen and, in general, it has survived well. Attacks on it have, however, been made, and they come from four directions.

1. There are some who still argue for the unity of the Pentateuch and even the Mosaic authorship. The great majority of scholars, however, believe that such a case cannot be maintained.

2. Some are not happy with a date for Deuteronomy in the seventh century. Some want to make it later, some earlier. In either case it upsets the pattern set out above.

3. Some scholars have examined the four sources and decided that they are not all homogeneous. So we hear of J1, J2, Pa, Pb and other hypothetical sources given the symbols, L, K and S. This is the most serious problem for the Wellhausen hypothesis. It seems necessary to conclude that the four source theory is oversimplified and that many sources, most of which were oral, are now brought together in the Pentateuch.

269

4. Some scholars have tried to put even more stress in oral tradition and have maintained that the four sources posited never existed as complete entities at all.

Two further points need to be made in this complex and difficult study. One is that the formation of the Pentateuch was not simply a literary undertaking. If we think of ancient scholars sitting at desks, we are surely wrong. The traditions were preserved by the people as expressions of their faith, which probably means they were preserved in the cult. These stories and laws were recited and acclaimed in public worship, not cut up and copied out in some private workroom. Secondly, there is no doubt that our Pentateuch is not quite the same as the cultic Pentateuch. The material has been brought out of its original context in worship and written up as a literary document. That document is now the cornerstone of Judaism.

Chapter 22

The Former Prophets

a THE Former Prophets is the name given in the Hebrew Bible to Joshua, Judges, 1 and 2 Samuel and 1 and 2 Kings (see above 20g). A more common name in works of scholarship is the Deuteronomic History, that is to say, a history informed by deuteronomic standards. It is generally agreed that in their present form these books represent one complete work with a consistent aim and point of view.

To discover what that point of view was it is best to turn to the book of Judges and especially *2.6–3.6*. Here the history of Israel is reduced to a simple pattern. It is as follows:

A. The Israelites deserted Yahweh for Baal and Ashtaroth (= Anath).

B. Yahweh punished them by delivering them into the hands of an oppressor.

C. When the punishment was complete or when the people were penitent, Yahweh sent a judge to deliver them and they enjoyed prosperity once more.

D. After the judge's death they fell back into baalism and the cycle began again.

So history is used to expound the Deuteronomic theology, which was discussed in the last chapter; it is a theology that centres on the covenant and maintains that obedience and disobedience are fairly rewarded and punished in the course of human affairs.

It is not easy to find any pattern in history, least of all one as simple as this. We may well think that a strict account of Hebrew history would not substantiate the pattern. But that is not the point. The deuteronomic writers were quite sure of their beliefs about God. Untimely events did not sway them from their beliefs. Their problem was to use a historical narrative as a medium for proclaiming that faith. They solved it by adjusting the proportions of their history so that godly figures who prospered were given plenty of space, whereas ungodly figures who appeared to succeed were passed over in a few verses. Two of the greatest kings of the northern kingdom were Omri and Jeroboam II. Omri's reign merits eight verses (1 K. *16*.23–7) and Jeroboam's seven (2 K. *14*.23–9), whereas much of 1 Samuel and the whole of 2 Samuel are devoted to David. From time to time in the text speeches are introduced to make the deuteronomic point (Jos. *24*, 1 Sam. *12*, 1 K. *8*) and other formulae are used such as Ju. *3*.7 f and 2 K. *18*.12. Kings are classified in terms of whether they did what was right in the eyes of the Lord or what was evil.

b   The contents of the books of the Former Prophets are as follows.

Joshua

1–12 report the conquest of the territory west of Jordan.

13–21 give an account of the distribution of the land among the tribes.

22–24 describe the last days of Joshua including two farewell addresses.

Judges

1.1–*2*.5 give a different account of the conquest from Joshua. There is no overall conquest. Battles are local and advances limited.

2.6–*3*.6 give an outline of the deuteronomic view of history.

3.7–*16*.31 describe the exploits of the judges, major and minor (see above 10d).

17–18 tell a story about the foundation of the sancturay at Dan.

272

19–21 tell of an outrage committed by men of Benjamin and the way in which it was punished.

1 Samuel

1–7 deal with the story of Samuel and the distress brought on Israel by the Philistines.
8–12 recount Samuel's dealings with Saul.
13–15 recall Saul's exploits as king.
16–31 tell the story of Saul and David as rivals concluding with Saul's death on Mount Gilboa.

2 Samuel

1–8 tell of the beginnings of David's reign, the capture of Jerusalem and the removal of the Ark to Jerusalem.
9–20 are part of the 'Court History'. They recount happenings at court especially the attempts to overthrow David. David's adultery with Bathsheba is included here.
21–24 provide a number of appended notes to the reign of David.

1 Kings

1–2 are also part of the Court History.
3–11 recount the events of Solomon's reign.
12–22 recount the affairs of the divided kingdom, dealing alternatively with Israel and Judah. 1 Kings ends with the death of Ahab in the north and the death of Jehoshaphat in the south, about 850 BC. Stories about Elijah are included in *17–19* and *21*.

2 Kings

1–9 describe the death of Elijah and recount the stories of Elisha.
10–17 continue the story of the divided kingdom down to the fall of Samaria.
18–25 tell the story of Judah up to the fall of Jerusalem in 587 BC and the departure of the Jews into exile.

Chapter 23

The Latter Prophets

a   THE Latter Prophets of the Hebrew Bible consist of four large
volumes that suggest four scrolls of roughly the same length.
They are Isaiah, Jeremiah, Ezekiel and the Twelve. The
Twelve are, broadly speaking, the minor prophets and we
now think of them as individual books. The fact that they
were once gathered together into a single book leads one to
wonder whether any of the other three is a collection of
different but unnamed prophets. The indications are that this
is, in fact, true of Isaiah. Note that the latter prophets do not
include Lamentations, which in our Bibles, follows Jeremiah,
nor Daniel, which is not a prophetic book at all. Both these
are discussed in the next section. The latter prophets do
include Jonah. In the list of heroes in Eccleciasticus, Isaiah,
Jeremiah, Ezekiel and the Twelve are all mentioned
(*48.22–49*.12). Jeremiah is mentioned again in Dan. 9.2.
This suggests that the prophets were hallowed as a collection
by about 200 BC.

The prophetic books belong to the years 750–350 BC or
thereabouts, which means that the early books are much
older than what we call classical literature. When Amos
prophesied, Rome was not yet founded and the great period
of Greece lay 250 years in the future. Almost certainly the
prophets themselves wrote nothing, though Jer. *36* contains
an obvious exception. The writing was done by others after
them, and their work was preserved in much the same way as
the legends and sagas and laws that had existed before them.
No doubt the editing involved modification and addition, but
we must beware of being misled by bogus arguments about

274

'genuineness'. In the last century scholars were wont to elimi-nate from a book everything that they considered could not have been written by the named author on the grounds that it was not 'genuine'. Only what was left was regarded as significant. This is absurd. The 'other material' is not neces-sarily inferior because its author is unnamed. Once again we must learn to see the books of the Bible as the product of a long literary process. The suggestion that only the first stage in the process was important and that the work of all the other devout men and women involved in the transmission must be set on one side as not genuine does not bear much scrutiny.

b   The prophetic books are made up of three types of material.

A. Oracles in the form of Hebrew poetry. (This does not mean oracles in rhyme, but rather oracles in rhythm.) These make up the largest part of the prophetic books. The oracles are usually short, dateless, and they rarely mention circumstances. This is unfortunate because they are usually addressed to a precise set of circumstances. Oracles often begin with, 'Thus saith the Lord'. The prophet never thought that he was giving his own opinion.

B. Biography in the form of prose. Most prophetic books have stories about the prophet as well as oracles pro-nounced by him. There are large tracts of such prose in Jeremiah, usually attributed to Baruch. (See, for example, chs. *36–45*.)

C. Autobiography in verse or prose form. This is quite differ-ent from the previous type. It is more like prophecy than narrative. Prophetic calls come in this category. (See Jer. *1*.1–14, *13*.1–14.)

We must now glance briefly at the books in turn. More time is given to Isaiah because it presents a special and important problem, though similar critical studies can and should be carried out on all the prophetic books.

c **Isaiah**

It seems certain that not all sixty-six chapters of the book can be fitted into the eighth-century background of Isaiah, son of Amoz (see above 19h). After ch. *40* the name of Isaiah does not occur at all (it occurs sixteen times in *1–39*), Jerusalem is in ruins, Israel is in exile and Cyrus is named as a contemporary figure (*44.28, 45.1*). At *40.1* there is also a change in style that can be detected even in the English translation. *1–39* are concise and restrained. After *40* the style becomes verbose and rhetorical, rich in imagery but not always clear. There are also changes in teaching. In *1–39* foreign deities are despised, but after *40* their very existence as real beings is denied and they are openly mocked. In *1–39* the prophet expects that Zion will be secure because of Yahweh's control of history. After *40* the scale is more vast. God is the universal creator and redeemer.

There are, of course, similarities between *1–39* and *40–66*, but it is common nowadays to conclude that *1–39* belong substantially to the son of Amoz and *40–55* to an unknown prophet writing towards the end of the Exile when Cyrus was already on the march. For various reasons *56–66* are dated even later.

The unknown prophet is referred to as Second Isaiah or Deutero-Isaiah. His work is well known and much loved. It contains the famous *servant passages, 42.1–4, 49.1–6, 50.4–9*, and *52.13–53.12*.

d **Jeremiah**

The first twenty-five chapters of the book deal with oracles against Judah, often expressed with much pain as Jeremiah knew himself to be one with the nation whose doom he was proclaiming. *26–35* are more hopeful and speak of a future salvation (see especially the New Covenant in ch. *31*). *36–45* tell the story of Jeremiah's sufferings. *46–51* contain oracles against other nations.

e **Ezekiel**

Much of his prophecy concerns the period before 587 BC

276

when Jerusalem finally fell. Ezekiel was a strange man. One has only to read the first chapter to see how strange his imagery is. His call in *2.1–3.3* is typically bizarre. Chapters *1–24* concern Judah and Jerusalem, *25–32* concern neighbouring nations, *33–39* contain promises of restoration and *40–48* give an account of the new Temple as it appeared to Ezekiel in a vision.

f **The Twelve**

These appear as the last twelve books in the English Bible: Hosea, Joel, Amos, Obadiah, Jonah, Micah, Nahum, Habakkuk, Zephaniah, Haggai, Zechariah and Malachi. For all these see the notes in 19h. Note that Daniel is not included in the Twelve. Jonah is, even though the book is a story about a prophet and not a series of prophetic oracles.

277

Chapter 24

The Writings

a ANOTHER name for the Writings is Hagiographa or 'holy writings'. They are a separate section in the Hebrew Bible, but they are scattered about in the English OT. They comprise three works of poetry, Job, Psalms and Proverbs, the 'Five Scrolls' of Jewish tradition (Esther, Song of Songs, Ruth, Lamentations and Ecclesiastes), Daniel, 1 and 2 Chronicles, and Ezra and Nehemiah. We will note them in the order in which they appear in English Bibles.

b **Ruth**

This is a story that is said to have happened during the period of the judges. That is why it follows Judges. This is an awkward position as it is now inserted into the middle of the Deuteronomic History. Date and authorship are unknown. It is an edifying story of faithfulness and duty. The fact that it suggests that David had a Moabitish ancestor (4.17) does not explain the book, as some have thought. This detail may be an afterthought.

c **1 and 2 Chronicles, Ezra and Nehemiah**

It is best to take these together because they are all part of the same work. 1 Chr. *1–9* are genealogies tracing Israel's family tree from Adam to Saul. 1 Chr. *10–29* deal with David's reign. 2 Chr. *1–9* deal with Solomon and *10–36* take the story on to the end of the Exile. Ezra and Nehemiah continue the history to their own day.

It is obvious that comparison between the Chronicler's History and the Deuteronomic History is easy because they cover much of the same ground. Indeed the Chronicler must have made use of the Deuteronomic History. The Chronicler had completely different aims and methods. There are additions, subtractions and alterations, not because fresh information had become available but because the Chronicler had different interests. The Chronicler used his history to magnify the Torah in the eyes of his generation and to enhance priestly institutions by giving them ancient origins. In the four books of Samuel and Kings there are three references to Levites. In the two books of Chronicles there are nearly 100 and nearly as many again in Ezra-Nehemiah. 1 Chr. *22–9* deal with the organization of the Temple and have no parallel in the Deuteronomic History.

Ezra *1–6* recount the events of the period 538–520 BC, concluding with the dedication of the rebuilt Temple. Ezra *7–10* deal with the work of Ezra himself as a religious reformer. The continuation of this story is in Neh. *8–10*. Neh. *1–7* and *11–13* tell Nehemiah's story of the building of the wall and his reforms. Which of these two comes first is one of the great historical puzzles of the OT. Most modern historians provide the evidence and vote for one solution or other. See above 10j.

d **Esther**

This story is a festival legend that provides the basis of the Jewish feast of Purim. It is a story of persecution and revenge. God is never mentioned. One can see the appeal of the story to more chauvinistic Jews, but it has little to say to Christians.

e **Job**

The basis of this great book is a dialogue between Job and his three friends, Eliphaz, Bildad and Zophar. The subject is not simply Job's calamities but the human tragedy in general. The dialogue is set out in three cycles beginning and ending with a speech of Job.

Chapters *32–7* recount the speeches of one Elihu who is not part of the discussion but rather passes comment on the whole problem. Many scholars take the view that the Elihu speeches were a later addition. In chapters *38–41* Yahweh himself intervenes and the majesty of these speeches is without parallel in the OT. The dialogue with its great climax has been set within the framework of an older prose narrative of a rich and godly sheikh who suffered a series of misfortunes.

No book in the OT has a higher place in the world's literature than Job.

f **Psalms**

There are various ways in which the psalms can be studied. In 15h we discussed Gunkel's form critical approach. The Psalms can also be divided into different collections, Yahwist psalms, Elohistic psalms, and so on. The titles provide an interesting study, and much labour has been spent on seeking dates and occasions for individual psalms. The modern trend is to see the psalms in a cultic setting, that is to understand them, not as great individual prayers, but as liturgies used again and again in the worship of the Temple. At one time it was common to give a late date to most of the psalms, but now, though the dating of individual psalms is rarely possible, there is a tendency to tie them in with the pre-exilic festivals.

A word of warning is necessary about psalms and festivals. Huge controversies rage over this subject. Some very novel theses have been put forward. The student is well advised to check one book against another before reaching any conclusions of his own.

g **Proverbs**

This book is attributed to Solomon, but it is hard to believe that any one man was responsible. Proverbs is the product of centuries of profound thought about the human condition. It is an anthology of wise sayings both Israelite and non-Israelite.

The book is made up of a number of different collections as is seen by the headings in *1*.1, *10*.1, *24*.23, *25*.1, *30*.1, and *31*.1. The section *22*.17–*24*.22 contains thirty sayings which are closely parallelled by the Thirty Sayings of Amenemopet, an Egyptian document.

The Wisdom literature, which in the OT means Proverbs, Job, Ecclesiastes and some psalms, is the most international strand in the OT. There is little reference to the facts of Israel's history, so often celebrated by the prophets, and much discussion of universal human experience. Wisdom literature also propounds its own way of salvation. There is little reliance on divine intervention and much concentration on learning the sound and wise way to live in God's world.

h **Ecclesiastes**

This is the work of a pessimist. 'Vanity of vanities, says the preacher; all is vanity.' The work is ascribed to Solomon in *1*.1, but it was probably one of the last books of the OT to be written. The book falls into two halves, *1–6* and *7–12*, but there is no difference in the philosophy that lies behind them. Both are concerned with the futility of human endeavour. It is not surprising that no NT writer quotes from Ecclesiastes.

i **Songs of Songs**

Also called the Song of Solomon. It is a collection of love songs that owes its place in the OT to allegorical interpretation.

j **Lamentations**

The book comes from Jeremiah's time and its theme fits the appalling situation, but there are no real grounds for attributing it to Jeremiah. The LXX moved the book to where it now is and gave it the title 'Lamentations of Jeremiah'. There is no such implication in the Hebrew. There are five lamentations portraying national rather than individual sorrow.

281

k Daniel

This book falls into two halves. Chapters *1–6* consist of stories about the period of Israelite captivity in Babylon. The heroes are Daniel and the three brave men, Shadrach, Meshach and Abednego. Chapters *7–12* describe four apocalyptic visions.

It is widely believed that Daniel was the last OT book to be written and that its date was 165 BC. The stories may be older. It is sometimes contended that the book is an exilic prophecy by Daniel himself, but the historical detail concealed in the vision of chapter *11* is decisive in favour of a date soon after these events occurred, that is, after the accession of the archpersecutor Antiochus IV Epiphanes.

Chapter 25

Deuteronomic History and the Chronicler's History Compared

a   As always, it is best to look at a particular instance, and we have chosen the account of David bringing the Ark up from the house of Obed-edom to Jerusalem, 2 Sam. *6*.12–23 and 1 Chr. *15.1–16*.6.

Deuteronomic History

2 Sam. 6

Chronicler's History

1 Chr. 15

15 David built houses for himself in the city of David; and he prepared a place for the ark of God, and pitched a tent for it. ² Then David said, 'No one but the Levites may carry the ark of God, for the LORD chose them to carry the ark of the LORD and to minister to him for ever.' ³ And David assembled all Israel at Jerusalem, to bring up the ark of the LORD to its place, which he had prepared for it. ⁴ And David gathered together the sons of Aaron and the Levites;

⁵ of the sons of Kohath, Uri'el the chief, with a hundred and twenty of his brethren; ⁶ of the sons of Merar'i, Asa'iah the chief, with two hundred and twenty of his brethren; ⁷ of the sons of Gershom, Jo'el the chief, with a hundred and thirty of his brethren; ⁸ of the sons of Eliza'phan, Shemai'ah the chief, with two hundred of his brethren: ⁹ of the sons of Hebron, Eli'el the chief, with eighty of his brethren; ¹⁰ of the sons of Uz'ziel, Ammin'adab the chief, with a hundred and twelve of his brethren. ¹¹ Then David summoned the priests Zadok and Abi'athar, and the Levites Uri'el, Asa'iah, Jo'el, Shemai'ah, Eli'el, and Ammin'adab, ¹² and said to them, You are the heads of the fathers' houses of the Levites; sanctify yourselves, you and your brethren, so that you may bring up the ark of the LORD, the God of Israel, to the place that I have prepared for it. ¹³ Because you did not carry it the first time, the LORD our God broke forth upon us, because we did not care for it in the way that is ordained. ¹⁴ so the priests and the Levites sanctified themselves to

bring up the ark of the LORD, the God of Israel. ¹⁵ And the Levites carried the ark of God upon their shoulders with the poles, as Moses had commanded according to the word of the LORD.

16 David also commanded the chiefs of the Levites to appoint their brethren as the singers who should play loudly on musical instruments, on harps and lyres and cymbals, to raise sounds of joy. ¹⁷ So the Levites appointed Heman the son of Jo'el: and of his brethren Asaph the son of Berechi'ah: and of the sons of Merafi, their brethren, Ethan the son of Kusha'iah; ¹⁸ and with them their brethren of the second order, Zechari'ah, Ja-a'ziel, Shemir'amoth, Jehi'el, Unni, Eli'ab, Benai'ah, Ma-ase'iah, Mattithi'ah, Eliph'elehu, and Mikne'iah, and the gatekeepers O'bede'dom and Je-i'el. ¹⁹ The singers, Heman, Asaph, and Ethan, were to sound bronze cymbals; ²⁰ Zechari'ah, A'zi-el, Shemir'amoth, Jehi'el, Unni, Eli'ab, Ma-ase'iah, and Benai'ah were to play harps according to Al'amoth; ²¹ but Mat-

tithi'ah, Eliph'elehu, Mik-ne'iah, O'bed-e'dom, Je-i'el, and Azazi'ah were to lead with lyres according to the Shem'inith. ²³ Chenani'ah, leader of the Levites in music, should direct the music, for he understood it. ²³ Berechi'ah and Elka'nah were to be gatekeepers for the ark. ²⁴ Shebani'ah, Josh'aphat, Nethan'el, Ama'sai, Zechari'ah, Benai'ah, and Elie'zer, the priests, should blow the trumpets before the ark of God. O'bed-e'dom and Jehi'ah also were to be gatekeepers for the ark.

25 So David and the elders of Israel, and the commanders of thousands, went to bring up the ark of the covenant of the LORD from the house of O'bed-e'dom with rejoicing. ²⁶ And because God helped the Levites who were carrying the ark of the covenant of the LORD, they sacrificed seven bulls and seven rams. ²⁷ David was clothed with a robe of fine linen, as also were all the Levites who were carrying the ark, and the singers, and Chenani'ah the leader of the music of the singers: and David wore a linen ephod.

12 And it was told King David. 'The LORD has blessed the household of O'bed-e'dom and all that belongs to him, because of the ark of God.' So David went and brought up the ark of God from the house of O'bed-e'dom to the city of David with rejoicing; ¹³ and when those who bore the ark of the LORD had gone six paces, he sacrificed an ox and a fatling. ¹⁴ And David danced before the LORD with all his might; and David was girded with a linen ephod. ¹⁵ So David and all the house of Israel brought up the ark of the LORD with shouting, and with the sound of the horn.

²⁸ So all Israel brought up the ark of the covenant of the LORD with shouting, to the sound of the horn, trumpets, and cymbals, and made loud music on harps and lyres.

29 And as the ark of the covenant of the LORD came to the city of David, Michal the daughter of Saul looked out of the window, and saw King David dancing and making merry; and she despised him in her heart.

16 And they brought in the ark of God, and set it inside the tent which David had pitched for it; and they offered burnt offerings and peace offerings before God. ² And when David had finished offering the burnt offerings and the peace offerings, he blessed the people in the name of the LORD, ³ and distributed to all Israel, both men and women, to each a loaf of bread, a portion of meat, and a cake of raisins.

16 As the ark of the LORD came into the city of David, Michal the daughter of Saul looked out of the window, and saw King David leaping and dancing before the LORD; and she despised him in her heart.

¹⁷ And they brought in the ark of the LORD, and set it in its place, inside the tent which David had pitched for it; and David offered burnt offerings and peace offerings before the LORD.

¹⁸ And when David had finished offering the burnt offerings and the peace offerings, he blessed the people in the name of the LORD of hosts, ¹⁹ and distributed among all the people, the whole multitude of Israel, both men and women, to each a cake of bread, a portion of meat, and a cake of raisins. Then all the people departed, each to his house.

20 And David returned to bless his household. But Michal the daughter of Saul came out to meet

287

GROUNDWORK OF BIBLICAL STUDIES

David, and said, 'How the king of Israel honored himself today, uncovering himself today before the eyes of his servants' maids, as one of the vulgar fellows shamelessly uncovers himself!' ²¹ And David said to Michal, 'It was before the LORD, who chose me above your father, and above all his house, to appoint me as prince over Israel, the people of the LORD—and I will make merry before the LORD. ²² I will make myself yet more contemptible than this, and I will be abased in your eyes; but by the maids of whom you have spoken, by them I shall be held in honour.' ²³ And Michal the daughter of Saul had no child to the day of her death.

4 Moreover he appointed certain of the Levites as ministers before the ark of the LORD, to invoke, to thank, and to praise the LORD, the God of Israel. ⁵ Asaph was the chief, and second to him were Zechari'ah, Je-i'el, Shemi'ramoth, Jehi'el, Mattithi'ah, Eli'ab, Bena'iah, O'bed-e'-dom, and Je-i'el, who were to play harps and lyres; Asaph was to sound the cymbals, ⁶ and Benai'ah and Jaha' ziel the priests were to blow trumpets continually, before the ark of the covenant of God.

b   The previous part of the story has been told in 2 Sam. 6.1–11 and 1 Chr. 13. The present passages deal only with the last stage of the journey. Notice that the Chronicler has a long introduction of twenty-four verses that does not appear in the Deuteronomic History at all. This is the more surprising when we note that from 15.25 to 16.3 the Chronicler is depending on 2 Sam. 6 and at times following it word for word.

The introduction is concerned exclusively with levitical order and the levitical hierarchy. None but Levites can carry the Ark (v. 2). There is a list of levitical families and the numbers of Levites involved. Priests and Levites sanctify themselves for the task (vv. 11–14) and the death of Uzzah is explained as due to a breach of levitical ordinances (v. 13). The chief Levite appointed singers and also 'brethren of the second degree' and doorkeepers and musicians. Everyone who can be named is named. Levites continue to appear throughout the Chronicler's account, but they are not mentioned at all in 2 Sam. 6.

In 2 Sam. 6.13 David sacrificed an ox and a fatling. The Chronicler makes it seven bullocks and seven rams, but it was not David who sacrificed. It is interesting that 2 Samuel mentions David sacrificing twice (vv. 13 and 17) and on both occasions the Chronicler changes the subject from David to 'they', but, in 16.2, the Chronicler says that David made an end of sacrificing. Was it carelessness on the part of the priestly writer? If not, why did he take the trouble to make the change in the two previous instances?

2 Sam. 6 is very frank about David's dancing. From v. 14 and v. 16 it is obvious that it was wild and uncontrolled. The Chronicler is much kinder to David (15.29). The Chronicler also describes a more elaborate orchestra. Compare 1 Chr. 15.28 and 2 Sam 6.15. But perhaps the most interesting fact of all is the way the two accounts end. The Deuteronomist recounts that Michal upbraided David for losing control of himself so that he danced naked before the on-looking women (v. 20). The Chronicler omits this detail altogether and concludes with more names and more technical details.

Chapter 26

The Growth of the OT

a THE main purpose of this diagram is to stress the very important fact that the OT came into existence very slowly. The OT was not written; it *grew*. Nobody knows when the process began, but we do know that from the time when someone uttered the first words that later became part of the OT to the time when it was all fixed and settled was much more than a

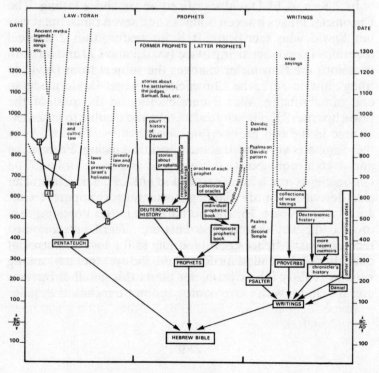

thousand years. It may have been nearer two thousand. It is not surprising, therefore, that we find much diversity in the OT.

b   Secondly, it must be stressed that very little on this diagram is *certain*. This is not an area in which it is possible to arrive at certainty. Instead we can say that most of it is very probable. Some parts are more probable than other parts, of course, but the whole has a greater degree of probability than any other hypothesis. The diagram cannot be regarded as complete or precise, but it gives a general picture of the way in which, most probably, the books came into being.

c   Thirdly, the funnel shapes represent *traditions*. A tradition is the process by which a saying or collection of sayings is passed down through history. The dotted lines are meant to suggest the period when the tradition was in oral form. The firm lines suggest written tradition, though the dates at which oral traditions became fixed and then written down are hard, if not impossible, to determine.

d   The boxes, square and oblong, represent sources that we either know or believe very strongly to have been *written*; and not simply written but edited as well. If we take as an example the 'wise sayings' from the right-hand side of the diagram, it is clear that such sayings must have existed for generations in oral form. At some time, however, a man of letters must have collected as many as he knew, edited them, and fitted them together. Probably several men of letters did this at different times and places. Then, later on, someone collected the collections and produced the book of Proverbs. The arrows in the diagram represent the incorporation of written sources into other, larger books.

e   There are some obvious imperfections in the diagram. The most serious is that the Deuteronomic History appears twice, once in the Former Prophets and again in the Writings, as a source for the Chronicler's History. There are not two Deuteronomic Histories. It is simply that a two dimensional diagram does not allow sufficient flexibility. Similarly, on the left-hand side of the diagram, it is hard to say whether D made use of J and E when they were separate or when they were combined. The diagram suggests the former, but it might have been the latter.

291

Chapter 27

Temple and Synagogue

a   No one who has read very far in the NT could confuse Temple and synagogue, but it is well to begin by stressing one or two fundamental differences. There was only one Temple and, after Dt. *12*, there could be only one. In the early days of the settlement there were many shrines (see above 17), and some of these shrines continued until the Exile, but they broke the deuteronomic law. After the Exile, the Samaritans built their temple on Mount Gerizim. But, for faithful Israel, there could only be one Temple, built on the spot that Yahweh had chosen, Mount Zion, a little to the north of David's city of Jerusalem. On the other hand in NT times there was a synagogue in every village. Wherever ten male Jews could form a group, they were obliged to join together to found a synagogue, so synagogues spread throughout the Diaspora.

    Secondly, the great industry of the Temple was sacrifice. Under the deuteronomic law, which was rigorously observed after the Exile, the open air altar on Mount Zion was *the only place in the world where sacrifice could be offered to Yahweh.* The great industry of the synagogues was the study of the Torah. The synagogue was a social centre, a place of worship, a school and a court-room, but all these activities were centred on the Torah.

    Thirdly, the staff of the Temple consisted of priests and Levites. They were all members of a single family group and they became the Sadducees. Many members of the tribe of

Levi could not find employment in the Temple and had to live on charity. Strictly speaking the synagogue had no necessary staff. The heads of local families were its elders and one of them might be chief elder. If the group became large enough, the elders might employ a scribe or a teacher, but the scribe was not necessary to the synagogue as the priest was necessary to the Temple.

Though there was only one place for the Temple, three Temples were built on the same spot and a fourth was imagined. The three were Solomon's, the second Temple, built immediately after the Exile, and Herod's Temple that was still being built in NT times. The imagined Temple is described in Ezekiel (Ez. *40–8*).

b **Solomon's Temple**

David could have chosen one of the ancient shrines for the national Temple, but, despite its lack of tradition, Jerusalem was a wise choice. It was a redoubtable fortress, David's capital, and it did not lie within the territory of any one tribe. It was a Jebusite city until David conquered it. Probably it was already a Jebusite shrine and Zadok may have been its priest. If so, it is an example of positive and constructive syncretism, for it became a sign of national unity and ultimately a bulwark of pure Yahwism. The Temple was also a sign of national self-confidence. In the desert no temples were possible. In the early days of the settlement the tribes were not wealthy enough to build on a grand scale. Solomon had the wealth because he inherited David's empire. The Temple was one indication of his magnificence.

The site of the Temple was indicated to David by Gad the prophet (2 Sam. *24*.18–25). It was the threshing-floor of Araunah the Jebusite, in actual fact, a large rock sticking out from the hillside, not unlike a small Dartmoor tor. The rock was outside David's city but inside the larger area fortified by Solomon and next door to the royal palace. The Temple consisted of three great courtyards with a relatively small shrine in the inner court. The buildings followed the line of the hill which runs roughly north to south, though the shrine itself, called the 'holy place', faced east.

The description of the buildings in 1 K. *6–7* is full of technicalities. Doubtless it has been worked over by later writers. None the less, a good idea of how the area was set out can be deduced from it. This is one of the points where archaeology can offer only limited help. Jerusalem was taken by Muslims in the seventh century and a mosque erected over the rock. Today a successor to that mosque stands over the site of Solomon's Temple. It is called the 'Dome of the Rock' and it must count as one of the most beautiful buildings in the world. Every photograph of Jerusalem shows its brilliant blue and white tiles and its golden dome. For aesthetic, religious and political reasons it would be quite impossible to disturb the area, though one wonders what secrets lie buried beneath the foundations.

This is a much simplified diagram and it is not drawn to scale according to the measurements given in 1 Kings, but it gives a general idea. The Holy Place was not large by our standards, about 35 yards long by 10 yards wide. It was divided into three. At the east end was the porch. Then came the Holy Place itself with the altar of incense, the table of shewbread and the ten candlesticks (1 K. *7*.48 f.). At the western end was the Holy of Holies, on a higher level and behind a screen (1 K. *6*.31). Inside the Holy of Holies was the Ark of the Covenant containing, so it is said, the two tablets of -stone that Moses brought down from the sacred mountain (1 K. *8*.5–11). The wings of the mysterious cherubim covered the Ark. The cherubim were composite figures with wings of a bird and the body of an animal. In Ps. *18*.10 Yahweh rides on a cherub. This is another syncretistic touch and a surprising one for, in later times, every kind of representation was banned.

Outside the porch were two free-standing pillars, called, in 1 K. *7*.21, Jachin and Boaz. Sacrifice took place on a huge altar outside the porch. Ahaz replaced this altar with one on an Assyrian model (2 K. *16*). Also in the inner court was a large tank, called 'the brasen sea', containing water for various purification ceremonies (1 K. *7*.23).

Even after the division of the kingdom the Temple maintained its hold on all Israelites. Jer. *41*.5 shows that, centuries

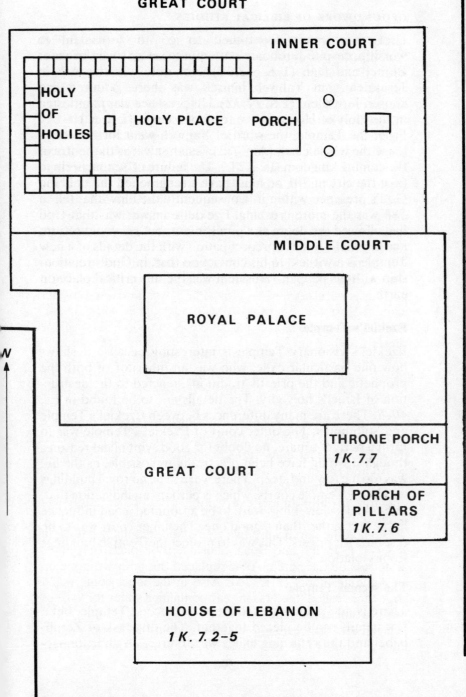

GREAT COURT

INNER COURT

HOLY
OF
HOLIES

HOLY PLACE

PORCH

MIDDLE COURT

ROYAL PALACE

N

GREAT COURT

THRONE PORCH
1 K. 7. 7

PORCH OF
PILLARS
1 K. 7. 6

HOUSE OF LEBANON
1 K. 7. 2-5

later, northerners continued to go to Jerusalem to worship, despite Jeroboam's attempt to set up rival shrines at Bethel and Dan (1 K. *12*.28). Not only was the Ark in Jerusalem, but Yahweh himself was there. Yahweh had chosen Jerusalem (1 K. *11*.32). His presence was manifested in the Holy of Holies in the form of a cloud (1 K. *8*.10–13). From the Temple, the word of Yahweh went forth to challenge the whole earth (Am. *1*.2). Isaiah saw it as the centre of the coming kingdom (Is. *2*.2 f.). The failure of Sennacherib to take the city in 701 BC must have strengthened the belief in God's presence within it. Consequently the blow that fell in 586 was the more crushing. Ezekiel's answer was that God had allowed the doom as a punishment; but he would return, and Ezekiel's intense preoccupation with the details of a new Temple is a witness to his conviction that, in God's relationship with his people, Jerusalem was the one critical place on earth.

c **Ezekiel's Temple**

Ezekiel's visionary Temple is interesting because it shows how one particular exile, who was an inheritor of both the prophetic and the priestly traditions, reacted to the destruction of Israel's holy city. The details are to be found in Ez. *40–8*. There are many differences between Ezekiel's Temple and Solomon's. The outer court of Ezekiel's Temple was to form a perfect square, no doubt for good symbolical reasons, though it would have been practically impossible, as the hill was too narrow and steep. There were to be no royal buildings within the Temple courts, which is perhaps an indication that, in Ezekiel's view, kings were to be accounted a bad influence in the cult rather than a good one. The inner court was to be reserved for priests. This was to protect the Temple buildings from violation.

d **The second Temple**

There is no systematic account of the second Temple, but a few details can be pieced together. The first task of Zerubbabel and the returning exiles was to erect an altar for sacrifice. This they did, probably on the same site as that of the one that had been destroyed. Then the foundations were laid amid general rejoicing, though some who remembered the old Temple had to weep (Ezra *3*.10–13). It is clear from Josephus that there were two courts with a wall between them (Ant. 14.16.2; cf. 1 Macc. *4*.38, 48). The Holy of Holies was separated from the rest of the Holy Place by a veil. The Ark of the Covenant had been destroyed, presumably when Jerusalem was sacked, so the Holy of Holies was empty. The work was finished and the Temple dedicated in 516 BC.

This was the Temple that was desecrated by Antiochus Epiphanes in 167 BC at the beginning of the Maccabaean War. Three years later the site was retaken by Judas Maccabaeus and the Temple rededicated, hence the feast of the Dedication mentioned in Jn. *10*.22. The story is to be found in 1 Macc. *4*.

e **The sacrificial system**

The rules for sacrifice, as they are laid down in Leviticus, come from the period of the second Temple. No doubt, in many cases, Leviticus is preserving ancient traditions. There is never any suggestion that the worship of Solomon's Temple was so corrupt that it needed to be scrapped and a new beginning made. None the less, the post-exile cult did produce some innovations and the difficulty is to decide what is new and what is old. There is much room for argument. Some maintain that the sin offering and the guilt offering arose in the period after the Exile when Israel had acquired an acute understanding of sin. Others argue that these offerings were firmly rooted in the pre-exilic cult.

Sacrifice is a very technical subject in the Bible and it is confused by a large number of terms. We shall confine ourselves to the two main types of sacrifice.

The most common sacrifice was the *peace offering* (Lev. *3*, 7.11–38, *22*.21–4). This was essentially a communal meal in which God, the worshipper, his friends and the priest all shared. There are many references to peace offerings in the historical books. Sometimes the sacrifice was connected with the conclusion of a vow, sometimes it was a free-will offering. The prescriptions are slightly more rigorous in the case of a vow (Lev. 22.23). The animal had always to be without blemish. The worshipper began by laying his hand upon its head. Much discussion has been inspired by this detail. It has been said that, by this act, the worshipper identified himself with the beast, but this cannot be pressed too hard as the carcase of the beast was finally eaten by the worshipper and his friends. It has been said that the worshipper transferred his guilt to the animal, but this cannot be right, as an animal so tainted would be unfit for sacrifice. The true explanation is probably much simpler. The action expressed the deliberate singling out of one particular animal to be the sacrifice of one particular worshipper. It was an act of specification. Perhaps on a busy day in the Temple such an action was necessary.

The worshipper himself killed the animal before the altar, cutting its throat and draining the blood into a bowl. The blood was then passed to the priest who sprinkled it on the altar. The rest of the carcase was then divided up. The fat, kidneys and liver were regarded as Yahweh's and they were burnt on the altar. Different traditions give different accounts of the priest's share. 1 Sam. 2.13 f. gives the priest the right, by custom, to all that he could hook out with a three-pronged fork. Dt. 18.3 stipulates the shoulder, two cheeks and the stomach. Lev. 7.28–34 and 10.14 f. stipulate the breast and the right thigh. The rest of the carcase belonged to the worshipper and he could eat it with his friends, though it all had to be finished in one or two days, depending on the kind of sacrifice (Lev. 7.15–17).

The second kind of sacrifice was the *whole burnt offering*. It had to be male and without blemish. The worshipper laid his hand on its head and then killed it, much as with the peace offering (Lev. 1). The important feature of this sacrifice is that the worshipper received nothing. According to Lev. 7.8 the priest had a small share in some cases, but substantially this sacrifice was what it says, an offering wholly given up to God by means of the altar fire.

In addition to these there were meal offerings and drink offerings and sin offerings and guilt offerings. The details can all be found in Leviticus. They are very complicated indeed. There was also the offering of the firstfruits at the great festivals. By offering the first sheaves or the first fruit of the harvest the Hebrew believed that he was making the rest of the crop available for common use.

One of the most important days in the Jewish year was the Day of Atonement. It has already been discussed in 7k. The first goat was offered as a sin offering, but the second was not a sacrifice at all. The high priest transferred all the sins of Israel onto the second goat (Lev. *16*.21) and it was then driven out into the wilderness to die. It was no longer without spot or blemish and it could not, therefore, be offered as a sacrifice to God.

f Herod's Temple

Herod was a grandiose builder and he thought, quite wrongly, that he could win the favour of the Jews by providing them with a magnificent Temple. The plan was so ambitious that it involved shoring up the hillside to enlarge the Temple area and erecting a new sanctuary from the foundation stones upwards. The work began in 19 BC. It had been in process forty-six years when the ministry of Jesus began according to the Johannine account of the cleansing of the Temple (Jn. *2*.20). The work continued until AD 64 and then the edifice was utterly destroyed a few years later in the Jewish War.

There are two sources of information about Herod's Temple, some chapters in Josephus (Ant. 15.11, War 5.5) and a tractate in the Mishnah (Middoth). Unfortunately they do not always agree. There is, as we have noted before, a tendency in these ancient texts to confuse the factual and the ideal. That is not an allegation against their authors, for they did not write to suit our standards of accuracy. The facts were probably not available and, even if they had been, the desire to represent the place of God's choice as perfect would have outweighed the desire for accuracy. None the less, this does mean that we cannot be absolutely sure of the lay-out of the Temple area where some of the formative events of the Christain faith took place.

The outermost court was the Court of the Gentiles. It was

TOWER
OF
ANTONIA

N

BALUSTRADE

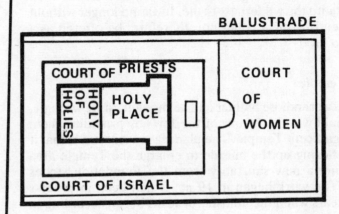

COURT OF PRIESTS

COURT
OF
WOMEN

HOLY
OF
HOLIES

HOLY
PLACE

COURT OF ISRAEL

COURT OF GENTILES

large, perhaps 200 yards square. This is smaller than the present court, called the Haram esh-Sharif, but only because of a later extension on the northern end. The east, south and west walls of the present court correspond roughly with the Court of the Gentiles in NT times. It was surrounded by colonnades, one of which may have been Solomon's porch mentioned in Jn. *10*.23, Ac. *3*.11 and *5*.12. Here the Temple traffic to which Jesus took exception took place. In the north-western corner was the strong-point called the tower of Antonia. This was the castle of Ac. *21*.34 where Paul was taken when he was arrested and from the steps of which he was allowed to address the crowd. (See also Ac.*22*.24, *23*.10,16,32.)

In the centre of the Court of the Gentiles was a stone balustrade about 4 feet high. This enclosed the true sanctuary area which was on a higher level than the outer court. Josephus tells us that notices in Greek and Latin warned that no foreigner should go within the sanctuary. In this Josephus was correct for two stones bearing such an inscription have been found. Inside the balustrade was the Court of Women and here were placed the trumpet-shaped containers into which people put their gifts (Mk. *12*.42). West of the Court of Women and on a still higher level was the Court of Israel and inside this, highest of all, was the Court of Priests, where was the place of slaughter and the open-air altar and the sacred building itself.

Like Solomon's Temple, this building was divided into three, a porch, apparently much wider than the building itself, a Holy Place, where were the altar of incense, the seven branched candlestick and the table for the shewbread (or bread of the presence), and a Holy of Holies, which contained no furniture at all. The Holy of Holies was separated from the Holy Place by a curtain (see Mk. *15*.38).

The synagogue

g The word means 'congregation', but it is more often used of the building. The true origins of the synagogue are unknown. The conservative view in Judaism is that there have been synagogues since the time of Moses, but there is little evidence for such a claim. The one possible reference in the OT, Ps. *74*.8, proves nothing as the dating of psalms is so difficult. It is reasonable to suppose that the synagogue came to prominence, if not began, when Jews found themselves separated from their homeland and the Jerusalem Temple. That suggests the beginning of the Dispersion and perhaps most of all the Babylonian Exile.

The logic of such a guess is faultless. Sacrificial worship could only take place on Mount Zion. None the less Yahweh must be worshipped even in an unclean land. So the faithful must gather to read, copy and reflect on the Law. Hence the synagogue. If this is sound, then the synagogue helped to produce the Law as much as the Law helped to produce the synagogue, for the Torah was not completed until 100 years after the Exile.

In post-exilic times the Temple was restored, but, at the same time, the Torah, or Law of Moses, became more and more important. Slowly the synagogue began to replace the Temple and the study of the Law to replace sacrifice. There were good reasons for the change. Synagogues were local. They were the focal point in the life of a Jewish village. They were part of the daily and weekly routine. They were bound to exert more influence than a distant institution that one might visit two or three times a year at most, or, of one lived in the Dispersion, perhaps once in a life-time. Moreover, in post-exilic times, the Temple staff became more notable for corruption than for piety. Corruption is always expensive to someone and usually to the common man, so it is easy to believe that the ordinary Israelite was more attracted to the simplicities of synagogue worship than to the lavish splendour of the Jerusalem cult.

The furniture of the synagogue was simple. The prime necessity was a cupboard or ark where the scroll of the Torah could be stored. For the rest all that was needed was a simple platform for reading and exposition, seats at the front for the elders, benches for the male congregation and separate seating for the women. Possibly a *menorah*, a seven-branched candlestick, stood before the ark.

In NT times the synagogue was under the control of a 'ruler of the synagogue'. Jairus was one (Mk. *5*.21–43). The ruler of the synagogue was a layman, the most dignified of the heads of families, or elders, in the neighbourhood. He presided at services and had the authority of a magistrate. According to Lk. *13*.10–17, one such ruler attempted to chide Jesus for healing in the synagogue on a Sabbath. Though he appears to have lacked popular support, the ruler was within his rights. The ruler of the synagogue also selected the readers for the day. He could invite suitable people to expound the readings. Paul was so invited at Pisidian Antioch according to Ac. *13*.15. Lk. *4*.20 refers to an attendant in a synagogue and this suggests the *hazzan* of the rabbinic writings. The hazzan was a general helper to the ruler of the synagogue, doing his bidding when he was present and carrying out his functions when he was away. No doubt he was also responsible for the care of the building.

The synagogue service was centred on the Law. It cannot be known precisely what the order of worship was in the first Christian century. Probably there was no universal pattern, but some general remarks can be made with confidence. The service would begin with the Shema, the prayer recited by every male Jew every day and found in Dt. *6*.4–9, *11*.13–21, and Nu. *15*.37–41. It was followed by a doxology. Then came prayers of thanksgiving and praise. We cannot be sure that the Eighteen Benedictions of later times were in use in the NT period, but some of them probably were. The readings of Scripture came next, one from the Torah and one from the Prophets. The Torah was read on a three-year cycle, but there was some latitude in the choice of the prophetic lesson. Jesus exercised choice in Lk. *4*.17. Then came the Targum, the translation of the Hebrew text into Aramic, one verse at a time for the Torah, a few verses at a time for the prophets. At this point the ruler of the synagogue called on someone to expound the readings (Mk. *1*.21; Mt. *4*.23; Ac. *13*.15). Finally there was a benediction (Nu. *6*.24–6).

The Temple was destroyed in AD 70, but in a large part of Judaism it had already become redundant. Judaism could exist without sacrifice and certainly without the Sadducean priesthood. In the synagogues the Jews learnt that obedience to the Torah was the best sacrifice possible.

303

Section 4

The New Testament

Chapter 28

Jesus

a THE Gospels are manifestos of faith, written by believers both for other believers and for the world. They are different from all other kinds of literature and they have to be studied, not as examples of this or that kind of writing, but *as Gospels*. They are the testimonies of brave and devout men eager to represent their Lord to friend and enemy alike.

Whenever the Gospels are studied as if they were something else, history or biography or great literature or whatever, serious mis-representations inevitably creep in. A classic example is the long series of books written fifty to a hundred years ago that treated the Gospels as biographies. Many of them bore the title 'The Life of Jesus', or something very similar. It is worth pausing to see how they went wrong.

The Gospels are relatively brief—Mark is about 11,000 words in Greek—and the Lives of Jesus were often very long—40,000 would be on the short side. The difference between the two was made up largely by inspired—or perhaps uninspired—imagination. The result was a portrait of Jesus *as the author liked to think of him*. There were many authors, so there were many portraits, and they were all different. This was not very helpful. A further point was that the imaginings of the authors were nineteenth-century imaginings rather than first-century imaginings with the result that Jesus was taken out of Roman Judaea and inserted into Victorian England. In this way the truth was obscured.

307

In modern studies of Jesus we ought not to make this mistake. Where the Gospels are silent, we should not try to fill the gap with imagination. Rather we should ask why they are silent and why, when space was short and writing difficult, they include the things they do.

Taking a brief look at Mark's Gospel we can see that the space is shared out between narratives about Jesus, including nearly twenty miracle stories, and teaching including several parables. The only continuous narrative is that relating the events of the last twenty-four hours. There is nothing about the childhood or upbringing of Jesus, nothing about his personal appearance and tastes, nothing about his social and economic existence and very little about the relation of one event in his life to the next. Even the vital fact about why he was betrayed is missing. On the other hand, some of the miracle stories appear to be repetitive. The feeding of the five thousand is soon followed by the feeding of the four. The healing of the deaf and dumb in 7.31–7 is much the same kind of story as the healing of the blind man in 8.22–6.

Even from so small an enquiry as this we are led to conclude that what mattered to the author of Mark were certain aspects of the teaching of Jesus, his works of saving power, if we may so describe his miracles, and the manner of his death. To understand Mark, therefore, we must understand these things.

The purpose of this chapter is not to write a life of Jesus, but to suggest ways in which the true emphases of the Gospel writers can be brought to the surface. We shall do this by studying the contents of the Gospels. After that we shall look at evidence from outside the Gospels to confirm that, at the heart of these unique writings, there was a firmly grounded historical person.

b   The Gospel story

The Synoptic Gospels (see below 30b) have broadly the same outline. John is quite different and needs a chapter on its own. Each of the Synoptics has its own identity, that is to say, each one has its own order and arrangement, its own peculiar material, its own theological emphasis. That leads scholars to conclude that each one had its own literary history, and that each one finally emerged in its own peculiar context as a result of an editorial process by which the Gospel was shaped for a particular purpose. Granted all that, it still remains that the Synoptics have a roughly similar shape. We must consider that shape now. It is best set out under eight headings.

c **1. Introduction** (Mk. *1*.1; Mt. *1*.1–*2*.23; Lk. *1*.1–*2*.52)

  (i) Here there is the greatest possible divergence between the Synoptics. Mark simply has a title.

  (ii) Matthew has two chapters including a genealogy and the stories of the Wise Men and the flight into Egypt.

  (iii) Luke has a four verse dedication to Theophilus and the stories of the appearance of Gabriel to Zacharias, the Annunciation to Mary, the meeting of Mary and Elisabeth, the birth of John the Baptist, the birth of Jesus and the coming of the Shepherds. Luke also refers to the circumcision of Jesus and his appearance in the Temple at the age of twelve.

d **2. The beginning of the ministry** (Mk. *1*.2–13; Mt. *3*.1–*4*.11; Lk. *3*.1–*4*.13)

  (i) All three synoptics begin the ministry in the same way, with the stories of the work of John the Baptist, the Baptism of Jesus, and the Temptation, though there is considerable divergence in content and in treatment.

  (ii) Mark is very brief especially in the Temptation narrative which he contracts into two verses.

  (iii) Matthew has a fuller account of the preaching of John the Baptist and also of the Temptation.

  (iv) Luke is similar to Matthew but adds further details of the Baptist's preaching.

309

e **3. The Galilean ministry** (Mk. *1*.14–*8*.26; Mt. *4*.12–*16*.12; Lk. *4*.14–*9*.17)

(i) This is a long section comprising nearly half of Mark and Matthew though rather less of Luke. Much of the material is shared, though there are wide divergences in the way that it is used. Four features of this section of the Synoptics need to be noted.

a The preaching of Jesus—the substance of the preaching is set out in these chapters. It is ad-dressed sometimes to the multitudes and some-times to the disciples and is sometimes direct and sometimes in parabolic form.

b The call of the first apostles and the mission on which they are sent.

c The large number of miracle stories—at least ten are to be found in all three Gospels and there are others in one or two.

d Controversy with the representatives of tra-ditional Judaism—Jesus is presented as going beyond the Law and doing what the Law could not do. Hence the opposition.

(ii) Matthew tends to gather the teaching of Jesus together in large blocks. Three such blocks occur in this section, the Sermon on the Mount (*5–7*), the Mission Charge (*10*), and the Parables of the King-dom (*13*).

(iii) Place names occur quite frequently but references to the passage of time are few. If only we could read, 'Jesus remained at Capernaum for three months', or, 'Jesus continued preaching and healing through that summer', but none of the three authors seems to be interested in that kind of story-telling. The incidents we have here are mostly recounted without a time reference. Much of the detail that could give ver-

310

isimilitude to the picture is missing. We cannot, therefore, speak of a coherent, least of all an ordered,
account of the ministry of Jesus, but we can speak of a
swift, positive affirmation of the kind of impression he
made and that he continued to make in the decades
when the Synoptics were being formed.

f **4. The watershed** (Mk. *8*.27–*9*.8; Mt. *16*.13–*17*.8; Lk.
9.19–36)

  (i) All three Synoptics come close together at this point.
  They all recount Peter's Confession at Caesaraea
  Philippi, Jesus' first prediction of his Passion, some
  searching words on discipleship, and the Transfiguration.

 (ii) This section represents the mid-point of the Gospel
  story. Before it there is the public, and often popular,
  ministry. After it the shadow of Jerusalem and the
  Cross looms larger and larger.

(iii) The section consists of a deliberate drawing together
  of three major themes, the confession of faith in Jesus,
  the inescapability of suffering in the mission of Jesus,
  and the glory of Jesus, hidden to the world but visible
  to the eye of faith.

(iv) Matthew inserts a passage of his own into
  the middle of the Caesaraea Philippi story (*16*.17–19)
  perhaps to meet particular problems that had arisen in
  the church from which Matthew's Gospel comes.

g **5. From Galilee to Jerusalem** (Mk. *9*.9–*10*.52; Mt.
17.9–*20*.34; Lk. *9*.37–*19*.28)

  (i) In this section Mark and Matthew are very similar,
  though Matthew makes certain additions (*17*.24–7,
  18.16–20, *18*.23–35, *20*.1–16 are the chief). Luke's
  variations from Mark, however, are very extensive.
  Mark and Matthew mention a number of place names

311

and, roughly speaking, they plot a course from Caesarea Philippi in the far north to Jerusalem, avoiding Samaria. The place names are Galilee (Mk. 8.31), Judaea beyond Jordan (Mk. 10.1), the way up to Jerusalem (Mk. 10.32), Jericho (Mk. 10.46), and finally, Bethany, the Mount of Olives and Jerusalem in Mk. 11.1. Time references are lacking, so it is hard to say whether this represents an actual journey or not.

(ii) Luke's account is much longer. It is set out much more obviously in terms of a journey, but Luke's route goes through Samaria. (See Lk. 9.51, 9.52, 17.11.)

(iii) In Mark the teaching of Jesus now centres on the themes of the cost of discipleship and the new standards of success and failure that belong to the Kingdom.

(iv) Luke includes in this section much of the teaching that Matthew fits into the Sermon on the Mount. Luke also includes a number of parables that are peculiar to him, the Good Samaritan (10.25–37), the Friend at Midnight (11.5–8), the Rich Fool (12.16–21), the Lost Coin (15.8–10), the Prodigal Son (15.11–32), the Unjust Steward (16.1–13), Dives and Lazarus (16.19–31), the Unjust Judge (18.1–8), and the Pharisee and the Publican (18.10–14).

(v) Matthew includes two parables that are peculiar to him, the Unmerciful Servant (18.23–25) and the Labourers in the Vineyard (20.1–16).

h **6. The last week** (Mk. 11.1–14.11; Mt. 21.1–26.16; Lk. 19.29–22.6)

(i) All three Synoptics follow much the same path. The section begins with the triumphal entry into Jerusalem, the cursing of the fig-tree (not in Luke) and the cleansing of the Temple.

312

(ii) An important feature of this section is the series of challenges to Jesus made by representatives of Jewish authority: they concern the authority of Jesus, tribute to Caesar, contemporary teaching about resurrection, and the question about the greatest commandment of all. The first three occur in all three Synoptics. Luke omits the fourth.

(iii) A second feature is the Eschatological Discourse, a long passage, present in all the Synoptics though in a different form in each.

(iv) Matthew has a number of additions that are peculiar to him, the parables of the Two Sons (*21*.28–32), the Marriage Feast (*22*.1–14, though compare Lk. *14*.15–24), the Ten Virgins (*25*.1–13), the Talents (*25*.14–30, though compare Lk. *19*.11–27), and the Sheep and the Goats (*25*.31–46, though this is more a discourse on the last judgment than a parable).

(v) The section concludes with the Anointing at Bethany (not in Luke, perhaps because Luke has a similar story in *7*.36–50) and the Betrayal by Judas.

i **7. The last twenty-four hours** (Mk. *14*.12–*15*.47; Mt. *26*.17–*27*.66; Lk. *22*.7–*23*.56)

(i) Broadly speaking the Synoptics follow the same path, that is to say, they describe the Last Supper, the Agony in Gethsemane, the Arrest, the Trial before Caiaphas, Peter's Denial, the Trial before Pilate, the Release of Barabbas, the Mocking and Scourging, the Crucifixion, and the Burial. While there is this broad agreement, each evangelist has his own way of telling the story of the Passion, and Matthew and Luke each introduce much material that is peculiar to them.

(ii) Matthew adds the details of the remorse of Judas (*27*.3–9), Pilate's wife dream (*27*.19), Pilate's hand-washing (*27*.24 f.), the earthquake and the resurrec-

313

tion of the saints (27.51–3), and the guard on the tomb (27.62–6).

(iii) Luke has very many additions and it is impossible to summarize them. Luke has two cups at the Last Supper, one before the breaking of the bread and one after. Luke refers to an angel being present at the Agony in Gethsemane, to the healing of the high priest's servant's ear, to the Lord turning to look at Peter after his denial, to the appearance of Jesus before Herod, to the repentance of one of the malefactors, and so on. It is difficult to understand the Lukan Passion Narrative simply as a series of additions to Mark. Despite the fact that Mark and Luke cover the same ground, Luke's account is best studied as an integrated narrative in its own right.

j   **8. The Resurrection** (Mk. *16*.1–8; Mt. *28*.1–20; Lk. *24*.1–53)

(i) Mark's version is only eight verses long. The present ending, that is *16*.9–20, is not to be found in the best MSS. It is a summary of stories from the other Gospels almost certainly added to Mark in the belief that the true Markan ending was missing. There is much debate whether *16*.8 is the proper ending of Mark or whether there was originally a longer ending now unhappily lost. In either case *16*.1–8 represents the only Markan resurrection story that is assuredly part of the Gospel as it first appeared.

(ii) The one story common to all three Synoptics is the finding of the empty tomb by the women. There are considerable variations in detail. Note, for example, the names of the women, Matthew's earthquake in *28*.2, the figure or figures who addressed the women, and the different references to Galilee. Mark and Matthew say that Jesus is going into Galilee to meet the apostles. Luke refers back to something Jesus said in Galilee and locates the meeting with the apostles in Jerusalem.

314

(iii) Matthew adds the story of the bribing of the soldiers and the appearance of Jesus to the eleven in Galilee where he charges them to make disciples of all the nations.

(iv) Luke adds the report of the women to the apostles, Peter's journey to the tomb, the Emmaus road, the appearance to the eleven in Jerusalem, concluding with the Ascension at Bethany.

k   **Evidence from outside the Gospels**

There are just a few references to the beginnings of Christianity in the writings of Roman authors who were by no means sympathetic to what one of them called 'the new superstition'.

Tacitus, who was born before Paul was martyred and who himself died around AD 115, was a Roman historian. In his *Annals* (XV 44) he explains how Nero, finding himself suspected of setting fire to Rome in AD 64, put the blame on the Christians and began a furious persecution of them. Tacitus continues:

> The name of Christian comes from Christ who, during the principate of Tiberius, was put to death by the procurator, Pontius Pilate. Checked for the moment, this detestable superstition broke out again, no longer simply in Judaea, where the evil took its birth, but even in the city (of Rome), where every kind of shameful frightfulness fetches itself and wins many followers.

Tacitus seems to be depending on hearsay. None the less, he has a number of facts right, or shall we say that he confirms that the NT says? He confirms the date and place. He confirms the name Christ. (To the pagan Gentile, 'Christ' was nothing more than a name.) Above all he confirms the execution under Pontius Pilate.

l   Another Roman historian, a decade or two later than Tacitus, was Suetonius. He chronicled the lives of various Roman emperors. His Life of Nero confirms that Nero made the Christians scapegoats for the fire of Rome. He describes Christianity as 'a new and mischievous superstition'. In his Life of Claudius he refers to the expulsion of the Jews from

315

Rome about the year AD 50. This is consistent with the statement in Ac. *18*.2, which also mentions that Aquila and Priscilla were among those expelled. It is interesting to note, however, that Suetonius gives as the reason for the expulsion the fact that the Jews were squabbling with each other over one 'Chrestus'. It is a reasonable guess that Suetonius had made a slight mistake in the name and that he was in fact referring to disputes in the Jewish community about Jesus Christ. If this is so, then it follows that Christian preachers had arrived in Rome by AD 50.

A letter written by Pliny the Younger around the year 110 also gives interesting information about early Christians and their worship. Pliny, who was asking for advice on how best to deal with Christians, mentions an early morning assembly at which Christians sing a hymn to Christ, 'as to a god'. Pliny is unsure whether there is anything treasonable in this conduct. It is fascinating that a pagan observer should see so clearly where the centre of Christian faith lay.

m The clearest of all references in Roman sources come from the Jewish historian, Josephus, who fought in the war of AD 66–70 and then went to Rome to write a history of the Jews. In Ant. *20*.9.1 (see note in 10k regarding references to Josephus) he refers briefly to the death by stoning of James, 'brother of Jesus, who was called Christ'. A few pages previously (Ant. *18*.3.3) there is a far more explicit statement. One paragraph refers to Jesus, his miracles, his teaching, his crucifixion and his resurrection. But this is just the trouble. It is only one paragraph. If Josephus was a Christian, and only a Christian could have written this paragraph, then it is amazing that other indications of his faith do not appear in his voluminous writings. It seems clear that Josephus was not a Christian and that this passage was added to his work by an unknown, Christian hand. Nobody knows when this might have been, so the value of the passage as evidence is slight.

n Apart from Roman sources, useful information comes from the Talmud, a collection of rabbinic writings completed in the fifth or sixth century AD. Various references to a Jesus ben Panthera imply that Jesus was the son of Mary and a Roman soldier, Tiberius Panthera. This is probably the origin of the rather crude suggestion that the tradition of Virginal Conception conceals the illegitimacy of Jesus. A further passage states:

> On the eve of the Passover Jesus was hanged. For forty days a herald went before him crying, 'He must be stoned, because he has practised sorcery, seduced Israel and enticed her into apostasy. Let anyone who has anything to say to justify him come forward and do so'. As nothing was said in his defence, he was hanged on Passover Eve.

The detail of the herald need not worry us. The author may be referring to some custom about which we know nothing and he may or may not have been correct. If the passage has the date right, then it contradicts the Synoptic Gospels which record that Jesus ate the Passover before he died. On the other hand the passage confirms the fourth Gospel which puts the crucifixion a day earlier. Most important is the description of Jesus as a sorcerer. It recalls the Beelzebub controversy in Mk. 3.22. The enemies of Jesus do not say that the rumours of his cures were false, but that they were carried out by an evil power. This confirms that the ministry of Jesus was attended by 'wonderful works', though it does not, of course, give support to any particular miracle story.

The most important material, however, comes from Christians sources. There is a large collection of early texts that were never included in the NT. Their value varies enormously and they represent a complex study in their own right. Readers of this book may not have much time to spare for NT Apocrypha, as these texts are called, but it is well to look sometime in a library at the books mentioned above in 13k.

o   **Conclusion**

This discussion brings us back to the books of the NT itself. The most important evidence of all is that they were written and preserved. Why were they written and preserved? Because of the unshakeable faith of the early Christians. On what was that faith founded? That is the historical question that leads us straight back to Jesus. Jesus lived and the

317

primitive Christians believed in him. Nothing can be more secure than that.

It might be useful now to summarize what might be called the bedrock facts of the beginnings of the Christian faith.

Jesus lived and taught in Galilee.

He gathered a band of disciples.

He carried out healings that onlookers regarded as miraculous.

He used parables.

He taught about God and his Kingdom in a direct way and not simply by discussing texts from the Torah.

He offended many, especially the Pharisees.

He was arrested in Jerusalem by Jewish authorities, tried before Pilate, and crucified.

Thereafter his followers, firmly believing that he had been raised from the dead, set out to preach that he was God's Messiah and that, in his life, death and resurrection, a new age had begun.

All these are facts, but they do not take us very far in understanding the Gospels, for the Gospels give us much more than facts. They also provide interpretation, that is to say, they are concerned with the *meaning* and the *significance* of the facts. To say that Jesus lived and died and rose *as part of the divine plan* is not to recite facts, though facts are involved, but to make a confession of faith.

This distinction follows us whenever we talk about Jesus. There are the facts that we share with all reasonable historians and there are the affirmations that we share only with other believers.

A difficulty arises when different people, sharing the same experience and addressing themselves to the same facts, none the less make different affirmations because their language and style is different. For example there is no more basic fact than the crucifixion. Matthew, addressing himself to this fact and anxious to proclaim Jesus to the Jewish world as the one in whose death the powers of good and evil came into violent collision, writes about an earthquake that accompanied the death of Jesus. This earthquake is not a fact in the way that the crucifixion is a fact and the other Gospel writers do not talk about an earthquake. None the less, it is an important part of Matthew's confession. What we, who live in altogether different circumstances, take from Matthew is his understanding of Jesus, not his witness to earthquakes.

We return to this most important subject in the last chapter of this book.

For further reading

F. F. Bruce, *Jesus and Christian Origins outside the New Testament* (Hodder and Stoughton, 1974).

Chapter 29

The Primitive Christian Community

a CHRISTIANITY began as an off-shoot of Judaism. The first Christians who gathered in Jerusalem in the weeks following the crucifixion were fired by two beliefs. One was that God had chosen Israel of old and had guided her through the turbulent centuries, giving her the prophets and the Law and sustaining her in the belief that all the old promises would, in the fulness of time, be fulfilled. This was the ancient faith that the first Christians shared with their Jewish compatriots. The other belief was new. It was that 'the fulness of time' had arrived, that the promises had, in part, been fulfilled and that they would soon be completely fulfilled, and that the focus of this new activity of God was the man Jesus, whom they had known in the flesh, who had been crucified but a few weeks before, and who, they believed, had risen from the dead and was present with them in their gatherings.

The task of the Christians in those early days was relatively straightforward. It was to convince those around them, that is to say, the Jews of Palestine, that God had acted decisively in Jesus. Straightforward the task may have been, easy it was not. The majority of Jews were unwilling to believe that the critical figure in Jewish history was a Galilean who had been condemned by the Jewish rulers and executed savagely, as if he were a slave, by the Romans. None the less, the battle lines were clearly drawn up. The Christians said that the fulfilment of the promises had begun with the coming of Jesus and that it would soon be completed with his return. The Jews said that the fulfilment had not yet begun at all.

So the whole argument turned on who Jesus was. It may appear to us that Jesus was obviously the Messiah, but that is, in fact, much too hasty a judgment as the difficulties experienced by the early preachers make clear.

How did those early Christians spend their time? According to Ac. *4*.32–5, they lived in a kind of commune. They sold all their goods and gave the proceeds to the apostles. If indeed there was such a commune, it must have been small and short-lived. It is entirely comprehensible that a group of excited believers, expecting the Parousia at any moment, might sell up in order to speed the work of preaching the Gospel. But the scheme cannot have lasted for long. Once the capital was spent, other policies must have been worked out. It is quite wrong, therefore, to look on 'Christian communism', as it is sometimes incorrectly called, as the one true Christian economic and political system. If the early Christians in Jerusalem did pool their goods, it was no more a political action than that of a group of explorers or mountaineers who might do the same thing to mount an expedition.

b **I. The early Christians at work**

The chief business of the community was *preaching*. And the preaching centred on Jesus. The thrust of the preaching was that God had acted through Jesus to bring salvation to Israel. It is an open question whether, in these early days, the Christians saw their movement as a *world* mission. The ministry of Jesus was largely limited to Israel. The environment of early Christianity was thoroughly Jewish. It is certain that, in the course of time, Christians saw their faith as a world mission but perhaps not at the beginning. On the other hand, there are passages like Mt. *28*.19 and Ac. *1*.8 that speak of making disciples 'of all the nations' and being witnesses 'unto the uttermost part of the earth'. Most scholars take the view that these charges represent the convictions of the Church rather than the actual words of Jesus. None the less, they demonstrate that, as the first century wore on, Christians began to realize more and more that they had a message of salvation for the whole world. The first stage, however, and the problem that confronted the small community in Jerusalem in the earliest days, was the conversion of Jewry.

c   How did Jesus bring salvation to Israel? By founding the Kingdom of God that would soon be completed in the Parousia. How could one be sure that this was so? The earliest Christian preachers answered this question by affirming that Jesus was God's Messiah. That was a message that Jews could easily understand, though they might have thought that all the evidence was against it. So the Christian preachers tried to prove that Jesus was Messiah in two ways, first by showing that Jesus fulfilled the Scriptures and secondly by bearing witness to his resurrection.

The early Christian preaching provided, without doubt, some of the raw material for the letters of Paul and for the Synoptic Gospels and for the book of Acts. Unfortunately it is hard for us to discover, from these later sources, exactly what the primitive preaching was like. It is true that Acts recounts a number of early Christian sermons, but we can hardly suppose that these are more than a general summary made some time afterwards. None the less, these sermons are worthy of the most careful study. They can be found in Ac. 2.14–39, 3.12–26, 4.8–12, 5.29–32, and 10.34–43. Ac. 4.24–30 is in the form of a prayer, but its structure is very similar to that of the sermons.

d   Let us take a closer look at Ac 2. The sermon begins with a quotation from the prophet Joel and the claim that the prophecy is now fulfilled and the last days have begun. Then the sermon focuses on Jesus. Certain statements are made to define him. But notice that the statements are of two kinds. There are those which might be called common knowledge, that he came from Nazareth, that he performed 'mighty works', that he was crucified and killed. And there are those that are positive statements of faith, that his works showed him to be approved by God, that his crucifixion was with the foreknowledge of God. No distinction is made between these two kinds of statement.

The sermon then moves on to the most crucial statement of

322

all, that God raised Jesus up. Because no distinction is made between the two kinds of statement, we cannot tell into which category the affirmation about the resurrection ought to fall. Does the sermon say: God raised him, as everybody knows, or, God raised him, as we believe? There is a great difference here, but the primitive Christians seem not to be aware of it, and they leave us to puzzle it out for ourselves.

Next comes the scriptural proof of the special nature of Jesus. The quotation is from Ps. *16*. It is worth reading Ps. *16* carefully from the OT before reading it in Ac. *2*. This exercise will show that the sermon uses the psalm in a way that we should nowadays think quite inappropriate, though it is typical of the way in which first-century Jews used Scripture. The sermon argues that the psalmist is not talking about himself at all but about Jesus. There is a secret meaning in the text, and whatever the psalmist and his original readers and hearers may have thought, the real truth in the psalm was a prophecy of Jesus.

So the sermon moves on to its climax. If all this is true, then you may be sure that this Jesus, whom you crucified, is, in fact, both Lord and Christ. All you can do, then, is to repent and believe.

e   Careful consideration of all the data in the NT about early Christian preaching leads to the conclusion that the basic outline was something like this:

Jesus (whom you/they crucified) is Christ/Lord.

       Proof 1: OT quotations
       Proof 2: his resurrection of which we are witnesses

      Conclusion: repent and believe!

That sermon was heard again and again within the walls of Jerusalem and beyond in the early days of the Christian Church.

f   Preaching is never sufficent by itself. It must always be followed with some kind of instruction if only because no sermon is long enough to say all that has to be said. This was

323

especially true in the early days. For the first few weeks it might have been possible simply to refer back to the Jesus whom everybody knew. But very soon converts would come along who knew very little about the life, words and acts of Jesus, and audiences, too, would be inclined to meet the proclamation, 'Jesus is Lord', with the rejoinder, 'But who was Jesus?'

So a new task appeared side by side with the preaching. This was the setting out, in an easily grasped form, of information about Jesus and his life and teaching, so that those who heard the preaching could know more about the one who was said to be Lord. Some of this must have been inserted in every sermon. Perhaps Ac. 2.22 f. gives a hint of what must have happened. But the real task of filling in the background could not have been done in preaching itself.

So, side by side with the task of preaching, comes the task of *instruction*. In the Christian community the words and acts of Jesus were remembered and passed on to the new converts. It is here that the methods of form criticsm have been most helpful. If we refer back to what was said in 15g about form criticism, we shall see that the so-called 'forms' appear in precise situations in life. The situation calls for a particular form of expression. If we imagine new converts to Christianity sitting down with the apostles at the end of the day, it is not difficult to see what the questions would be, nor what kind of answers would be necessary. What kind of person was Jesus? What did he teach about this and that?

The answers would come in the form of short, easily memorized passages very much like the pericopes of the Synoptic Gospels. (See below 30a.) It is claiming too much to suggest that the Synoptics can be fully explained in this way. Years of usage and transmission moulded the pericopes and the evangelists themselves had a large hand in the final version. None the less, the situation that we now have in mind, that of the apostle and his convert, probably supplied the occasion for the composition of some of what we read in the Synoptic Gospels today.

g It is clear that the instruction, like the preaching, made no distinction between facts of the what-everybody-knows kind and affirmations of the what-we-believe kind. We, with our analytical minds, might think this a pity. Hundreds of publicly known facts must have been referred to in the instructions, but because these facts were mixed up with what-we-believe statements, it is impossible for us now to have any certainty in sorting out facts from statements of faith; our analytical minds are leading us to ask questions that the NT does not answer.

One final comment needs to be made on this matter of instruction. The convert and the apostle met only after the resurrection. The ministry of Jesus, of course, took place before the resurrection. That means that there was a decisive difference between the instruction Jesus gave to his hearers, even the disciples, and the instruction the apostle gave to his converts. Jesus spoke largely about God and the good life and only sparingly about himself, his death and the glory beyond. The apostle spoke in the light of the crucifixion and the resurrection and he made them his central theme. For him Jesus *was* glorified. We reach, then, the paradoxical conclusion, that the essence of the Christian faith is to be found more in the teaching of the apostles than in the teaching of Jesus himself. Much the same can be said about Christian preaching. Both preaching and instruction sound a new note, a note that could not have been sounded during Jesus' own ministry. That note was that Jesus is now the crucified, risen, ascended and reigning Lord.

h   If the first task was *preaching* and the second *instruction*, a third came very close behind it. That task was *worship*. It is unthinkable that devout Jews would cease to worship God. The difference their Christian faith made was that now they worshipped God *through Jesus Christ.* Christian worship was not addressed to a different God. There is every reason to suppose that the early Christians went on worshipping Yahweh in the synagogues with their Jewish friends, wherever they were allowed to do so. But synagogue worship was not enough. The name of Jesus was not honoured in the synagogue, nor, among God's mighty acts, was the latest and greatest ever mentioned.

So the Christians had to have meetings for worship of their

325

own much as the early Methodists went to the parish church in the morning and to their Methodist class meeting at night. It is not possible to speak with certainty about these early Christian meetings for worship. The direct evidence is scanty and different scholars draw different inferences. None the less, three things can be said with reasonable confidence.

i 1. The worship was centred on a *meal*. Meals are of the utmost importance in the Gospels. Some important miracle stories are concerned with meals. The Last Supper is given that name because it was the last of a series. In the resurrection narratives meals occur again. The climax of the Emmaus road story is a meal (Lk. *24*.30). In Lk. *24*.42 Jesus eats broiled fish with the disciples. Similarly in Jn. *21*.13 there was a meal of bread and fish by the lakeside. Acts refers to the early Christian meal as 'breaking bread' (Ac. *2*.42, 46), and says that Christians did it regularly.

2. The meal was *linked with the Last Supper*. No doubt it was linked in some minds with all the other meals that Jesus had had with his disciples, but the Last Supper was uppermost. In two accounts of the Last Supper (Lk. *22*.19 and 1 Cor. *11*.25), Jesus gives an explicit command to 'do this in remembrance of me'. It is hardly likely that these words would have been set down if the Church did not, in fact, continue in the practice. We can, therefore, reasonably assume that the earliest Christian services were what we could call services of Holy Communion.

3. The meals were occasions of *great joy*. The word 'remembrance' is a poor translation of the original. When we remember we cast our minds back to the long ago. When the Hebrew remembered he believed that the past was actually brought back into the present. This is still true of Jewish worship. The modern Passover is not a memorial of an escape that took place in ancient times. It is an experience of release *now*. The modern Jew has the sense of standing on the shores of the Red Sea and the service still ends with, 'Next year in Jerusalem'. So Christian worship did not mourn a departed Jesus or strive to recall experiences of days gone by. It cele-

brated the presence of Jesus who was recalled into the midst of his people as they broke bread together. That is why Ac. 2.46 speaks of them breaking bread with joy. It is true that 1 Cor. *11*, the earliest account of the Christian Lord's Supper that we have, draws attention to the suffering and death of Jesus. Paul was anxious that the Corinthians, who had become shallow and careless about the whole matter, should not forget this aspect. But Paul's account does nothing to weaken the contention that, in the Lord's Supper, the early Christians believed themselves to be meeting their crucified, risen and ascended Lord.

j   Finally, the early Christians concerned themselves with the *baptism* of converts. Again the details are not clear, but we can be sure that the rite of baptism implied not simply a washing away of the sins of the past, but a complete re-birth of the individual. The waters, in Hebrew mythology, stood for death. When the convert was plunged into them, he died. When he emerged, he was a new being. Conversion to Christianity in those days was a radical experience and the sign of it was no less radical. The question arises as to who was baptized. In the early days the answer was simply— those who believed that God had acted decisively in Jesus. There is a debate about whether children were baptized in the early days, but among adults the situation was clear. Either you believed, and were baptized and became a Christian (and were probably disowned by your family as well), or you did not. There were no half believers in those circumstances.

Candidates for baptism would, therefore, confess their faith in Jesus. This was an important part of the baptismal service and, in one form or another, it has been present ever since. This is probably where creeds began. Candidates were asked if they believed in Jesus. They had to make a reply in the form of a short creed, 'Jesus is Messiah' or 'Jesus is Lord'. Then they were plunged into the water and the new life had begun.

So the early Christian community preached and taught and worshipped and baptized *and grew*.

327

k **II. The early preachers' audience**

The story of Pentecost in Ac. 2 lays special stress on the many parts of the world that Peter's audience had come from, and Luke, as we shall try to show later (31j), was very interested in the world mission of the Christian Church. But the important divisions, as far as the Christian preachers were concerned, were not geographical. Jews would be Jews whether they lived in Mesopotamia or Rome. The critical factor was what the religious background of the audience was, and this varied enormously. It is convenient to divide the audience into a number of different categories, though this, of course, is bound to involve an over-simplification.

1. Jews of Jerusalem and Judaea

These reckoned themselves to be the truest Jews of all. They lived in the shadow of the Temple. In this small locality they outnumbered people of other races. The culture and convention of the area was predominantly Jewish. Here the Sadducees and the Jewish aristocracy were in control, at least as far as the Romans permitted. The Christian message in this situation was a straightforward affirmation that Jesus was the expected Messiah. The opposition, and very serious it was, derived from the fact that the Jerusalem hierarchy were the very people who had co-operated in, if not engineered, the crucifixion of Jesus on the grounds that he was a blasphemer. Jerusalem Jews were likely to be conservative in matters of religion and there are good reasons for thinking that the mission among Judaean Jews did not go well.

l *2. Hellenistic Jews*

These were Jews who lived away from the Promised Land. The word 'Hellenist' derives from the Greek word for 'Greek' and means here those who are exposed to Greek culture. Ever since the year 721 BC Jews had been scattered round the then known world by a series of historical chances. Unlike other tribal groups who suffered similar disasters, the Jews faithfully preserved their religion and so their identity. So Jewish settlements appeared in every big city of the Mediter-

328

ranean world, and, in NT times, the Jews outside Palestine greatly outnumbered those within it. These Jews of 'the Dispersion' had had much more to do with Gentiles than their Judaean brethren. Many of them spoke Greek as their first or only language and they were necessarily more liberal in their attitudes than the Judaean Jews. Their faith, however, was fundamentally the same and the Dispersion Jews tried to visit Jerusalem at least once in their lifetime. The Dispersion Jews gave Paul his greatest opportunity, for, on one hand, they were thoroughly versed in the Scriptures, and, on the other, they were not as conservative as their Judaean counterparts. The Jews of Galilee and other parts of Palestine came somewhere between these first two groups. Jerusalem Jews had little respect for them (Jn. *1*.46).

m *3. Proselytes*
These were Gentiles who had espoused the Jewish religion completely. This means that they had given up their family and friends and, if males, been circumcised, and undertaken to obey the Jewish Law in every respect. Proselytes were not numerous in NT times, though they are mentioned three or four times in the NT. They are important because they witness to the fact that the one mysterious God of Israel did attract those of other races, presumably because they found the religions of the Roman Empire to be shallow and unsatisfying.

n *4. 'God-fearers'*
These were Gentile men and women who were attracted to the Jewish faith but who stopped short of becoming proselytes. Jews might respect them as Gentiles who feared God, but proselytes were not allowed to participate fully in the synagogue. Cornelius was a godfearer and so, surely, was the centurion of Lk. *7*. God-fearers were far more numerous than proselytes, if only because becoming a proselyte involved the dangerous operation of circumcision. The god-fearers provided a splendid audience for Paul, because they could understand Jewish expectations and Jewish terms and yet they were, as uncircumcised Gentiles, given no status in Judaism.

The Gospel was eventually preached to god-fearers on the same terms as to Jews, and there is every reason to suppose that they responded in large numbers. When Paul spoke in the synagogue of Pisidian Antioch, according to Ac. *13*.16, he began his speech, 'Men of Israel (Jews sitting in front of him) and ye that fear God (god-fearers gathered round the door)'.

o   *5. Samaritans*

As far as the Jews were concerned these people were half-castes and outside the Covenant, whereas the Samaritans regarded themselves as the true guardians of the Law. (See above 10j.) As far as Christian preachers were concerned the Samaritan community must have seemed to offer a natural extension of their mission. There is a record of a mission to Samaria in Ac. *8*.

p   *6. Gentiles*

Preaching to the Gentiles involved the Church in enormous problems. To begin with, most Gentiles were not monotheists and had no conception of Israel's God and the divine plan for salvation that was basic to Israel's faith. Consequently the Christian preachers could take nothing for granted. The phrase, 'Jesus is Messiah', would have meant nothing to the average Gentile. He could only reply, 'Who is what?' Reframing the Gospel message so that it made sense to the Gentiles must have taxed the powers of preachers like Paul. The difficulty is still with us and we must not underestimate it. A further complication was the fact that, once Christians began to invite Gentiles to share their faith and their worship, opposition from Judaism was redoubled. Eating with Gentiles was absolutely forbidden to the Jew. Not only did Jews outside the Church cause trouble but Christian Jews had grave doubts about this policy. Solving the problem of whether to preach to Gentiles and how to preach to Gentiles was, perhaps, the gravest of all the issues that confronted the primitive Church.

q   **III. The admission of Gentiles**

It appears that, for the first few years, the Christian preachers offered the Gospel to Jews only. But, before very long, Gentiles began to show an interest and so presented the infant Church with a massive theological problem. The problem is summed up in the question: can Gentiles be admitted into the Christian faith without first becoming Jews? To us a positive answer seems obvious, but it was by no means clear in the early days, and—let it be honestly admitted—the opponents of free admission had a very strong case. Let us look at the arguments of three typical people in, let us say, the second decade of the Church's life.

First, consider the *typical Jew*. He believes firmly in Yahweh, rejoices in the Torah that Yahweh has given to his people, recognizes Yahweh's hand in the experiences of both chastening and salvation that have come upon Israel, and looks forward to the final deliverance that must come soon. He does not believe that Jesus was the Messiah because Jesus was not a victorious leader, he did not bring deliverance, he did not inaugurate a new age. On the contrary, he was executed shamefully by the Romans. He objects strongly to Christians sharing food with Gentiles because it breaks the Law. As for the Church's claim to be the true Israel, this is absurd. Israel, as a people, has rejected Jesus. If Israel is wrong and the Christians right, it means that the people that God had prepared by the Law and the prophets through the centuries had failed to recognize the Messiah when he came, while heathen Gentiles, whom God had not prepared, did recognize him. This is to suggest that God's plans have miscarried hopelessly, which is blasphemy.

r   Secondly, consider the *strict Jewish Christian*. (We will not use the word Judaiser as scholars differ about how this term is to be used, but see note at 37i.) He believes that God called Israel and that salvation will come to Israel first. There is no other way. If, due to the perversity of Israel's present leaders, Israel as a people does not believe in Jesus, that is one further judgment on Israel. If Gentiles do believe, they must, of course, enter Israel by circumcision first, for only so can they become heirs to the promises which God has made to Israel and which are now being fulfilled.

s   Thirdly, consider the *Pauline kind of Christian*. He has no doubt that God called Israel and prepared his people for the coming of Messiah. He has no doubt that Jesus fulfils all the expectation of the OT for a deliverer. But one element in God's plan is that all the world should believe, that the Israel of physical descent should be replaced by a larger Israel of faith. So God planned that, for the time being, the physical Israel should not believe. This drove the Christian preachers out to the Gentiles. The Gentiles did believe and so were admitted to the renewed Israel by faith alone. When this development has run its course, the physical Israel will be released and will come to believe, so that, in the end, all the world will be saved.

There was a fundamental argument between the Jews in the first group and the Christians in groups two and three. But within Christianity there was a very serious disagreement between the strict Jewish Christians and the Paulinists. It lasted for decades, it divided many local churches, it was Paul's chief worry, and it threatened to destroy Christianity from within.

The Book of Acts is not very clear or consistent on this matter. In Ac. *8.* there is a record of a mission to Samaria. Samaritans were certainly outside the covenant community by Jewish standards, so the fact that Samaritans seemed to be acceptable suggests that there was no problem. But in Ac. *10.* it is clear that there was a problem, though the solution is presented there in the clearest terms. Peter had his vision at Joppa telling him, in effect, to baptize Cornelius, a Gentile. If the vision and its consequence had been taken seriously, then the problem would have been over. The third group and the third group alone must have been right. But the problem apparently continued and in Ac. *15* we find an account of a general council to settle the matter. There are many difficulties with this council. Suffice to say here that the matter appears not to have been settled even there, and the solution related in *15.*20 would not have satisfied Paul anyway (see 34c).

The depth at which the Church was troubled is best revealed in Paul's letters. Again and again he returns to the question of the old Israel and its relation to the Church. Again and again he sets himself against those who would tie Christian converts back to the Jewish Law. His own answer is worked out in three chapters in Romans (*9–11*) where he tries to show that all that has happened fits in to the divine plan. The argument is tortuous and needs to be read several times. The one thing that stands out clearly is that, if Paul and his supporters had not won this argument in the end, Christianity would never have become the world religion that it is.

Chapter 30

The Synoptic Problem

a THE Synoptic Problem can be summed up in two questions. *Why are Matthew, Mark, and Luke so similar* in style, contents, order and actual wording? And if, as seems reasonable, the similarities can best be explained by supposing that they copied from each other, *why are they so different?* Why did they not copy consistently and accurately?

The similarities are very striking, especially when the first three Gospels are set over against the fourth. If one compares Mark and John, it is clear that both books are *Gospels*, they are both concerned to present the good news that Jesus is Lord, but their manner of doing so is quite different. Mark is made up of short, terse paragraphs (called *pericopes*) relating incidents or recording teaching with no exposition or ornamentation at all. John consists of long, discursive passages in which incidents and teaching are expounded at length. But if one compares Mark and Matthew, the similarity of treatment is at once evident. Matthew is made up of the same kind of short sections as Mark. Luke, too, follows a similar pattern.

As far as contents are concerned, simple statistics are impressive. There are about eighty-five of these short sections in Mark, and perhaps three of them do not occur in either Matthew or Luke. As many as seventy-five occur in some form in all three. But, despite the fact that John is apparently addressing himself to the same subject, less than thirty of Mark's sections have any parallel in John, and, as we shall see below, there are considerable differences between the first three Gospels and John regarding contents.

The question of order is also interesting. We have already seen in the chapter on 'Jesus' that the first three Gospels have roughly the same over-all order. More detailed study confirms this. Mark sets out his pericopes in one order, Matthew usually follows suit. And if Matthew does not, Luke does. Nothing similar can be said about Mark and John. One cannot ask questions about order when the contents differ, but even when the contents are broadly the same, Mark and John arrange their sections in their own way regardless of each other. The only points at which they come together are towards the end of the Gospel story and even here the differences are as impressive as the similarities.

The most important evidence comes from the actual wording. Again statistics are enough. In the first of the two passages we consider below there are, leaving aside the introductory verse, fifty-two words in the Greek in Matthew. Thirty-eight of these, that is to say seventy-three per cent, are also to be found in Mark's version. Luke compares with Mark in the same way. His account has eighty-eight words and about forty of them are also found in Mark. There are several runs of five or six words that occur in the same sequence in two of the Gospels, sometimes in all three. If one encountered that kind of similarity in examination papers, there could be only one conclusion.

b   This makes it clear why the first three Gospels are called *Synoptics*. They see things the same way. Synoptic means 'seeing together'. What is not so clear is how the Synoptics came to be so similar. The simple answer is that the authors copied from each other. If that is the case, then the most probable hypothesis is that Mark was the first Gospel to be finished and that the authors of Matthew and Luke copied from him independently.

On this reckoning we would have to imagine Matthew and Luke sitting down with a copy of Mark, a few private notes of their own, a pair of scissors and a bowl of paste. At the end of the day each had a new Gospel and a pile of cuttings.

c   A complication appears straight away with this simple

picture. It is not difficult to show that Matthew and Luke had *other sources beside* Mark. At least one of these sources they shared with each other. For example, Matthew and Luke both have beatitudes while Mark has none. And each of them also had *at least one source of his own*. For example, the birth stories in Matthew and Luke are quite different.

The source Matthew and Luke shared was, at one time, also thought to be a document. German scholars called it *Quelle*, which means 'source', hence the sign Q. Matthew's own special source is called M and Luke's L. So, if we still think in scissors-and-paste terms, the simplest solution to the synoptic problem is as follows;

There are two good reasons why this solution must be rejected as too simple. In the first place we have to think of differences as well as similarities. This is the other half of the synoptic problem and it is every bit as important as the first half. Why, *if Luke had Mark to copy from*, did he copy only forty words when he might have copied the whole passage? In the second place the whole conception is too static. It implies that the gospel material was fixed, like a series of articles in a newspaper, that might remain unchanged for decades. It seems far more likely that the gospel material was assembled to be used, and that *much of the usage was oral*. The Gospels as we have them are the final literary result of long decades of such usage.

This conclusion greatly increases the number of possible explanations of the synoptic problem. For example, the fact that Matthew and Luke have words in common does not necessarily mean that the borrowing was a single literary operation. It may be that it took place at various times before the final stage.

d   The fact that there are so many different ways in which one Gospel might have contributed to another means that the scissors-and-paste explanation must be abandoned, and that we can no longer be as confident about the solution to the synoptic problem as were the scholars of thirty or forty years ago. It is still probable that Mark's version came first and that Matthew and Luke borrowed from him, but at what stage the borrowing happened and under what circumstances is hard to say.

Perhaps this accounts for the tendency of modern scholars to concentrate on the individuality of the Gospels rather than on their inter-dependence. There has to be a word of warning here. If, in any given instance, we do not know the exact form of a pericope when Matthew borrowed it, we cannot be sure what changes he made in it. What we do know is that, when the final version of Matthew appeared, it revealed a large number of differences from the final version of Mark. These changes point to a Matthean editor, probably not the Matthew who was a disciple, with his own particular point of view. But how much of the particular Matthean character belongs to this editor and how much to the intermediate stages of development is difficult for even the most meticulous scholar to determine.

It is reasonable to suppose that changes were made at the time of borrowing, either to improve the pericope—that is to say, to make it shorter or less clumsy—or to make it more applicable to the precise circumstances of the borrower. To get the complete picture all the variations between Mark and Matthew and between Mark and Luke need to be studied, but we have no space to do that. None the less, it is time to cease generalizing and to consider the text itself. We shall consider two pericopes which will be enough to suggest that the Markan version was the earliest one and that Matthew and Luke were the borrowers, and also to reveal something of the special character of the Matthean and Lukan traditions.

e **The healing of a leper**

Matt. 8.1–4	Mark 1.40–45	Luke 5.12–16
1 When he came down from the mountain great crowds followed him; ²and behold, a leper came to him and knelt before him, saying, 'Lord, if you will, you can make me clean.'	⁴⁰And a leper came to him beseeching him, and kneeling said to him, 'If you will, you can make me clean.' ⁴¹Moved with pity,	12 While he was in one of the cities, there came a man full of leprosy; and when he saw Jesus, he fell on his face and besought him, 'Lord, if you will, you can make me clean.'
³And he stretched out his hand and touched him, saying, 'I will; be clean.' And immediately his leprosy was cleansed.	he stretched out his hand and touched him, and said to him, 'I will; be clean.' ⁴²And immediately the leprosy left him, and he was made clean. ⁴³And he sternly charged him, and sent him away at once, ⁴⁴and said to him, 'See that you say nothing to anyone; but go, show yourself to the priest, and offer for your cleansing what Moses commanded, for a proof to the people. ⁴⁵But he went out and began to talk freely about it, and to spread the news, so that Jesus could no longer openly enter a town, but was out in the country; and people came to him from every quarter.	¹³And he stretched out his hand, and touched him, saying, 'I will; be clean.' And immediately the leprosy left him. ¹⁴And he charged him to tell no one; but 'go and show yourself to the priest, and make an offering for your cleansing, as Moses commanded, for a proof to the people. ¹⁵But so much the more the report went abroad concerning him; and great multitudes gathered to hear and to be healed of their infirmities. ¹⁶But he withdrew to the wilderness and prayed.
⁴And Jesus said to him, 'See that you say nothing to anyone; but go, show yourself to the priest, and offer the gift that Moses commanded, for a proof to the people.'		

1. Notice that Matthew and Luke are more economical in

words than Mark, an important point when one remembers how costly and difficult writing was. A true comparison must, of course, deal with the Greek versions, not the English. In the main body of the story, which is common to all three accounts (that is, vv. 40–4 of the Markan account), Mark has sixty-nine words in Greek, Luke sixty-one, and Matthew fifty-two.

2. Each Gospel has its own connecting link. At this point Mark has very little over-all structure, so he just adds the passage to the preceding verse which summarizes the Galilean ministry. Matthew has inserted the Sermon on the Mount at this point, so he links this miracle with the end of that sermon. Luke ties the story rather loosely to the story of the call of Simon, James and John, an incident which comes a little earlier in Mark and Matthew.

3. The man was a leper, but Luke is not content simply to call him a leper. Luke says he was 'full of leprosy'. Either 'full of leprosy' belongs to the earliest version and Mark and Matthew shortened it, or 'leper' is the earliest version and Luke, for a special reason, lengthened it. Col. 4.14 describes Luke as a physician, but there is no reason to suppose that the phrase he uses is more apt medically than the 'leper' of Mark and Matthew. By making the diagnosis worse, however, Luke heightens the miraculous element. It is noticeable that he often does this and it may explain the longer form.

4. Notice the differences in the description of what the leper did. Mark has beseeching, kneeling, saying, which is very impressive. Luke, however, has 'fell on his face, and besought him', which is several words longer in Greek. Luke's version is the more dramatic and more exaggerated. The man saw Jesus and instantly fell on his face. Matthew's version is shorter than Mark's and there is an even more important difference. In Matthew the leper *knelt before* Jesus. One explanation, though not the only one, is that Luke's version is an attempt to make it a more exciting story, Matthew's is an attempt to make it more theological. For Matthew it is the leper's devout attitude to Jesus that counts.

5. Mark has an unnecessary 'to him' in v. 40. Matthew and Luke save a minute by leaving it out. But in the very next line both Matthew and Luke add a word, the word 'Lord'. These two details are significant and they both point in the same direction. Later scribes will save time if they can. So out goes 'to him'. But later scribes were also familiar with long arguments about the honour due to Jesus. They hesitate over a form of address that lacks a sense of respect. So in comes the word 'Lord'.

6. Mark includes a reference to Jesus being 'moved with pity'. Matthew and Luke leave this out. Some Greek texts, however, have a different word at this point. They read, 'being angry' or 'being indignant'. If this is the word Mark had originally, it is easy to see why Matthew and Luke left it out.

7. Several of the lines here are identical or almost so, showing that there is a close relationship between the Synoptics. In the last line of v. 41 Mark has another 'to him' that the others leave out.

8. In v. 42 Mark has two descriptions of the cure, one medical, one ceremonial. Matthew has the ceremonial one, for he was interested in Jewish ritual. Luke has the medical one. It is just possible that Mark knew the other two and combined them, but it is more likely that Matthew and Luke knew Mark and that they each selected the statement that interested them.

9. In v. 43 Mark uses a powerful word translated 'sternly charged'. Matthew and Luke will have none of it. The words 'said' and 'charged' are in a much lower key. It is easy to see why. The leper did not obey. Matthew and Luke could not have Jesus sternly enjoining something that was immediately disobeyed.

10. Mark has three verbs, 'charged', 'sent', 'said' at this point as well as an unnecessary 'at once'. Matthew and Luke simplify and abbreviate.

11. Jesus' speech in Mk. *1*.44 is longer and more awkward than either Matthew or Luke's version.

12. Why does Matthew leave out 'for your cleansing'? Because he has already spoken about cleansing in v. 3. Luke did not mention cleansing in his v. 13 so he brings it in here. Mark has it in v. 42 and v. 44 which again suggests that his version was first and the others were able to improve on him.

13. Mark is a little vague about what the leper ought to offer as a result of his cure, Luke even more so. One gains the impression that Matthew is the only one who was concerned with the requirements of Lev. *14*. It would be quite reasonable for Matthew to correct Mark by making the phrase more precise, but it is unreasonable to imagine Mark deliberately altering Matthew to make it more vague.

14. At this point Matthew finishes the story. Mark goes on to speak about the disobedience of the man and the great stir the cure aroused. Matthew is embarrassed by the disobedience. It does not suit the picture of the lordly Messiah that he is presenting. And he does not need to mention the great stir as the point is made in his introduction, 'great crowds followed him'. So Matthew leaves out Mark's v. 45 altogether.

15. Mark makes the man plainly disobedient in v. 45. Luke softens it and suggests that the onlookers, who had not been told to be quiet, did the damage, not the man himself.

16. Mark describes Jesus in difficulties. He could not enter the city. He had to stay outside in the desert places. Luke does not allow that. His vv. 15 and 16 have only a slight connection with Mark. He shows Jesus first of all healing great multitudes and then withdrawing himself deliberately into the desert. This is an important difference. In Mark Jesus was a man who could be harassed. In Luke he was in charge of every situation. As time went on the limitations of Jesus became less and less important, and more and more stress was laid on his power.

17. In Luke Jesus withdrew himself in order to pray. This is a typical Lukan touch. Luke often mentions that Jesus prayed when the others do not mention the fact.

f Peter's confession at Caesarea Philippi

Matt. *16*.13–23	Mark *8*.27–33	Luke *9*.18–22
13 Now when Jesus came into the district of Caesarea Philippi,	27 And Jesus went on with his disciples, to the villages of Caesarea Philippi; and on the way he asked his disciples,	18 Now it happened that as he was praying alone the disciples were with him:
he asked his disciples, 'Who do men say that the Son of man is?' ¹⁴And they said, 'Some say John the Baptist,	'Who do men say that I am?'	and he asked them, 'Who do the people say that I am?' ¹⁹And they answered,
others say Elijah, and others Jeremiah or one of the prophets.'	²⁸And they told him, 'John the Baptist; and others say, Elijah; and others	'John the Baptist; but other say, Elijah; and others that
¹⁵He said to them, 'But who do you say that I am?' ¹⁶Simon Peter replied, 'You are the Christ, the Son of the living God.'	one of the prophets.' ²⁹And he asked them, 'But who do you say That I am?' Peter answered him, 'You are the Christ.'	one of the old prophets has risen.' ²⁰ And he said to them, 'But who do you say that I am?' And Peter answered, 'The Christ of God.'
¹⁷And Jesus answered him, 'Blessed are you, Simon Bar-Jona! For flesh and blood has not revealed this to you, but my Father who is in heaven. ¹⁸And I tell you, you are Peter, and on this rock I will build my church, and the powers of death shall not prevail against it. ¹⁹I will give you the keys of the kingdom of heaven, and whatever you bind on earth shall be bound in heaven, and whatever you loose on earth shall be loosed in heaven.' ²⁰Then he strictly charged the disciples to tell no one that he was the Christ.	³⁰And he charged them to tell no one about him.	²¹But he charged and commanded them to tell this to no one,
²¹From that time Jesus began to show his disciples that he must go to Jerusalem and suffer many things	31 And he began to teach them that the Son of man must suffer many things, and be	²²saying, 'The Son of man must
from the elders and chief priests and scribes, and be killed, and on the third day be raised.	rejected by the elders and the chief priests and the scribes, and be killed and after three days rise again.	suffer many things, and be rejected by the elders and chief priests and scribes, and be killed, and on the third day be raised.'

²²And Peter took him and began to rebuke him, saying, 'God forbid, Lord! This shall never happen to you.' ²³But he turned and said to Peter, 'Get behind me, Satan! You are a hindrance to me; for you are not on the side of God, but of men.'	³²And he said this plainly. And Peter took him, and began to rebuke him. ³³But turning and seeing his disciples, he rebuked Peter, and said, 'Get behind me, Satan! For you are not on the side of God, but of men.'

1. The most obvious factor here is the long insertion in Matthew (vv. 17–19). Matthew is, therefore, longer than Mark or Luke. Serious questions must be asked about this, but first we can note that, in Greek, Mark's first three verses contain sixty-eight words, Matthew's first four verses contain sixty-four and Luke's first three, fifty-eight.

2. Mark and Matthew have a similar beginning, but Matthew leaves out the unnecessary detail, 'on the way', and avoids a double reference to the disciples. In setting up the story, that is to say, in the first four lines of the synopsis given above, Mark uses twenty-four Greek words and Matthew fifteen.

3. Luke has a different beginning altogether. He leaves out the reference to Caesarea Philippi, perhaps because his readers would have no interest in the name of a small Palestinian town. Instead he concentrates on his favourite theme of prayer and says something rather contradictory. Jesus was praying alone and his disciples were with him. This is an interesting example of the editorial process of redaction. (See above 15r) Luke forges a connecting link that expresses his own particular interests and, in doing so, overlooks the fact that, in the rest of the story, Jesus and his disciples were together.

4. Mark refers to the villages of Caesarea Philippi, but Caesarea Philippi was a town, not a region. Matthew's 'district' is vaguer but a little more accurate.

5. The question Jesus asks is different in all three Gospels. Mark has the straightforward question. Luke heightens it by bringing in 'the people'. Matthew, however, makes a

343

significant change. Instead of 'I', Matthew has, 'the Son of Man'. Why? It may simply be that Matthew believed that 'the Son of Man' was the usual way in which Jesus described himself. Or it may be that we need to look ahead to v.16 and consider these two verses together. The use of 'the Son of Man' rather than 'I' in the question gives Jesus a rather mysterious dignity. (Ezekiel appears to have used the same term of himself in a similar way in Ez. *2*.1, *3*.6, etc.) The use of 'the Son of the living God' in the answer does the rest. Together the two terms reveal Matthew's great concern with the question of who Jesus was and how he could be described.

6. Mark's 'And they told him', uses up five Greek words. Matthew reduces it to three. Luke uses four and is more precise than the others.

7. The disciples' reply is different in all three. Mark is the shortest, but the extra elements in Matthew and Luke are important and seem deliberate, so the verse still counts in favour of the hypothesis that Matthew and Luke knew and made use of Mark. Matthew adds the name 'Jeremiah' to make a point for his Jewish readers. Jeremiah, like Elijah, was expected to reappear as the end approached. (See 2 Macc. *15*.12–6; 2 Esdras *2*.18.) Luke's readers would be ignorant of Jewish apocalyptic expectations and he has to spell it out to them.

8. Jesus' second question is the same in all versions, though Mark's 'And he asked them' uses four Greek words while Luke manages with three and Matthew with two.

9. In the next line (the first line of Matthew's v.16), Matthew adds the name Simon to Peter. This is necessary because Matthew is about to introduce an insertion that plays on the names Simon and Peter.

10. Peter's answer varies. Mark has the simplest version; it is the confession any Jew would make when he was first converted. Luke adds the words 'of God', presumably because some of his readers would not realize what the word 'Christ' meant. Matthew goes much further and gives an interpretation of 'Christ', which suggests that, by the time Matthew's

344

Gospel was written, there had been much discussion of how to describe Jesus to the world.

11. Now comes the famous insertion that is in Matthew alone. The implication seems to be that Peter was originally called Simon, that he was given the nickname Peter on this occasion, and that he was known thereafter as Simon Peter. Much has been written about the passage. Roman Catholics base their belief about the primacy of Peter upon it. From the point of view of synoptic criticism there are two questions. First, why does this passage occur in Matthew at all? Is it because Peter's simple statement needed elaboration in the light of a few decades of corporate Christian experience? It appears that Matthew wrote in a time when various versions of the Christian faith were abroad and the primacy of Peter was, for Matthew, the guarantee of the true one. We might be tempted to think of Corinth (see 1 Cor. *1*.12), but there is nothing to connect Matthew's Gospel with Corinth. Secondly, why does the passage occur in Matthew *alone*? Mark and Luke may have left it out because their situations were different, but it seems too important a statement to be so discarded if they knew about it. Alternatively the passage may have come into being in Matthew's community in which case Mark and Luke do not reproduce it because they knew nothing of it. Early Christian communities could be creative in this way. It may seem to us like forgery, but the early Christians believed that they were faithfully drawing out the meaning of the teaching of Jesus, not forging it. (See above 15p.)

12. When we pick up the story again in the three versions Matthew has to be the longest because he has to reintroduce the subject he left behind in v.16. Luke's v.21 is very forceful, but in Greek it is no longer than Mark.

13. In v. 21 Matthew adds, 'From that time', making the point that it was only after he was recognized as the Christ that he could talk about his future suffering. Mark is less clear on this and Luke does not make the point at all.

14. In Mark and Luke Jesus calls himself 'the Son of Man' at

this point. Matthew does not, perhaps because he has made use of the designation already.

15. Matthew adds the words, 'go to Jerusalem'. Matthew's interest in all things Jewish means that he is more critical of Judaism as well as more concerned with it. He does not want it to be forgotten that Jesus suffered rejection and death in the very centre of the Jewish world.

16. Matthew makes the charge against the elders, chief priests and scribes slightly worse. In Mark and Luke Jesus suffers many things but the elders are accused only of rejecting him. In Matthew Jesus suffers many things directly through them.

17. Assuming that all the Synoptics are referring to the same interval, that is from Friday to Sunday in our notation, then Mark's expression, 'after three days' represents the Jewish way of counting. Matthew and Luke use what is, to us, a more accurate expression and one that recalls Hos. 6.2.

18. Mark has an active verb suggesting that Jesus himself rose again. Matthew and Luke have a passive verb suggesting that Jesus was raised up by God.

19. The prophecy of suffering and resurrection is made 'plainly' in Mark, a fact that Matthew and Luke do not record.

20. The last two verses tell of Peter rebuking Jesus and Jesus rebuking Peter. Luke misses them out, perhaps because he does not wish to record a clumsy mistake made by the chief apostle. Mark includes them, which is interesting if he really was 'the interpreter of Peter' as tradition says. (See below 31a.) It is also interesting that Matthew includes them. Evidently, in Matthew's eyes, the fact that Peter was the rock on which the Church was built did not mean that he was free from error. Matthew, in fact, includes Peter's speech in full and so stresses his error more than Mark.

21. Once again, in v. 33, Mark has the longer introductory formula (twelve words in Greek against Matthew's six).

22. Matthew's version of the rebuke to Peter includes an extra phrase, 'you are a hindrance to me'. Only a few verses before

346

Peter was the 'rock', understood as a foundation stone. Now he is a 'hindrance' or 'stumbling-block', understood as a great danger. Matthew could not resist pointing out the two different aspects of the boulder and relating both to Peter. Mark has not alluded to the first earlier so he can hardly allude to the second here.

Chapter 31

The Synoptic Gospels

a **THE GOSPEL ACCORDING TO ST. MARK**

Authorship

NONE of the Gospels name their authors, but our St. Mark has traditionally been attributed to the Mark mentioned in the NT. The word 'author' needs careful definition. To say that Mark was the author of his Gospel means that Mark was the person who shaped the final version. Much of the material was already in existence, probably in oral form. Mark took it and arranged it into a complete work.

There is no reason to doubt the tradition of Markan authorship. About the year AD 140, a bishop of Hierapolis, called Papias, affirmed that Mark was 'the interpreter of Peter' and wrote down accurately, though not in order, what Peter remembered of Jesus' acts and words. At one time it was thought that Mark wrote the complete Gospel from first to last after he had met Peter in Rome not long before the latter's death. Now, after a few decades of form criticism (see above 15g) less reliance is put on Papias' statement. It seems more likely that much of the material reached a fixed, oral form long before Mark set to work. None the less Papias need not be discarded altogether. Peter may have had some influence on Mark's editorial work, that is to say, on what Mark selected, how he adapted and arranged it, and how he linked one section to the next.

b **John Mark**

Mark was not one of the Twelve, though many scholars
believe that he was the young man who was present in Gethsemane at the time of the arrest and who ran away without his
loincloth. This detail is mentioned in Mark's Gospel only
(*14*.51 f.).

Assuming that all the references to Mark in the NT refer to
the same person, we can conclude that Mark's other name
was John (Ac. *12*.12), that he lived with his mother Mary in a
substantial house in Jerusalem, that they were both Christian
believers, that he went with Paul and Barnabas, his uncle, to
Cyprus (Ac. *13*.5; Col. *4*.10) but left them when they crossed
to Perga (Ac. *13*.13), that Paul and Barnabas later disagreed
over him and Paul refused to have him as a travelling companion again, that he went to Cyprus a second time with Barnabas
(Ac. *15*.37–9), that he was eventually reconciled with Paul
and was with him when he wrote Philemon (v. 24). Further
references state that Mark became a helper to Paul in his
imprisonment (Col. *4*.10; 2 Tim. *4*.11). In 1 Pe. *5*.13 the
author, not necessarily Peter himself, describes Mark as 'my
son', which is plainly a figurative statement to show the relationship between Peter and Mark.

Date, place of origin, readership

It is very often said, though with little hard evidence, that
Mark completed his Gospel around AD 65 in Rome. It
appears that the Gospel came from a Jewish hand but it was
intended for Gentile Christians. The Pharisaic practice of
washing before meals is explained in 7.2–4. So, too, is 'the
Preparation' in *15*.42. Matthew does not explain these
details. Mark uses Aramaic words several times (*3*.17, *5*.41,
7.34, *10*.46) but translates them for the benefit of readers
who knew no Aramaic. Similarly, in *12*.42, the two mites,
which were Greek coins, are explained in terms of Roman
coinage (cf. Lk. *21*.2), and in *15*.16, the courtyard is given
both a colloquial and a technical name.

349

c **Distinguishing characteristics**

1. The *urgency* of the narrative. Incidents follow one another in rapid succession with no hint of a pause for reflexion. The word translated 'at once', 'immediately' or 'straightway' occurs in Mark over forty times, whereas it is found only seven times in Matthew and only once in Luke.

2. *Vividness*. Mark has a number of touches lost by the others. The grass is green in 6.39, a significant detail in a hot country. Jesus was asleep on 'a cushion' (4.37 f.). The people sat down 'in ranks' (6.40). Note, too, the harrowing details in 9.14–29 that are not in the parallel passages Mt. 17.14–20 and Lk. 9.37–43. There are many such examples.

3. *Emphasis on exorcism*. Miracles stories occur in all the gospels. Mark has a particular interest in the power of Jesus, where faith is present, to drive out devils. Exorcism is as much a part of the mission as preaching in 1.39 and 6.7.

4. Deep concern with the *passion* of Jesus. The destiny of Jesus to suffer is first stated in 8.31, only half-way through the Gospel. The passion dominates the remaining eight chapters.

5. *Down to earth elements* in the picture of Jesus. Jesus was plainly upset in 1.41. He was disobeyed in 1.45 and embarrassed as a consequence. He was frustrated by public unbelief in 6.5. The disciples were almost rude to Jesus in 4.38.

6. The *Messianic secret*. Mark insists that Jesus did not want the affirmation of his Messiahship to be made in public. Demons are commanded to keep silence about it (1.25, 34, 3.12; see too 8.30). Apparently the truth was to be veiled until the great moment when Jesus stood before Caiaphas (14.62).

Matter peculiar to Mark

Many words and phrases occur in Mark but not in the other two synoptics, but only three complete pericopes are his alone, the parable of the seed growing secretly (4.26–9), the healing of the deaf and dumb man (7.31–7), and the healing of the blind man at Bethsaida (8.22–6).

d THE GOSPEL ACCORDING TO ST. MATTHEW

Authorship

Papias, the bishop of Hierapolis, also had something to say about Matthew. 'Matthew, however, wrote the *logia* in the Hebrew tongue and everyone interpreted them as he was able.' On the face of it this is fine, for it is much easier to believe that Matthew the apostle wrote certain *logia* or sayings, later incorporated into a Gospel by someone else, than that Matthew lived long enough to write the whole Gospel himself. The final editing of Matthew was probably carried out fairly late in the century after Judaism and Christianity had gone their separate ways.

But what were the *logia*? The word simply means 'sayings'. One explanation is that the term refers to the source we call Q, the source that Matthew and Luke (but not Mark) have in common. Q is largely made up of sayings, but there is no evidence that it ever existed in a Hebrew version. Matthew and Luke share some material. That is all we can be sure of. To identify this material with the *Logia* to which Papias refers is simply to fall back on guesswork. Another explanation is that Matthew the apostle compiled a list of OT passages that were used by Christian preachers as proof texts. Matthew's Gospel, as we shall see, was certainly interested in this line of argument. The passages might reasonably have been called *logia*. But again there is no good evidence that such a list ever existed in Hebrew or in Greek.

In the end, therefore, we have to admit that Papias' statement is obscure, and that we do not know what part the apostle played in writing the Gospel, or, to put it another way, we do not know why this Gospel is linked with the apostle Matthew.

e Date and place of origin

It has often been said that the critical factor in dating Matthew is how the Gospel stands in relation to the horrors of the Jewish War of AD 66–70, but it is really impossible to say whether a passage like *24*.15–22 is a prophecy of a future event or a recollection of a past one set out like a prophecy. It might, of course, be a little of both, for a genuine prophecy could be adapted afterwards to make it conform with what actually happened. In the latter case, the final version of the Gospel would have to be later than AD 70. We have also supported the common view that Matthew used Mark. Equally important, as far as dating is concerned, are the indications in Matthew that Christianity and Judaism had developed in different ways for some time and had had several confrontations. It is hard to believe that *16*.17–9 and *18*.15–20 could have been written in the first two or three decades. Both suggest a Christian community where the first ardour had cooled and a second, more formal, phase had begun. The frequent harsh references to the representatives of Judaism and *their* synagogues suggest a time when the breach had become final. Considerations like these suggest a date between AD 80 and 90.

The place of origin is often thought to be Antioch in Syria because it was a great Jewish and Christian centre and the Gosple was intended for Jewish readers who were in danger of missing the distinctive nature of Christianity. Matthew often appeals to the OT to show that the Church and not the Israel he so frequently attacks was the true heir to the promises of the old covenant and that Jesus was the fulfilment of the Law.

f **Distinguishing characteristics**

1. Matthew's peculiar source. It is clear from the amount of material that is peculiar to Matthew that Matthew had a source that was not known to the other evangelists. This source is commonly called M. It is not known whether the source was oral or written, nor is it always clear whether scholars who talk about M include Matthew's nativity stories in it or not. These stories are peculiar to Matthew, but they are also unlike the rest of M, so perhaps it is best to regard them as a fourth possible source. One is tempted to produce a mathematical formula, Mt. = Mk. + Q + M + nativity

352

stories, but this makes the whole matter too clear-cut. Sources cannot be defined with that kind of clarity.

2. *The five discourses.* Matthew arranges the teaching of Jesus into five large blocks each concluding with some such formula as, 'and when Jesus had ended these sayings . . .' The five blocks are: the Sermon on the Mount (5–7), the mission charge (10), the parables of the Kingdom (13), the sayings on greatness and forgiveness (18), and the apocalyptic discourse (24–5). These five blocks form the framework of the Gospel. Some have maintained that this scheme was an attempt to provide a new, Christian Torah.

3. *Fulfilment of Scripture* Matthew often makes use of some such formula as 'that it might be fulfilled which was spoken by the prophet . . .' The purpose of the formula is to match an incident in the life of Jesus with an OT text which it is held to 'fulfil'. Matthew is thus pursuing a form of argument that was widely used in Judaism. The Scriptures were the repository of all truth. Every event of significance to the human race would, therefore, be foreshadowed within them. If Jesus were indeed the Messiah, then the Scriptures would prove it. It is clear that the Scriptures did not prove it to everybody's satisfaction, but Matthew tries to show how the Christian case can be argued in this way. His notion of proof is different from ours. Careful comparison of Mt. 2.15 and Hos. 11.1 leads us to conclude that Hosea was talking about something quite different from what Matthew implies. But it was usual in contemporary Judaism to suppose that the Scriptures were inspired on several different levels. Besides the obvious meaning, an OT passage might have a secret meaning, hidden even from the OT author himself, a meaning that would be revealed only on some distant occasion when it would become relevant. Hosea may have thought that he was speaking of God leading Israel out of Egypt, but in fact he was speaking more wisely than he knew. God would one day lead his son, the true personification of Israel, out of Egypt. Unbeknown to Hosea, this prophecy also was hidden in his words. Such argumentation would not be widely accepted today, but for Matthew's readers it was the most telling argument of all. It is interesting that

Matthew sometimes adjusts details in order to make incidents fit more closely an OT passage. For example, in Mk. *15*.23, Jesus was offered myrrh to ease his sufferings. Matthew, with Ps. *69*.21 in mind, changed it to gall, thus improving the parallel but spoiling the point.

4. The Christian community. Matthew writes as if the Church had established its identity over against Judaism, determined its mission, and gone some way to working out its organization. The only references to the Church in the Gospels are Mt. *16*.18 and *18*.17. The former deals with Peter as the foundation stone, the latter with some kind of disciplinary procedure in the congregation. The whole passage *18*.15–20 is an interesting sidelight on the life of the Christian community and no clearer account of the mission and the security of the Church can be found than *28*.19–20.

5. Christology. Matthews sees Jesus as the majestic Son of God, worthy to receive worship and obedience. Some of the more homely touches in Mark which reveal the human limitations of Jesus are missed out (e.g. Mk. *1*.45, *3*.5, *5*.30 f, *6*.5) while in other cases, details which affirm the authority of Jesus are added (see Mt. *5*.17, *11*.28–30, *12*.6, *14*.33, *19*.25, *23*.8–10).

g **Matter peculiar to Matthew**

1. The nativity stories including the genealogy tracing the lineage of Jesus back to Abraham, the appearance of the angel to Joseph, the visit to the Wise Men, the flight into Egypt, and the slaughter of the innocents.

2. The narratives of the healing of the two blind men (*9*.27–31), the payment of the half-shekel (*17*.24–7), the death of Judas (*27*.3–10), and the guard on the tomb (*27*.11–15).

3. Several parables: the wheat and the tares (*13*.24–30, 36–43), the hidden treasure (*13*.41), the pearl of great price (*13*.45 f.), the drag-net (*13*.47–50), the unmerciful servant (*18*.23–35), the labourers in the vineyard (*20*.1–16), the two

sons (*21*.28–32), the wise and foolish virgins (*25*.1–13). The marriage feast (*22*.1–10) is similar to Lk. *14*.15–24, but Matthew adds a peculiar ending. The parable of the talents (*25*.14–30) is similar to Luke's parable of the pounds (Lk. *19*.11–27).

4. Many additions to pericopes in Mark such as Mt. *16*.17–9. Also many additions to the teaching of Jesus, some quite extensive (e.g. Mt. *25*.31–46).

h **THE GOSPEL ACCORDING TO ST. LUKE**

Authorship

Very little can be known about Luke with absolute certainty, but, as we have often said, in biblical studies, absolute certainty is all but impossible to attain. By a process of deduction it is possible to reach some *probable* conclusions and the fact that these conclusions fit in well with other NT probabilities makes them the more interesting.

The place to begin is the Acts of the Apostles. Most of Acts is written in the third person, that is to say, it is about what *they* did. But in *16*.10 the person changes and it becomes, '*we* sought to go forth'. The first person continues for eight verses and then the third person returns. The 'we' reappears in *20*.5–16, *21*.1–18, and *27*.1–*28*.16. All these passages have to do with journeys and it seems reasonable to suppose that they were written by a companion of Paul. Of all the companions of Paul mentioned in the NT, none is more likely than Luke. This is not all. The first person travel passages do not differ in style from the rest of Acts and it is again reasonable to suppose that the person who wrote the travelogue was also responsible for the rest of Acts. In some places he could rely on first-hand experience, in others he had to rely on hearsay or on other sources.

Now, if we compare the beginning of Acts with the beginning of Luke's Gospel, Ac. *1*.1 with Lk. *1*.1–4, it seems clear that both were written by the same person. Both are dedicated to one Theophilus and Acts refers to a previous volume already completed. By this roundabout way it is possible to affirm with some confidence, though not with certainty, that the traditional attribution of the third Gospel to Luke, Paul's companion, is correct.

What more can be known about him? He is mentioned three times in the NT. In Philemon *24* Paul describes Luke as a fellow-worker with him. In Col. *4*.14, Luke is 'the beloved physician'. Commentators have seized on this phrase and searched the two books to find evidence that they were written by one who had technical knowledge of disease and its cure. On points like this it is all too easy for imagination to run away with the commentator; the evidence is not sufficient to prove that the author of the third Gospel had an interest in illness. Finally, in 2 Tim. *4*.11, it is said that only Luke was with Paul at the end. Long and difficult arguments have taken place over the authorship of the Pastorals (1 and 2 Timothy and Titus), but they need not concern us here. The verse simply adds a little weight to the supposition that Luke was a companion of Paul.

Everything else about Luke has to be inferred from his writings, and here we leave probability behind and enter the realms of mere hypothesis. Consequently there is little profit in pursuing the quest further. It cannot even be known whether Luke was a Jew or a Gentile. He has a very firm grasp of the OT and the Jewish style of writing, and yet he is familiar with the Roman world and has a better grasp of the Greek language than any of the other evangelists. He might have been born a Gentile and then been converted to Jusaism. Or he might have been a Jew who lived most of his life outside Palestine. The one thing we can be sure of is that he was an educated, much-travelled, and profoundly sensitive Christian.

i **Date, readership and purpose**

There is very little evidence about the date of Luke's Gospel. Many think that the reference to Jerusalem surrounded by armies in *21*.20 means that Luke must have written after the fall of Jerusalem in AD 70. There is also the presumption that

Luke must have written some time after Mark. But this evidence is not very imposing. Most scholars think of Luke as belonging roughly to the same period as Matthew, that is, between AD 80 and 90, but nobody can be very confident on the matter.

The purpose of Luke is again difficult to ascertain with precision. Nothing is known of Theophilus to whom the book is addressed. It is not even certain that Theophilus was a real person, for the name means 'lover of God' and it might be simply a way of addressing the god-fearing public. There is evidence that Luke was meant for a wider audience than Matthew. His genealogy is traced back to Adam, the father of all men, not to Abraham, the father of Israel. Luke tends to substitute Greek words for Hebrew words. For example he never uses the term, 'rabbi'. He used 'Lord' or 'master' or nothing. Sometimes he prefers the widely understood word 'lawyer' to the rather technical Jewish word 'scribe'. Similarly the dates in chapters 2 and 3 are tied to Roman rulers as well as to Jewish. All this suggests that Luke was addressed to the Gentile as well as to the Jew. It is a Gospel for the whole world.

If the Gospel is coupled with Acts there is some ground for the theory that Luke was trying to prove to the Roman world that Christianity was not a seditious sect despite its origins in a distant and rebellious country. On the contrary, Christianity was a faith to commend the respect of all, Jew or Roman, outcast or ruler.

j **Distinguishing characteristics**

1. Luke's peculiar source. The material peculiar to Luke is extensive (see below) and many scholars envisage a special source which they call L. There is no proof that it was a *written* source, but Luke plainly had access to material that escaped the other evangelists. Apart from the nativity stories, which are very distinctive, and some very important parables, this source contained narrative material that adds considerably to the Markan outline and is sometimes at variance with it. This additional material is particularly important in the passion narrative.

357

2. The role of the *Holy Spirit.* Luke's Gospel, more than any other, sees the Christ event as the work of the Holy Spirit. The Holy Spirit comes upon John the Baptist (*1.*15), Mary (*1.*35), Elisabeth (*1.*41), Zacharias (*1.*67), and Simeon (*2.*25 f.). Jesus himself begins his mission 'full of the Holy Spirit' (*4.*1, 14) and his first public address begins with the words, 'The Spirit of the Lord is upon me' (*4.*18).

3. The *reversal of fortunes.* Luke takes especial pleasure in the fact that the coming of Jesus upsets the established order and makes the last first and the first last. To quote the Prayer Book version of the Magnificat,

> He hath put down the mighty from their seat: and hath exalted the humble and meek.
> He hath filled the hungry with good things: and the rich he hath sent empty away.

The Magnificat, of course, comes from Luke's Gospel (*1.*46–55). Luke alone records details of the sermon at Nazareth in which Jesus, quoting from Is. *61,* describes his ministry as bringing good tidings to the poor, release to the captives, sight to the blind, and freedom to the oppressed (*4.*18). Luke, like Matthew, has Beatitudes in which the lowly are exalted, but Luke adds, his own series of woes on those who are rich and full and happy *now* (*6.*24–6, *11.*42–4). Luke alone tells the parable of the Good Samaritan, in which the priest and the levite are found wanting and the Samaritan is proved virtuous (*10.*30–7), and Luke alone tells the parable of the publican who was justified and the Pharisee whose prayers died on his lips (*18.*9–14). Clearest of all is the parable of the rich man and the beggar, Lazarus (*17.*19–30). It is not said that one was wicked and the other righteous. It *is* said that the rich man went to the place of torment and the beggar to Abraham's bosom.

4. Concern for *the outcast.* All four Gospels have a story of a woman anointing Jesus. Luke alone describes the woman who performed this devoted action as 'a sinner', and Luke follows the story with the parable of the two debtors, showing that the devotion of the sinner who repents may be greater

358

than that of the righteous (7.36–50). Luke alone preserves the parables of the Good Samaritan (10.30–7) and the publican and the Pharisee (18.9–14). Luke alone tells the story of the grateful Samaritan (17.11–9), who was a leper and an outcast; Luke alone records Jesus' happy encounter with Zacchaeus (19.1–10) who was one of the hated publicans; and Luke alone records the penitence of one of the crucified thieves (23.39–43).

5. Concern for *women*. Luke mentions many women in his story and always with sympathy. He, alone of the Synoptists, refers to Elisabeth and Anna, to Joanna and Susanna (8.3), to Mary and Martha (10.38–42), to the widow of Nain (7.11–7), and to the daughters of Jerusalem (23.27–31). All the Gospels mention Mary Magdalene. Only Luke adds the sympathetic detail, 'from whom seven devils had gone out' (8.2). All this is symptomatic of Luke's approach to salvation. Salvation is not for the high and mighty. It is for those who, in the old dispensation, were of no account. Outcasts, Samaritans, women, beggars, these are the aristocracy of the kingdom Luke proclaims.

6. Concern for the *world mission* of Christianity. The angels in the nativity story proclaim peace of earth, and Simeon sees in the infant Jesus the salvation prepared for all peoples and 'a light to lighten the Gentiles' (2.31 f.). In 3.5 f. Luke extends the quotation from Is. 40, which is found in all the Synoptists, to include a positive reference to 'all flesh'. Is. 40 speaks of all flesh seeing the glory of the Lord. Luke with perhaps a memory of Is. 52.1 in his mind, changes it to 'all flesh shall see the salvation of God'. If this was a mistake, it looks like a deliberate mistake, for the adapted quotation admirably summarizes Luke's true interests. In the sermon at Nazareth Jesus, in Luke's version, cites two occasions in the OT where blessings fell on those outside Israel (4.24–7). The last words of the risen Jesus to the disciples in Luke refer to the preaching of repentance and remission 'unto all the nations, beginning from Jerusalem' (24.47).

7. An interest in the *prayers of Jesus*. Luke, more than the

others, sees Jesus as a man of prayer. After healing the leper, Jesus withdrew to pray (5.16). All the Synoptists refer to the calling of the disciples. Only Luke introduces the story by saying that Jesus first prayed all night (6.12). Similarly the request of the disciples that he should teach them to pray is preceded by the statement that Jesus was himself praying (11.1). Jesus prayed for Peter (22.32) and Luke alone records the agony of prayer in 22.44 and the prayer, 'Father, forgive them' in 23.34.

8. *The journey to Jerusalem.* In Lk. 9.51 Jesus sets his face steadfastly to go to Jerusalem to face the final trial. This is odd, because 9.51 is less than half way through the Gospel and many events and much teaching that have nothing especially to do with Jerusalem or the journey there, come in the second half. It seems that Luke has used the idea of a journey as a literary device to give shape to his Gospel. So the story moves from Galilee, through Samaria, through various towns and villages, to Jericho, and finally to Jerusalem in 19.27. (See 9.57, 10.38, 13.22, 17.11, 18.31, 35, 19.1, 28.) This is particularly interesting because, in Acts, Luke appears to have done something similar with the life of Paul. Important events have been linked together into the form of missionary journeys. (See the discussion of Paul's journeys below—34d.)

k **Matter peculiar to Luke**

1. The nativity stories. These are very extensive filling two long chapters. They include the promise of a son to Elisabeth and Zacharias, the Annunciation, the visit of Mary to Elisabeth, the birth of John the Baptist, the journey of Joseph and Mary to Bethlehem, the visit of the shepherds, the presentation of Jesus in the Temple, and the visit of Jesus to the Temple as a boy. In addition, these chapters contain three hymns that have become familiar in Christian worship, the Magnificat (1.46–55) the Benedictus (1.68–79) and the Nunc Dimittis (2.29—32).

2. The number of parables peculiar to Luke depends, to some

360

extent, on how we define the word parable. Some passages might be called parables or again might not, for example *14*.28–33 and *17*.7–10. Even so, the following clearly defined parables are peculiar to Luke: the two debtors (*7*.41–3), the Good Samaritan (*10*.30–7), the friend at midnight (*11*.5–8), the rich fool (*12*.16–21), the Barren Fig Tree (*13*.6–9), the Lost Coin (*15*.8–10), the Prodigal Son (*15*.11–32), the Unjust Steward (*16*.1–13), the Rich Man and Lazarus (*16*.19–31), the Unjust Judge (*18*.1–8) and the Pharisee and the Publican (*18*.10–4).

3. Several miracles are recorded by Luke alone: the miraculous draught of fish (*5*.4–11, though see Jn. *21*.6), the raising of the widow's son at Nain (*7*.11–7), the woman with an infirmity (*13*.10–7), the man with dropsy (*14*.1–6), the ten lepers (*17*.11–19) and the healing of the high priest's servant's ear (*22*.50 f.).

4. Luke has a number of additions to the Passion narratives. In Luke's account of the Last Supper there are two cups, one before and one after the meal. Luke alone refers to Jesus' promise to pray for Peter (*22*.31 f.), to the angel of the agony (*22*.43 f.), to the healing of the high priest's servant's ear (*22*.51), to Jesus looking at Peter at the time of the denial (*22*.61), to a trial before Herod (*23*.4–12), to a second appearance before Pilate (*23*.13–19), to the lament of the daughters of Jerusalem (*23*.27–31), to the penitence of one of the malefactors (*23*.39–43), and to three separate words from the cross (*23*.34, 43, 46).

5. There are many other narratives and sayings that can only be isolated by the use of a synopsis.

Chapter 32

The Fourth Gospel

a THE first question is: *how does the fourth Gospel differ from the Synoptics?* In that they are all concerned with the life, death and resurrection of Jesus of Nazareth, all the Gospels are similar. They have a common purpose, too, in the sense that they were all written to inspire faith in him. Beyond these important but general points, however, there are significant differences between John and the Synoptics. What follows here is a summary of the more obvious points, since we cannot deal with the questions in detail.

1. In the Synoptics the scene of the ministry is Galilee. Jesus travels around and teaches in the villages but does not approach Jerusalem until the time comes for the final visit when he is arrested and put to death. John records visits to Jerusalem (*2*.13, *5*.1, *7*.10, *10*,22, *12*.12), so that one might almost speak as if the ministry was centred in Jerusalem. Jesus appears not to leave Judaea after Jn. *7*.10.

2. The Synoptics have few references to time, but the whole story seems to last little longer than a year. John has many references to Jewish feasts (*2*.13, *6*.4, *7*.2, *10*.22, *11*.55, *12*.1, *13*.1) and they require a ministry of between two and three years in length.

3. The contents are very different. The Synoptics do not mention the miracle at Cana of Galilee (Jn. *2*.1–11) or the

362

raising of Lazarus (Jn. *11*.1–44). John does not mention the baptism of Jesus, the Temptation, the Transfiguration, the institution of the Lord's Supper, or the agony in Gethsemane. Closer study reveals much larger divergence in contents than this.

4. In John the cleansing of the Temple comes at the beginning of the ministry (*2*.13–22). In the Synoptics it comes at the beginning of the last week.

5. In the Synoptics the Last Supper is a passover meal and Jesus is crucified on what, to us, would be the next day. (The Jewish day began in the evening at sunset, so by Jewish reckoning the crucifixion was on the *same* day but some twelve hours *after* the Passover supper.) In John Jesus was arrested, condemned and crucified *before* the Passover supper (*18*.28, *19*.14). This means that he was put to death at the same time as the Passover lambs were being sacrificed. The final meal with the disciples was not, therefore, the Passover.

6. In the Synoptics Jesus begins his ministry after John the Baptist has been arrested. This accords with the idea of John the Baptist as a preacher of repentance and a forerunner of Jesus. In John, the two ministries overlap (*3*.22–30, *4*.1), which emphasizes the idea of the Baptist as primarily a witness to Jesus.

7. There is a marked difference in style between the Synoptics and John. We have often referred to the short pithy sayings and brief anecdotes to be found in the Synoptic pericopes. In John the discourses are long and elaborate, and it is sometimes not possible to distinguish what are meant to be the words of Jesus from the comments of the evangelist.

8. In John, Jesus is recognized as the Messiah from the beginning (*1*.34, 41, 45, etc.). In the Synoptics there is no such recognition. The disciples first grasp the truth at Caesarea Philippi. This points to a deep difference in the way the evangelists think of Jesus. The Synoptic evangelists are sure of Jesus' real status, but they begin by talking about him as a man in whom God's power was at work. John sees Jesus as the divine son from the beginning, completely in control of

affairs. Opposition frustrates Jesus in the Synoptics. In John it simply provides incident on the road to his glorification. In John, even the cross reveals Jesus' glory (17.1.).

9. In the Synoptics the miracles are usually directly related to illness, and to the power that works through Jesus to bring healing. Many of the miracles are exorcisms and rarely do the accounts involve much explanation. In John there are seven miracles, all in the first twelve chapters, all referred to as signs; in each case John is less concerned with the recipients themselves than with the implication regarding the status of Jesus. In some cases the teaching based on the miracle is very extensive. John's seven signs are to be found in 2.1–11, 4.46–54, 5.1–9, 6.1–14, 6.15–21, 9.1–12, and 11.1–44.

10. Many terms, familiar from the Synoptics, are missing from John. In John there is only one parable (10.6) and it is quite different from the Synoptic kind. Demons are few in John though very common in the Synoptics. The central theme of the teaching of Jesus in the Synoptics is the kingdom of God. Only two passages in John (3.3–5 and 18.36) mention it. The Greek word that lies behind 'preaching' and 'Gospel' occurs frequently in the Synoptics but not at all in John. John never talks about repentance, though the Synoptics often do. Curiously, John talks much about the Jews, much more than the Synoptics, but he never mentions the Sadducees. So we could go on. The differences in vocabulary and presentation are enormous.

The 'I am' sayings in the fourth Gospel

The majesty of Jesus is nowhere more clearly demonstrated than in seven sayings which begin with the words, 'I am'. In them Jesus makes the most far-reaching claims about himself and these claims are heightened if they are linked with Ex. 3.14 and 6.2. All the statements come from the fourth Gospel. None is found in any of the Synoptics. The seven sayings are as follows (but see also 8.24, 28, 58, 13, 19, 18, 6):

6.35 the bread of life

> 8.*12 the light of the world*
> 10.*7 the door of the sheep*
> 10.*14 the good shepherd*
> 11.*25 the resurrection and the life*
> 14.*6 the way and the truth and the life*
> 15.*1 the true vine.*

b **Did John use the Synoptics?**

As we shall see, it is generally agreed by scholars that John was the last Gospel to be written. How does it come about, then, that John is so different from the Synoptics? To some extent the answer lies in the evangelist's situation and his purpose. But this leaves unsolved the question whether John knew about the Synoptics and used them. There has been a long and inconclusive debate among NT scholars on this subject. Some have held that John did not know the Synoptics at all. This seems hard to believe. It is very unlikely that he did not know the general outline of one or other of them, even allowing for the fact that the other Gospels were probably composed and preserved in cities far from his own.

It is, however, difficult to prove more than that John had general knowledge of one or other of the Synoptics. There are endless small points to be pursued, such as the 'two hundred pennyworth' in Mk. *6.*37 and Jn. *6.*7, the 'take up thy bed' in Mk. *2.*11 and Jn. *5.*8 or the references to Mary and Martha (Lk. *10.*38–41; Jn. *11*) and to the anointing of the *feet* of Jesus (Lk. *7.*36–9; Jn. *12.*1–8). At the end of the day, however, there will be no certainty. This evidence is quite inadequate and the problem remains unsolved.

c **Hebrew or Greek?**

Another problem on which scholars have concentrated for many years is the question whether the fourth Gospel is essentially Jewish or Greek in its thought structure. The problem is posed in the first verse, 'In the beginning was the Word'. What does the word 'Word' mean? In the world of Greek culture, *logos* (which is the Greek word John uses for 'Word') was widely used for the fundamental and essential rationality of the creation. The creation worked. It made sense. It was orderly. All this was due to a principle of reason-ableness that permeated everything. Any biblical student can see that this Greek idea of *logos* is impersonal and foreign to the Bible. In the Bible, things are orderly because God wills it so. There is no 'principle of reasonableness', but a God who wills things to be as they are.

What then does *logos* mean in John? Could it possibly be the Greek *logos,* or is it the divine creative word of Gn. 1, 'God spake, and it was so'? This is what the discussion is about.

There are other indications of Greek ways of thinking. Instead of the kingdom of God, which is a Jewish idea, we read about eternal life, which could be a Greek idea. Instead of concrete and practical actions, which represent the Jewish style, we read about abstract ideas like truth and life, which represent the Greek style.

It is hard to believe that judgments of this kind are very reliable. They rest so much on the subjective judgment of the scholar. On the other side, John has a deep interest in the Hebrew OT, he is familiar with the Jewish festivals, he under-stands Jewish expectations and Jewish customs. His know-ledge of the geography and topography of Palestine and Jerusalem is remarkable. It is, in fact, much easier to argue that John is thoroughly Jewish than it is to argue that he is thoroughly Greek. The truth probably is that the author was a Jew, immersed in Jewish culture but living in a Greek city in the days when Christianity had been separated from Judaism. His audience was Greek and he had to commend the Gospel in Greek terms or not commend it at all. This is probably enough to explain the Greek atmosphere. Some scholars have pored over ancient texts that derive from other contemporary religious sects in the hope of showing that John was really linked with them, but it is doubtful if they have proved very much. The need to speak to Greeks in Greek terms is prob-ably sufficient explanation.

d **Authorship and provenance**

The problem of authorship is no easier to resolve than the

other problems we have looked at. Chapters *1–2* do not name their author; *20*.30 f. looks like the end of a book, and there are other reasons for supposing that chapter *21* is an appendix. But chapter *21* does say something about authorship. Verse 24 looks like an appendix to the appendix, added deliberately to say who the author was. The reference, however, is not clear. Verse 24 plainly refers to the 'the disciple whom Jesus loved' (see *21*.20). This disciple is mentioned several times in the Gospel (*13*.23–5, *19*.26, *20*.2–8, *21*.7, *21*.20–4). But who was he? He reclined in Jesus' bosom; he asked who would be the betrayer; to him Jesus, on the cross, commended his mother; he outran Peter to the tomb; he recognized the risen Jesus on the shore; but he is never named. The traditional view has always been that he was John the son of Zebedee and that he wrote the Gospel at an advanced age in Ephesus. This view finds support in a clear statement by Irenaeus, bishop of Lyons, dated about AD 185.

The problem begins with the question of date. Nearly every scholar who turns his attention to the matter concludes that John was written very late in the first century or even in the beginning of the second. When it was written, it was not immediately accepted by the Church and it needed some spirited defence before it attained a status equal to that of the Synoptics. The question is therefore raised whether a contemporary of Jesus would have been writing at that date, and also why a Gospel, known to have been written by 'the disciple whom Jesus loved', was not immediately accepted by the Church at large.

A complication arises from the fact that Papias, about whom we have already heard (31a), mentions two Johns living at Ephesus, one a disciple of Jesus, the other an elder or presbyter. Some think it reasonable to suppose that there was a mix-up between the two Johns, that the elder was the true author, but that the credit went to the apostle. This supposition would solve both the problems raised in the previous paragraph. John the elder might have been in his prime in AD 100, but he might have been a nobody to the Church at large.

A further problem that militates against authorship by any

one man is the immense range of the Gospel. At one moment the author writes as a typical Jewish resident in Palestine at the time of the ministry, at another as one who knows well the ways of the Gentile world, understands its various challenges to the Church, and attempts to meet them at a time and place far removed from Jerusalem in AD 30. This is sometimes explained by the supposition that the Gospel was composed in two stages. The first stage provides the Palestinian colouring and may well be directly attributable to John the Apostle. The second stage emerged only after decades of struggle and development. If the second editor was also called John (whether the elder or not), this would account for the mix-up.

All these Johannine problems reveal to us how difficult it is to know anything with complete certainty after so long a time. They do not, however, affect the contents of the Gospel. To say that the background is problematic is not in any sense to say that the Gospel is inauthentic. Criticism in the literary sense must never be confused with criticism in the every day usage. (See above 1e.)

e   **The historical value of the fourth Gospel**

The differences between John and the Synoptics raise a question about the historical reliability of John. The Synoptics are nearer to the event. They must surely be more reliable. Their view was countered by claims that John contained evidence of 'eye-witness' material such as could have come only from one who was with Jesus. More recently some scholars, impressed by the Greek elements in John, have represented it as a theological and philosophical tract having no interest in the facts at all. But equally recently others have reckoned to discover evidence of a sound historical tradition in John.

There can be no doubt that much of the Gospel is reflexion rather than reportage. But that does not mean that there is no historical tradition in John, nor that, where he contradicts the Synoptics, they must be preferred. It can be argued that, at times, John clarifies a Synoptic story by giving its proper historical context. For example, why did Jesus suddenly turn on the disciples in Mk. *8.*27 and ask, 'Who do men say that I am?' Perhaps John supplies the answer. He reports that many disciples were deserting and it had become necessary for each person to make up his mind where he stood (Jn. *6.*66–8).

Perhaps the theory of two stages in the composition would help here. If the final editor had a source that contained the earliest Palestinian traditions, then local knowledge and contemporary observations would show through in the final version, no matter where and when it appeared. There is, of course, no evidence for a written source, but the argument would still hold if the source were oral. At any rate, it will not do to say simply that there is no historical material in the fourth Gospel. The truth is more complicated than that.

The purpose of the fourth Gospel

f

There may be many problems surrounding the fourth Gospel, but there can be no doubt about its depth and its insight. No document that has ever been written expresses the pure spirit of Christian faith better. Indeed, so rich and many-faceted is the fourth Gospel that scholars find it difficult to agree about the purpose for which it was written. It serves so many ends now, and it might have served any number of ends in AD 100.

One suggestion is that John was written to add to what was already known from the Synoptics. This argument rests on the supposition that John knew the Synoptics, but even if he did not, it is reasonable to suppose that what he wrote was an interpretation of the tradition that he did know.

Some suggest that John wrote to translate the Gospel from Jewish terms into Greek. Much of the earlier tradition would have been hard for a person of Greek culture to grasp. One had only to think of the difference between the Hebrew idea of the resurrection of the dead and the Greek idea of the immortality of the soul. Is John attempting to build a bridge between the two cultures? The Gospel is certainly grounded in the Hebrew world and yet it was produced and circulated far from Palestine.

Some think that the Gospel was directed to Jewish readers rather than to Greeks, and that it was a missionary document intended to convince the Jews of Asia Minor that Jesus was the Messiah. It is quite clear that John has some very hard things to say about 'the Jews' who did not believe (5.16, 18, 45 f., etc.). They fail to understand Moses, he says (5.45 f., 7.19). The true disciples of Moses are Christian believers. The approach may appear undiplomatic, but it is precisely the kind of argument that would make sense to Jews though not, of course, to Gentiles.

Some maintain that the Gospel is primarily concerned with false doctrine. One of the reasons why the Gospel is dated as late as AD 100 is that it seems to be concerned with corruptions of the Christian faith that would have taken some decades to develop. One such corruption was the belief that Jesus was not a real man at all. He was a heavenly being who only pretended to suffer. This may seem odd to us, but, just as there have been many who have denied the divinity of Jesus, so there have been some who denied his humanity. (See note on Gnosticism and Docetism at 37o.) John's Jesus is certainly the heavenly Son of God, but he was tired and wept and thirsted, all of which underlines his humanity.

Some have thought that the key to the Gospel is the fact that John the Baptist is clearly subordinated to Jesus in it. There is some evidence that there was a sect that derived from John the Baptist (see, for example, Ac. 19.1–7) and it is possible that one aim of the Gospel was to resist this sect by subordinating the Baptist to Jesus.

The last word should rest with Clement of Alexandria, a distinguished Christian scholar who was born probably within half a century of the appearance of the fourth Gospel. He wrote, 'Last of all, John, because he perceived that the bodily things were presented in the other Gospels, in consultation with his friends and motivated by the divine Spirit, created a Spiritual Gospel.' The meaning of the words 'bodily' and 'spiritual' may have changed through the centuries, but some of what Clement meant is still clear to anyone who reads through all four Gospels. The Synoptics begin with a mundane and earthy Jesus and yet they show him to be the

Messianic figure. John begins with the Jesus who was glorified in the Church's faith. He does not forget the earthy, but he is more concerned to move on to the Jesus to whom all time and space belong. Without the fourth Gospel, Christianity would be a different kind of faith.

Chapter 33

Jewish Sects and Parties

a **Sadducees**

THE name comes from Zadok, David's priest in Jerusalem. The Sadducees were not so much a party as a club of aristocratic priestly families. They had much political power in the Hasmonaean period and under the Romans, so that the aristocratic element was more significant than the priestly. They tended to be worldly in their tastes and ready to compromise with Greek and Roman overlords, even though their centre was the Temple. One of the tragedies of Judaism was that the holy place was in the hands of such an uninspiring group. The Sadducees not only allowed the Temple market, about which Jesus protested, they also profited from it. It hardly needs to be said that they were unpopular and out of touch with the common people.

The Sadducees were rigorous in their application of the Torah, perhaps more so than the Pharisees. The story of the trial of the apostles in Ac. 5, in which Gamaliel makes a wise interjection, suggests that the Sadducees were not only rigorous but wooden in religious matters. The Sadducces had little regard for the prophetic literature or for the volumes of interpretation of the Torah that had appeared in Pharisaic circles in the previous two or three centuries. They rejected beliefs that had no basis in the Torah; hence they did not believe in the resurrection of the dead nor in the coming Messianic kingdom. In Mk. 12.18–27, where Jesus argues with the Sadducees about resurrection, he proves his case with a quotation from the Torah.

372

Josephus gives an account of the Sadducees in Ant. 18.1.4 and Wars 2.8.14 and draws attention to their remarkable belief in free will.

b **Pharisees**

The origin of the Pharisaic movement is to be found in the conflict between Israel and the invading Greek culture in the third century BC. One group refused to compromise. Originally they were called Hasidim, and out of them grew the Pharisees. The root of the name is not clear but it probably has something to do with 'separation'.

Unlike the Sadducees, the Pharisees did not represent one profession. They were a guild or party and most members were laymen. A few priests were Pharisees because they were devoted to Pharisaic ideals, not because they were priests. Similarly many scribes (copiers and teachers of the Law) were Pharisees, but not all Pharisees were scribes. Whereas the Sadducees were strong in the Temple at Jerusalem, the Pharisees were strong with the common people all over the country. Their influence was felt in the synagogues.

The Pharisees revered the Torah, the Prophets and the Writings, though they regarded the Torah as unique. To defend it they built up a tradition of what must be done and what must not be done in order to ensure that the Torah was not broken even by accident. This was known as 'the fence about the Law'. Rabbis, that is teachers of the Law, who were the backbone of the Pharisaic party, argued endlessly about this tradition and their various interpretations became known as 'the tradition of the elders' (Mk. 7.3). The complexity of this teaching was in sharp contrast to the simple and direct teaching of Jesus (Mk. 1.22).

The Pharisees were enthusiasts for the Jewish faith and given to making converts or proselytes (Mt. 23.15). According to the Gospels they were ostentatious in their devotions, but it is a grave historical error to dismiss them all as hypocrites. As a party they were deeply religious and thoroughly committed. If they were scathing about Gentiles and recalcitrant Israelites, it was because their faith in the God of Israel

373

required them to be so. Josephus refers to them in Ant. 18.1.3 and Wars 2.8.14, and he gives them a good report for both sincerity and humility.

In NT times there were two parties among the Pharisaic scribes, followers of Rabbi Hillel who were slightly liberal and who were willing to ask whether a particular ruling was practicable, and followers of Rabbi Shammai who were strict and unbending in all things. All the Pharisees believed in the resurrection, and rewards and punishments after death, and in the Messianic kingdom.

The Sanhedrin

The Jerusalem Sanhedrin (from the Greek word sunedrion *meaning 'council') was the supreme court of Israel. It had seventy-one members, including the high priest as chairman. Its members were mostly Sadducees, though there were some Pharisees. Jesus, Peter and John, Stephen, and Paul are all said to have appeared before this Sanhedrin (Mk. 14.55; Ac. 5.27, 6.12, 22.30). Every town also had its local Sanhedrin to deal with breaches of the Law. Its members were local elders and they had jurisdiction over all criminal, civil and religious matters, for the Mosaic Law covered everything.*

---

c **Essenes**

This group is not mentioned in the NT, but Josephus describes them at length (Wars 2.8.2–13, Ant. 18.1.3). Much of the description, though not all, fits the Qumran community who were responsible for the Dead Sea Scrolls, so the majority of scholars hold that the community was a sect of Essenes. The Essenes, like the Pharisees, derive from the Hasidim. No satisfactory explanation can be give for the name.

The Essenes were a celibate and monastic order spread throughout Palestine. They lived and worshipped in community but worked in secular tasks during the day. Like the very early Christians, they pooled their goods and appointed stewards to administer them. The Essenes were rigorists in every way. They rejected pleasure as an evil, embraced poverty, rose early to pray, and made a virtue of meekness. They took frequent ritual baths and wore white garments when they were not at work. Their devotion to the Torah verged on the fanatical. No one was admitted to their communities before completing a three-year novitiate, which is, perhaps, just as well.

The surprising thing about them is that some of their doctrines are most un-Jewish. They espoused a Greek doctrine of immortality, their devotion to the sun is open to various interpretations, but it diverges from traditional Judaism. They did not deny Temple sacrifice but took no part in it themselves.

d **Zealots**

The zealots were guerilla fighters. They were Pharisaic in their religious outlook, but, unlike the main body of Pharisees, they believed in direct action. The movement probably began when one Judas (variously called the Gaulonite, the Galilean, or Judas of Gamala) led a rebellion against the census instituted for tax purposes by Quirinius, the Roman governor of Syria, in AD 6. They were strongly Messianic in their outlook even believing that their acts of insurrection would hasten the coming of the Messiah. Their movement reached its zenith in the war against the Romans in AD 66–70 when zealots fought and died with fanatical heroism. See Josephus, Ant. 18.1.6. It is probable that one of Jesus' disciples was formerly a Zealot (Lk. 6.15).

e **Herodians**

This group is mentioned in Mk. 3.6, 12.13 and Mt. 22.16. Luke avoids the term. Presumably they were a group of residents in Palestine who approved the policy of the Herods, though it is difficult to understand how anyone could. The really remarkable fact is that the Pharisees, who detested the Herods, were willing to make common cause with them against Jesus. Bad causes make bad bed-fellows.

Taxes

Palestine, particularly Judaea, was not prosperous in the first century AD. *The Jews bitterly resented paying taxes to the Romans because they also had to pay their own taxes. It was a double burden, and, to make it worse, the Roman system was open to corruption. The purpose of the census was to assess the population for tax. The right to collect was then sold to a publican in Rome. The publican then raised his own local collectors. Each collector had a fixed profit margin, but it was easy for him to collect more and keep it. Taxes were raised in various ways (customs, poll-tax, property tax, etc.) and they were used for roads, bridges and for 'protection' by the army. Certain taxes are laid down for Jews in the Torah, particularly the half-shekel (Ex. 30.31) and the tithe (Dt. 14.22). Beyond this there were various firstfruits and offerings for the Temple. It is easy to see why the matter was a sensitive one and why publicans were readily classed with sinners.*

Chapter 34

The Acts of the Apostles

a Authorship and date

WE have already argued that Luke's Gospel and Acts were by the same author, and that he was most probably Luke, the companion of Paul (31h). Acts was written after the Gospel (Ac. *1*.1), so a date fairly late in the century is probable. Acts does not refer to the death of Paul and some have argued that it was written while he was still alive. This would create havoc with the usual theories about the chronology of the NT. Assuming that the tradition that Paul died under Nero is correct, Acts would need to be written before AD 64, Luke some time before that, and Mark some time before that. Granted we have no certainty in the matter of dating NT books, none the less this theory is less probable than the common supposition that Acts does not mention the death of Paul, though it had already taken place, because Luke's purpose would not have been served by recounting it.

Towards the end of the century Josephus' work was published and Paul's letters were collected and circulated. There is, however, no evidence that Luke made use of either of these sources, so we can conclude that the most likely date for Acts is around AD 85–90. The place or origin is unknown. Most scholars assume that it was Rome, but it might have been anywhere.

b Sources

There is a strong probability that, in writing the Gospel, Luke used Mark and another source we call Q. Are there sources behind Acts? Unfortunately we do not have two other versions with which to compare Luke's version. It does seem, however, that there was a travel diary, which first appears in *16*.10 (see above 31j 8). That very fact suggests that Luke was not present throughout the rest of Paul's mission, that is to say, in those parts of Acts where he uses the word 'they' and not 'we'. Moreover, the first part of Acts deals with the early Church in Jerusalem and the missions that took place from there. It is unlikely that Luke, who first appears in Philippi, and who was probably still working in AD 90, was present in Jerusalem in the early days. We can therefore infer three sources, one from Jerusalem, one concerned with the Pauline mission, and the travel diary. There are no grounds for saying whether the first was written or oral. The second was probably oral. There may also have been traditions from other places, but we do not know.

c **Historical reliability**

Acts, like the Gospel, was written to unfold the plan of salvation, to show how the Gospel marched on from Jerusalem, its birthplace, to Rome, the capital of the world. This is history with a theological slant. It is more concerned with interpreting events than with recording them. It has sometimes been said that Luke is a very reliable historian and that he makes few mistakes in geography and the organization of the Roman Empire. This is true, but there are difficulties of two kinds.

In the first place, Luke does not fulfil the requirements of *modern* historians, that is, he does not aim at complete and impartial coverage of his area, he does not prove his case by providing evidence, he does not aim at precision in detail. But why should he? He was not a modern historian. His purpose was quite different from theirs. The fault here lies with those who expect him to be what he could never have been, and who read his history as if it had been written in the light of modern disciplines.

In the second place, Luke's theological aim leads him to

construct a plan that is not entirely consistent with what we know from other sources, particularly Paul's letters.

In Gal. *1* Paul is anxious to establish his independence of the Jerusalem apostles, so he lists every occasion on which he had come into contact with them. We may reasonably assume that Paul would know the facts, and, with the kind of critics he had in Galatia, he would want to get it right. He mentions two visits to Jerusalem:

1. A visit three years after his conversion lasting a fortnight (*1*.18).
2. A visit with Barnabas and Titus, fourteen years later, to discuss the Gospel he was preaching (*2*.1).

Acts records a visit of Paul to Jerusalem immediately following his conversion, indeed before the facts of the case were known to the Jerusalem apostles. It is very hard indeed to suppose that Luke intended to imply a gap of three years between *9*.25 and 26. Then Acts records another visit in *11*.30 in which Paul and Barnabas bring up the proceeds of a collection. There is no mention of this visit in Galatians. Ac. *15* describes a third visit, the so-called Council of Jerusalem, which was certainly concerned with the terms of the Gospel that was being preached, but the account of the discussion given in Ac. *15* is very different from that in Gal. *2*.

The Acts account of this council gives rise to several problems. The whole matter appeared to have been settled in Ac. *11*.18. The conclusion reached in *15*.20 (which describes the 'minimum law' that Gentile converts must keep) contradicts the tone of the speeches, and it is a conclusion Paul would never have agreed with. It is impossible to imagine the author of Galatians delivering decrees about ceremonial requirements to his converts as Ac. *16*.4 states. In Ac. *21*.25, James seems to be telling Paul about these decrees for the first time. A further point is that the decrees of Ac. *16*.20 would have been impossible for the Gentile church to keep, as they required the co-operation of Jewish butchers.

The difficulties can be solved if we assume that Paul is more likely to be correct about his own actions than Luke, especially if we take into consideration Luke's understanding of the plan of salvation. In his writings, the Gospel moves in an orderly progress from Galilee to Jerusalem and from Jerusalem to Rome. Luke is anxious to work Paul into this plan, so he makes sure that every phase in Paul's life *begins and ends in Jerusalem.* He sets out five phases.

Conversion *9.1–26*
Caesarea, Tarsus, Antioch *9.30–11.30*
First journey *12.25–15.4*
Second journey *15.30–18.22*
Third journey *18.22–21.15.*

In *23.*31 Paul sets out under guard from Jerusalem to Caesarea and Rome.

In this scheme Luke banishes the idea of Paul as the free-lance evangelist and fits him into his careful plan. It is entirely consistent that he should do so. But we are bound to conclude that Gal. *2* is more likely to be accurate in its account of the Jerusalem conference than Ac. *15.* Indeed, it is reasonable to suppose, from Paul's ignorance in Ac. *21.25,* that most of Ac. *15* relates to a council at which Paul was not present. One supposition is that there were two councils, one without Paul, concerned only with Jewish areas, and one, recorded in Galatians, at which the work was divided up. The decrees of Ac. *15.*20 would be perfectly appropriate in Judaea where Judaism was dominant.

d **Paul's journeys**

One of the gravest injustices that was ever done to a NT author is to be found in the emphasis we place on Paul's missionary journeys. Schoolboys learn them for their homework, maps of them are bound into Bibles, examination questions are set on them, tourists pay large sums to follow in Paul's steps. This is much to be regretted, for it is a capital example of gazing at the frame and ignoring the picture. There is a journey in Luke's Gospel, but we do not ignore the teaching and the events in order to study the journey as a journey. Why do we do it with Acts? It is hard to escape the conclusion that we teach Paul's journeys because they are easy to teach, easy to illustrate, and easy to learn. We seem to forget that, as journeys, they are of little consequence.

To begin with, a mission that involves long stops in places like Corinth and Ephesus is not well described as a journey or several journeys. Secondly, it is the preaching that matters. The travelling and the route tell us nothing about the Gospel. Thirdly, according to Paul's own account of things. he spent long periods preaching and teaching in different places (and suffered many privations that Luke does not mention according to 2 Cor. *11*.23–8) without being aware that he was on the first, second or third journey. Fourthly the 'journey' provided a useful literary scheme for Luke, which he had already used in his first volume, and which enabled him to show that Paul fitted into the Galilee–Jerusalem–Rome plan. Luke simply organized Paul's missionary activity into phases that began and ended in Jerusalem. Later generations have tended to magnify 'the three missionary journeys'.

It would be good for our understanding of Luke if we turned from the classroom maps and gave more attention to Luke's plan and to the meaning of the events which occurred as the Gospel marched on to Rome.

e   **The purpose of Acts**

Luke's purpose in Acts is in keeping with that in the Gospel. That means that he is concerned to show that Christianity was not a dangerous and subversive religion but a wholesome faith for the world. Consequently he records that Paul is always being exonerated by the Roman authorities (Ac. *16*.39, *17*.7–9, *18*.12–7, *19*.37–41, *23*.29, *25*.25, *26*.31 f.). At the same time he describes the progress of the Church under the Spirit as it overcomes every obstacle on its way to Rome. Luke's two volumes attempted to unfold a history of the work of the Holy Spirit in the first Christian century.

Chapter 35

Cities of St. Paul

a   NEITHER the map nor the list of cities that follows is exhaustive. Acts mentions many towns through which Paul passed, Seleucia, Attalia, Rhegium, etc., but there seems little point in taking note of these towns when no incidents are reported as having taken place there. On the other hand, the more we can known about the towns and cities where Paul did preach, the better we shall understand his message.

Much of Paul's work was done in great city centres like Corinth and Ephesus, but it does not follow that the important cities in the Christian story were identical with the important cities of the ancient world. There were great cities, like Pergamum, that Paul appears never to have visited, and others, that figure largely in Paul's life story but were not so important by the standards of the day. There is no better example of this than Jerusalem, the centre of the universe for Jews, and the place where it all began to Christians, but, to Romans, a small, distant and insignificant town.

b   **Antioch in Pisidia**: a city important in both Greek and Roman worlds. It was a junction on the Roman road system and was consequently busy with both civil and military traffic. It was also a Roman colony which means that settlers had come from many parts to live there. Paul and Barnabas visited Antioch and preached in the synagogue two sabbaths running

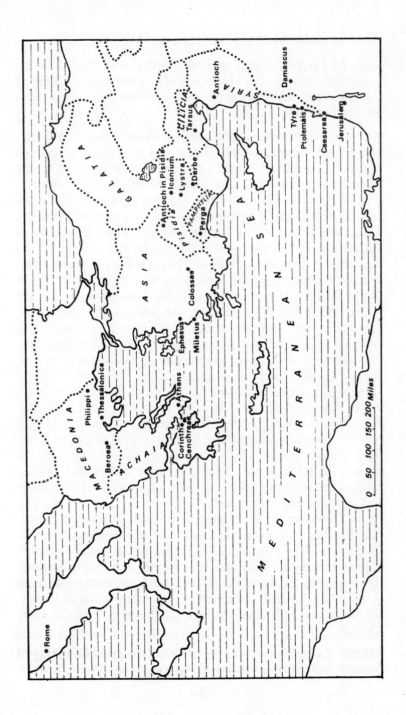

(Ac. *13*.14–50). There was opposition and Paul left the synagogue to preach to Gentiles who were showing a lively interest. Paul and Barnabas were expelled, and angry Jews pursued them to Lystra.

Antioch in Syria: one of the greatest cities of both the Greek and Roman empires. Only Rome and Alexandria exceeded Antioch in political and cultural importance. Situated on the river Orontes, Antioch was ideally placed to be a centre of trade between east and west. Roman government, Greek culture and oriental religion met in the streets of Antioch. There was also a strong Jewish element. After the death of Alexander the Great, Antioch became the capital of the Seleucid or Antiochan empire. Thus it had a profound influence on the history of the Jews, especially after 198 BC, when the land of Israel was included in the Seleucid domain. (See above 10k.) The Maccabaean war was fought against the Seleucids. The Romans made Syria into a province with Antioch as its capital. A government was installed there who had authority over a huge area including Galilee and Judaea. All the various rulers of Palestine in NT times were subservient to him. Christianity reached Antioch due to the scattering of disciples after the death of Stephen (Ac. *11*.19–26). Barnabas and Paul worked there for a year and Ac. *11*.20 reports that they preached to Greeks, that is to say, to Gentiles. Some ancient MSS, however, change 'Greeks' to 'Greek-speaking Jews'. This difference in the text plainly reflects the controversy in the early Church about whether it was legitimate to preach to Gentiles or not. (See 29q–s.) The name 'Christian' was first used in Antioch. It was from Antioch that Paul and Barnabas set out on their missionary travels (Ac. *13*.1, *14*.26). Ac. *15*.22–30 records that a special report of the conclusions of the apostolic council was sent to Antioch (but see 34c). Paul and Peter had a confrontation at Antioch (Gal. *2*.11). Antioch remained an important centre of Christian work and influence throughout the period of the early Church.

c **Athens**: this noble city was the centre of the great flowering of culture that the western world has ever seen. The Athens of

Socrates and Plato, however, was but a memory in NT times. The city was of no great importance in the Roman world and there is little evidence that Paul did very much work there. Paul stayed in Athens according to 1 Thess. *3*.1 and preached according to Ac. *17,* but he seems never to have returned and perhaps never founded a church there. Ac. *17* shows that Athens, like all Greek and Roman cities, was given up to popular cults known as 'mystery religions'. These cults kept their rituals secret. Each had its own god (or Lord, as he was called) and each professed to provide certain forms of protection. Only initiates could benefit, so a prudent (and wealthy) citizen joined as many cults as possible in order to gain the maximum number of benefits. Doubtless misfortune still struck, even when one had subscribed to all the temples there were. Perhaps this explains the existence of an altar 'to an unknown god'. The great philosphers had their successors in contemporary Athens, and Paul addressed them. It is not clear from Ac. *17*.19 ff. whether he was giving a lecture or facing some kind of trial. Similarly, it is not clear whether Areopagus refers to a court of that name or the place, Mars Hill.

Beroae: a city of Macedonia where Paul and Silas were well received by the Jews (Ac. *17*.10–4).

Caesarea: an important sea-port twenty miles south of the Carmel range. The town was given to Herod the Great by Augustus and Herod rebuilt it in his usual lavish style. The work included a large artificial harbour. It was finished in 10 BC and named after Augustus Caesar. The procurators established their HQ in Caesarea, presumably because it was the port nearest to the world that mattered to them. It was badly placed to be the administrative centre of Judaea and Samaria, but it was very near to Galilee. Cornelius the centurion (Ac. *10*) and Philip the deacon (Ac. *21*.8) lived in Caesarea. Paul was imprisoned there for two years and faced trial from two procurators, Felix and Festus, and from Agrippa II who was on a visit from over the border (Ac. *23*.31–*26.32*). The Jewish War of AD 66 began with an incident that took place at Caesarea.

Cenchreae: the eastern harbour of Corinth leading to the Aegean Sea. When Paul sailed away from Corinth he embarked there (Ac. *18*.18). There is no record of Paul working at Cenchreae but Ro *16*.1 refers to a church there, so here is a further indication that Acts is not to be regarded as a complete history of the early days.

Colossae: an important Greek and Roman city just over 100 miles east of Ephesus. The city is in the valley of the Lycus, and Laodicea and Hierapolis are near by. Philemon and Onesimus lived there (Col. *4*.9).

d **Corinth**: A great sea-port and capital of the Roman province of Achaia. A glance at the map reveals how important Corinth was. The journey between Italy and Asia Minor could be shortened by hundreds of miles if travellers sailed up the Gulf of Corinth and crossed the narrow neck of land that joined the north of Achaia to the south. This was the common military and trade route. Small ships were actually hauled across the isthmus. Larger ships had to unload and their cargoes were taken overland and loaded on to other ships at Cenchreae. Corinth was the city that stood astride this east-west and west-east route. Corinth had been refounded and resettled as a Roman colony in 44 BC. Hence it was a relatively new city with no ancient traditions in NT times. The colonizers were Roman freedmen who might have been of any nationality and Corinth is, therefore, aptly described as a cosmopolitan city. Paul stayed in Corinth eighteen months. (See below 37d.) Archaeologists have uncovered a rostrum that may well be the actual place where Paul was charged before Gallio (Ac. *18*.12). They have also uncovered a number of shrines, including one of Aphrodite, the goddess of love. Information from secular sources is entirely consistent with what Paul implies in his Corinthian letters.

Damascus: the ancient and modern capital of Syria. Like so many other ancient cities, Damascus owed its importance to being situated at the junction of trade routes. The routes from the Fertile Crescent to Egypt and from Arabia to the north crossed at Damascus, an ancient oasis where water was plentiful. In NT times the city was in eclipse, as far as political power goes, for it came under the Nabataean kingdom (an Arab kingdom subservient to Rome) and Aretas IV, the Nabataean king, had installed a governor there (2 Cor. *11*.32). There was a large Jewish population and it appears that Christian missionaries were at work there within a few years of the crucifixion. Ananias was their leader (Ac. *9*.10–19). Paul preached there after his conversion and escaped over the wall when opposition was aroused (Ac. *9*.25; 2 Cor. *11*.32 f.). Gal. *1*.17 implies a second visit. Legally it is unlikely that the high priest in Jerusalem had any power over Jews in Damascus, as Ac. *9*.2 implies, but the Jews did not think of their nation in territorial terms. Jews were a people and a nation under covenant to God, wherever they happened to be living.

Derbe: a town on the borders of the Roman provinces of Galatia and Cilicia in a district known as Lycaonia. Paul visited the town twice (Ac. *14*.20, *16*.1).

e   **Ephesus**: an important sea-port and capital of the Roman province of Asia. The fame of Ephesus, however, rested even more on the famous shrine of Artemis, a goddess of fertility. The Roman name for the goddess was Diana, though Diana had slightly different characteristics from Artemis. Female images with many breasts reveal the true nature of the Ephesian goddess. The shrine was centuries old. It had been rebuilt in the fourth century BC and was regarded as one of the seven wonders of the world. Due to the silting up of the river, the population of Ephesus had moved away to the west, but it made no difference to the popularity of the shrine. The whole site has now been excavated and, apart from the shrine, remains of the stadium, rebuilt under Nero, have been discovered. Similarly the theatre has been found where Paul confronted the mob (Ac. *19*.29). Paul spent three years in Ephesus (Ac. *20*.31), encountering opposition from Jews as well as from the silversmiths. Later he bade a moving farewell to the Ephesian elders at Miletus as he made his way back to Jerusalem in Ac. *20*.16 f. Much must have happened at Ephesus about which we know nothing. Christian tradition connects John the Apostle with Ephesus, but there is no hint of this in Acts.

Iconium: a large city of the Roman province of Galatia. Paul and Barnabas visited it and met opposition from the Jews (Ac. *13*.51, *14*.21).

f   **Jerusalem**: Jerusalem was the centre of the Jewish world, though the Romans put the administrative centre at Caesarea. A Roman presence was maintained in Jerusalem at Herod's palace and at the tower of Antonia. The most important factor about Jerusalem was that it was the place that God had chosen. There his altar and Temple were built. (See above 27a–f.) All Jewish longing stemmed from this fact. (See Ps. *122, 137.*) The leader of the church in Jerusalem was James, the brother of Jesus (Ac. *15*, Gal. *1*.19). The Ac. *15* council met under his direction (but see 34c). The Jerusalem church was poor because the city had little industry apart from that connected with the Temple, and Christians were probably excluded from that. If, as is probable, there was a famine in the mid forties (Ac. *11*.28), the need for Paul's collection for the poor saints at Jerusalem is easily explained (R. *15*.25 f.; 1 Cor. *16*.1–4). The number and circumstances of Paul's visits to Jerusalem are matters of scholarly debate. (See above 34c.) Paul was arrested and made his first defence there (Ac. *21–3*). When the Jewish revolt began in AD 66, the whole population suffered terribly. The city was sacked by Titus in AD 70.

Lystra: a Roman colony in the Roman province of Galatia. It was visited by Paul at least three times (Ac. *14*.6, 21, *16*.1). Barnabas and Paul were taken for gods there after they had healed a cripple (Ac. *14*.8–18). Timothy came from Lystra.

Miletus: an important sea-port just south of Ephesus where Paul met and said goodbye to the Ephesian elders (Ac. *20*.17–38). 2 Tim. *4*.20 suggests another visit.

Nicopolis: a town mentioned in Tit. *3*.12. Several cities bear this name. The most likely one is on the western coast of Greece.

Paphos: a sea-port in the west of Cyprus, the capital city of the island and seat of the pro-consul. Paul had a confrontation with the local sorcerer, Elymas, that resulted in Elymas losing his sight and the pro-consul, Sergius Paulus, being converted (Ac. *13*.6–13).

Perga: a large city in the Roman province of Pamphylia. Paul apparently stayed there only a short time, though he passed through the place twice. We know no more than that he preached at Perga and that Mark left him there (Ac. *13*.13 f., *14*.25).

Philippi: a town of Macedonia named after Philip of Macedon, the father of Alexander the Great. It was situated on the Egnatian Way, that great highway, the M4 of the ancient world, that linked east and west. Philippi was also a Roman colony. It was the site of one of the great battles of Roman history, when Antony and Octavian (later Augustus Caesar) defeated Brutus and Cassius in 42 BC. Paul preached for the first time in Europe by a river to the west of Philippi (Ac. *16*.13). The story continues with Paul and Silas being beaten and imprisoned. (See Ac. *16*.11–40.) Paul had the happiest relations with the Philippian church. They contributed generously to the cost of his travels (Phil. *4*.10–20).

g   **Rome**: the imperial city which Paul longed to visit and where he arrived, a prisoner, in Ac. *28*.16. He addressed his greatest letter to the Christians there. Rome was built on the east side of the river Tiber on seven hills with the names Capitol, Palatine, Aventine, Caelian, Esquiline, Viminal and Quirinal. Originally Rome was a monarchy, but it became a republic in 510 BC. Roman rule then expanded by conquest till it covered the whole area from Scotland to India. Rome was a city of sumptuous buildings and many of them can still be seen. Of all the remains of NT times, perhaps the most interesting is the Arch of Titus, a triumphal arch built to celebrate the victories of Titus in the Jewish War. Rome was the scene of chariot racing, gladiatorial combats, theatrical performances and, in the course of time, the persecution of Christians. Both Peter and Paul probably died there. The

389

Circus Maximus and the Colosseum are witnesses to many martyrdoms. In NT times there was a large foreign population including many Jews. There was a multiplicity of cults and religious philosphies imported from all over the world.

Roman citizenship

Rome controlled its conquests overseas by establishing colonies that were intended to be extensions of the great city itself. The colonies were populated by settlers who might be government officials, wealthy traders, officers of the garrison, or others of similar class. All these possessed Roman citizenship, which was a status and not to be confused with actual residence in Rome. Certain members of the native population who had been especially helpful to the empire might be given Roman citizenship. In the course of time corruption set in and the status could be bought. (See Ac. 6.37, 22.25, 28). Certificates were issued so that citizens could prove their status when away from home.

Salamis: a town in the east of Cyprus where Paul and Barnabas preached in the synagogue (Ac. *13*.5). Mark was with them.

h **Tarsus**: one of the oldest cities in the world and the place where Paul was born. Tarsus was the capital of the Roman province of Cilicia. It was an important commercial city in the midst of a fertile plain. Most of all it owed its importance to the pass through the Taurus Mountains called the Cilician Gates. Tarsus controlled this pass. Like many other towns of the NT it was half oriental and half Greek. Tarsus had a famous school of philosophy that vied with Alexandria in learning. Was Paul educated in this atmosphere? It seems unlikely. The best way to understand Ac. *22*.3 is to suppose that Paul was born at Tarsus and educated in Jerusalem. There was a tent-making industry in Tarsus, which may possibly be an argument the other way (Ac. *18*.3).

390

Thessalonica: the capital city of the Roman province of Macedonia. The city was situated on the Egnatian Way. In 42 BC it was made a 'free city' and ruled by dignitaries called 'politarchs'. This is an unusual term, but inscriptions have been found that confirm the usage in Ac. *17*.6, 8. Paul visited the city more than once and what are probably his first letters were addressed to the church there. Jason, Paul's host, was dragged before the politarchs by the Jews and falsely accused (Ac. *17*.7).

Troas: a large and important port in the north-west corner of Asia Minor in the Roman province of Asia. Paul was there when he had the vision of the man of Macedonia (Ac. *16*.6–11). He also preached at a Eucharist when Eutychus fell out of the window (Ac. *20*.7–12). Troas was also a Roman colony. It is not far from though not identical with, the Troy of classical literature.

Tyre: an ancient Phoenician port on a small island. It is frequently referred to in the OT. Jesus visited Tyre according to Mk. *7*.24. There was a Christian settlement at Tyre when Paul finally came back to Palestine on his way to Jerusalem (Ac. *21*.3–7). He stayed seven days and the local Christians did their best to persuade him not to go further. He was adamant, however, and he departed after an emotional farewell on the beach.

Chapter 36

NT Chronology

a IN the early days of the Christian faith, the years were reckoned from the supposed founding of the city of Rome. Not until the sixth century AD did Christendom abandon this method of counting and turn instead to the idea of 'the Christian era'. A Roman monk was responsible for the change. His name was Dionysius Exiguus, which means 'Dionysius the insignificant'. Whether that is a witness to his stature or his humility is not clear. Insignificant or not, Dionysius was a great ecclesiastical lawyer and he began the system we have been using ever since.

Unfortunately he did not get it quite right. Jesus was born rather earlier than he thought. By comparing the old system with the new we can fix the death of Herod the Great at 4 BC. It is probable that Jesus was born while Herod the Great was still alive, so we are led to a date of 5 or 6 BC. Scholars have tried hard to find a date for the census of Lk. 2.1 f., but there are so many difficulties and the evidence is so contradictory that one has to admit that the attempt has failed.

There are no historical grounds for regarding December 25th as the correct birthday. This date was not adopted by Christians until the fourth century and then it was almost certainly to provide a Christian alternative to pagan midwinter festivals. There is little on which we can base even a reasonable guess as to the correct date.

The baptism of Jesus is said to be in the fifteenth year of the reign of Tiberius Caesar (Lk 3.1). At this time Jesus was about thirty (Lk. 3.23). The reign of Tiberius is usually dated from AD 14, but there is some uncertainty about this because he was regent before he was emperor. None the less, we can reasonably conclude that the ministry began between AD 24 and 29. The three-year ministry of the fourth Gospel is no more probable than the much shorter period of the Synoptics, which gives us AD 24–32 for the crucifixion.

In these matters of dating it is common to make use of the Latin word 'circa', which means 'about' or 'approximately'. We therefore say that the crucifixion took place circa AD 30.

Nearly all the other dates in the chart are approximate. In some cases they are only guesses. The purpose of setting them out is not to suggest that all this is established but rather to show the probable relationship of one set of events to another.

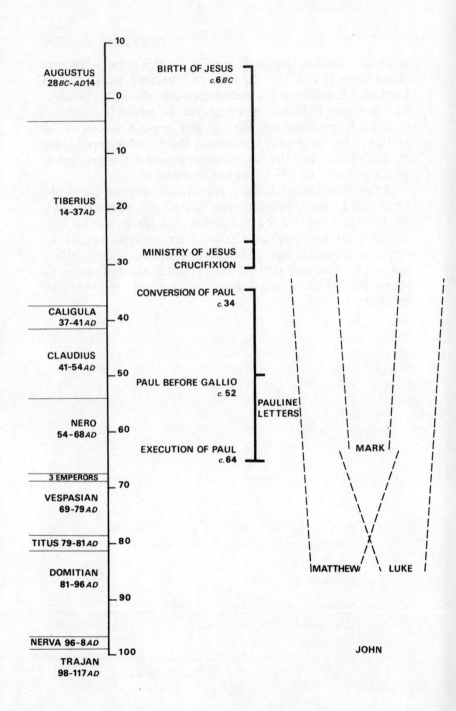

AUGUSTUS 28BC-AD14	10	BIRTH OF JESUS c.6BC
	0	
	10	
TIBERIUS 14-37AD	20	
	30	MINISTRY OF JESUS CRUCIFIXION
		CONVERSION OF PAUL c.34
CALIGULA 37-41AD	40	
CLAUDIUS 41-54AD	50	PAUL BEFORE GALLIO c.52
NERO 54-68AD	60	EXECUTION OF PAUL c.64
3 EMPERORS	70	
VESPASIAN 69-79AD		
TITUS 79-81AD	80	
DOMITIAN 81-96AD	90	
NERVA 96-8AD	100	
TRAJAN 98-117AD		

PAULINE LETTERS

MARK

MATTHEW   LUKE

JOHN

Chapter 37

The Pauline Epistles

a Romans

ROMANS has always been regarded as the quintessence of the Pauline Gospel. It was used and quoted by other Christian writers almost at once. No serious doubt has ever been cast on its authorship. The one critical problem concerns its ending. Scholars have sometimes wondered how Paul could send greetings to so many people (see Ro. *16*) in a church he had never visited. Moreover, the concluding doxology at the end of chapter *16* tends to wander about. In some versions it appears at the end of *14*, and, in one Greek papyrus, at the end of *15*. It is quite possible that so important an epistle was sent to more than one church, in which case, perhaps the long version with all its greetings was sent to a church Paul did know, such as Ephesus. In one group of MSS the words 'at Rome' are missing. None the less, nobody doubts that the body of the epistle was sent by Paul to Rome.

b The Roman Church

We know nothing about how it was founded. The Roman Catholic view is that, after the Council of Jerusalem (Ac. *15*), Peter went to Rome, founded the church, and became its first bishop. If this is true, it is odd that Luke does not mention it in Acts and that Paul sends no greetings to Peter.

The church was probably established before AD 50, for, at that time, Jews were expelled from Rome for disputing about 'Chrestus', surely 'Christus'. (See above 28 l.) We can infer from Ro. *1*.13 and *11*.13 that the church was predominantly Gentile, but Paul's method of argument is thoroughly Jewish (note the abundance of quotations from the OT) and he is deeply concerned about the place of Israel in the new dispensation (Ro. *9–11*).

The important fact is that Paul had never been to Rome. He is writing a letter to introduce himself. It does not deal with the local situation as the Corinthian letters do. Instead Paul sets out his Gospel at length. It is for that reason that the letter is so valuable to us.

c **Summary of Romans**

1. Introduction
   Long theological greeting including a summary of the Gospel (*1*.1–7)
   His wish to preach in Rome (*1*.8–17)
2. Universal need of man for the Gospel
   Proof of man's guilt with special reference to Gentiles (*1*.18–32)
   Proof of man's guilt with special reference to Jews (*2*.1–*3*.18)
3. God's new plan of salvation
   Summary of the doctrine of justification through God's grace (*3*.19–31)
   Abraham was saved by faith, not by obedience to the Law (*4*)
   Those justified by faith have nothing to fear (*5*.1–11)
   Christ has reversed the fall of Adam (*5*.12–21)
4. The new life of the Christian
   The Christian has died with Christ, so the sinful self is gone for ever (*6*)
   The role of the Law and its inability to deal with sin (*7*)
   The freedom of the Spirit (*8*)
5. The problem of unbelieving Israel
   Why Israel has been rejected, why the Gentiles have

heard the message, and how Israel will at last return (*9–11*)

6. Practical problems
   A Christian's duties (*12*)
   Attitudes to the state and one's neighbour (*13*)
   Protecting the weak (*14*.1–*15*.13)
7. Personal matters
   Plans for the future (*15*.14–33)
   Greetings (*16*.1–23)
   Closing doxology (*16*.25–7)

d **The Corinthian letters**

Paul had founded the Corinthian church (Ac. *18*) and kept in touch with it. There had been trouble and Paul had heard about it (1. Cor. *1*.11, *16*.17). Indeed the Corinthians appear to have written to Paul asking his advice (1 Cor. *7*.1). Nobody doubts that Paul wrote 1 and 2 Corinthians. The difficulty is to know just how many letters he wrote to this church and whether some of the lost ones are hidden in the two letters we possess. 1 Cor. *5*.9 shows that Paul had already written to Corinth before 1 Corinthians and that the letter was about relationships with Christians who were immoral. It has been suggested that part of this lost letter is found in 2. Cor. *6*.14–*7*.1, but that passage is about unbelievers and no MS has ever been found from which it is missing, so the suggestion has little to be said for it.

2 Cor. *2*.4,9 and *7*.8 refer to a letter written by Paul to Corinth that was very severe in tone. Can this be 1 Corinthians? Hardly, for apart from the early chapters, 1 Corinthians is quite a friendly letter. Some believe that part of the severe letter is found in 2 Cor. *10–3*, but again there is no MS evidence.

From 2 Cor. *12*.14 and *13*.1 f. we learn that Paul paid Corinth at least three visits. Acts records only two (*18*, *20*.2), which confirms that Acts cannot be taken as a full account of Paul's movements.

In general the Corinthian letters were written by Paul to a

church he knew well to answer their questions and to resolve their feuds.

e The Corinthian Church

Corinth was a port and a provincial capital. Its residents included all sorts from high Roman officials to low debauched sailors. The church reflected this social background. Some of the lowest types had been converted (1 Cor. 6.9–11). So, too, had some of the wealthiest, and they were turning the Lord's Supper into a private dinner party from which the poor members of the congregation were excluded (1 Cor. 11.17–22). Plainly it was a divided community. Neither was it a simple division of rich and poor. 1 Cor. 1.12 suggests that three or four parties, which might or might not have coincided with social divisions. Apollos, a cultivated Christian Jew from Alexandria, had also worked in the city (Ac. 18.27 f.). From 1 Cor. 3.1–9 it appears that his presence made matters worse. Apollos and Paul were very different and appealed to different types of people.

It is easy, therefore, to see where the Paul party and the Apollos party come from, but why a Peter party? As far as we know Peter never went near Corinth, but we do not know everything. As for the Christ party, was there one? The words might refer to a holier-than-thou group in Corinth, but, alternatively, they might represent Paul's own confession. Paul attacks the divisions roundly. For him, unity was an essential feature of the Church.

Acts records two visits by Paul to Corinth (18.1–17, 20.1–3). On the first occasion he stayed with Aquila and Priscilla. He had a bitter confrontation with the Jews in the synagogue and so moved his preaching place to the house next door. Crispus, the chief Jewish elder, was converted. The Jews took their case against Paul to Gallio, the pro-consul, but he was not interested.

f Summary of 1 Corinthians

1. Introduction

Greetings (*1*.1–3)
Thanks for their gifts (*1*.4–9)
2. Divisions in the Church
An attack on divisions coupled with an exposition of the
Gospel as 'the foolishness of God', and a defence of his
own apostleship (*1*.10–*4*.21)
3. Cases of immorality
The evil-doer should be expelled (*5*)
Christians should not go to law in heathen courts
(*6*.1–11)
The body is not for fornication (*6*.12–20)
4. Topics raised in their letter
Sexual relations (*7*)
Meat sacrificed to idols, including a lengthy illustration
of his own forbearance in *9* (*8*.1–*11*.1)
The place of women in public worship (*11*.2–16)
Spiritual gifts, their multiplicity, the pre-eminence of
love, the need to use spiritual gifts—and this particularly applies to 'tongues'—to build up the Church and
to enrich its worship (*12*–*14*)
The resurrection: Paul gives an outline of the Gospel
followed by a list of resurrection appearances, followed by a defence of the Christian hope of the resurrection (*15*)
News of the collection for poor Christians in Jerusalem
(*16*.1–4)
5. Personal matters
Personal plans for the future and requests (*16*.5–18)
Final salutation and blessing (*16*.19–24)

g **Summary of 2 Corinthians**

1. Introduction
Greetings and thanksgiving (*1*.1–7)
News of his misfortune in Asia (*1*.8–11)
2. Paul's self-defence—first phase
His absence from Corinth was not due to fickleness but to
concern for them (*1*.12–*2*.17)
Paul's ministry: he is minister of a new covenant (*3*)

The glory of the Gospel is the glory of Christ revealed through weakness and death (*4*)

Though confident about the life to come, his present concern is preaching the Gospel (*5*.1–*6*.10)

Appeal to the Corinthians to be reconciled to Paul (*6*.11–*7*.16)

3. Appeal for contributions to the Jerusalem churches (*8–9*)
4. Paul's self-defence—second phase

They should not under-estimate him or compare him unfavourably with others (*10*)

Rudeness in speech and unwillingness to be paid do not negate his apostolic authority (*11*.1–15)

His record of suffering can bear comparison with any (*11*.16–33)

His visions were equally striking (*12*.1–13)

He is coming again to Corinth ready to be severe (*12*.14–*13*.10)

5. Final salutation and blessing (*13*.11–14)

h **Galatians**

For generations scholars have argued about whether the Galatians were a people called the Galatae, who lived in northern Asia Minor, or the inhabitants of the Roman province of Galatia further south; and students have patiently studied their arguments. It is an arid discussion, probably impossible to resolve, and certainly less important than the theological argument pursued in the epistle. No one doubts that the letter was written by Paul.

A serious situation had arisen in the Galatian church. The argument whether Gentile converts to Christianity should submit to the whole Jewish Law (see above 29q–s) had broken out in an acute form. Enemies of Paul had arisen who insisted that only Jews could be Christians, and they had persuaded Gentile converts that they could not become Christians unless they were circumcised. Further, they denied, not only Paul's practice of admitting Gentiles on confession of faith in Christ, but also his apostleship and his entire Gospel.

400

Paul was not the kind of man to take this quietly. He argues vigorously that his call and his Gospel came from God, that he owed nothing and was not subservient to the Jerusalem apostles (which suggests that their views were different from his), that whatever they did in Jerusalem, they acknowledged him to be the apostle of the Gentiles, and that his Gospel was the true Gospel. He summed up his Gospel as free forgiveness and redemption through the grace of Christ and not through any legal obedience whatever.

Visits to Galatia are mentioned twice in Acts (*16*.6, *18*.23). Iconium, Lystra, and Derbe were in the Roman province of Galatia, so it is possible that the first visit to Galatia is described, not in *16*.6, but in *14*.1 when Paul came to Iconium. In that case, Ac. *14* and *16*.1–4 describe incidents in the life of the churches to which this epistle was sent.

i **Summary of Galatians**

    1. Introduction
        Greetings (*1*.1–5)
    2. Defence of his apostleship and his Gospel
        Sorrow over their lapse (*1*.6–10)
        His independence of the Jerusalem apostles (*1*.11–*2*.21)
    3. The Galatian error
        The gift of the Spirit depends on faith alone (e.g. Abraham) (*3*)
        Christians are free sons of God, not slave children (e.g. Abraham's two children) (*4*.1.–*5*.1)
        To accept the Law means to turn away from Christ (*5*.2–12)
        Christian freedom involves high moral standards (*5*.13–26)
    4. Conclusion
        General instructions to the faithful (*6*.1–10)
        Reiteration of the message (*6*.11–17)
        Blessing (*6*.18)

Judaisers

'*Judaiser*' *is the name given to those who argued that Gentiles must first be circumcised before being admitted to the Christian faith. (See above 29q–s.) What is not absolutely clear is whether those Judaisers who attacked Paul's teaching were conservative Jews who accepted Christianity but regarded it as an element within Judaism, or fanatical Gentile converts who found it impossible to accept Jesus as the fulfilment of the Jewish Law without accepting the Law itself with all its demands.*

j   **The captivity epistles**

Four of the letters commonly attributed to Paul contain numerous references to his being a prisoner. (See Eph. *3*.1, *4*.1,*6*.20; Phil.*1*.7,13,14,17; Col.*4*.3,10,18; Philemon 1,9, 10,13,23.) It is hard to believe that they are all metaphorical. If Paul was in prison when he wrote these letters, we need to ask where. He proudly states that he had been 'in prisons more abundantly' than his rivals (2 Cor. *11*.23), which does not help us. Acts refers to imprisonments at Philippi (*16*.24), Jerusalem (*22*.24), Caesarea (*23*.35), and Rome (*28*.16), but there may well have been more. Philippi can be counted out because it was only an overnight affair. So, too, can Jerusalem, because Paul stayed only a short time and was much too busy there. We do not have to assume that all the letters were written from the same prison.

On the face of it, Rome was the most likely place for writing letters, for Paul had considerable freedom there (Ac. *28*.30). On the other hand, he was at least two years at Caesarea with time on his hands. Some have argued that Paul was imprisoned at Ephesus which is an attractive hypothesis because Colossae, where Philemon lived, was close at hand. An Ephesian imprisonment would suit Colossians and Philemons well.

To some extent, arguments about the prison are bound up with arguments about date. If the letters did come from Rome, they would all be very late. By the same token any that could be proved to be early could not have come from Rome.

k **Ephesians**

Ephesians is a profound, theological document, but it raises certain difficulties.

1. There are no greetings in it at all, though Paul had preached in Ephesus for two years according to Ac. *19*.10, and he would have known countless people there.

2. Two of the best Greek MSS omit the words 'at Ephesus' in *1*.1.

3. There are no references to particular problems in the church. Other letters are full of them.

4. Marcion, a heretic who produced a list of NT books in the second century AD, calls this letter the epistle to the Laodiceans.

One reasonable explanation is that this was a circular letter sent round to several churches. Marcion had seen the copy from Laodicea, but the copy from Ephesus became the best known.

There are, however, a number of further difficulties that lead many scholars to conclude that Ephesians was written by a disciple of Paul rather than by Paul himself. It is important to remind ourselves yet again that, by the standards of the day, this would not necessarily constitute forgery. Rather it might be the act of a devout and modest man anxious to render credit where he thought it was due. The difficulties are as follows:

1. All the epistles we have looked at so far are concrete and practical. Even Romans, sent to a church of which Paul had no direct knowledge, deals with immediate issues. The author of Ephesians is not concerned with practical problems. There are no angry charges, no self-defence, no controversy at all. Instead the author explores the vast theme of the divine plan of redemption, and the cosmic significance of Christ. Typical of this change is the fact that Paul speaks often of *the churches*, meaning

403

actual communities in particular places. Ephesians speaks of the one *Church*, a divine and mysterious unity, that has significance, not simply for the world of men, but for the heavenly beings as well.

2. Paul's style is usually vigorous and impulsive. Sentences are often short and spontaneous. In Ephesians sentences are long, involved, and hard to unravel. *1*.3–23 consists of two sentences.

3. Many words and phrases from Ephesians are not found in the other letters and vice versa. For example, 'the devil' comes twice in Ephesians and not at all in Romans, 1 and 2 Corinthians, and Galatians. 'Satan' comes ten times elsewhere, but not at all in Ephesians. The force of this argument depends on the number of examples and the number is impressive.

4. In *3*.5 we read of 'holy apostles and prophets'. This witnesses to a time when these people had become institutional figures in the Church. In Paul's day things were still in a state of flux and the arguments were still going on.

5. There are many verbal similarities between Colossians and Ephesians, far more than between any other two letters. About a third of the words in Colossians reappear in Ephesians. The only reasonable explanation of this, if Paul was the author of both, is that he wrote them at the same time. In those days one could not keep carbon copies for future use. He must have written one letter within a few days of the other. But then the differences come into play. The differences in style and subject matter and in the meanings given to the same words and phrases are so great that a long gap between the two is demanded. Considerations of this kind lead to the conclusion that the author wished to sound like Paul and quoted him as much as possible, but his situation was, in fact, different. There are echoes of other epistles, too, in Ephesians, but they create no difficulty.

Against this it must be said that all the concerns are

Pauline. Ephesians is about grace and salvation and unity, and above all, the greatness and the glory of Christ, all themes that Paul would readily have written about and probably did in Colossians.

There is further the question of 6.21 f. These verses contain practical details which would not have made sense in a general epistle written after Paul was dead. But these words are also in Colossians. It is hard to believe that Paul spelt out the same practical plan involving the same person at the same time to two different churches. One turns, therefore, to the alternative explanation that the author included this practical detail from Colossians in order to make the letters seem more like Paul's own. This leads many scholars to conclude that Ephesians was written for general circulation by a disciple of Paul who applied the message of the great apostle, particularly the teaching of Colossians, to his own later situation. Pauline authorship was not questioned in the early Church but the doubts go back to the sixteenth century, to Erasmus.

1 **Summary of Ephesians**

   1. Introduction
      Greetings (*1*.1 f.)
   2. The mystery of the Gospel
      Prayer of thanks and blessing with a summary of the
         Gospel (*1*.3–14)
      Thanks and prayers on their behalf (*1*.15–23)
      The privileged place of believers in the divine plan (*2*)
      His own position as preacher to the Gentiles (*3*.1–13)
      Further prayer for them and doxology (*3*.14–21)
   3. Practical exhortations
      The need for unity (*4*.1–16)
      They must live no longer as Gentiles do (*4*.17–32)
      They must shun every kind of immorality (*5*.1–21)
      Exhortation to wives, husbands, etc. (*5*.22–*6*.9)
      The whole armour of God (*6*.10–20)
   4. Conclusion, personal reference and blessing (*6*.21–4)

m **Philippians**

This letter was sent by Paul to Philippi to thank them for a gift. Apparently they had made gifts to him twice before, but then there had been a break while Paul was away. (See *4*.10–20.)

3.1a suggests that the letter is about to end—presumably with some words about his gratitude for the gift—but instead, in *3*.1b, Paul launches into an attack on 'evil workers' who put their trust in 'the flesh'. Paul is given to such digressions. Attempts have been made to dissect Philippians into two or three letters, but they have gained little support. The Pauline authorship seems secure.

When Paul first visited Philippi and founded the church there (Ac. *16*.11–40) he was dragged before the local magistrates and falsely accused (v. 21). Acts describes the night in gaol, the earthquake and the conversion of the gaoler. Paul's relations with the church seem to have been very happy, though *3*.2–19 show that trouble was never far away.

n **Summary of Philippians**

1. Introduction
   Greetings (*1*.1 f.)
   Thanksgiving and prayers for them (*1*.3–11)
2. Personal news (*1*.12–26)
3. Exhortations
   They must stand firm in the faith (*1*.27–30)
   They must be united in love (*2*.1–11). (This passage includes in vv. 6–11 what may perhaps be a quotation from a Christian hymn)
   They must be peaceable (*2*.12–8)
4. He is sending Timothy and Epaphroditus to them (*2*.19–30)
5. Warnings against Judaisers
   He contrasts the attitude of those who put their trust in the Law with his own spiritual struggle (*3*.1–21)
6. Further admonitions, particular and general
   They must stand fast and rejoice (*4*.1–9)

Thanks for their gift (4.10–20)
7. Salutation and blessing (4.21–3)

o **Colossians**

Colossae was a small town in Asia Minor about 100 miles east of Ephesus. Apparently the church there was founded, not by Paul, but by Epaphras (1.7). 2.1 suggests that Paul had never been there. Epaphras, however, was a companion of Paul, and no doubt Paul assumed some kind of responsibility. Epaphras, who was a Colossian (4.12), was with Paul in prison at the time of the writing of the letter, so it was carried by Tychicus (4.7). Philemon was also a Colossian. This is clear from the fact that Onesimus, his slave, was sent home with Tychicus (4.9).

Paul finds it necessary to warn the Colossians against false teaching that is abroad, and many have thought that there was a particular false teacher at Colossae. Chapter 2 gives some clues to this false teaching. 'Philosophy and vain deceit' (Col. 2.8) is a good description of a strange movement called Gnosticism, which proved a great threat to the Christian faith towards the end of the first century and throughout the second. A few Gnostic terms occur in this chapter. 2.16 is a warning against a renewal of legalism. 2.18 talks of bogus angel worship. 2.20–3 returns to the theme of legalism. Paul's answer is to show that Christ is sufficient for everything and that all other means to salvation are false.

There is here a clear development of Paul's thought, so much so that some have argued that Paul did not write Colossians. The vision is much broader than in the earlier epistles. The work of Christ is not simply to bring salvation to men but to redeem the whole universe. The argument is, of course, complex and no answer can be taken as proved. One reasonable supposition among others is that Colossians represents the full flowering of Paul's theological imagination.

Gnosticism and Docetism

1. Gnosticism was a mixture of philosophy and religion. It

407

was an attempt by imaginative intellectuals to draw all religious ideas together into one comprehensive system. 2. Each Gnostic thinker did it in his own way, so no two systems agree, save that they were all complicated and all eclectic (that is, constructed of bits and pieces from all over the place).

3. Angels and demons in various ranks figure in all the systems.

4. The way of salvation was to know the system (the name Gnosticism comes from the Greek word for knowledge) and how to ascend it. This was often thought to be a dark secret, so Gnosticism had the attraction of being an esoteric cult.

5. This made it the antithesis of Christianity which rested on faith and not on knowledge.

Docetism, *was the belief that Jesus was never a true man but a spirit who inhabited a human body. The true Jesus escaped from the Roman soldiers and allowed someone else to be crucified in his place. Docetism comes from a Greek word meaning 'to appear'. Jesus appeared to be a man but in fact was not one.*

p **Summary of Colossians**

1. Introduction
   Salutation (*1*.1 f.)
   Thanksgiving (*1*.3–8)
2. Christ's glory
   Prayer for them which turns into a glorification of Christ (*1*.9–23)
   His awareness of his own duty to preach Christ (*1*.24–2.5)
3. Timely warnings
   They should beware of those who would offer their own sophistries in place of Christ (*2*.6–23)
4. The risen life of Christians
   They must live the life of those risen with Christ (*3*.1–4)

They must put away all malice and immorality (3.5–11)
They must put on godly virtues (3.12–7)
Advice to wives, husbands, etc. (3.18–4.1)
They must be constant in prayer and thanksgiving (4.2–6)
5. Personal messages and greetings (4.7–17)
6. Blessing (4.18)

q **The Thessalonian letters**

Paul's visit to Thessalonica is described in Ac. 17.1–9, but the reference to three sabbaths in 17.2 can hardly mean that he stayed only three weeks. The relationship seems too deep for that. While Paul and Silas were at Thessalonica, there was a disturbance caused by the Jews, and Jason, Paul's host, was brought before the magistrates and falsely accused. Paul and Silas escaped by night. From Athens Paul sent Timothy to Thessalonica to gather the latest news (1 Thess. 3.1 f.).

The Pauline authorship of 1 and 2 Thessalonians raises problems, the chief of which is that, at one point, the two letters seem contradictory. 1 Thess. 5.1–11 speaks of a *sudden* coming of the day of the Lord; 2 Thess. 2.1–12 speaks of a number of preliminary events which make it appear that the end cannot come yet. Some scholars are inclined, therefore, to accept 1 Thessalonians as Pauline and 2 Thessalonians as a later pseudepigraphical work written perhaps to explain the delay in the parousia. Paul is not the most consistent of writers and the eschatological hopes of both Judaism and Christianity are full of contradictions. This argument alone cannot, therefore, tell against Pauline authorship, and other more technical arguments are not very strong. In the circumstances it is perhaps best to suppose that Paul wrote both letters, the second a little while after the first to correct a misunderstanding.

The Thessalonians were in some doubt about matters relating to the end of the age. They did not know what would happen to those who were dead at the time of the Parousia. They also wanted to know when it would be. Some apparently had given up work and were waiting for the day. The first letter attempts to deal with these points and to offer the usual defence against detractors. The second letter attempts to clear up the misunderstandings left by the first. The key passage is 2 Thess. 2.1–12, which asserts that the Parousia is not to be yet. From 3.6–15 we can infer that the problem of idleness, briefly alluded to in 1 Thess. 4.1–11 f., had grown worse.

r **Summary of 1 Thessalonians**

1. Introduction
      Greetings (*1*.1)
      Thanksgiving (*1*.2–10)
2. Paul's self-defence
      Vindication of his behaviour against accusers (*2*.1–16)
      He had not forgotten them and was eager for news (*2*.17–*3*.13)
3. Exhortation
      They should abstain from fornication (*4*.1–8)
      They should carry on working honestly (*4*.9–12)
4. Teaching on the Parousia
      The dead would share in its glory (*4*.13–8)
      The end would come suddenly (*5*.1–11)
5. Conclusion
      Further admonitions (*5*.12–22)
      Salutation and blessing (*5*.23–8)

s **Summary of 2 Thessalonians**

1. Introduction
      Greetings (*1*.1 f.)
      Thanksgiving for their faithful endurance (*1*.3–12)
2. Teaching on the Parousia
      They should not be misled: many things had to happen first (*2*.1–12)
      They should stand fast (*2*.13–17)
3. Admonitions
      They must pray for him as he does for them (*3*.1–5)
      They must carry on working diligently (*3*.6–15)

4. Concluding salutation and blessing (*3*.16–8)

t **The Pastoral Letters**

This is the name given to 1 and 2 Timothy and Titus because these letters consist of directions to younger men on the care of the churches. They are so similar that they must be taken together.

Timothy and Titus were both companions of Paul. Timothy came from Lystra where Paul first met him (Ac. *16*.1–3). He travelled extensively with Paul and was often sent on special errands. He is mentioned frequently in Paul's letters. Phil. *2*.19–30 show how Paul esteemed and trusted him. Curiously Acts does not mention Titus, but Paul mentions him in 2 Corinthians and Galatians. He was a Gentile convert to Christianity (Gal. *2*.1–3) and, therefore, one of those around whom the great controversey raged. Should he be circumcised or not? Paul said no and held his ground. (See above 29s.) Titus was also used as a messenger and an ambassador for Paul (2 Cor. *7*.6, *8*,6, 23).

Fixing the background of these letters has caused much difficulty. The personal and geographical references are hard to fit in with the other letters of Paul and also with Acts.

1 Timothy: Timothy appears to be at Ephesus (*1*.3) and Paul hopes to come to him soon (*3*.14, *4*.13). In the only visit of Paul to Ephesus that is recorded extensively in Acts, Timothy left Ephesus ahead of Paul (*19*.22). A brief visit is recorded in Ac. *18*.19, but Timothy is not mentioned.

2 Timothy: Paul is now in prison in Rome and is suffering hardship (*1*.15–17). Luke alone is with him (*4*.11). His first defence is over and it went badly (*4*.16). He looks back on his former sufferings in the cause and prepares for the end, which seems not far away (*3*.11, *4*.6–8). Yet, on the other hand, he appears to have been recently at Corinth and Miletus (*4*.20), and he urges Timothy to come to him bringing Mark and also a cloak and books from Troas (*4*.11–13, 21). The difficulty here is how, if Paul had 'finished the course', he could expect to profit from books brought from the other end of the

411

Mediterranean. If we allow time for Paul's letter to reach Timothy and then for Timothy to go to Troas and Rome, we are in difficulties with the words, 'the time for my departure is come'.

Titus: Paul is free and has left Titus in Crete (*1*.5). He hopes to meet him in Nicopolis, where he will spend the winter (*3*.12). Crete is mentioned in Ac. *27*.7–21 as a stop on the way to Rome. Wintering in Nicopolis after that is scarcely possible, unless there is a chapter in Paul's life, after his arrival in Rome, about which we know nothing.

u   It is clear already that the Pastoral Letters present problems, but there are others.

1. The Pastorals do not read like private letters to individual friends but rather like official communications.

2. Letters of this kind to Timothy and Titus were hardly necessary, for they were constant companions of Paul. The instruction here is directed to churches.

3. The ecclesiastical atmosphere revealed in the letters does not belong to the time of Paul. The bishop has now arrived, the undoubted head of the local church (1 Tim. *3*.1–8; Titus *1*.7–9). This suggests the time, not of Paul, but Ignatius, early in the second century.

4. There is false teaching in the background and the author attacks it in a most un-Pauline way. He rules against it with an air of confident if rather fussy authority. Paul was never so cool. He always attacked with vehemence and passion. The teaching referred to, a mixture of Judaism and Gnosticism, is reminiscent of what we know about the second century rather than the first.

5. 'Faith' in Paul means a personal relationship with Christ. In the Pastorals, '*the faith*' means formal Christian teaching and practice (1. Tim. *4*.6, *5*.8, *6*.10, 21). Similarly we now hear of

'good doctrine' as if Christianity now had its body of dogma (1 Tim. *4*.6, *6*.3; Tit. *2*.1, 10).

6. The greatest problem is the style. Even in English the difference in style between Romans and the Pastorals is immediately obvious. There are ways in which comparisons of vocabulary and style can be assessed mathematically. Scholars working in this way have shown that it is most unlikely that the author of Romans, Galatians, 1 and 2 Corinthians was the author of the Pastorals.

There is a strong presumption, therefore, that the Pastorals were not by Paul, but such a negative statement leaves their existence and use by the Church unexplained.

A pointer to a possible explanation is to be found in 2 Tim. *4*. Here, side by side, are two passages, one suggesting that martydom is already at hand, the other that he needs comfort and support throughout the coming winter. Paul would not write in such a contradictory way himself, but neither would anyone trying to give the impression he was Paul. Let us suppose that a number of fragments of genuine Pauline letters survived into the second century and fell into the hands of a teacher and pastor who was earnest enough, but who lacked Paul's inspiration, and who, of course, addressed a different situation. What would that teacher do? He might weave together the fragments into a series of continuous letters presenting Paul's teaching, as he understood it, to his own day. The result would be something very similar to our Pastoral Letters.

This suggestion is unproven. It does, however, deal with all the problems we have raised, and it reminds us of the important fact that the apostolic age did not end suddenly on the day that the last of the apostles died. Teaching and letter-writing went on unhindered and they have continued to this day. The formulation of a canon of Scripture and the exaltation of the Bible above all other literature tends to obscure this important fact. The Pastoral letters are, perhaps, best seen as a bridge between the pioneering days of Paul and the equally important but less exciting period when the Church settled down to its long sojourn in history.

v **Philemon**

A slave, Onesimus, had stolen money from his master, Philemon, escaped, and then, in some way, met Paul, who was in prison. Paul converted Onesimus (10) and would have liked to keep him by his side, but instead sent him back to his master at Colossae with this letter—and also with Tychicus and Colossians (Col. 4.7–9).

Philemon was a notable Christian of Colossae. Paul appears to have converted him (19) and the church now met in his house (2). Paul does not ask Philemon to free Onesimus but to take him back as 'a brother beloved' (16).

It is interesting that Paul asks Philemon to prepare a lodging as he hopes to be out of prison soon. We would like to know which prison this was, but we lack evidence. There is no reason to doubt that this is a genuine Pauline letter.

Chapter 38

The General Epistles

a THE arrangement of the books in the NT can give a false impression. It can suggest that the books decline in importance as the reader proceeds. Perhaps the OT provides encouragement for this view, for, according to the traditions of Judaism, the Law, the Prophets and the Writings are arranged in a descending order of authority. Preachers tend to confirm the notion by their neglect of the later books.

The impression is unfortunate for it misrepresents primitive Christianity. The early Church was not 'Paul's show'. He laboured for thirty years, travelled extensively, and founded many churches, but the Roman empire was big enough to soak up all his energy and still leave huge tracts for others. We know that there were great churches, such as Rome, Antioch in Syria, and Colossae, that Paul did not found, and that there were many other evangelists at work. The Gospels themselves prove that other people were engaged in preserving the traditions, and the non-Pauline letters give further evidence of the vigour of the Church in places where Paul was not pre-eminent. These 'other books' witness to types of Christian faith and types of Christian affirmation that are different from those we associate with Paul. They are, therefore, worthy of serious study.

The name, 'the General Epistles', is the rather vague title given to those NT letters that make no claim to be by Paul. In theory the name means that the letters were written to the

Church at large and not to a particular church for a specific purpose. For this reason Hebrews is sometimes not included among them. The name may be a useful term for biblical students to use, but the justification is not sound. Some of the 'General' epistles were written to particular communities, just as Romans was. Another name for the same writings is 'Catholic Epistles'. The word 'catholic' means 'world-wide', and the implication, not wholly accurate, is that all the letters were written for the Church throughout the then known world.

b **Hebrews**

The first problem is authorship. AV and RV head the letter, 'The Epistle of Paul to the Hebrews'; but the ancient MSS do not have this title. Modern scholars are unanimous in believing that it was not written by Paul. The arguments against Pauline authorship are as follows.

1. The first word of every Pauline letter is 'Paul', and there follows a personal introduction. Hebrews does not begin in this way and it does not name its author.

2. Early tradition is against Pauline authorship. Origen, in the third century, made the famous remark, 'Who wrote the epistle only God knows certainly'. Various suggestions were made, but they were all guess-work.

3. The NT letters were arranged in order in ancient lists according to various different principles, but Hebrews always appeared at the end of the Pauline group. The Pauline letters were often arranged in order of length. If Hebrews had been regarded as Pauline, it would have followed Romans.

4. The theme of Hebrews is consistent with Pauline teaching but it is expressed in a different way. The Jewish Law and the Jewish sacrificial system are interpreted as a shadow of the Gospel and the death of Christ. This suggests that the author was influenced by Platonic philosophy which made considerable use of the distinction between shadow and reality. Paul's way of arguing was quite different.

5. Basic Pauline terms are missing. 'Christ Jesus', a favourite term of Paul, nowhere appears. Nor does 'in Christ'. 'Faith' appears in the famous chapter *11* and elsewhere, but Hebrews lays the stress on clarity of vision and firmness of intention, whereas Paul stresses the personal relationship with Christ.

6. Paul's style is vigorous but erratic. His enthusiam tends to run away with him. The author of Hebrews writes in a more polished and regular style.

7. Paul was quite sure that he was a first-hand apostle. He could never have written Heb. *2.3*.

If Pauline authorship is excluded, we are left with the question: if not Paul, then who? Barnabas, Apollos, Luke, Silas, Priscilla and others have been suggested. The truth is that nobody knows.

It is also impossible to determine the recipients of this letter. *13*.23 suggests one particular church, but we cannot tell whether it was at Antioch or Caesarea or Rome or some other place. The balance of probabilities is that the readers were Jews, though there are scholars who would contest this. The title 'to the Hebrews' cannot be used as an argument, but the fact that the epistle is based upon the OT and that the Christian faith is expressed throughout as the perfection of Judaism points to a Jewish community.

The purpose of Hebrews cannot be easily summarized as it fulfils a number of purposes. The main intention is to strengthen Jewish Christians in the faith so that they do not slip back into Judaism; and further to show the unlimited range of the Christian Gospel in contrast to Judaism. Those who think the community addressed was primarily Gentile tend to reverse these aims and put the stress on the range of the Christian Gospel.

The theme of this work, more a treatise than an epistle, is set out in the first few chapters. God has often spoken before, but Jesus, the Son, the heir, the means of creation, the effulgence of his glory, the image of his substance, is his unique and final word. Jesus has effected something that none

417

else could effect, the redemption of mankind. He is thus superior to Joshua (*4*.9), to Moses (*2*.3), to the angels (*1*.4). He is a priest of a new order, far greater than the high priests of Judaism. His sacrifice, in which he is both priest and victim, never needs to be repeated (*10*.12).

c **Summary of Hebrews**
1. The supremacy of Christ
    The superiority of Christ to angels (*1*.1–*2*.18)
    The superiority of Christ to all who have gone before (*3*.1–*4*.13)
    The superiority of Christ as High Priest (*4*.14–*7*.28)
    The superiority of Christ's sacrifice (*8*.1–*10*.18)
2. Exhortations
    They must be⁻ faithful (*10*.19–30), learn from the examples set before them (*11*.1–*12*.2), expect chastening (*12*.3–17), and be ready to endure (*12*.18–29).
    Further admonitions (*13*.1–17)
    Conclusion (*13*.18–25)

d **James**
This letter was written by James to the twelve tribes of the Dispersion. The twelve tribes must be a metaphorical way of referring to Jewish Christians generally, but who was James? Two apostles were called James (Mk. *3*.17 f.) and Jesus had a brother called James (Mk.*6*.3). The last became head of the church in Jerusalem (Ac. *15*.13) and it has commonly been supposed that he was the author. There is little to substantiate this belief and equally little to undermine it.

At first sight the letter reads like a bad sermon. It contains no 'good news' but is full of exhortations. Someone has calculated that there are sixty direct commands in a work of 108 verses. But this author understands religion primarily in moral terms. His use of the word 'faith' in *2*.24 is very different from Paul's which explains why they use the same OT text in such different ways (cf. Jas. *2*.23 with Ro. *4*.3).

The most important factor in understanding James, however, is to grasp his relationship with the Wisdom tradition.

418

(See above 20m, 24g.) Books like Proverbs and Ecclesiasticus and Job represent an approach to religion that is far removed from Pauline Christianity. This is a reminder that the OT is a much *broader* book than the NT and OT religion has a much wider range. James stands in a true OT tradition, and is a witness to the diversity of primitive Christianity. Something similar can be said about Revelation and the apocalyptic tradition. This is not a problem. It only becomes a problem if we try to reduce the NT to a single, consistent message. The fact is that both James and Revelation have a place in the canon and the NT would not be the NT without them.

e **Summary of James**

1. Introduction (*1*.1)
2. Encouragement in temptation (*1*.2–18)
3. Wise counsels for the Christian
   Pure religion involves purity of thought and action (*1*.19–27)
   The true Christian is not impressed by wealth (*2*.1–13)
   Pure religion involves works as well as faith (*2*.14–26)
   The true Christian guards his tongue and is peaceable (*3*)
   True wisdom is to be humble before God (*4*.1–12)
4. Denunciations
   Of those who forget that life is ephemeral (*4*.13–17)
   Of the rich (*5*.1–6)
5. Further counsels of patience (*5*.7–20)

f **1 and 2 Peter**

1 Peter was written from 'Babylon', which is surely Rome, to Christians in Asia Minor to encourage them in a time of persecution. There is a sharp difference among scholars regarding authorship. Some argue that the claim of *1*.1, that the author was Peter the apostle, cannot be sustained. They point out that the Greek of the epistle is far too good for an unlettered, Aramaic-speaking fisherman, that persecution in Asia Minor in Peter's lifetime is hard to substantiate, and that

419

a number of passages in 1 Peter seem to be borrowed from other epistles.

In answer it is said that the author claims to be Peter (*1*.1) and an eye-witness of Christ's sufferings (*5*.12), that the letter was accepted as genuine very early, and that the good literary style might be due to the skill of Silvanus (=Silas), the secretary who did the actual writing (*5*.12).

Many theories have been put forward about the structure of 1 Peter. Some have suggested that a number of primitive hymns have been incorporated into a letter. Others hold that the letter is based on a baptismal sermon, others that the letter is really a baptismal liturgy. Some have argued that there is a sharp break after *4*.11, and that *4*.12–*5*.14 is an addition to render the first part into a credible letter. We can agree that the style is sermonic and that parts of the letter sound as if they had been used over and over again (e.g. *2*.21–5, *3*,18–22). We can agree that the baptismal idea is central (*3*.18–22). But, beyond that, all that is necessary is to imagine a Christian teacher and preacher of great experience sitting down to write a letter into which he crowds many of his most familiar affirmations and exhortations. 1 Peter is not the kind of letter one writes to a friend on a wet Sunday afternoon; rather it is the letter of an elder statesman, feeling a great sense of responsibility, and writing to a community of Christians many of whom were unknown to him and some of whom were facing persecution.

g **Summary of 1 Peter**

1. Introduction (*1*.1 f.)
2. Praise and thanks (*1*.3–12)
3. Exhortation to be holy as befits the redeemed (*1*.13–2.10)
4. Particular injunctions
    To be good citizens (*2*.11–7)
    To be good servants, wives, husbands (*2*.18–*3*.7)
    To be faithful as befits those who share, through baptism in Christ's sufferings and exaltation (*3*.8–22)
5. The nearness of the end—they must be sober and be ready to suffer (*4*)

6. Further counsels (5.1–11)
7. Conclusion (5.12–14)

2 Peter bears little resemblance to 1 Peter, and yet there is a positive attempt in *3*.1 to suggest that this is the author's second letter, and he calls himself 'Peter, a servant and apostle of Jesus Christ' in *1*.1. Moreover he claims to have been present during the ministry of Jesus (*1*.14, 16, 18). So, without doubt, the author was anxious to make this appear to be a letter of Peter the apostle.

None the less, few modern scholars are convinced. The letter seems to have been written to keep spirits from flagging, even though the return of Jesus was long delayed. The 'fathers' of the faith have been dead for some time (*3*.4). Paul's letters are so well known that they are gathered together and regarded as Scripture (*3*.16). Chapter *2* is verbally dependent on the Epistle of Jude. These points suggest a date long after Peter's lifetime, perhaps even in the second century. Origen and other scholars of his period were very suspicious of 2 Peter and it was a long time before it was accepted as canonical.

Very probably it is another case of what we know as pseudonymity. This suggests that the author was an admirer of Peter. He published what he thought Peter might have written. His letter is full of exhortations to watchfulness and diligence, and warnings against false teaching.

h **1, 2, and 3 John**

All three of these epistles probably come from Asia Minor at the end of the first century. They are sufficiently similar in style to suggest a common author. There has been much debate on the question whether the author of the epistles is the same as the author of the Gospel, and the evidence is probably against it. There are theological differences that would be hard to explain on the hypothesis of common authorship. For example, the Gospel is centred in Christ, whereas the epistles focus on the Father. This does not involve a contradiction but a significant difference of emphasis.

If we are concerned with two authors, then they had much in common, and many scholars hold that the author of the epistles was a disciple of the author of the Gospel. It is not certain, however, whether Gospel or epistles was written first.

1 John does not look very much like a letter. It does not begin with a name and a greeting as most NT letters do. It does not end with personal remarks and good wishes. Its contents are general, and one cannot deduce much about the people to whom it was sent, if letter it was. 1 John contains the simplest Greek in the NT. Beginners with the language often begin here. Yet the simple phrases have depths that have given rise to some of the richest writings of Christendom. This suggests that the author was a profound and sensitive Christian and the letter is really a pastoral address.

1 John consistently attacks false teaching. There are many 'anti-Christs' about (2.18), and the readers must be careful not to be led astray (2.26, 3.7, 4.1, 3). These false teachers appear to have been both docetists (see above 37o) and antinomians. 'Antinomian' is the name given to those Christians who believed that being in Christ and being free from the Law meant that they could do exactly as they liked. Their lack of moral restraint was reckoned to be a sign of their great faith!

The docetism appears in the background behind such verses as 4.2. To confess that Jesus Christ is come *in the flesh* is 'of God', but those referred to in v. 3 deny this. Of course it is not enough to say that Jesus was a man of flesh. One must also confess that Jesus is the Son of God (4.15, 5.5, 10). This also was denied, which suggests that there was a group who said: either Jesus was a man of flesh or the Son of God; he could not have been both. This was the docetist position. The author of 1 John argues strongly against it. Jesus is the Christ, begotten of God, and God abides in him, but he is still a man of flesh.

The antinomianism appears in 2.4, 3.8–10, 17, and 4.20 1 John will have none of it. For him, God is love (4.16), and his love is expressed in Christ (4.9), and love is, therefore, the supreme mark of the believer (3.11, 4.7, 20). The man who does not love his brother cannot protest that he is a Christian. These five chapters make this point unmistakeably clear.

2 John is more like a letter. It is written by 'the elder' and addressed to 'the elect lady and her children', which most scholars understand as a church and its members. This letter, too, is about love, and it attacks docetism and antinomianism (6f). The writer hopes to visit the church soon and sends greetings from his own comminity, 'thine elect sister' (12f).

3 John is a letter addressed to one Gaius, a faithful disciple and a friend of the writer. The beginning of 3 John is an echo of the beginning of 2 John and the endings are very similar. In 3 John, however, there is a passage (9–12) censuring one Diotrephes and commending one Demetrius. The letter contains the familiar emphasis on doing good (against antinomians) and walking in the truth.

i **Jude**

Jude is a short tract written by Judas, the 'brother of James', to 'them that are called', which means to all Christians. Who Jude was cannot be established. There was a Jude or Judas who was a brother of Jesus and James (Mt. *13*.55), but there are no adequate grounds for attributing the letter to him. One or two phrases, (see, for example, vv. 3 and 17) imply that the apostles had been dead some time and that the faith had solidified into a body of doctrine. This suggests the very end of the first century. Whoever the author was, he knew Jewish literature well, for the work is full of allusions to the OT and to Jewish pseudepigraphical literature.

The theme is the now familiar one of an attack on 'certain men crept in privily' who are denying the faith and behaving badly. They have, it appears, committed every sin in the book. In immoderate and colourful language Jude denounces them and warns them that the fate of Sodom and Gomorrah awaits them. The book continues with a warning not to follow their example.

Jude preserves one of the best known of all doxologies in 24f and the much quoted phrase, 'the faith which was once for all delivered to the saints' in 3.

Chapter 39

Revelation

a   BY common consent the book of Revelation stands out from all the other books of the NT. It is a strange book. Strange doctrines have been based upon it. Strange sects make use of it. It is difficult for the simple believer to read very far in it without becoming bewildered. There is something ironic about the title. A revelation is supposed to make things clear. On that reckoning, this is perhaps the one book in the NT that is *not* a revelation.

Another name for the book of Revelation is 'the Apocalypse'. 'Apocalypse' is the English form of the Greek word that is translated 'revelation', but 'Apocalypse' is a better name because it directs attention to that type of literature to which this book belongs, that is, the apocalyptic literature. (See above 201.) A great flood of apocalyptic literature appeared in Judaism in the last two centuries BC and the first century AD. It is worth noting here some of the more important features of that literature.

1.   It grows out of a deep despair of this world and of human history generally. Whereas the prophets expected salvation in this world order, the apocalyptists believed that the only possible end for this world was utter destruction. They pinned their hope on what lay after the destruction.

2. The apocalyptic writers expected a catastrophic divine intervention. Whereas human figures of one kind and another might have measured up to the task in the days of the prophets, no human son of David, no matter how gifted, could be expected to bring about the dissolution of the age.

3. In line with this other-wordly hope, the apocalyptists looked, quite literally, for a new creation, a new heaven and a new earth. Rev. *21* gives a clear account of that hope.

4. The apocalyptists' message was that the climax of history was near. The sufferings of the faithful were offered as proof. 'The darkest hour is just before the dawn' admirably sums up this aspect of the message.

5. The purpose of the apocalyptic literature was to encourage the faithful to hold out just a little longer. The ultimate hope was painted in glowing colours in order that the agony of the present might be accepted and endured.

6. The literary form of an apocalyptic book is usually that of a vision in which weird creatures appear and odd things happen. Some apocalyptic visions have a nightmarish quality. The phrase 'bizarre imagery' crops up in nearly every description of an apocalyptic writing. One does not have to read far in Revelation to see that it is justified.

b   Despite the fact that apocalyptic is a Jewish form of writing, Revelation is a Christian book. James and Revelation, in their different ways, both reveal how a Jewish literary style appears in Christian dress. The agony behind Revelation arises from a vicious persecution of Christians by the Roman Empire, described as 'the beast' in Rev. *13* and 'the great harlot' in Rev. *17*. The hope lies in the return of Christ who would come soon to inaugurate the judgment (*22.*7, 12, 20).

The book begins in a fairly low key. The author, called John, describes a vision that came to him on the Lord's day in the island of Patmos, where he was an exile. He was instructed to write letters to seven churches in the Roman province of Asia. The churches were all within 100 miles of Ephesus and they can easily be picked out on a map. They were Ephesus, Smyrna, Pergamum, Thyatira, Sardis, Philadelphia and Laodicea. The letters appear in chapters 2 and 3. There is plenty of bizarre imagery in these chapters, but none the less a fairly clear message to each of the churches can be picked out. But once the door in heaven opens at the beginning of chapter 4 and the trumpet speaks, all clear discourse seems to disappear, until 22.6 when the final section begins.

It has to be clearly stated that the meaning of many of the details is lost. One can guess, but guessing is dangerous. Even more dangerous is wishing onto the book a meaning of our own. This has happened too many times. Self-acclaimed prophets continually emerge who announce that 'the beast' is Soviet Russia, or the trade unions, or the World Council of Churches. And the Pope has always been a candidate among Protestants. This kind of thing is both false and wicked. Some of the detail is clear. Some is lost. Even where the detailed meaning is lost, often the total impact of a passage will come through. There is more revelation than secret about chapters such as 7 and 21. Revelation is a book of great devotion and immense confidence, and both are focused on God in Christ. That is enough. We should not be disturbed if the Bible still keeps some of its secrets.

c   The circumstances under which this book was written reveal a Church under greater pressure than ever before. False teachers are still around and their heresies now seem to be multiplied as fresh groups, such as the Nicolaitans (2.6, 15), appear to complicate the picture. Jewish opponents continue to harass the faithful. But, far worse, the Roman Empire has now turned its hand against the Church. 'The scarlet woman' is 'drunk with the blood of the saints' (17.6). 'The hour of trial' has come upon Christians (3.10). The prospect of martyrdom is before many of them (12.11, 20.4). The saints in white are those who have come out of 'the great tribulation' (7.14).

The immediate problem was emperor worship. Worship of

426

the emperor seemed a reasonable thing to a Roman. If a man had six or seven gods to whom he paid service, what possible harm could there be in paying service to a seventh or eighth? All the Christians were asked to do was to sprinkle a little incense on a flame before a bust of the emperor. They could then go on their way and worship whom they liked. Romans could never understand why Christians refused, and why they pursued their stubborn stance to the point of martyrdom. But for Christians the point was absolutley crucial. 'One God, one faith, one Lord,' allowed no compromise. It was either the arena or apostasy.

Against such a background Revelation was written. The emperor in question was probably Domitian (81–96). He was not the first emperor to demand worship from his subjects. Neither was he the first to persecute the Church. But his predecessors had been less efficient in the matter. Domitian made emperor worship compulsory and enforced the demand with rigour. Thousands of Christians died and John could reckon himself lucky to be surviving on lonely Patmos.

Who was this John? He does not claim to be an apostle or an elder. His Greek is sometimes appalling. It is unlike that of the fourth Gospel and of the Johnannine Epistles. The tradition that he was John the apostle has little to support it. We can only say that the author was a man called John who was familiar with the Christian churches of Asia, who had suffered exile for his faith, and who was in such a position of authority that he could pass judgment on the various churches.

d Summary of Revelation

Title (*1*.1–3)
The vision which gives rise to the book (*1*.4–20)
Letters to the seven churches (*2–3*)
The visions
  The throne in heaven (*4*)
  The Lamb (*5*)
  The seven seals (*6*.1–*8*.5)
  The seven trumpets (*8*.6–*11*.19)
  The dragon (*12*)

427

Chapter 40

Epilogue—History and the Gospel

a   IT must often appear to the young student that critical studies transform the Bible from a simple document of faith into a catalogue of conundrums that have no answer. This final chapter is an attempt to reassure the student. First let us be clear that truth has nothing to fear from scholarship. True faith is not damaged when awkward questions are asked and faithfully answered. Some cherished illusions may disappear, but not true faith.

Most of the queries come back to the same point. It is that, very often, the conclusions of the scholars contradict what the Bible appears to say quite explicitly. The Bible says that sixty-six chapters were written by Isaiah, and the scholars say that this is not so. The most painful point is often the historical one. The Bible says that this or that happened and the scholars doubt it. How can this be anything other than a disaster for faith?

b   The first thing to recognize is that the word 'history' has two meanings. It can refer to *happenings*, like the battle of Waterloo; and it can also mean *words written in a book* about the happenings. History in the second sense is about history in the first sense.

On the face of it, the words written in a book, that is, the record, are a perfect account of the happening. Read the record and know all about the happening! But it is not as easy as that. A happening is made up of thousands, indeed

429

millions, of facts, for every bullet at Waterloo had a few hundred facts attendant upon it. *Absolutely never* does the historian know all the facts. Even the people on the spot do not know all the facts. Private soldiers in battles normally know very few of them. Even the best historian can know only some of the facts and his history will, therefore, be less than perfect.

c   Next one has to consider the historian himself. This brings us to the third important element in the complex idea of history. After *happening* and *record*, we have to consider *interpretation*. Interpretation has to do with seeing meaning in happenings; and, to some extent, the meaning we see is determined by the attitude of mind we bring to the record.

Think of a bull-fight. Three people will see the same happenings and interpret them in three different ways. One will say it was a bad fight because the toreador lacked style. He has the devotee's point of view. Another will say it was a good fight because the crowd was large. He is the promoter. Another will say it was a bad fight because it was cruel. He is a member of a reforming body. All see the same happening, but they each interpret it in a different way. Each is right *within his own terms* but, of course, his attitude is something that he brought to the event. The three were devotee, promoter and reformer the night before the bull-fight, so they came to the bull-ring with different intentions in their minds.

It is not much good asking which of the three is right. The one we agree with is right, and for most of us, that will be the last one, because most of us will share his attitude.

The point of view of the historian is therefore all important. This is as true of the Gospel as of anything else. Hundreds of people saw Jesus at work and listened to his preaching and did absolutely nothing about it. Why? Because of their point of view. They brought nothing positive to the happening and so saw nothing positive in it. Some saw Jesus at work and interpreted what he was doing as blasphemy. Why? Because they came along with the idea in their minds that God could not act through someone whose teaching did not agree with their own. So, when Jesus taught and acted as he did, they rejected him outright. And, of course, some saw and believed.

The Gospels were created by those who saw (or heard) and

believed. We agree with them, because we share that faith. We disagree with the Pharisees, because although they saw what we did not see, they interpreted it in a way we think is wrong. This is an interesting point. They had a far better grasp of the facts than we have, but we believe and they did not. Plainly the argument we should like to have with those Pharisees is not about the facts, where they have the superior knowledge, but about interpretation, where we believe ourselves to be right.

d   From this we can draw out three principles concerning history and the Gospel.

1. As far as facts and happenings are concerned, we have to recognize that our picture is not complete, and in many areas we have to be content with probabilities rather than certainty. This is true about events that took place last week (race riots, football supporters' clashes, and so on). How much more true is it of ancient events!

2. The facts alone do not create faith anyway. They did not then and they do not now. Everything depends upon what we bring to the event or the record. The Gospel writers brought faith and they saw the Gospel story as the supreme event in the world's history. The Pharisees brought suspicion and they saw it as an outrage. We see it in the same way as the Gospel writers, not because we are compelled by the facts to do so, but because we share their faith.

3. Faith and facts—or should we say probabilities?—live together in a creative tension. We cannot create further facts or further evidence, but we can build up further understanding. One of the facts—the most certain of all—is the faith of the early Christians. The more we study their records, the more we can understand why they write as they do.

e   Let us now have a look at the Apostles' Creed, not because it was written by the apostles, but because it is a short statement of the faith much as the Gospels are long statements of the faith. The middle section of the Apostles' Creed contains

431

a number of affirmations about Jesus. They all seem to be historical and they are all affirmed as essential, Christian truth. But, as we look closer, it appears that this section contains at least three different kinds of statement. Consider, for example, these three lines:

> I believe in Jesus Christ, his only Son, our Lord.
> He was conceived by the power of the Holy Spirit and born of the Virgin Mary.
> He suffered under Pontius Pilate, was crucified, died, and was buried.

If we take the third line first and work backwards, we find, first of all, a series of *happenings*—Jesus was crucified, he died and was buried. Believers and Pharisees would agree that these things happened. The evidence about them is very strong. It would be hard to find a serious person today, *whether Christian or not*, who denied them. This may be because the happenings belong to the normal programme of human history. There is nothing at all improbable about a Jewish teacher under the Romans being crucified and buried.

The second line is rather different. It also refers to a happening, the fertilization of an egg cell in Mary's womb, but this happening is not part of the normal human programme. Indeed, it is quite the reverse. If it happened, it was a unique happening and it can only be explained as a once-for-all action on the part of God. For this reason, many serious people have difficulties with the virginal conception of Jesus.

The first line is different again. To say, 'Jesus was the Messiah and God's Son' looks like a historical statement, but in fact it is subtly different from the statement, 'Thomas Cranmer was Archbishop of Canterbury at the time of the English Reformation'. We must return to this matter as we look at all three statements more closely.

About the first there is little more to be said. There are certain facts about Jesus that nobody wants to deny. From time to time, in the past, odd scholars have tried to argue that Jesus was the figment of someone's imagination, but they have not got very far. There may be an anti-Christian case for opponents of the faith to argue, but this is not it. Furthermore, the evidence is strong that wonderful cures were attributed to Jesus. Both friends and enemies record that he was, in this regard, a most remarkable person. There is no reason why anyone should doubt this. Plenty of modern, clinical evidence suggests that certain people have a gift of raising the morale of the sick and restoring their confidence, and that this alone is sufficient to improve and sometimes cure their physical symptoms. It is entirely consistent with the evidence that Jesus was such a person. So we can go beyond what the Creed says. Jesus lived, taught, healed, raised a following, and then was crucified and buried. That part of the Gospel rests on the firmest possible foundation. So far very little interpretation has entered into our historical reconstruction.

The virginal conception, some of the other miracles, like walking on water and turning water into wine, and the bodily resurrection of Jesus come in a different category. One reason is that there is no corroborating evidence from non-Christian sources. But a far more important reason is that these miracles require us to believe that, on certain occasions in the life of Jesus, the natural order operated in a different way from that to which we have become accustomed. When we try to walk on water, we sink. If Jesus did not sink, then the force of gravity must have acted differently from what we should expect. Considerations of this kind have led scholars to ask whether we can speak of these miracles as historical in the way that the happenings discussed in the previous paragraph were historical. The answer is that it depends upon our point of view and our interpretation.

f Broadly speaking, there are two ways in which we might approach this question. The *first*, the traditional one, is to say that these miracles are indications of a special activity of God which showed itself in the world at that time. God is free to show himself in whatever way he likes. In fact he showed himself fully in Jesus, and it is not, therefore, surprising that the water became wine and that the loaves and the fishes were multiplied. The pattern is quite coherent. God would not be God if he were not capable of such activity. There is no great problem about evidence: the Gospel record is enough.

This argument will seem persuasive to many faithful Christians, but it will not persuade the uncommitted historian. It is easy to see why. The argument rests to some extent on the Gospel record but much more on the theological presupposition that God was at work in Jesus in a special way. Historians, particularly non-Christian historians, do not take account of theological convictions in reconstructing the past. They reach the conclusion that, *historically speaking*, the miracles in question are unlikely to have happened. None the less, it is open to Christians to hold, on other grounds than the purely historical, that they did happen.

The problem then is how Christian and non-Christian can converse with one another. The Christian puts forward the two ideas, that God was at work in Jesus, and that a number of miracles attended this supreme event, as a kind of package. He invites belief in both. The non-Christian may be converted, in which case his view of what happened in history will change. On the other hand, he may resist, in which case Christian and non-Christian will continue to differ about the historical probablilty of the Gospel record.

g   The *second* way of meeting the difficulty caused by these stories of exceptional miracles—they are sometimes called 'nature miracles', though the name is not a good one as it presupposes that we know how nature works—is much more modern. It is often, though not always, pursued by scholars who find the idea that God's self-revelation in Jesus was attended by stunning physical happenings unhelpful and contradictory.

They begin with the observation that the Gospels provide us with a narrative, not necessarily with a historical record. It may be that the narrative serves some other purpose than historical record. The parables are examples of narratives that are profoundly true without being historical records. Is it possible that some stories in the Gospels have to be understood in the same way?

One of the features of the Hebrew and Aramaic tongues is the sparsity of abstract words of the kind we find essential in talking about theology. A first-century Jew did not talk about God as self-existent being or the uncaused cause. What he did

434

was to tell stories because his language was ideally suited to telling stories. These stories are not less expressive than the theoretical language used by later theologians. On the contrary, more people will attend to and be able to understand the stories than will ever ponder over the theoretical language. The narrative style of first century writing is a great boon to us all.

If this is so, then the purpose of those miracle stories, even the most fantastic of all, is more easily seen. It is to affirm beliefs about Jesus that could not, at the time, be expressed in any other way. The miracle stories make their points about Jesus more directly and more memorably than did the complex abstract language that abounded in later Christian discourse.

This does not necessarily mean that the miracle stories are not historically true, but simply that recording historical events may not be their primary purpose. This brings the miracle stories—and the Gospels—in line with other great narratives of Israel's history, particularly the story of the Exodus. Undoubtedly there is a historical core to the account of the Exodus, but the primary function of the narrative was to enable Jews of later days to worship and glorify the God who had led them through countless crises and continued to be their hope in every contemporary situation.

The right question to ask, therefore, is not 'Is this miracle story historically accurate?' but 'What does this story affirm?' From this point of view the Gospels are to be seen more as affirmations about Jesus than as historically accurate records.

Scholars who argue in this way have no difficulty in conversing with other historians. Neither should they have difficulties in finding common cause with other Christians, since they are at one with those who take the other view, in making positive affirmations about Jesus. It has to be admitted, however, that the historical accuracy of the Gospels has often been a matter of deep contention in Christianity. Those who hold the views outlined here have sometimes found themselves out of sympathy with each other. It is important, therefore, to stress that both views are held with equal conviction and honesty.

h   This brings us finally to the first line of the quotation from the Creed, 'I believe in Jesus Christ, his only Son, our Lord'. Are we making a historical statement, when we recite this line?

The question is best answered if we concentrate on one of the three titles given to Jesus in this sentence. Let us take 'Christ', or, as it is in the Hebrew form, 'Messiah'. When Jesus confronted Pilate, one might say that the Messiah was confronting the procurator. But are these titles similar? 'Procurator' was a title given in the Roman empire to an official who exercised authority in a particular area. The title was controlled from Rome. Nobody else could set up a procurator or call himself procurator. The appointment of a procurator and his deposition, if he was deposed, were straightforward constitutional happenings.

That is not true of the Messiah. God alone 'appoints' the Messiah. He has no uniform or badge of office to say he is Messiah. If we maintain that Jesus was the Messiah, it is because we believe him to be so, not because of any official documentation. It is difficult, therefore, to put this title in the same category as that of procurator.

If we look at the NT carefully we shall discover that Jesus is given a large number of different designations, the Messiah, the Son of Man, the Son of God, the Lord, the Son of David, etc. The more we look at them, the more clear it becomes that they are not at all like 'procurator of Judaea' or even 'Archbishop of Canterbury'. They are not clearly defined titles officially conferred upon one person so that all the world knows to whom the title belongs. Rather, they are designations, conjuring up various notions of virtue and authority, that are applied to Jesus by those who wish to do him honour. Pilate was procurator to friends and enemies alike. Jesus was Messiah only to believers. To this day the Jewish people do not regard him as Messiah. These designations are, therefore, matters of faith; they are a means of exalting Jesus and saying about him what the believer longs to say.

Jesus, my Shepherd, Brother, Friend,
My Prophet, Priest, and King,

My Lord, my Life, my Way, my End
Accept the praise I bring.

One has the impression that John Newton, the hymn-writer, would have been happy to go on with line after line of designations in order to get his point over. Indeed, a similar hymn by Isaac Watts speaks of joining all the glorious names that are and concludes,

All are too mean to speak his worth,
Too mean to set our Saviour forth.

Much more can be said on this matter. Here we point out that Jesus was none of these things in the way that Pilate was procurator. As a matter of *faith*, he was all of them and more.

i We can best close this book with a summary of what is said in this chapter.

First, criticism cannot destroy true faith. If questions arise, they must be fairly and honestly answered. The true unbeliever is the person who refuses to face the questions.

Secondly, the great statements of the faith are only partly historical. There are facts, but there is also interpretation. Not all the facts can now be known. The Christian student has first to consider the probabilities and then how to interpret them.

Thirdly, Christians think their way through this problem in different ways. Some conceive of a special kind of history in the biblical events. Others concentrate on the record and find in it a proclamation of the writers' faith. Both positions can be conscientiously held.

Fourthly, the quest must go on. Bible study must never end. The new convert and the most learned scholar have this in common: they can begin each day expecting to find new riches in the biblical text; and they are rarely disappointed.

Further Reading

On the whole Bible

Matthew Black and H. H. Rowley (eds), *Peake's Commentary on the Bible*, Thos. Nelson, 1963
Lucas Grollenberg, *Rediscovering the Bible*, SCM, 1978
John H. Hayes, *Introduction to the Bible*, SPCK, 1973
Richard N. Soulen, *Handbook of Biblical Criticism*, Lutterworth, 1977

On the OT

C. Westerman,, *Handbook to the OT*, SPCK, 1969
Robert Martin-Achard, *An Approach to the OT*, Oliver and Boyd, 1965
Harry Mowvley, *The Testimony of Israel: An Introduction to OT Literature*, REP, 1971
R. de Vaux, *Ancient Israel: Its Life and Institutions*, rev. ed. 1965

On the NT

Brian Beck, *Reading the NT Today*, Lutterworth, 1977
Ralph P. Martin, *NT Foundations: A guide for Christian Students*,
Vol 1, *The four Gospels*, Paternoster, 1975
Vol. 2, *Acts–Revelation*, Paternoster, 1978

Robert A. Spivey and D. Moody Smith, *Anatomy of the NT: A guide to its Structure and Meaning*, Macmillan, 1969
G. Bornkamm, *The NT: A Guide to its Writings*, SPCK, 1974
Robert Grant, *A Historical Introduction to the NT*, Collins, 1963
Bruce Metzger, *The NT: Background, Growth and Content*, Lutterworth, 1969

These are but a few of the enormous number of books covering the whole Bible or one of the testaments. Good as they are, they will not satisfy the student for long. He will want to read books that deal with smaller areas in more detail, books on the prophets, or the parables, or Pauline theology, or the titles of Jesus. To give a complete list of these would be impossible; even a select list would be a considerable undertaking and of doubtful value. Each year the SCM Press publish *Religion and Theology: A Select Book Guide*. This is well worth the pound or so that it at present costs. Beyond that the student is best advised to read all the reviews he can and to haunt the bookshops. Knowing books is a skill on its own. It is all part of the task of studying the Bible.

Index

Aaron, 246
Abdon, 128
Abel, 254, 263, 267
Abijah, 131
Abimelech, 118, 128, 227
Abner, 258
Abraham, 79 f., 118 f., 122 f., 151 f., 159 f., 224 ff., 253 f., 263, 354, 357 f., 396
Absalom, 130, 225
Acco, 78
Achaia, 383, 386
Achan, 118
Actium, 141
Adam, 119, 255, 265, 278, 357, 396
Adonijah, 248
Aegean, 79
Aelia Capitolina, 148
Aetiological myth, 252 ff.
Ahab, 131 f., 221, 233, 237, 240 f., 244, 273
Ahaz, 21, 132 f., 217, 294
Ahaziah (Judah), 132
Ahaziah (Northern Israel), 131
Ahijah, 133, 227, 237, 240 f.
Ai, 267
Aland, Kurt, 189 f.
Albright, W. F., 129, 132 f.
Alexander the Great, 78 f., 137, 160, 164, 223, 384, 389
Alexander Jannaeus, 139
Alexandra, 140
Alexandria, 137, 164 f., 221, 384, 390, 398
Alexandrian text, 184–8, 197
Alt, Albrecht, 257
Amalekites, 127
Amaziah (king), 132, 254
Amaziah (priest), 237
Amenophis IV = Akhenaton, 153
American Bible Society, 53
Ammon, 84, 127, 217, 219, 228
Amon, 133
Amorites, 265, 267
Amos, 86, 133, 140, 225, 237, 239, 241, 257, 274
Amphictyony, 128
Ananias, 387
Anath, 231 f., 271
Anath-Bethel, 155
Anathoth, 117

Anderson, B. W., 148
Andrew, 143
Antigonus, 140
Antinomian, 422 f.
Antioch (Pisidia), 303, 330, 382 f.
Antioch (Syria), 137, 139 f., 145, 156, 221, 352, 380, 383 f., 415
Antiochus III, 137
Antiochus IV (Ephiphanes), 103, 138 f., 282, 297
Antonia, tower of, 300 f., 388
Antony, 140 f., 389
Aphrodite, 386
Apocalyptic, 176, 260 f., 344, 353, 419, 424 f.
Apocrypha, 41, 44, 46, 48, 51, 54, 168–72, 176, 317
Apodeictic law, 257
Apollos, 398, 417
Ap-Thomas, D. R., 191
Aqaba, gulf of, 219
Aquila (from Acts), 316
Aquila (version), 166, 181, 398
Arabah, 85
Arabia, 77, 80, 125, 386
Aram, 81, 123, 217
Aramaic, 158, 161, 182, 207, 303, 349, 419, 434
Araunah the Jebusite, 293
Archaeology, 27 f., 149–57, 225, 386
Archelaus, 142 f., 147
Areopagus, 385
Aretas IV, 387
Aristeas, letter of, 164, 172
Aristobulus I, 139
Aristobulus II, 140
Ark of the Covenant, 36, 128, 131, 227, 245, 249, 263, 273, 284, 289, 294, 297
Armageddon, 85
Arnon, 84, 87, 218 f., 228
Artemis, 387
Asa, 131 f.
Ascension, 99, 112
Ashdod, 226, 228
Asherah, 232, 234
Ashkelon, 151, 226, 228
Ashtoreth, Ashtaroth, 231 f., 271

441

INDEX

443

INDEX

INDEX

446

447

INDEX